NATIVE AMERICAN RELIGIONS

A Geographical Survey

John James Collins

Native American Studies
Volume 1

The Edwin Mellen Press
Lewiston/Queenston/Lampeter

Library of Congress Cataloging-in-Publication Data

Collins, John J. (John James), 1938-
Native American religions : a geographical survey / John James Collins.
p. cm. -- (Native American studies ; v. 1.)
Includes bibliographical references
ISBN 0-88946-483-9
1. Indians of North America--Religion and mythology. I. Title. II. Series.
E98.R3C69 1990
299'.7--dc20 90-33942
CIP

This is volume 1 in the continuing series
Native American Studies
Volume 1 ISBN 0-88946-483-9
NAS Series ISBN 0-88946-482-0

A CIP catalog record for this book is available from the British Library.

The Edwin Mellen Press
Box 450
Lewiston, New York
USA 14092

The Edwin Mellen Press
Box 67
Queenston, Ontario
CANADA L0S 1L0

The Edwin Mellen Press, Ltd.
Lampeter, Dyfed, Wales
UNITED KINGDOM SA48 7DY

Printed in the United States of America

NATIVE AMERICAN RELIGIONS

A Geographical Survey

TABLE OF CONTENTS

Part I
Southwest and West

Part II
Central, East and Northwest

Chapter

CULTURE AREA MAP

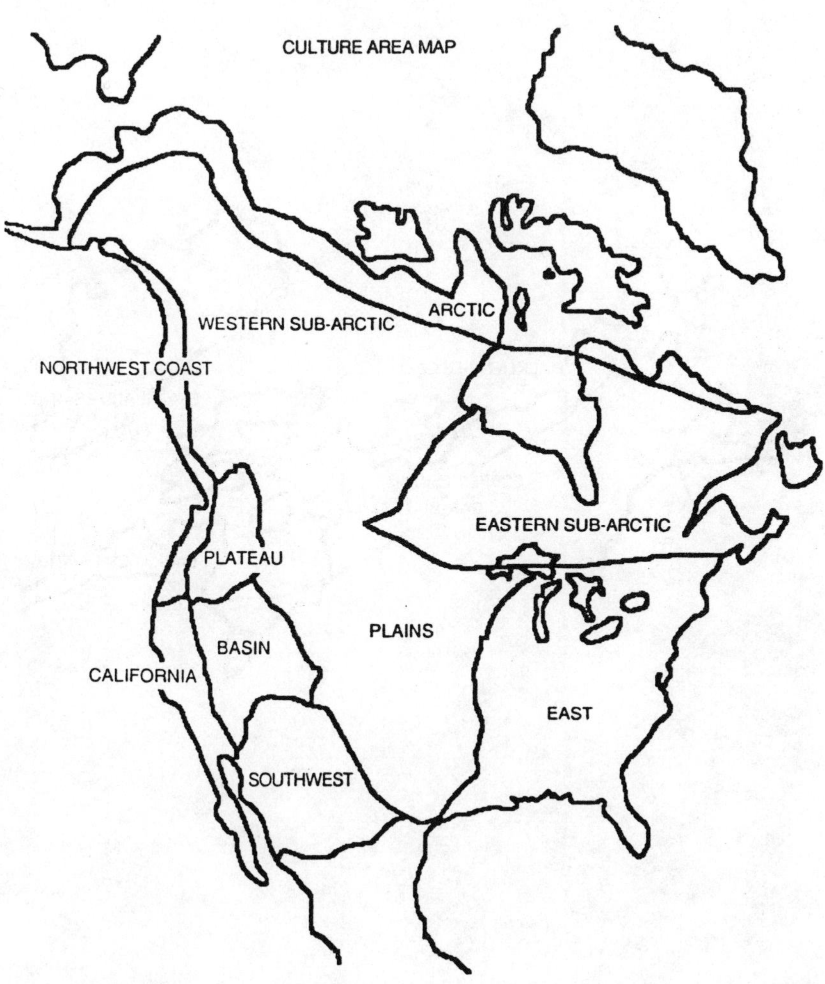

ARCTIC

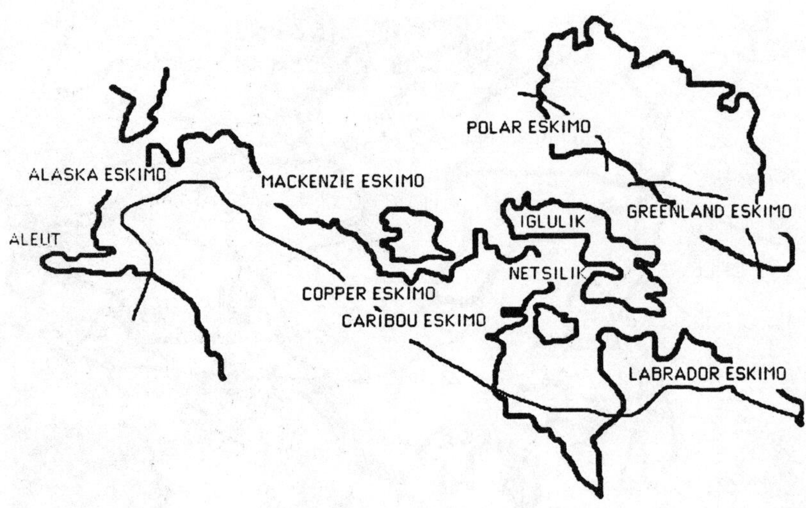

POLAR ESKIMO
ALASKA ESKIMO
MACKENZIE ESKIMO
IGLULIK
GREENLAND ESKIMO
ALEUT
NETSILIK
COPPER ESKIMO
CARIBOU ESKIMO
LABRADOR ESKIMO

EASTERN SUB-ARCTIC

WESTERN SUB-ARCTIC

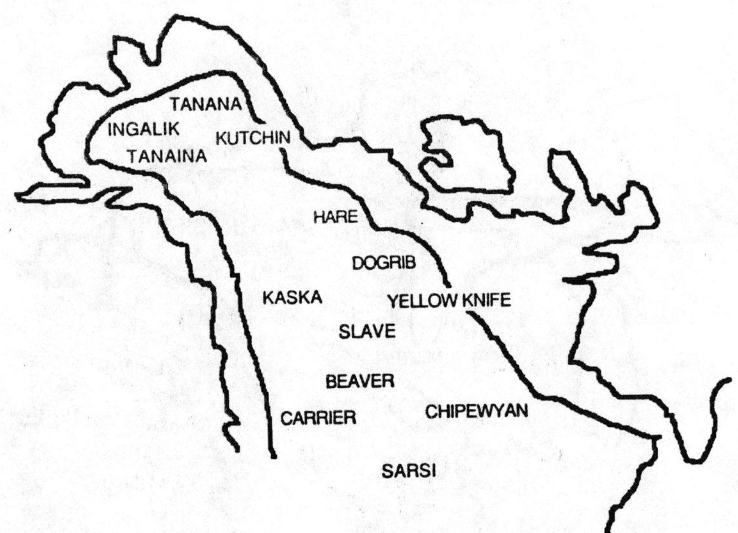

NORTHEAST AND GREAT LAKES

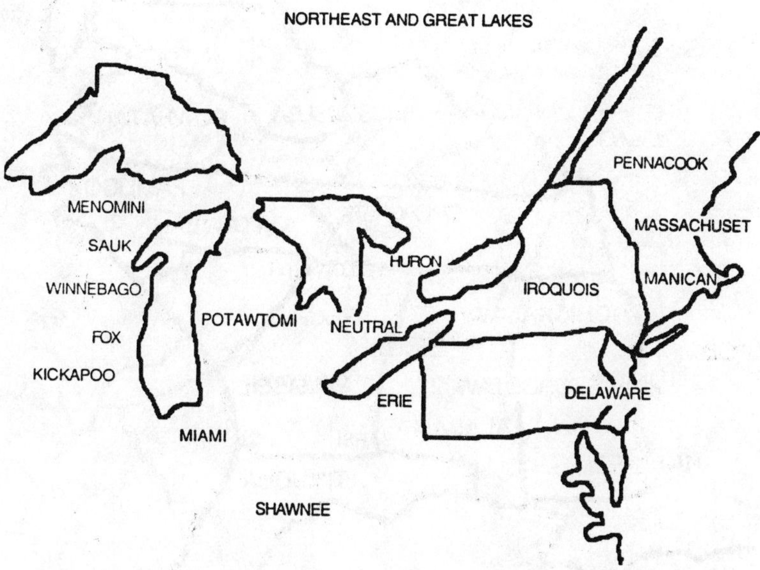

SOUTHEAST

ERIE
OSAGE
MOSOPELEA
POWHATAN
PAMLICO
CHEROKEE
CATAWBA
CHICKASAW
YUCHI
CREEK
CADDO
TUNICA
CHOCTAW
YAMASEE
ALABAMA
NATCHEZ
TIMUCUA
CALUSA

NORTHWEST COAST

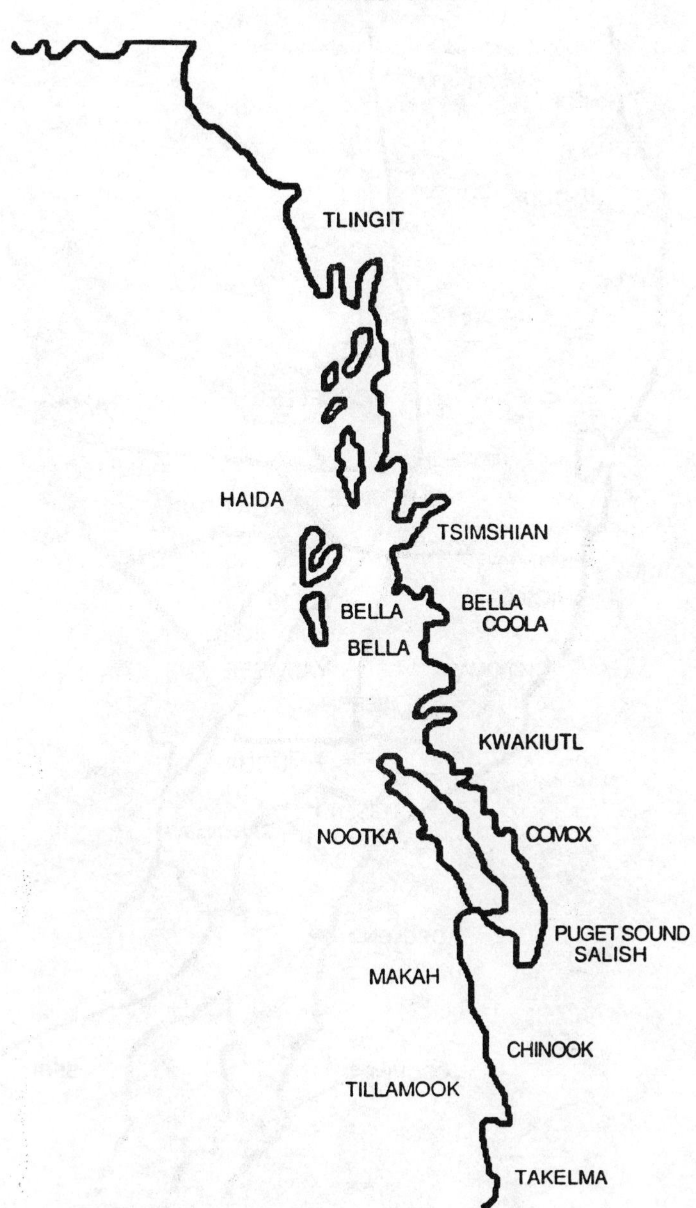

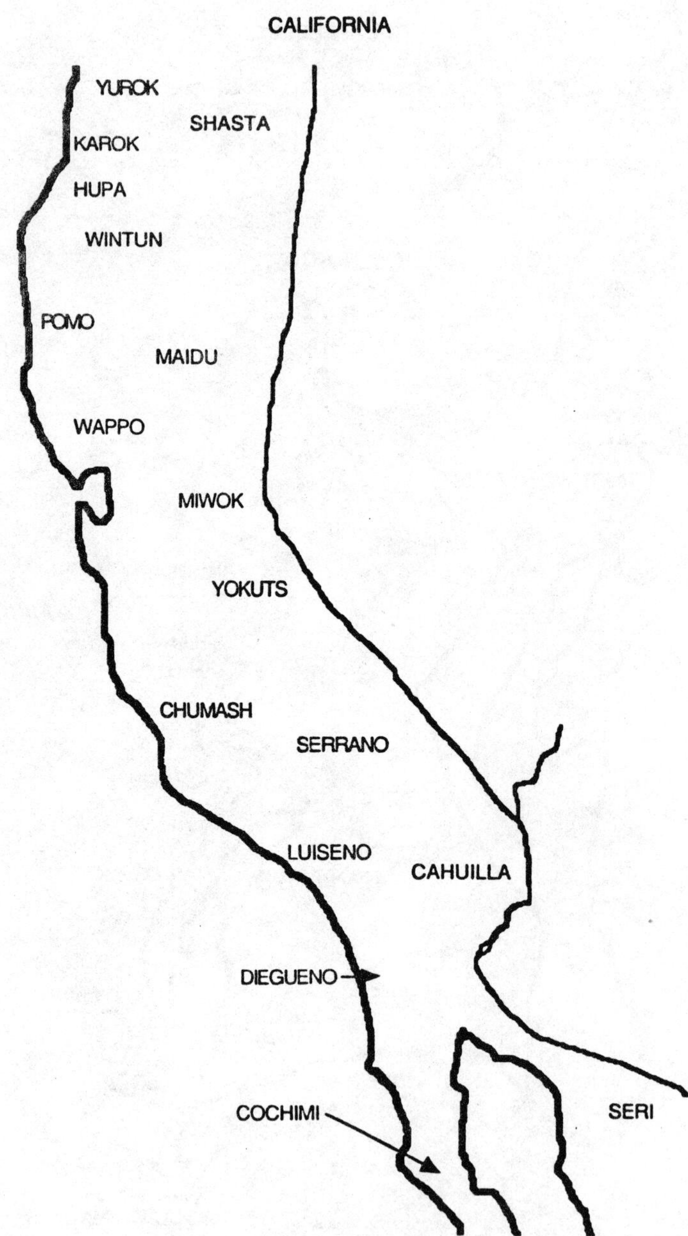
CALIFORNIA
YUROK
SHASTA
KAROK
HUPA
WINTUN
POMO
MAIDU
WAPPO
MIWOK
YOKUTS
CHUMASH
SERRANO
LUISENO
CAHUILLA
DIEGUENO
COCHIMI
SERI

PLATEAU

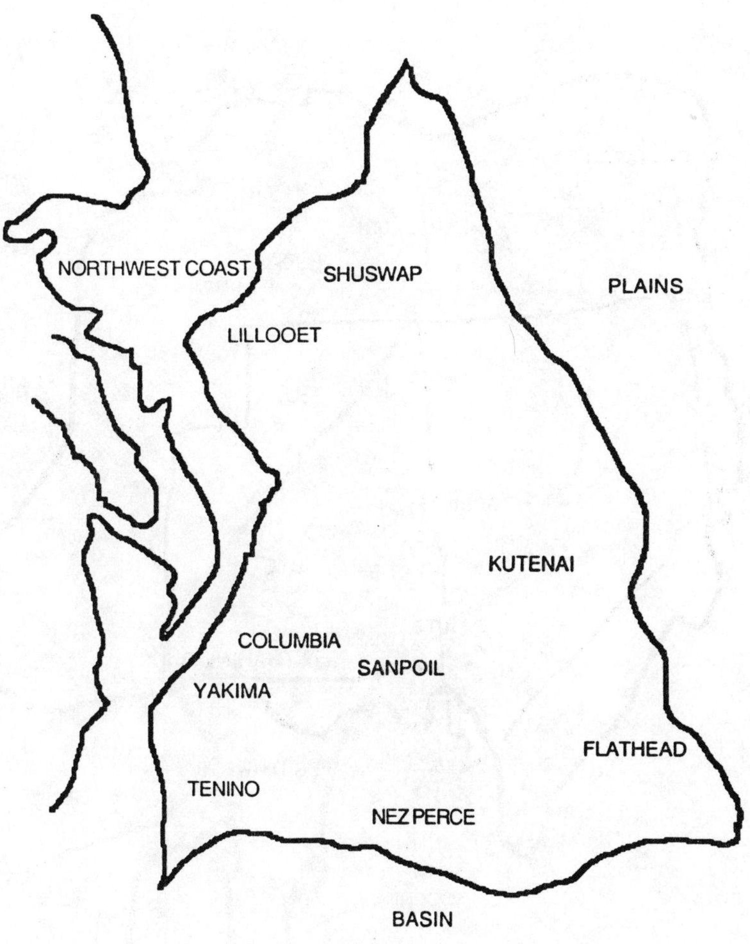
NORTHWEST COAST
SHUSWAP
PLAINS
LILLOOET
KUTENAI
COLUMBIA
SANPOIL
YAKIMA
FLATHEAD
TENINO
NEZ PERCE
BASIN

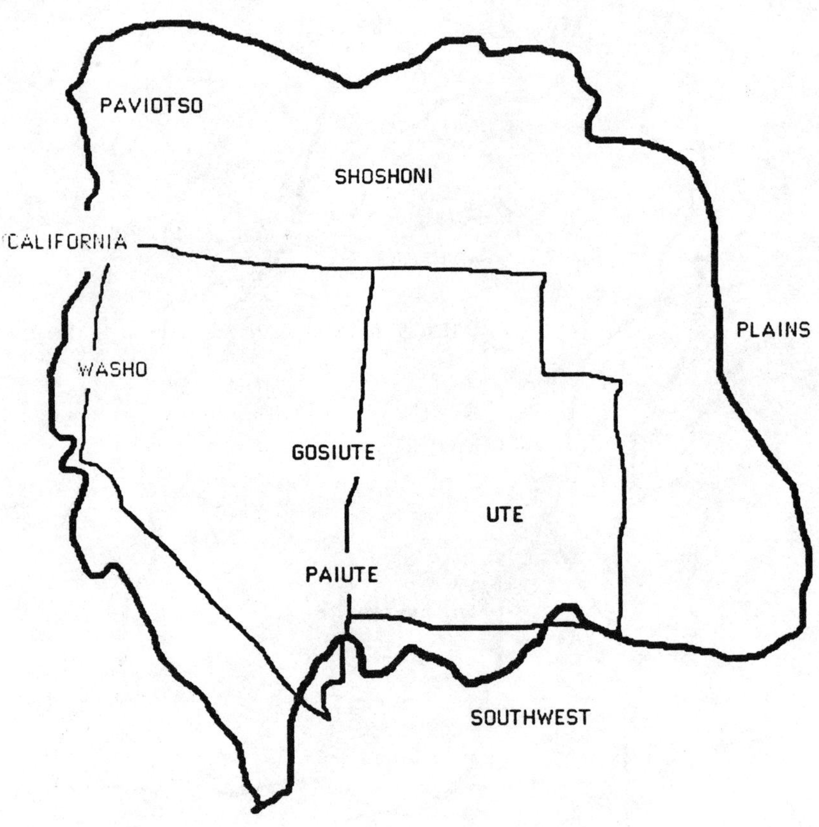
GREAT BASIN
PAVIOTSO
SHOSHONI
CALIFORNIA
PLAINS
WASHO
GOSIUTE
UTE
PAIUTE
SOUTHWEST

PLAINS

SARSI
BLACKFOOT
CREE
ASSINIBOIN
GROS VENTRE
HIDATSA
MANDAN
CROW
ARIKARA
YANKTON
TETON (SIOUX)
SANTEE
KICKAPOO
ARAPAHO
OMAHA
PAWNEE
IOWA
CHEYENNE
UTE
OSAGE
KIOWA
NATCHEZ
CADDO
COMANCHE

SOUTHWEST

SOUTHWEST

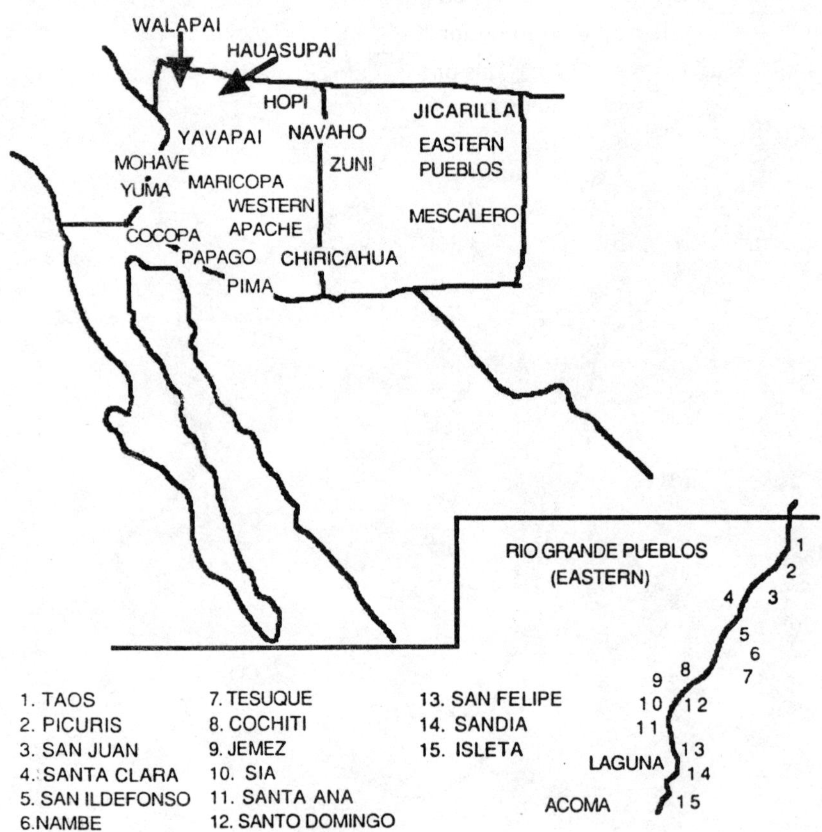

ACKNOWLEDGEMENTS

I would like to thank the staff of the Edwin Mellen Press for their prompt help, kind considerations, and infectious enthusiasm. This book could not have come to fruition without the assistance of my college inter-library loan staff at Jamestown Community College. Their help over a number of years was incalculable. Having dedicated past books to my parents and to my family I would like this one to be for Katie and all her kin who watched my labors and accept me as I am. This one is for you.

PREFACE

This book describes the religion of Native Americans (American Indians) north of Mexico as it existed at the time of European contact. It presents data primarily on rituals and religious practitioners and does so by considering such information on a culture-area basis. Religion is surveyed from the Arctic to the Southwest and brief accounts are given on the general culture background of each area. This book brings together data from sources not generally available to readers wishing to learn about this topic.

INTRODUCTION

This is a volume dealing with the topic of Native American religion. It provides a primarily descriptive account of the supernatural beliefs and ritual practices of the first Americans. The two parts of this book are based upon a great many source materials that are inaccessible in even regional libraries and so they should appeal both to the general reader and to college students who are interested in American Indian culture or in comparative religion and who have no way to consult such basic literature. This account is not intended to be a final professional summation of scholarship on Indian religion. It is not meant for the specialist in such studies. The limits of length precluded a truly in-depth treatment of such behaviors, even if a single writer had such knowledge at his disposal. It should also be pointed out that the focus of this book deals primarily with rituals and the organization of their participants. This information is the most consistently reported upon facet of supernaturalism represented in the literature. As such, it provides good comparable materials for each culture area. Other aspects accordingly are highlighted only when they are of importance in specific religions. A discussion of myth, which is certainly of significance, is not included in the present work since to treat it adequately would have doubled the size of this volume. I have also not taken up the complex topic of area stimulus and diffusion.

The data that are presented have been arranged by culture areas: geographical regions where it is assumed that some basic communalities of cultural adaptation occur. This has been a time-honored approach in anthropology and in American Indian studies even though it is quite apparent that tribes within such regions are not duplications of each other and in fact may vary widely in such respects. Nonetheless this approach is still the easiest way to present comparative materials. This book also includes a brief and non-technical account of each culture area so that technological and social behaviors may provide the appropriate context and background for the more specific religious beliefs and behaviors.

The first part, Southwest and West, begins with a very brief introduction to American Indian cultural development. It deals with data secured primarily by archaeologists. This information puts American Indian culture into a general context. Two major areas of religious significance are then surveyed – the Southwest and West which taken together form a large portion of North America. They are also areas having links together in the past. The Southwest was truly the most complex as well as diverse culture area and much of this part is taken up in dealing with it. The West culture area also had varieties in it although the levels of religious development are roughly comparable. The second part covers Central, East and Northwestern areas. It takes into account the Plains, the Arctic and Subarctic, and the Northwest Coast as well as the Eastern Woodlands. A number of comparative and perspective topics are dealt with in the second section as well as recent cults and religious movements. Each descriptive section contains a bibliography both for sources cited in the texts and for further reading.

It must also be mentioned that the accounts presented in the present work are given as nearly as possible in the sense that such beliefs and rituals were being practiced at the time of European contact or shortly thereafter except in the cases so noted. Since no consensus exists, or is ever likely to, on the precise developmental stages and influences involved in aboriginal supernaturalism in North America, we are dealing in most culture areas with unknown mixtures of behaviors and time frames. However, we are probably not too far off base in most area descriptions. Added to this general problem is the more specific difficulty of the materials themselves. This can be seen in various aspects (other special comments are given for the areas themselves). Accounts of American Indian customs are uneven and often lacking, given the differing emphasis of the "reporters" involved. To this can be added the problem of more simple unconscious misrepresentation of materials due to the lack of true understanding by outsiders. And, of course, much important data is lacking due to secrecy or being forgotten by Indian informants themselves. I believe that the present study, despite such difficulties, does adequately represent the major ritual and other dimensions of aboriginal Native American religion.

PART I

SOUTHWEST AND WEST

CHAPTER I

THE DEVELOPMENT OF AMERICAN INDIAN CULTURE

The ancestors of the American Indian came to the New World as the first of a long line of immigrants. While it was once believed that humans might have developed here independently, scholars have yet to find old skeletal remains or cultural artifacts that clearly demonstrate an early state of humanity. Apparently humans developed to the modern Homo sapiens level in the Old World and then made a fairly recent entry into the Americas. Most scholars also suggest that the earliest migration point into the New World was in the area of the Bering Straits which, several times during the ice ages, had land exposed to provide a "bridge" between northeastern Siberia and northwestern Alaska. This is called Beringia. While entry may have been somewhat earlier, the best time frame presently accepted for such migrations is between 27,000 and 12,000 years ago.

We are not entirely sure as to the motives behind such population movements. Probably people came unconsciously, following big game animals in their migrations. Population pressure or shifts in the positions of major ice sheets may have also been significant factors. Since the "bridge" was about one thousand miles wide, newcomers were hardly aware of their momentous discovery. Once humans had entered the Americas, it would seem that population growth would trigger subsequent movements of people although there was certainly more than a single migration of people here. Great debate currently surrounds what the culture of the first comers might have been like and the nature of its links to Old Stone Age cultures in Asia.

While further research will soon clarify these issues, archaeologists do generally agree on five stages of cultural development. In this very brief chapter, we characterize these in a nontechnical manner so that the reader can gain a general impression of both time and cultural aspects of the background of American Indian prehistory.

The first well-documented stage is called the Paleo-Indian or Lithic state and is generally equated to the Old Stone Age of Europe, Asia and Africa. This stage dates generally back beyond 12,000 years ago and for many New World areas it represents a time of specialized big game hunting. One of the best-known sequences is in the Southwest of North America and consists chiefly of "kill sites" where mammoth, bison, and other animals were killed and butchered. Culture phases such as the Llano, Folsom, and Plano are distinguished in terms of spearhead types used in hunting, the animals focused upon, and the associated techniques; from driving animals into boggy areas and herding them over cliffs. Evidence also exists for rather more generalized cultures developing at this time. A fairly nomadic existence was common as well as a "poverty" of cultural remains.

As early as 10,000 years ago a new way of life appeared called the Archaic stage. This at least partially coincided with the extinction of many types of big game animals. This necessitated readaptation to altered environmental circumstances although some stimulus arose from cultures not so specialized. This new stage was certainly more totally exploitative of food varieties and other resources in its adaptation to the environment and in some culture areas it persisted up into historic times. General traits included a great variety of spear and arrow points, the use of bone and other raw materials for making tools, heavy ground stone tools including food-grinding stones (mortars and pestles) for use with wild plants. A seasonal pattern of life is generally well attested to as people moved from place to place to take advantage of locally differing resources. Refuse accumulation testifies to people spending some time in each area; these sites are usually not just temporary camps. It should also be mentioned that as population expanded people began to move into hitherto unoccupied New World areas. While hunting, fishing, and gathering wild plants were Archaic bases of existence, there were a few areas in Mexico, Peru, and other places where archaeologists have uncovered the beginnings of agricultural experimentation. From these areas higher levels of cultural development would soon emerge. Finally, differences in the inventory of artifacts and style of life from one major region to another suggest that the beginnings of differentiation were developing that culminate later on as the culture areas described in this volume.

The next stage of cultural development is called the Formative or Pre-Classic. It begins somewhat earlier than 1500 B.C. in some New World areas. This level is identified by the presence of developed agriculture, evidence of sedentary village life, the remains of pottery and other arts and crafts, and, among other things, considerable religious developments. Perhaps the most important sequence of development, and perhaps the oldest, occurred along the Gulf Coast of Mexico and is known as the Olmec culture. Ritual centers existed there probably containing an elite population that held sway over more rural, farming people. At the site of La Venta, for example, a large earth "pyramid" structure 420 feet in diameter and over 100 feet high dominated a series of religious constructions mixed with stone stelae, "altars," giant sculptured heads, and other monumental art forms. Figurines, pottery, carvings, and other artwork suggest a cult of a feline deity possibly associated with rain. Military activity, and extensive trade and political and economic control existed over a vast area. The Olmecs may well have been the "mother culture" that influenced many developments elsewhere and later in the New World. Comparable developments were underway in South America, especially along the west coast where ritual centers also provided nuclei of influence over large regions.

In North America two major Formative sequences are worthy of mention. In the Eastern United States a sequence of primarily burial-mound cultures existed running approximately from 800 B.C. right into historic times. The phases of these have been designated the Adena-Hopewell and Mississippian; the latter perhaps demonstrating more direct Mexican influence. They all involved massive earthworks and the burial of elite individuals along with substantial grave goods and other evidences of arts and crafts. Village sites also accompany these remains as well as data indicating an agricultural basis for life. In the Southwestern area, another elaborate Formative sequence existed which archaeologists have designated as three culture types: the Mogollon, Hohokam, and Anasazi; the cliff-dwelling remains of the latter people being perhaps the most popularly known sites. These people did not emphasize the burial aspects of their eastern contemporaries, but arts and crafts, especially pottery, were excellent. Communal types of housing plus special religious structures were common, and such groups appear to have been directly ancestral to the Pimans and the Zuni and other Pueblo peoples dealt with in this volume.

The next and probably greatest stage of cultural development in the Americas is known as the Classic. It began as early as 300 B.C. and was limited to only a few areas of Middle and South America. It represented a high point in arts and crafts, monumental architecture, and perhaps religion and is accompanied by intensive agricultural techniques and population growth. Social class distinctions and political development also occurred as well as specialization in all facets of life. The most famous site in the Mexican region at this time is that of Teotihuacan in the central valley which consisted of about eight square miles of building projects literally "topped off" by the great sun pyramid measuring 700 feet along the base and rising to a height of more than 200 feet. This site was not only a ritual center but a city estimated by scholars to have contained more than 100,000 inhabitants. Palaces, apartment complexes, broad avenues, and areas given over to ceremonial activities bespeak centralized planning. Murals, pottery, stone work and other crafts were seldom equalled in later times. Many famous Mayan sites also date from this stage as do the famous Mochica, Nazca and other cultures along the west coast of South America.

The last stage prior to authenticated European discovery of the New World is called the Post-Classic and began perhaps around 600 A.D. It is represented in Middle America by the Toltecs and many other peoples and eventually the Aztecs. In South American the Chimu date from these times, eventually eclipsed by the rise to dominance of the Inca. This stage represents a somewhat new way of life in these areas – a glorification of war resulting in political development, professional military groups, empire building on a grand scale, and many fortifications and architecture. The military person dominates the priestly type as perhaps never before.

Population numbers are greater during these times, and while city building continues, there was a decline in some arts and crafts due to mass production techniques. There may well have been an even greater age following this period, but with the arrival of the Spanish in both Mexico and Peru, such possibilities were forever terminated as were other stages elsewhere in the Americas. The reader should be reminded that when Europeans came here and began exploration and conquest they found not only the civilizations of the Post-Classic stage but discovered populations of Native Americans existing on most of the other levels of cultural development as well. This helps explain the differences existing between various Indian groups. Part two (in chapter nineteen) deals with the effects of European contact on New World culture. This brief account does not deal with the complex problems of Old World influences on New World cultural development after the first migration but prior to known outside contact. We can now deal with the general culture and the religious beliefs and practices of those Native Americans who lived in the Southwest and in Western North America.

CHAPTER II

THE SOUTHWEST CULTURE AREA

Some of the best-known tribes of North American Indians in popular imagination as well as in anthropological literature are found in the Southwest culture area. Not only are these people perhaps the best preserved "aboriginal" cultures – still clinging to many of their ancestral traditions and avoiding full integration into the national society – but a rather complete archaeological record allows us to trace the origins of many groups back a considerable distance in time.

Basically, this area encompasses Arizona, New Mexico, Southeast Utah, Southwest Colorado, and parts of Texas. The so-called "greater southwest" also includes northern Mexico. Indeed some scholars would extend the area, with divisions into arid hunting-gathering and oasis-farming peoples, into parts of adjacent culture areas. Since the scope of the present section is limited and since the second part will deal with religious behavior in other culture areas, we restrict our discussion to the original geographical region. Culture areas within it have traditionally been based partly on linguistic and partly on other cultural similarities. Four major divisions are generally discussed: the Pueblo, Piman, Athabascan and Yuman. We can briefly discuss each of these in turn.

The general Pueblo division is based upon similarity in architectural and other material cultural and social considerations and less perhaps upon language. The number and variety of groups subsumed within it, however, have led to further subdivision. The Western Pueblos consist of the numerous villages of the Hopi, the Zuni, and the villages of Acoma and

Laguna. Linguistically, the Hopi, along with the Pimans to be described later, are linked to a major language stock, the Uto-Aztecan. The Zuni appear to have a rather distinct language. Acoma and Laguna are classified as Keresan and are linguistically linked to other Pueblos in the Eastern grouping. Keresan is a language not yet clearly associated with a larger grouping. The Eastern Pueblos in the Rio Grande area include five other Keresan villages: Cochiti, Sia, Santa Ana, San Felipe, and Santo Domingo. They also include the various speakers of the Tanoan language family. The divisions here are the Tewa, which includes the villages of San Juan, San Ildefonso, Santa Clara, Nambe, Pojoaque, and Tesuque; the Tiwa including the villages of Taos, Picuris, Sisleta, and Sandia; and the Towa of which the village of Jemez is the sole surviving representative. One Tewa-speaking Pueblo–Hano–took up residence among the Hopi in historic times. The Tanoan language family is perhaps closest in relationship to Uto-Aztecan. It should be pointed out that formerly a considerably greater number of Pueblo villages existed; in 1540 (at the time of the Coronado expedition) there existed about eighty villages. Even before this time, drought conditions and warfare had reduced Pueblo populations.

Despite differences between Pueblo divisions, it is obvious that considerable similarities existed. Agriculture was the basis of life, supplemented by hunting and gathering activities. Corn, beans, and squash were basic food crops; tobacco and cotton were also raised. Surplus was stored against poor growing seasons. Much of the work of agriculture was in the hands of men. Along the Rio Grande, irrigation made the occurrence of rain less a necessity; a fact reflected in their religious behavior. In the West, dry farming was practiced, locating fields so as to take advantage of rain runoffs from washes. Wild plant foods such as cactus fruits and piñon nuts were collected, and a fair amount of hunting took place. Deer, antelope, and rabbits were of chief importance. In the Rio Grande area, buffalo were also taken.

Each of the Pueblo villages was an autonomous political entity, even among the Hopi where they were often located close together. Theocratic (priest-chief) control occurred with the heads of religious societies and/or moieties forming the government unit, with one of their number being the head chief of the village. A separate chief occupied a position of war leader and generally was responsible for the maintenance of internal order. Such leaders determined village affairs, judged "crimes," and scheduled religious events. Today among Rio Grande villages, an additional set of officials introduced by the Spanish makes the aboriginal structures of government somewhat more difficult to determine. Government control over village members was absolute, and in such villages the desires of individuals were carefully socialized into feelings for the welfare and solidarity of the group. Conformity was the rule. Despite theocratic leadership, there was no real wealth or social differences although some people had more "status" due to their intimacy of religious involvement. Warfare in aboriginal times appears to have been primarily defensive in nature although after Spanish contact groups of Pueblo Indians often served as auxiliary forces, aiding the Spanish in their subjugation of other Indian groups. This leaves recollections by informants less than adequate testimony for original conditions.

The second grouping of Southwest Indians to be examined is that of the Pima and Papago who are the Pimans. This language group is also included in the Uto-Aztecan stock, and the two languages represented hardly differ from each other. The major differences between the two groups are basically tied to environment. The Pima lived along the Salt and Gila rivers and constructed irrigation ditches, permitting rather intensive farming. The Papago lived under more arid, riverless conditions, and while they did some farming, they were more dependent upon hunting and gathering activities which contributed up to three quarters of their food supply. Corn, beans, pumpkins, and squash were agricultural staples; wild vegetable foods included roots, stalks of certain plants, and mesquite beans. Cactus fruits were extensively used. Among the Pima, both men and women did agricultural work, but among the Papago, because of the greater need for wild plant foods, the women spent their time in pursuit of these. The animals hunted included deer, rabbit, rats, and several species of wild fowl.

Villages of the Pima were fairly large due to the concentration of much of their food supply and were permanent. The Papago were seasonally nomadic, moving from summer areas where they planted their crops to mountain areas where hunting was more rewarding in the winter. As a result, the Papago dwellings were less substantial, consisting of a framework of branches covered with brush and earth. Both groups made excellent basketry, carrying bags, mats of vegetable fiber, and pottery.

Differences in the style of subsistence were carried over into social behavior. The Pima had a sense of total tribal identity. A tribal leader existed, chosen by the local village chiefs. Such individuals had some degree of power and directed the necessarily communal and organized irrigation activities. Papago leadership was more fragmented. Each village was a separate entity and consisted of fewer people than among the Pima. Members seem mostly to have been patrilineal kinsmen who lived under the more informal leadership of a headman, along with hunt and war leaders assisted by a council of the adult males. Such officers had priestly functions as well; the village headman apparently being the chief ceremonial official. Both Pima and Papago had patrilineal clans and were divided into moieties. Marriage was mostly monogamous with the patrilocal extended family a major social and work unit. Warfare for both groups appears to have been primarily of a defensive nature – they faced the same threats as the Pueblos. In actual fighting, the Pima seem to have organized large numbers of fighters who marched to meet the enemy. The Papago got a few men together for a revenge raid, fighting in a much less deliberate fashion.

The third division included speakers within the Athabascan family of languages. These were the various Apache groups and the Navaho. These groups had moved into the Southwest somewhat prior to 1600 A.D. The Apache were semi-nomadic peoples who raided extensively. Five large "divisions" existed: Jicarilla, Lipan, Mescalero, Chiricahua, and Western; the latter had a number of subgroups. Each differed somewhat in its subsistence activities although they all originally entered this area as hunters and gatherers. Subsequently, some developed some dependence upon agriculture. The Cibecue (Western) Apache, for example, planted small plots of corn, beans, and squash in the mountains in the spring, left older people to care for them, and then left to collect wild plant foods – cactus fruits, acorns, mesquite beans, etc. – and returned in the early fall to harvest, and spent late fall in hunting. Raiding other groups was also a means of augmenting the food supply. Dwellings were simple, and basketry the most outstanding craft.

None of these groups had any real political unity. Locality groups of matrilocal extended families formed the basic economic cooperating unit, and a number of these joined on occasion into a band, chiefly under the stimulus of warfare motivation. Marriage was chiefly monogamous and mostly within the local group. While the Western groups developed a matrilineal clan system, the other Apache traced descent in a bilateral fashion. Each extended family had its own headman as did the local group. Such leadership was built heavily upon personal qualities and was of an informal nature. When local groups combined for war, most of these leaders met to select a common leader. Smaller raids, however, were separately organized. War was considered a prime masculine activity, and Apache warriors became extremely feared throughout the Southwest.

The Navaho also originally entered the area as hunters and gatherers but learned agriculture from Pueblo sources and gained heavier dependence upon it than did the Apache. Hunting and gathering retained some importance however. After Spanish contact, the herding of animals became significant. Their typical dwelling was the Hogan, constructed of logs covered with mud. Basketry and pottery were rather poor in comparison to other peoples. The basic economic group was the matrilocal extended family, and descent was matrilineal, forming people into clans. The basic social unit was a locality group consisting of a number of cooperating extended families, the leader of one also assuming the general headmanship of all. Each such group also had a war leader. Decisions involving the whole "community" were apparently based upon consensus. Like the Apache, the Navaho raided neighboring peoples for food and women although they were perhaps a little less motivated along such lines.

The last of the Southwestern groups are the Yuman language speakers. Here again there are two divisions. The Upland Yumans, consisting of the Yavapai, Walapai and Havasupai, lived under very arid conditions and were similar to Great Basin peoples to the north. These people had a knowledge of farming but relied chiefly on hunting and gathering activities. Deer, antelope, and rabbits were taken, and wild seeds, fruits and roots were collected. The Havasupai relied somewhat more on agriculture. These peoples lived in dome-shaped huts, and marriage and the family were simple with bands of families loosely united under the headman types of leaders. Such leadership was based upon skill in hunting and oratorical ability. There was no sense of total tribal identity. Warfare was primarily of the raiding variety. The Havasupai, situated in the bottom of the Grand Canyon, seemed insulated even from that.

The River Yumans included the Mohave, Yuma, Cocopa, and Maricopa. In some respects, they represent cultural forms transitional between California and the Southwest. These peoples generally lived in small farming villages scattered along river-bottom lands. Some engaged in agriculture more than others. Corn, beans, and pumpkins were major crops. River flooding provided irrigation and aided in the dependability of this mode of subsistence. Some fishing as well as gathering of wild vegetable products occurred, but hunting appears to have been limited chiefly to small game such as rabbits.

The patrilocal extended family was an important economic unit, and patrilineal clans occurred. These tribes did have a sense of tribal identity, and hereditary chiefs helped to keep internal peace within them. However, they were only informal leaders. These groups did exhibit a degree of aggressiveness. Boundaries within and between tribes were defended, and both small raiding parties and larger groups led by special war chiefs engaged in hostilities. Young men used war as an avenue for gaining prestige, and scalping and taking of captives were practiced.

Having now very briefly characterized the various Southwestern groups, we will now turn to their supernatural beliefs and practices.

CHAPTER III

PUEBLO INDIAN RELIGION: WESTERN VARIETY

This chapter deals with the western variety of Pueblo Indian religion. It will be remembered that this encompasses the various Hopi villages, plus the Hano on first mesa, and the Zuni. It also includes Acoma and Laguna. These last, the western Keresan groups, will be considered in the succeeding chapter. Before beginning, it is necessary to make brief mention of the difficulty of studying and learning about Pueblo Indian supernatural behavior. As Byron Harvey has put it:

> Historically, the progress of studies on Pueblo religion have been hindered by several adverse factors facing the student:
>
> 1. The defensive stance of Pueblo religion, first as a reaction to repressive measures in the 1600's and later as a reaction to further repression and conflicting Anglo values....
>
> 2. Difficulties presented by multiple explanations of symbols and mystical or secret aspects to the beliefs and ceremonies.
>
> 3. The existence of six languages....Few non-Indian workers have even one of these under control.
>
> (Harvey 1972:198-99)

We can add to this the sheer complexity of their system of beliefs and practices and the great number of variations on the common Pueblo theme. Since many would-be informants are not members of the esoteric religious groups, we can also only obtain informed guesses on many topics. There is the related problem of shifts of people from one Pueblo to another altering what might have been more individualistic religious behavior. Nonetheless, some broad descriptive outlines are possible, and it is to these that we now turn.

Hopi Religion

A great deal of literature exists on the supernatural behavior of the Hopi, and they appear to represent the most comprehensively studied Pueblo Indian group. The present account basically follows accounts given for the Pueblo of Oraibi. Their behaviors are reasonably typical for the Hopi in general. Fred Eggan has neatly summarized the major elements of the organization of these people: "The ceremonial organization of the Hopi is highly complex and includes the kachina cult, the men's societies concerned with tribal initiation, the Winter Solstice ceremony, and the various societies concerned with rain, war, clowning and curing. The ritual activities are organized in terms of a ceremonial calendar and each major ceremony is associated with a clan, a society, and a kiva" (Eggan 1950:89). Perhaps the key concept here is that of the clan, a social group we have previously discussed. A specific clan (occasionally two) had charge of each society and the ritual activities for which that society was held responsible. Generally, the clan leader was also the society chief, and important ritual paraphernalia were kept in his possession. The actual society membership consisted of some related clansmen, but members of other clans might also be initiated. Hence, society membership crosscut those of clans in a unifying manner. Members were sponsored by a ceremonial "father" who already belonged to the group in question. While some rites might be held in the house belonging to the clan, most such rites were held in the kivas, (ceremonial chambers). These structures symbolized the underworld from which, in myth, the ancestors of the Hopi emerged. Kivas were also owned by clans.

The ceremonial calendar of the Hopi was a rather fixed structure of annual rites. The dates of performances were determined mainly by the position of the sun, observed by a special priest, the sun watcher. The year was divided into ritual seasons, the period between winter and summer soltices being the time for most of the important rites. Generally speaking, each ritual followed a nine-day schedule of activities. "As a rule, the first seven days...are given over entirely to esoteric, kiva ritual; the eighth day sometimes combines public activities with private; and the ninth day is generally featured by a public exhibition commonly called a dance" (Titiev 1944:105). The time period was extended in some cases. Most of the secret rites on the initial days consisted of the following activities: smoking tobacco, singing, and praying seemed central, plus the manufacture of prayersticks (carved cylinders of wood with attached feathers) and other offerings which could later be deposited at sacred places. Altars were also constructed and consisted of an upright portion in front of which various cult objects were placed. Symbolic drawings on the floor were made by using sand and colored cornmeal. Another important activity was the making and drinking of medicine water. A common purifying act consisted of the washing of the hair with suds manufactured from the yucca plant.

There were many specific rituals which follow the Hopi calendar. Some of the most important included the following. In December was the *Winter Solstice* ceremony (soyal) which was perhaps the keystone of Hopi ceremonialism. It emphasized the annual cycle of the sun but had many other natural elements and symbols incorporated within it. At this time, the sun is thought to start back towards its summer home which will bring the warm weather necessary for planting the fields. In February, there was the "bean dance" or *Powamu* ceremony, designed to aid in the germination and fertility of crops. This was also the occasion for initiation into the Kachina cult which will be described presently. Kachina dances during the summer continued the theme of fertility and rain, and rites performed by the Flute and Snake and Antelope societies in August also aided in rain-bringing and ripening of crops. In September was the main harvest, and in November the cycle was terminated by performance of the *Wuwutcim*. This not only served to initiate young males into full adulthood but also incorporated many other seemingly diverse elements, including the notion of life after death, human fertility, and the emergence myth. Rites by female membership groups stressed fertility along with thanks for the harvest. Other more minor rituals might be interspersed between all the above activities.

We can now look at some of the above rituals in more detail and also at some of the groups associated with them. The first real connection between the Hopi individual and ritualism began with initiation into the Kachina cult. These rites were to convert the child (6-10 years old) into a youth and linked the living with the Kachinas as well as bestowing a new name and the opportunity to return to the underworld at death. It should be mentioned that the Kachina cult was the only tribal-wide ritual grouping that initiated both boys and girls. "The Kachinas are associated with the cult of the dead and are thought of as generalized ancestors who return with the clouds and rain to help the community. They normally come in groups to dance in the plaza, being impersonated by the men. The more important Kachinas...are thought of as clan ancestors and are impersonated by clansmen in connection with important ceremonies" (Eggan 1950:91). These latter Kachinas were represented by permanent masks; others seem subject to variation and innovation. Hopi theology suggests that once an impersonator put on a Kachina mask he "became" the particular Kachina he was representing.

These Kachina spirits were thought to visit the realm of the living during half of the year – winter to summer solstice – and, with one exception, return to their home in the underworld for the duration of the other half. As previously mentioned, when visiting, their impersonations usually were dramatized in group dances. Dancers wore the masks and decorated and painted their bodies in a fashion appropriate to the Kachinas being represented. Two clans cooperated in conducting the annual cycle of dance performances. The first Kachinas represented are special types; later on in the cycle any Kachinas might be impersonated. During colder weather, dances were held in the kivas; later on they occurred in the village dance plazas. Each kiva group impersonated a type of Kachina. The visit of the Kachinas was concluded shortly after the summer solstice in a lengthy ritual called the Niman or homegoing dance.

Young children, of course, believed that these dancers are the spirits themselves. Since this belief would not persist past adolescence, they must be initiated into the cult.

> During the Kachina initiation the child learns that the supernatural beings whom he has known from infancy as bringers of gifts and rain and also as dispensers of punishment, are really only people he knows dressed up to impersonate

> them, but he also learns of the Kachinas' key role in the scheme of things and his own part in the cosmic exchange for the mutual welfare of all. His godfather gives him a new name and from now on he may participate in the Kachina rites and gradually assume his share of responsibility for the great annual cycle of ceremonies which gives significance and zest to Hopi life. He has acquired a certain status in the tribe as a whole and may return to the underworld when he dies (Thompson and Joseph 1945:56).

Since this initiation occurred during the February Powamu ceremony, we may now briefly describe this rite.

The ritual itself (led by the heads of the Powamu and Kachina societies) was preceded by an introductory rite, the Powalawu. Indeed most major rites are so preceded. During this rite, prayersticks were manufactured and a sand painting was made with a sun symbol as its center. It was surrounded by supernatural objects including a corn ear fetish. Smoking, a prayer, and singing followed. Many of the songs involved the function of blessing. Objects were taken and deposited outside the village. Prayersticks were taken to the different kivas, and the chief priest told the leaders that they might now plant beans in the kivas. This planting "...seems to symbolize the planting of corn, beans, etc....of the coming season. He expresses a prayer that these ceremonies may give them blessings, that no evil may befall their crops, that they may come up, have plenty of rain, grow well..." (Voth 1901:83). During the interval before the Powamu rite itself, kivas were repaired, small children were given special haircuts, and informal dances took place.

The first four days of Powamu seem relatively unimportant. Paraphernalia were collected, and the chief priest blessed the growing beans. On the fifth day, prayersticks were manufactured, and the altar was prepared. It was on this day of the ritual (every few years) that initiation into the Powamu society itself occurred. Candidates were brought into the kiva and songs and prayers occurred. A special Kachina (Chowilawu) centered and danced around the altar while other participants sprinkled medicine water and corn meal upon him. The chief priest made an address to the initiates, urging them not to reveal what they have witnessed. The initiates have now become members of the Powamu society and could learn its secrets. They also might act later as Kachina Fathers–those who led the dancers to the plaza and gave them offerings. On the sixth day, those who were to be initiated into the ordinary Kachina cult underwent their rituals in a separate kiva, and other rites occurred. The altar for this initiation consisted of three figures representing Kachinas pictured holding whips of yucca leaves. After preliminary ritual, the candidates arrived. The chief priest, now representing the god of germination and growth, entered and recited a considerable body of sacred lore. He then sprinkled medicine water on the candidates and left the scene. After some ritual, three Kachinas arrived and danced in a rather frenzied fashion. An initiate was placed on the sand painting and was whipped by one of the Kachinas–generally four strokes. Girls remained dressed, but boys were nude. The whipping continued until all had gone through the ordeal. "When all the children had been flogged [one] Kachina steps on the sand mosaic...and is then severely flogged by both Kachinas, after which the two latter apply a thorough scourging to each other in the same manner..." (Voth 1901:104). They then retired. The initiates were admonished not to reveal the secrets they had learned.

The seventh day was primarily given over to preparation of paraphernalia. On the eighth day, altar rites occurred as it was taken down, and purification of the participants with ashes took place. The ninth day consisted of a complex series of rites. These involved ritual maneuvers, the making of cornmeal designs, gift distributions, and the walking about of Kachinas. Some of these latter were of a type ("angry") which supposedly punished disobedient children. This was done chiefly by visiting their homes and frightening them into good behavior. At night the Powamu Kachina dance (bean dance) was held, one of the few unmasked dances of this type. "Inasmuch as the performers announce on entering a kiva that they are real Kachinas...it does not take long for the recent initiates to discover that the Kachina impersonators are their relatives and fellow villagers. In such dramatic fashion is the most important of all Kachina secrets revealed to Hopi children" (Titiev 1944:119). As previously mentioned, a major function of the Powamu was to aid in crop growth, hence the planting of beans in the kivas.

As children mature, they undergo further ritual attendance. Girls (16-20) underwent a puberty rite. This was not, at Oraibi, correlated with the onset of the menstrual cycle. It occurred in June at the home of a paternal aunt of one of the girls. For four days, the girls would grind corn in a dark room and observe several food taboos. Aunts came in the evenings to bring more corn and take away that which had been ground. On the fourth day, the girls baked bread and had their hair specially arranged in the fashion worn at rituals. This made the girls eligible for marriage as they had demonstrated competence in adult female accomplishments. Rites transferring boys from youth to adult status were more complex. Prior to marriage a boy had to go through a second initiation into one of four tribal societies. These were Singers (Tao), Wuwutcim, Horns (Al), and Agaves (Kwan). The Wuwutcim group comprised the greatest number of members, and, in fact, the ritual itself is known by this name. The chief priest of this group was from the controlling clan, and he was simultaneously the tribal initiation leader. These groups cooperated together in the performance of the ritual but appear to have different functions and symbolic referents. The Agaves and Horn groups paid homage to the destructive aspects of life. The former was especially associated with the god of death. The Singers and Wuwutcim venerate powers of germination and life.

The ritual only occurred when sufficient initiates existed. The basic ritual was structured along the following lines. After preliminary rites, two fires were kindled, and fire was taken to participating kivas. The Kwan chief impersonated the death god. Members went to sacred spots away from the village where they would pray to the Kachinas for rain, harvest, and health and deposit offerings. The dead were asked to join with the living. The next day there was a dance and ritual smoking. The third day exhibited dancing, and some Wuwutcim members dressed as pregnant women and were decorated with phallic designs. The fourth day had more dances by some groups plus altar rites for others. On the fifth day, the image of the goddess Dawn Woman (obtained on the first day) was returned to a shrine, and the fertility oriented groups would carry on in symbolic fashion.

> In the afternoon, the Singers, naked except for breech clouts, and adorned with or carrying realistic phallic representations, revile the women in bawdy, rowdy, exhibition to which the women retaliate by dousing them liberally with water and urine and by smearing them with filth. Sometime later, the

> Wuwutcim men, likewise featuring a variety of phallic signs, emerge from their kiva and try to outdo their predecessors in obscenity, while the women ply them with refuse and even with human ordure (Titiev 1944:132).

On the sixth and seventh days, no major rites were held. On the eighth day, a dance symbolic of corn germination occurred. On the ninth day, there were secret dances and rites and the sprinkling of a line of cornmeal which was then later obliterated. This line represented the path of the homeward-bound dead. Throughout the ritual, the initiates received attention. On the first day, they were taken to a shrine and led back in a fashion that suggests they cannot walk by themselves – here they are children waiting to be reborn and Dawn Woman represents their mother (in her mode as goddess of childbirth). Later (on the fourth day), four Kwan men dress in the costumes of corpses and visit the initiates waiting in the kivas. Apparently at this time, the initiates were "killed" by the Death God and are reborn as men. Having met with the dead, they were assured of a reception in the other world of spirits. Finally, their heads were ritually washed and they received new names. In essence, this rite not only created men, but it also reestablished the link between the living and the dead, this world and the next, while introducing the ever-present fertility and germination motifs.

Perhaps because of the efficacy of this rite, rituals and conceptions of death are underemphasized among the Hopi.

> Mortuary rites are simple and quickly accomplished, the Hopi showing a marked aversion to anything connected with death. The hair of the deceased is washed by his paternal aunt and the body is wrapped and quickly buried by the oldest son on the day or night of death. It is placed in a flexed position with a 'cloud' shroud over the face and a stick is inserted upright in the grave to serve as an exit for the soul, which is believed to stay in the grave for three days and on the fourth to begin its journey to the land of the dead. The spirit of the deceased is propitiated with prayer feathers to forget and not to bother the living and the trail back to the village is ceremonially closed (Thompson and Joseph 1945:64).

The *Soyal* or winter solstice celebration was probably the most important ritual. Any of those persons who belonged to one of the four tribal initiation societies might take part in this rite, and, in fact, it followed the initiations in a year when those rites occurred. The rite itself was under control of the village chief who was assisted by leaders drawn from the important societies. Preliminary ceremonies occurred the day before it commenced and consisted of smoking and the manufacture of offerings. The first three days of the rite involved relatively minor activities. Prayer offerings were manufactured as well as altar paraphernalia. On the fourth day, war fetishes were brought into the chief kiva, and offerings taken and deposited at shrines. The war priest dressed like one of the war gods. War medicine was made, and during a series of songs, this was smeared on the bodies of the participants. During the seventh song, one of the participants pretended to stab the war priest a number of times; he fended him off with his shield. After the singing had been completed, all drank some medicine water and retained some in their mouths which was later rubbed on their kinsmen for health and bravery. That evening, an assistant chief danced.

The fifth day was mainly comprised of a number of evening impersonations of the Hawk Man (war bird). In these, a number of participants imitated the actions of a hawk. The dancers flopped symbolic wings and ritually handled a bow and arrow, screeching all the while in vigorous imitation. The sixth and seventh days were mostly given over to preparing alter paraphernalia and the making of a great number of prayersticks. On the eighth day, cornmeal and pollen were taken throughout the pueblo so people might breathe on them (perhaps as a charm against illness). The altars were also erected, and corn ears collected and brought to the kiva. Special Kachina dancers (Mastop) appeared who pantomimed sexual desire. "They began running among the spectators outside the kiva, taking a hold of a woman from behind here and there and going through the motions of copulation..." (Dorsey and Voth 1901:45). After the Kachinas leave, the war priests repeated their medicine-making rites, and in the evening, the hawk dance was repeated. Before dawn on the ninth day, some Agave society members brought a screen fixed with the picture of the main god of germination into the kiva. This representation held a grown cornstalk in one hand, and there were symbols of rain and lightning over his head. Moon and sun symbols were represented. A variety of seeds had been affixed to the screen, and these were then scraped off ritually by the Soyal chief. Then the sun (star) priest entered and performed a dance while chanting in accompaniment. His costume included a headdress in the shape of a four-pointed star. His dance was climaxed by the twirling of the sun symbol – a disk with a face in the center and with feathers radiating out from its edges. The twirling of this symbol represented, among other things, the going and coming of the sun.

All these ritual activities concluded prior to sunrise, at which time all of the participants went to deposit offerings at shrines. They made prayers for success in hunting, for males, and long life and fertility, for females. In the late morning, the altars were dismantled, and the corn returned (now consecrated) to be kept until spring planting. In the afternoon, the first group of Kachina dances (Qoqoqlom) of the season occurred. The dances really opened the season for such activities, and cornmeal was rubbed on the kivas to consecrate them. For the next three days, rabbit hunts occurred, and on the fourth day the Soyal members were ritually bathed and ate rabbit stew to finally terminate this major ceremony.

There certainly were many elements involved in this rite. The progress of the sun from one solstice point to another must have been the central element; to aid in this journey and bring the necessary warm weather for crops. Fertility, bravery, good health, and crop germination were other motives plus general blessing for all pueblo members.

The last major Hopi rituals were in the possession of two Flute societies, the counterparts of the Snake and Antelope groupings, and in the hands of three women's societies. We will make only a few comments on these. The rites of the former groups were held in August, and those of the Blue and Gray Flute groupings alternated every other year with those of the Snake and Antelope societies. The general purpose – accomplished via prayers to the sun and other ritual activities – seems to have been for rain to nourish the growing crops and for their fertility. In the case of the Flute ritual, it also aided the sun in its return from summer to winter, acting in the reverse fashion of the Soyal. Because of popular familiarity of Hopi snake dances, we can briefly describe their rituals.

As usual, there were preliminary rituals involving smoking and the manufacture and disposition of prayer offerings and they made prayers for rain. There were also initial rites in the Snake kiva contained within the main rites themselves, and these included collection of altar paraphernalia including images of the god of War and goddess of Germination. Men also went out periodically to search for snakes in the surrounding countryside. On the fifth day, members of the Antelope society became more active, and the two groups met for joint participation. Also on this day, if necessary, initiation of new members took place. Now was also the occasion for a man and woman to dress as "Antelope Youth and Maid" (mythic heroes). Both groups gathered in the Antelope kiva. After singing, impersonation took place with the intention of securing long life for the participants. These rites were repeated on the sixth day. The seventh day mostly involved preparations.

On the morning of the eighth day, members of the Snake group went through both kivas and imitated the thunder and lightning. A ritual race to the village occurred, and some earlier rites were repeated. In the afternoon, members of both groups danced around a previously erected structure of cottonwood in the plaza. The two lines of dancers danced facing each other. The Snake chief priest and antelope counterpart did a solo dance in which the latter held a cluster of vines in his mouth helped by the Snake chief. Then the groups danced around the structure and returned to their kivas. On the concluding day, the rites and races of the previous day were repeated. In the snake kiva, the snakes previously captured were ritually washed with yucca suds. They were then later placed in bags outside the plaza structure. Again the two lines of dancers formed. After singing, the snake members paired up behind each other with the second placing his hand on the shoulder of the front man. The front man was handed a snake. "This he places between his teeth, grasping its body with both hands, both move slowly around in a sinistral circuit, the holder of the snake moving it and also stepping to the time of the singing.... Every dancer drops his snake after a few minutes and gets another one, the snakes thus dropped being picked up by another set of men..." (Voth 1903:346). All the snakes were employed in the dance. A circle of corn meal was made, and the snakes were handed to Antelope men. "The girls and women then throw their meal into the circle, whereupon all who hold snakes throw them on one pile in the circle.... No sooner has the last reptile been thrown down than each snake dancer...grabs from the pile of snakes with both hands as many as they can get and dash with their handfuls of writhing reptiles from the village..." (Voth 1903:347). These were then deposited at shrines in various directions.

There were three women's societies: the Maru, Lakon and Oaqol. Of these, the first was most important and had its own kiva. Their nine-day rite in January involved singing and dancing, some of which was obscene and phallic, a sort of counterpart to male activities during the Wuwutcim rites. Fertility certainly seems to have been a motive here. There were also fall observances by this group in which expression of germination and rain symbols played a prominent part, along with war elements. The rites of the other two groups also emphasized germination and fertility.

As among other Pueblo Indian groups, there was a *War Association* among the Hopi and a corresponding war ritual. Some interpretative difficulties occur here. There was a warrior group, the *Momtcit*, which every able-bodied male apparently had to join. A subgroup comprised of those who had killed and scalped an enemy – "real warriors" – appears to have had special initiation/purification rituals of membership and put on a victory war dance in the fall featuring war weapons and scalps and involving gift distributions. Scalps were also ritually cared for during the year. The general warriors society also held regular fall observances involving medicine made from scalps and the ritual "swallowing" of sticks. Also during war, the Agaves and Horns groups were relied upon to supernaturally weaken the enemy (because of their death associations).

We may conclude this incomplete presentation of Hopi ceremonial groups and their rituals with brief mention of three other sets of groups. Some scholars assert the presence of a Hunt group. Among Pueblo groups elsewhere, there appears to have been a permanent association of this sort with a chief priest. They offered prayers for hunting success and for the fertility of game. This is less clear for the Hopi. At Oraibi, for example, any man, regardless of clan membership, may have become "hunting Chief" and was able to perform appropriate rituals in honor of the patron deity of game animals. He also participated in leading the actual hunt activities. Certainly, the Horns group had some hunting powers. Nonetheless, the Hopi situation appears to be somewhat less formal than that found among some other Pueblo societies.

The existence of ritual Clown groups is also a point of difficulty in our understanding of their supernaturalism. Elsewhere, these, even today, often accompany Kachina dances with grotesque, comic antics in the course of which they violate normal social taboos, behaving in the reverse of normal ways as well as providing a counterpose to the sanctity of the occasion. There appear to have been no permanent associations of this sort among the Hopi although on an ad hoc basis some such activities did occur. There is also remembrance of more formal groups as having been active in the past, and the usual two formal groups may have been formally recognized. It is possible that the Wuwutcim and Singers groups had taken these functions over, as had perhaps the Horns partially in the case of hunting and the Agaves somewhat in the case of war.

The apparent lack of specific curing groups to rectify supernatural illnesses, especially witchcraft, has also puzzled scholars. Each of the societies mentioned previously had control of some illness (their "Whips"), which they themselves can bring about, but they are certainly not curing societies per se. Eggan (1950) suggests the presence of actual curing groups – fire-doctors and eye-seekers – for burns and witches especially. But Dozier (1970) suggests the activities of individual curers rather than the existence of specific societies. Certainly such practices lacked the complexity found elsewhere in the Pueblo area even though accounts exist of initiation into regular ritual groups as a response to illness.

Hano Religion

Before turning to the Zuni variety of Western Pueblo religion, we can briefly examine the Hano, the Tewa group that took up permanent residence among the Hopi of first mesa. In some respects, their system of supernaturalism approximates that of the Hopi, from whom they have obviously borrowed more than just traits of social organization. Yet, due either to loss of complexity or incompleteness of study, there are descriptive uncertainties of reference to these people.

> Hano religious organization and ceremonies are not as complex as the Hopi, but bear similarities to those of the latter. Yet, despite these resemblances, affinity to the New Mexico Tewa is also evident in virtually all areas of Hano religion and ritual. Basic in the organizational pattern of the religion are the two-kiva pattern and the clans associated with the kivas. The core of the ceremonial system of the Kachina cult and the ceremonial association system. Kachina performers are drawn from members of clans which belong to the kivas and the performances are fitted into the Kachina cycle of Walpi (Dozier 1966:72).

As indicated above, two kiva groupings occurred among the Hano, court and outside kivas, with the clans in court kiva furnishing the impetus for much of the ritual activities. The head of this group (Bear clan leader) was the village chief and was concerned with watching over the village. This he accomplished by prayers for rain and similar acts. He was assisted by a sun watcher who set the dates for rituals and, in a capacity as a "talking chief" for the village chief, communicated that person's wishes and other information. The outside kiva group furnished leaders associated with more secular groupings and activities. The assistant to the head of this group was the war chief who was charged with protection of the village from enemies. In such capacity, he also opposed the activities of witches and guarded the sanctity of the people. He appears to have had additional functions in leadership of communal hunting activities.

There were a number of religious groups or associations found among the Hano. The *Kachina cult*, as previously mentioned, occupied the center of their ritual stage. Initiation into this group occurred between the ages of six to ten for both males and females. The rite follows essentially Hopi lines. Originally the dance cycle was composed of four one-night dances throughout the year held in the kivas. More recently, however, they have meshed such activities into the Hopi ritual cycle, and now Hano dance groups (after first visiting their own kivas) visit the Hopi kivas on the appropriate occasions. Of some interest is the notion that some of their Kachina dances appeared to have curing functions, a trait of uncertain nature among their neighbors.

After Kachina initiation, boys next joined the *Winter Solstice Association*, entry into which usually required a new ceremonial sponsor.

This initiation was actually into the kiva grouping and is somewhat like the initiation of Hopi boys into their tribal associations. During solstice celebrations, the initiates learned the appropriate songs, prayers, and legends. Girls underwent a puberty observance at the time of their first menstruation. This rite is nearly identical to that for Hopi girls. At this point in the life cycle, both males and females are considered ready for marriage.

Along with the above associations, other Hano religious groupings are comparable to those found elsewhere in the Pueblo area although complete information on them appears to be lacking. A *clown* organization, the Koyalah, now extinct, seems to have accompanied Kachinas and other dancers to amuse spectators with their antics and to heap ridicule on transgressors of social custom. There was also a *curing* association, the Sumakolih, with abilities to cure a specific illness–sore eyes. They appear also to have engaged in rites designed for collective benefit. A number of individual curers also existed. As among their Hopi neighbors, there are a number of more secular observances.

> Social dances are of many types, but animals and war dances probably prevail. Some of these dances are obviously very old, going back to early Tewa-Plains contacts. Social dances are performed...primarily for entertainment; they also differ from the more esoteric rites in that novel forms are permitted and improvisations are constantly being introduced....The songs and dance steps retain basic Indian patterns, however, and Euro-American features are absent (Dozier 1966:80).

We can now turn to the last group to be described in the present chapter.

Zuni Religion

It has been said by some scholars that the supernatural beliefs and practices of the Zuni represented the highest degree of Pueblo theology and complexity. Indeed this does appear to be the case. Their system was, however, a variation on common Pueblo themes, most of which have already been discussed for the Hopi. Speaking of the Zuni, Leighton and Adair observe:

> This is a religion of great formalism, precision and compulsion. Nothing is left in the balance; there is room for free play and individual variation in song, costume and dance only as

> secondary features, as embellishments to the basic form....In Zuni religion the gods must be compelled by precise action. Once these ritual acts are performed, they automatically bring the desired results. The organization of priests and the part each plays in the working whole are as precisely defined as the prayers they utter for the public good. Each of the priests is trained to carry on his own duties, which interlock with those of other priests like the gears of a delicate machine (Leighton and Adair 1966:45).

The ritualists devoted to the above included a great number of elements and paraphernalia. Prayers were very important and appeared to be very mechanistic; articulated correctly, they were automatically effective. Fetishes of various sorts existed in many forms–feathered corn ears, stone objects, masks and, of course, the altars themselves. These included upright portions as well as the meal/sand paintings. Prayersticks were common items. In theology was the notion that the spirits nourish themselves on the food offerings and clothe themselves in similar fashion from the feathers on the prayersticks. Medicine water was drunk as well as sprinkled on things to induce rain. Along the same lines, the blowing of smoke was said to produce "clouds." Yucca suds were also whipped up in bowls manufactured for this purpose. Head-washing was an act of purification. Singing and dancing were usual accompaniments of most rituals although public performance of them often seems subsidiary to more important esoteric rites performed by major priests. Sometimes "...the dance is not performed by the same group that hold the core of the rite, but by some cooperating group or by an organized group of laymen...." "...the complexity of ritual is more apparent than real. All ceremonies have five principal aspects–the manufacture and veneration of sacrosant objects, offerings, purification, abstinence and seclusion, recitation of sacred formulas, public celebration" (Bunzel 1930:507-08).

Zuni rites occurred on an annual calendar from winter solstice to winter solstice with the period of the solstice being considered the "middle" or center of time as the pueblo itself was the center of space. Other ceremonies fall into place on a cycle laid down along the same lines as those previously described for the Hopi. Ruth Bunzel distinguishes seven cults or major cult groups, and the present work follows her simplified presentation of these.

Perhaps the only truly tribal-such cult was that of the *ancients* or *ancestors*. This was the popular cult in as much as there were no special priests or fetishes. People would pray to ancestors in general and give them offerings, especially prayersticks. There was some ambivalence since some fear existed that the dead, in remembrance of their former human lives, would long for relatives and trouble them in dreams from which they might sicken and die. On balance, however, the ancestors were beneficent. "They are identified with the greatest of all blessings in this arid land, the clouds and rain. In prayers they are referred to as 'those who have attained the blessed place of waters' and when they return they came clothed in the rain" (Bunzel 1930:510). Upon this stratum of supernaturalism rested the esoteric cults with their priests, fetishes, and calendrical rites.

The *Sun* was referred to as "our father" and was considered the source of all life. A special priest, the Pekwin, was one of the most important Zuni leaders. As the priest charged with observing from shrines outside the village the passage of the sun (like the Hopi sun watcher), it was he who set the dates for the solstice rites and hence the other ceremonies. He appears in the past to have also had charge of a special sun-worship public ceremony.

A second cult was that of the *Uwanami*, or water spirits. As the name implies, these lived in the waters of the earth. They appear to be bringers of rain par excellence as well as crop fertility and were worshipped by twelve priesthoods comprising two to six members each drawn from specific matrilineage family groups within clans. They retained the appropriate fetishes (etowe) within their own possession. These fetishes were considered the most powerful supernatural objects employed by the Zuni. The groups of priests appear to have been hierarchically ranked with those of the north, east, south, and west; these directions being the most important. The village chief was also the head of the chief of these priesthoods, that of the north. This group also had a permanent altar that was said to represent the center of the world. Like the Pekwin, the rain priests were extremely sacred personages who were removed from worldly affairs and activities.

Most of their rituals took place during the summer when the growing crops required rainfall. The various groups went into retreat in their ceremonial houses in a series, aided by the Pekwin and chief war priest, from the end of June to September. Major groups retreated for eight days, and minor ones for four. They could hold no public rites at this time. "The purpose of these retreats is to secure rain – immediate rain for the thirsting young plants. Should the days of any group fail to be blessed with rain it receives the censure of the community, and one of its members will surely be suspected of laxness in the observance of his duties" (Bunzel 1930:515). Kolowisi, the Horned Water Serpent, was also associated with the worship of those water spirits in as much as he was the guardian of sacred springs.

A third body of Zuni ritual involved the *Kachina cult*. This comes close to being a tribal-wide cult, but, unlike the Hopi, generally only adult males were members. The Kachinas represent the lost children of mythic ancestors. Apparently the dead joined the Kachina in their village but were not identical to them as in Hopi belief. Moreover, only dead people who had been initiated into the cult could join them. This leaves unexplained the fate of women and children. Predictably, the wearing of masks transformed the impersonator into the god, and the dancers now represented these beings who no longer came in person to the pueblo. The cult society was led by a chief priest and a set of lesser officers. This director appears to have come from a specific clan. They performed the associated esoteric rituals.

The organization was divided into six subgroupings, each of which was associated with a kiva. Membership by subgroup was basically decided at birth by the choice of a ceremonial father. Each group had to dance on at least three formal occasions during the year. Winter dances, free from the need for rain, were more lighthearted affairs. Initiation into Kachina groupings follows Hopi practice with an initiation into the secret knowledge and revelation of the human nature of the participants. Whipping inspired awe of the Kachina but also was considered as a form of blessing.

A possible subcult within the Kachina cult itself was that of the Kachina Priests. This society concerned itself with the worship of a somewhat different type of supernatural being. While they could bring rain, as did most Zuni supernaturals, their major contribution was that of aiding human fertility. The masks, that were used in their impersonation, which were great fetishes, were of tribal rather than individual ownership and were kept in the possession of certain matrilineal descent groups. The spirits themselves, thought to dwell with the regular Kachina at their village, as their name implies, are their leaders. Each of the gods of this group had a distinct nature, and each had its own cult group composed of past impersonators. New members learned the ritual from those already in the group although they might choose an impersonator from among the present membership. Each of these gods appeared in the village to carry out his own particular ritual. The chief of these spirits was Pautiwa, representing beauty, dignity and kindliness, and the mythic references to his sexual exploits with human females are testimony to the fertility nature of this class of deities. The famous Shalako (messengers) also belonged to this group as did the Koyemci, the sacred clowns who participated throughout the year in dance and other ritual activities. The phallic significance of much of their activity was again a reflection of their role in fertility.

The cult of *Animal Spirits* (beast gods) was highly developed among the Zuni. These gods were thought to have the ability to give curing powers and medicines and were associated with the various directions. They were also considered the source of disease and death. The bear was the most powerful of these spirits. Both males and females might be initiated into these societies of curers, and there appears to have been twelve such groups.

> The mode of joining the different esoteric fraternities in which the sick are healed through Mystery medicine is substantially the same. Although those restored to health usually join the fraternity to which the theurgist called upon belongs, to do so is not obligatory.
>
> ....
>
> When a restored patient desires to join the order, a small quantity of sacred meal...is deposited in a corn husk. It is then folded in rectangular form, tied with the greatest care, and carried in the right hand of the restored invalid to the theurgist who effected the cure....The theurgist carries the package at night to one of the points of the compass, makes an excavation, and sprinkles the contents of the husk into it as an offering to the Beast Gods (Stevenson 1904:415).

Only males seem to have held offices of leadership, and each curing group had two divisions. One consisted of members with full knowledge of the secrets and curing techniques. The second division appears to have had an apprentice-like status. A few curing societies also had other suborders which functioned in weather control and performed stick swallowing and eating activities. Each such society had specific ritual knowledge that permitted it to control a specific illness as well as more general functions in controlling witchcraft – that great threat to the natural order of things.

> These groups had highly developed rituals and paraphernalia and held collective performances in the fall and winter, especially at the winter solstice at which time there was a more general curing rite that did not involve the "patients" joining the societies. Their other rites occurred periodically and were for regular curing purposes and the initiation of new members. It should be mentioned here that one of these societies, the Newekwe, while maintaining curing functions also played a role as ritual clowns, like the Koyemci. Their behavior, however, appears to have been more contrary to custom, and these clown groups were not coequals.
>
> ....
>
> While the Newekwe are considered great theurgists, one of the organization is seldom called upon except in extreme cases, from the fact that the invalid, if cured is expected to join the fraternity and one naturally hates to indulge in its filthy practices, but after joining the new fellow seems as eager as the others to excel in their disgusting acts.
>
> ....
>
> To add to the amusement of the spectators, members of the Newekwe frequently appear in the plaza with the Koyemci between the dances of the gods, and whenever this occurs they play the fool generally, but it is when the Newekwe appear in large numbers that their conduct is shocking.
>
> ....
>
> Each man endeavors to excel his fellows in buffoonery and in eating repulsive things, such as bits of old blankets or splinters of wood. They bite off the heads of living mice and chew them, tear dogs limb from limb, eat the intestines and fight over the liver like hungry wolves (Stevenson 1904:430, 437).

Among these groups, there was also a Hunters Society. Apparently they had some functions relative to hunt activities since prayerstick offerings could only be made when members of a household belonged to this society and its controlling clan. Society members also possessed medicine to help in hunting and participated in rites after a successful hunt, helping to dip fetishes in the blood of the slain animal. Fetishes appeared to be the property of individuals, however, and did not belong to the ritual group. A portion of the animal was also offered to the animal spirits. We observed similar confusion in such practices among the Hopi.

The last major esoteric grouping surrounds the cult of the *War Gods*. "The gods of war in Zuni are the Ahayuta, twin children of the sun begotten...when the Zunis, wandering in search of the middle, were in dire need of military leadership" (Bunzel 1930:525). These beings lived in the surrounding mountains, and their worship was under the control of two chief priests – Elder and Younger Bow Priests – who were selected by the chief rain priest. There were also minor priests in whose custody fetishes and scalps were entrusted. This cult practiced various war rituals which gave victory in battle. Membership was restricted to those who had killed and scalped an enemy. Initiation was accomplished in the scalp dance ritual which celebrated the victory and also transformed the malevolent power of the scalps into positive form as rain fetishes. In fact, part of the ritual itself concerned rain symbolism, highlighting once again such a necessity in the life of the Zuni. Those warriors who had not met the conditions prerequisite for such initiation apparently joined another group – along the lines of Hopi practice.

The Bow Priests and their assistants also functioned as a mechanism for internal religious control. That is to say, since the priests of other groups were aloof from mundane things, it was this group which executed their orders, defended the faith, and especially sought out witches (assisted by the curing groups) and tortured confessions from them. To aid in the performance of the above activities, members of this society were assigned to most of the other religious groupings. While the scalp dance was formally held at regular intervals, this cult group also performed at the winter solstice and after the harvest in the fall. Of course, such individuals also assumed positions of leadership in warfare.

We can now briefly examine a Zuni ritual, selecting as an example that which enables a descriptive extension of the range of such rites for Pueblos in general. As one writer has generally summarized.

> The ceremonial calendar co-ordinates and interrelates the various cults and ritual activities in a complex way. Each cult has a cycle of ceremonies starting and ending with the winter

> solstice, where all are fitted into a twenty day period of ceremonial celebration....The winter ceremonies are primarily concerned with medicine, war and fertility, while the summer ceremonies are concerned with rain and crops. At the solstices there is a convergence of these various activities in honor of the sun (Eggan 1950:209).

Perhaps the most impressive Zuni ceremony is known as the "Coming of the Gods" and was part of the cult of the Kachina Priests and involved their impersonation. General blessing, rain and fecundity are its benefits. "The coming of the gods...(or Shalako) so called from the most conspicuous participants, is the great annual cycle of ceremonies of the Kachina Priests. The esoteric ceremonies last throughout the calendar year, starting with the appointment of impersonators at the winter solstice and culminating in a public festival of fourteen days duration in the early part of December, shortly before the winter solstice" (Bunzel 1932:941). This rite continues at present. The Shalako costumes themselves are probably the most unique among the Pueblos. They are perhaps ten feet in height and are supported by poles attached to the waist of the impersonators. The masks surmount a long cylindrical structure which narrows at the top and covers a skirt-like bottom. The impersonator looks out a hole in the middle of the costume.

During the previous winter solstice, the head priests select the impersonators of the various masked spirits who will be involved. Acceptance of special wooden shafts (crooks) indicates formal appointment. At this time period, too, those people who will undertake the expense of holding public rites in their houses volunteer to do so. There should be eight such houses. This involves not only building extensions onto or renovating houses but also supplying food. As such, "The richer class is likely to entertain the Shalako most frequently, as they are better able to remodel and enlarge their houses from time to time, yet those who are very poor sometimes aspire to this honor" (Stevenson 1904:230). During the year the various impersonators begin meeting to learn the prayers, etc., requisite to their positions. During this time they must also offer special daily prayers and offerings. Especially from about midsummer on, they must also work in the fields of those who are opening up their houses, and they must aid in the construction or reconstruction of these. A flurry of such activity occurs as the time for the public rites begin.

The coming of the Koyemci signals that the time is at hand. These gods come and visit the various plazas, announcing that the other gods will come in eight days time. They then go into retreat in their ceremonial house. On the eighth day, prayersticks are offered to summon the gods, head Kachina Priests and the Shalako from their place of residence. The gods approach the pueblo. The Shalako remain outside the village until later while the other gods involved enter the village and plant prayersticks in six excavations in the village streets. They then go to a house and dedicate and bless it. Six other houses are blessed by the six Shalako, and the remaining one by the Koyemci. When the Shalako come, they are met by priests who pray and sprinkle them with cornmeal. They go to the houses they are to dedicate followed by the Koyemci who sing for them and then finally go to the house that they themselves will bless. The process of blessing is approximately the same. The gods place prayersticks inside the threshold and deposit seeds in an excavation in the center of the house. The host questions the gods as to why they have come, and they reply with a long formalized recitation and invoke their blessings, especially fecundity. About eleven in the evening, there is a feast, and the masked gods dance in the houses until about dawn. Sometime prior to noon the next day, the Shalako, followed by the other Kachina Priests, leave the houses. Cornmeal is again sprinkled on them, and they make offerings and deposit prayersticks to fructify the earth with rain. They then leave for their own village. The Koyemci do not appear at this time but have other ritual responsibilities later on.

CHAPTER IV

PUEBLO INDIAN RELIGION: EASTERN VARIETY

This chapter deals with the Eastern variety of Pueblo Indian religion found among the Eastern Keres and Tanoans. Brief mention is also made of the Western Keres who form a link to those groups discussed in the previous chapter. We can begin by discussing the Eastern Keresan Pueblos: Cochiti, San Felipe, Sia, Santo Domingo, and Santa Ana. While variations occur among these groups with respect to their supernatural practices, we can, for general comparative purposes, present a sort of amalgamated account.

Eastern Keresan Religion

We have already observed that in the West, weather control – rain and sun for crop germination and growth – was important and central to religious motivations. Perhaps because of better water resources and irrigation in the East, the basic concern appears to have shifted to curing groups and rituals concerning themselves with human illness.

> Prominent in the Keresan pueblos are the medicine societies. They are secret organizations of doctors whose chief function is the curing of disease. But they have other functions as well. They are important as rain-makers, they are indispensable at the solstices, and they function at births and deaths. Supreme political control of the village rests, virtually, among the medicinemen (White 1928:604).

So such groups have both specific and general functions. Since they occupy the center of the supernatural stage for the Keres, we can begin our discussion with them.

A number of medicine societies occurred. Perhaps the most common were the Flint, Giant, Fire, and Cikame. They were primarily concerned with the treatment of illness caused by witches although they had full power to cure many other things. The other, less widely distributed societies, for example, Ant, Snake and Lightning groups, gravitated more towards specific ailments. Membership in these medicine societies was usually for life and was generally in response to having been cured of illness by the members of that group. Members could also be "trapped"; if they broke some ritual taboo related to the group in question, they might be obligated to join it. Occasionally, a person could join voluntarily. Initiation consisted of the common Pueblo pattern of learning secrets and ritual techniques followed by public demonstration of the candidate's abilities. Each society had a house, and members received power from "animal doctors," especially the bear. Effigies of these animals were placed on altars as supernatural objects. Generally, the oldest member of the group served as its leader. Before returning to a brief consideration of other functions, we may describe that of curing since this area of supernaturalism has not been presented for Western groups and the techniques are generally equivalent.

Curing procedures at Sia Pueblo were more or less typical. White (1962) distinguishes three types of curing ceremonies: clearing-away, halfway, and all-the-way doctoring. In the first case, the initiative was taken by the sick person or a relative by taking cornmeal to the appropriate shaman. This individual then went to the patient's house. He sang songs (to gain power) and diagnosed the patient. He brushed away evil with eagle wing feathers and deposited offerings to his helping spirits. He would visit the sick person up to four successive nights. Medicine might be given to the patient.

In more serious cases, the latter two types of curing were employed. Here petition must be made to the village and war chiefs for the cure to take place. Cornmeal was taken to a society leader who discussed the case with his members. Four days of preliminary activities occurred during which there was vomiting by the shamans for purification and songs and prayers for the benefit of the sick person. On the evening of the fourth day, altars were constructed, and they went to the house of the patient or brought him to their ceremonial chamber. First there were prayers and songs and the shamans (in turn) purified the house of the patient. They then diagnosed the patient; often sucking out "disease objects," giving him medicine water to drink, and washing him. Prayersticks were deposited for his recovery. If the case was serious – a lost heart – divination of the whereabouts of the witch responsible took place. This was done by looking into a bowl of medicine water or into a crystal. Some shamans go

> ...outside the village, looking for witches. Sometimes they fight them....
>
> ....
>
> If they have been out after the patient's stolen heart they invariably return with it. The "heart" is a ball of rags, in the center of which is a kernel of corn; the corn is the real heart. The doctors unwrap the rags and examine the corn closely...he is given the corn to swallow and a draught from the medicine bowl. All the relatives of the patient are given medicine to drink from the bowl (White 1962:298).

Near the end of winter, the village chief also ordered a communal curing rite to drive out evil spirits and witches and purify the village. This ceremony ran about the same as described above except that the village chief symbolically occupied the place of the patient and was cured by all the shamans, who spit disease objects into a bowl and "captured" witches and "killed" them.

As previously mentioned, the Keresan medicine societies added to their curing activities a number of other functions and associations. At the solstices, they performed rituals to reverse the direction of the sun. In times of drought, it is they who went into special retreat and, at regular intervals, it is they who undertook four-day rainmaking activities featuring the performance of esoteric rites. The medicine societies also aided the Kachina dancers in their preparations and in their performances. It is also of interest to note that two of these groups, Flint and Cikame, are often associated intimately with the closed associations – holding membership in these groups. Finally, among some of the Keres, the village chief had to be a member of one of these groups. Quite often, there is an association devoted to war activities as well – keeping of scalps, choice of war chief or participation in war dances.

A second grouping which occurred in Keresan Pueblos is the Moiety division. Each pueblo divided its people into two groups based upon kinship or residential lines, and each of these groups was associated with one of two kivas. Generally speaking, one obtained one's membership from one's father. A wife joined the kiva grouping of her husband. Some shifting of membership was possible. These groups, most commonly called Turquoise and Squash, do not function at the present as marriage-regulating devices. Their function is and was ceremonial. They are charged with dance and other ritual activities.

> In most of the Keresan pueblos, the Kachina cult is associated with the kivas as a dual organization. Zia and Santa Ana pueblos depart from this pattern, however. In Zia, some seven medicine associations, including one of the clown associations have masks and each may conduct its own ceremony. Participants are drawn from males who are inducted into the cult on a village-wide basis. Santa Ana's Kachina cult is divided into five groups, each managed by a medicine association. In all the Keresan pueblos medicine associations and the clown organizations...control and manage the cult and its activities (Dozier 1970:156-57).

In general, the Kachina cult of the Keres approximated practices already described. The organization existed for the purpose of impersonating Kachina spirits (Shiwana) in masked dances at specific times of the year. Initiation into the organization sometimes did not involve whipping, but masks were removed to show children the human nature of the impersonators, and vows were exacted not to reveal the secrets. The general dance pattern involved a number of dancers wearing the same mask (line dancers) who danced together single file accompanied by groups of two or three persons (side dancers) who danced in and around them and who wore different masks. Female Kachinas also occurred sometimes acting as musicians. The purpose was for rain, fertility, and general well-being.

> The Shiwana live in a pueblo at a place...called Wenima. When a person dies, he eventually becomes a katsina. The chief function of the shiwana is to bring rain. They used to come to the pueblo in person to dance for the people and to bring rain to their fields. But for some reason they quit coming, long ago. Nowadays, in order to get the rain-making powers of the shiwana, men and women dress up with mask and costume and impersonate them in dances. When they do this they possess the power of the real shiwana: their dancing brings rain (White 1942:210).

It should be pointed out that the scholars possess less full accounts of various types of Kachinas for the Keres and other Eastern groups than they do for the Hopi and Zuni. This arises from the conscious effort on the part of these peoples to guard such knowledge of the cult from outsiders–as a result of early Spanish attempts at suppression. The Western Pueblos encountered less difficulties and are hence less cautious about guarding their secrets.

A religious organization closely related to the Kachina cult was the two clown groups, generally called the Koshare and Kwirena. As elsewhere, their function was to provide comic relief at rituals and to function as agents of social control; among other things ridiculing during the rites spectators who have broken custom. They also aided in the conduct of ceremonial activities, assisting the medicine societies and accompanying Kachina dancers. At Cochiti, for example, "Of major concern to the Ku-sha-li [Koshare] Society was weather control, fertility of the animal and plant worlds and, related to these, the supervision of many ceremonies" (Lange 1959:298). At this pueblo (and apparently elsewhere), the two groups alternated with each other in activities although the Kwirena group was said not to engage in actual clowning activities. Of some interest is the notion that the Koshare (or both groups) had curing functions, although perhaps less power in this regard than regular medicine societies. Each of these groups was composed of males who are full-fledged members and a few women who act as assistants. The motive for joining was voluntary, or a parent may dedicate a child to the group. Trapping also apparently occurred.

Another basic grouping among the Eastern Keresans was the Warriors Association (Opi). This group apparently was structured along Western lines although there does not appear to have been any woman's groups to care for scalps. This group was headed by two war priests (sometimes only one) representing the twin war gods Masewi and Oyoyewi. Along the lines of the Zuni bow priests and at Hono, the Keres war priests (given the sanctity of other ritual leaders) functioned in the maintenance of internal social order and ensured the rituals were properly carried out. Of course, their primary function was in actual war activities.

> The purpose of the warriors' society in the old days was two-fold: military and ceremonial. In case of war the Opi were

> supposed to be the first to fight and the most effective. In taking scalps of slain enemies, in "taking care of the scalps" in the pueblo and in performing rituals and dances with the scalps, the Opi brought ianyi (power blessing) to the pueblo. This in concrete terms of pueblo ideology meant bringing rain – and, perhaps health and strength (White 1942:132).
>
> Although every able-bodied man was a warrior as well as a farmer, the Opi were regarded as especially fitted for war; they were man killers and they had supernatural power (White 1942:305).

Among some Keres today, there are "animal Opi" that have been instituted to take the place of man-killers – men who have killed bears or mountain lions. This may be a functional replication of older practices or by analogy have existed concurrently with them in the past.

Finally, as an organized group, there was the Caiyaik – the Hunters Association. This group, which has only male members, secured its power from various prey animals, especially the mountain lion. It was considered as a sort of curing society although its powers in this regard were apparently limited to hunting accidents and related illnesses. They did not take part in the annual curing rituals. It is not entirely clear who might join this group although scholars list the same motivations as for joining a medicine group. Formal initiation occurred in the past. The major function of the Caiyaik was to help the hunters in securing game. Prior to communal hunts (which were usually led by other officials) the hunting shamans performed rituals which gave the hunters power over game animals. They blessed weapons, talked of hunting to draw game close to the village, engaged the hunters in songs and dances, and deposited prayersticks. They also staged animal dances in which buffalo, antelope, and deer were impersonated. At Santa Ana, for example, "...two bison, four or five deer, and twelve or fifteen antelope are represented as a rule....The bison dancers stand and dance erect; the impersonators of the other animals walk on all fours, holding sticks in their hands for forelegs" (White 1942:298). This dance was performed around Christmastime in response to a request from some individual, and its performance required the assent and assistance of the Caiyaik leader. Sometimes towards the end of a series of such dances, the animal impersonators were symbolically killed by men not taking part in the dance itself. They were then treated as if they were real dead animals after a hunt. Such dances not only gave hunters power over game but are said to have brought moisture (snow).

The existence and function of a Woman's Society is not known for the Eastern Keres. While women may have formed subgroups within other organizations, whether there was a distinct group or groups as among Western peoples is difficult to determine at this point in time. It has been marked for Cochiti that

> At present, there are four members of Women's Society (Koyawe)....Informants insisted that this society has no connection with scalps or war. The principal function of the group is the ceremonial gathering of corn to make prayer meal...(Lange 1959:283).

As a final point on ceremonial structure, we may mention the position of village chief, the Cacique. The principal duty of this sacred official was (as elsewhere) to watch over the pueblo and to pray and fast for its welfare. In so doing, he possessed an important fetish and remained aloof from ordinary village affairs. In addition, he appears to have functioned as the sun watcher, setting dates for rituals and taking prominent part in some of them. He represented the mythic goddess of creation and so was referred to as the "mother and father" of the people.

The ceremonial calendar and components of ritual of Keresans are similar to those already presented for the Hopi and Zuni. Solstice rites, rain retreats, Kachina dances, harvest rites, curing rituals, and other esoteric activities all occurred. Whether due to less compete fieldwork or natural conditions, most rites appear to be less complex than those of Western groups. To such ceremonies can be added a number of rites that appear to be of Spanish or of Mexican Indian derivation, missing in the West because of their greater isolation from such contacts. While there are definite Pueblo overtones to such rites–in terms of content and staging–they are usually interpreted as late increments of Pueblo ceremonialism and not treated here. So too are Spanish-Catholic activities at birth, baptism, marriage, and death. We can turn now to the Tanoan component of Eastern Pueblo supernaturalism.

Tanoan Religion: Tewa

While a number of Tewa pueblos exist, certain generalizations are possible relative to their supernatural beliefs and practices. Study of these societies has been uneven, San Juan being perhaps the best studied at present. Where specific examples are necessary, they will mostly be drawn from this pueblo.

The moiety divisions of the Tewa are generally called Winter and Summer. The population belongs to one or the other based upon the membership of the father, and at some villages there exists a tendency to marry like-associated people. The kivas are associated with this dual division, the usual pattern being one large and one small kiva similar to the Hano situation. Sometimes one kiva was used for Kachina cult activities while the other was for practice and other types of dances. The position of village chief is of great interest among the Tewa. It was based upon the dual kiva-moiety division. One half of the year, the Winter moiety chief fulfilled this role; the other half, he is replaced by the chief of the Summer division. "...only among the Tewa is there a double caciqueship or town-chieftaincy with a divided charge of the people according to season, and only among the Tewa is the alignment into Summer people and Winter people, the outstanding principle of social classification..." (Parsons 1929:89).

The occupant of the position of village chief functions very much like his counterpart elsewhere. He is called "father and mother" of the people, has custody of important fetishes, conducts or assists in solstice rites and rain rituals, and generally remains aloof from secular affairs. He makes prayersticks and other offerings on behalf of the people whose welfare is his sole concern.

At San Juan, the natural and supernatural worlds are each divided today into three hierarchically ranked categories. In the natural world are "dry food people" – the common person who is outside the religious system, the Towae – who are special "political" officers, and the Patowa or "made people" – who are society members. In the supernatural world are the counterparts of these: the souls of ordinary people, spirits of mythical emergence significance, and a category of deities who existed prior to the emergence of the Tewa ancestors and who are joined by the souls of Patowa after they die. Against such a canvas of belief are superimposed people and groups and ritual motivations and functions.

The common Tewa (dry food people) undergo six rites of passage. At birth mother and child are secluded, and naming of the child occurs on the fourth day which gives the child a general social identity. During the first year, a water giving rite is held. The appropriate moiety chief prays over the child and gives it medicine water and its moiety name. The child is now close to being "human." Between the ages of six and ten, the child undergoes the water pouring rite which completes the transition to the dry food category. It is again presided over by the moiety chief. Spirit impersonation occurs, and the children are instructed in traditions, are bathed, and have medicine water poured over them.

When a sufficient number of children over ten years old exist, the finishing rite is held. This is also by moieties. The child is awakened at night and taken to the kiva. Boys and girls are separated at this point. The chief Kachina spirit of the moiety (they are organized by moiety division) appears and lightly whips the girls, who are then taken home. The boys are then whipped more severely, following which (as elsewhere) the mask is removed and the secret of impersonation is revealed. Other masks are taken from their place of safekeeping and are presented for examination to the young male initiates. Marriage and death complete the life cycle stages, but rites of passage at such times are less significant, the latter being accompanied by the same ambivalence as noted for other Pueblo groups.

The Towae transcend the moieties being drawn from both and function on a village level of activity. The nominees – selected for a one year term from among the dry food people – for this position "...are those known to have a firm commitment to and knowledge of native ritual" (Ortiz 1969:69). They function to protect society members during their rites, in witch hunts and as protectors of custom. "However, their primary and most time consuming duty throughout the year is to coordinate...all rituals planned and directed by the Made People and participated in by the Dry Food People" (Ortiz 1969:72). They serve also as a check on the power of ritual officials. They may whip with impunity (while impersonating certain gods) any person who has deviated from the norms. In such activities, they appear to function much like the war priests at other pueblos.

When we examine the nature of Patowa, we arrive at the other ritual organizations. These groups of Made People also cut across the moiety division. Membership comprises a large proportion of the entire village population and is recruited without regard to moiety affiliation. Each society has a leader and two assistants, his right and left "arms." The specific recruitment process is as elsewhere: dedication by parents, voluntarily, or by trapping. Initiation of members involves the usual acquisition of ritual knowledge and demonstration of newly acquired skills. We may briefly examine each of these groups.

The Medicine Societies (Pufona) exist to cure illness as well as to perform other functions. There appears to have been only two such groups among the Tewa, and at some there appears to be only one medicine group at present. Given the apparent individualistic nature of curing among Tanoans in general, the actual number in the past is dubious although two would carry out the theme of their dualism nicely. Cures themselves involve many Keresan-like traits–use of fetishes, division into minor and major illnesses, sucking out of disease objects, fighting of witches, and restoration of stolen or lost hearts. There was also a communal rite held periodically for the benefit of the village as a whole.

There are two Clown associations. They are generally called Kossa and Kwirana. "Like any true clown, the ceremonial clowns are more than just funmakers and entertainers. They are, first of all, masters of ceremony who introduce the characters; secondly, they are the 'bringers of the Kachina.'...The clowns also have a moral function" (Laski 1959:13).

A Hunters Society exists among the Tewa, generally with the mountain lion as a patron saint. Prayers for the success of hunting expeditions and the fertility of game and the performance of animal impersonation dances were its chief occupations. A Warrior society formerly existed. It is hard to resurrect data on this group. One assumes that, as elsewhere, at least its inner membership consisted of scalp takers and that there were war dances and rites of initiation. "From a folktale one may infer that there were war songs, sung on going forth and on the return. Against the return a fire was built in the kiva and all the men were summoned and the warriors had to tell their story....The folktale suggests that until after the war dance...in four days, the warriors had to stay in retreat" (Parsons 1929:138). Members of this group apparently also retained scalps in their possession and, except on special occasions, "fed" them. The existence of a Women's society among the Tewa appears much confused. Some scholars suggest a scalp association to care for enemy scalps on formal occasions and to aid human fertility. It is possible that different groups seasonally or in some other way divided these functions. Speaking of San Juan:

> The Women's society presents an insight of special significance. Within the group of three (or more) women who comprise the society, there are two divisions. The head, who is called "Red Bow Male Youth," has a white corn mother (fetish), but the other two, who are called "Blue Corn Women," have blue corn mothers.
>
> ....
>
> The principal duty of the Women's society is to care for the scalps in the possession of the Scalp society. The head is called "male youth" because she represents the Winter moiety and maleness, although she may be recruited from either moiety. The Blue Corn Women, in turn, represent the Summer moiety and femaleness, although they, too, may be recruited from either moiety (Ortiz 1969:89).

As elsewhere in the Pueblo area, there is an annual cycle of ritual activities. In order to ensure the cyclical events of nature will reoccur each year, each society meets in retreat for a number of days until all have met. These "works" are repeated by each group until all have so met. They then repeat the process for the next event. The major rites would be ineffectual without these more esoteric activities. Such major rites include weather rites, germination and fertility activities, harvest, the transfer of seasonal responsibility between moieties, solstice rites, and ceremonies of Mexican derivation. One rite of great significance to these people is the Raingod (Kachina) ritual for which an excellent description exists (Laski 1959). At present this is performed only once each year.

Prior to the actual ritual itself, a number of days are spent in preparation of the masks, in choosing impersonators, in purification of participants, and in dance practice. The ritual itself takes place in the large kiva. People enter as does the town chief and his alternate. Soon two ceremonial clowns come to the kiva, descend the ladder, and walk around among the people. They eat a small meal and tell jokes and give bits of food to the audience. The clowns then blow ashes and try to "see" the Kachinas coming. Three special women sprinkle a line of cornmeal from the ladder as a sacred path for them. Some men take blankets and make a screen around the ladder area, and the impersonators line up behind it. Suddenly, a fearsome noise is made; the clowns appear frightened but welcome the gods. The chief Kachina steps from behind the screen. "The people perform the Feeding Rite by taking cornmeal in their hands, exhaling their breath upon it, and then throwing the cornmeal to 'feed' the gods, all the while praying..." (Laski 1959:49).

More Kachinas make their entrance. The chief Kachina asks to speak to the caciques, and they talk of their concern for the people and their fear that people have not been good. The gods are assured that people have been good. The gods then individually return behind the screen after first giving a general blessing by moving their hands and arms in various directions in a sweeping motion–"...to take in the Great Goodness, that is, the powers of rainmaking and of raising corn and squash, beans and watermelons, the powers of killing deer, buffalo, and rabbits; in short, the blessing of fertility and abundance" (Laski 1959:52).

After the Kachinas have left, a special "clownish" Kachina enters and looks around. The clowns engage him in conversation. The god requests a young virgin, and eventually a young girl stands up. The god gives her a freshly killed rabbit. She takes off her shawl and hands it to one of the clowns who arranges it in human shape (as a person ready for copulation) on the floor. The Kachina goes through the blessing rite, and when he had taken the Goodness, clasps his hands and throws it at the girl. He repeats this fertility-oriented rite with three other young girls and retires. The clowns take the sacred melons (which the raingods had earlier brought in with them) and break them into small pieces for all present to eat. They retire, and the caciques give a prayer of thanksgiving. The people leave, and all those who actively participated pray and later deposit prayer offerings. In such a way, do the Tewa of San Juan achieve contact with the realm of the supernatural.

> But while the characters of the drama appear as individuals – each Raingod having his specific function, appearance and vocal sounds – this ritual drama is not the story of an individual person or god, but rather the drama of a group experience, the dramatic meeting of a people with their gods. In it, the spiritual powers are personified and dramatized....
>
> ....
>
> Because this drama is not the story of individuals and their destiny, but the story of a people and their gods, the dramatic projection of the very soul of each and every Tewa, everybody in San Juan participates in the ceremonial event (Laski 1959:60).

Such aspects are certainly true for Pueblo rituals elsewhere, at least in the past.

Tanoan Religion: Tiwa

Tiwa religion is incompletely known. For the Southern Tiwa, some data exists for Isleta, but Sandia is an ethnographic blank at the present time. In the north, Taos has been somewhat studied, but Picuris has not yielded substantive data. We can look briefly at Isleta and Taos.

A number of ceremonial cults or groups appear at Isleta, generally comparable to those found elsewhere. Each had a leader and two assistants. There is a town chief who was "...constantly referred to as the source of all ceremonial life, in the sense that permission to hold ceremonies or dances must be sought from him....On his own initiative he may ask for ceremonies....The summer rain ceremony the town chief appears to conduct himself" (Parsons 1932:256). He was also the custodian of a fetish and other ritual supplies. He remained, as elsewhere, remote from normal secular affairs, and the welfare of the people is said to rest in his hands.

The moiety organization existed including all pueblo people: The Shifun (black eyes) winter division and the Shure (red eyes?) or summer division. As among the Tewa, they divided up the year in terms of ritual responsibilities, a child belonging to the moiety of its parents or if parents belong to different divisions, the oldest child joined that of his father and subsequent children alternate membership. Each moiety had its own ceremonial chambers and "In all moiety ceremonials the two groups act separately, with the Black Eyes...being thought of as senior to the Shure..." (Parsons 1932:263). Each moiety appears to have had four special persons ("grandfathers") who may have had disciplinary functions.

A rather unique series of ritual associations at Isleta were the Corn groups. There are seven of these ceremonial groups, some of which appear to have subdivisions, and everyone joined one, generally that to which one's mother belonged. Initiation occurred at solstice periods. While data are incomplete, it is possible that the town chief was selected from the corn groups on a rotating basis. In some respects, these groups appear to have been a substitute for clans at Isleta. These ceremonial associations went into retreat at solstices and might engage in dancing and other ritual activities.

Of considerable importance were the Medicine societies. Although some scholars suggest the existence of only individual shamans, actual formal societies seem to have existed. As elsewhere, the chief technique in curing was brushing away and object sucking as well as dealing with witches. There was also a rite of general curing to exorcise evil spirits from the village. They also functioned in weather control and assisted at the solstice ceremonies. The catching of thieves – because of their divinatory potential – appears to have been a special function of some members. Parsons asserts the existence of two such groups: the "Town fathers" and the "Laguna fathers," some of the members of Laguna pueblos having migrated to Isleta in historic times and founded this group.

As indicated above, control of witches was a major function of these curing societies. Witches projected disease objects into the body.

> The witch comes as a light in the night....The witch light jumps from place to place. Witches are abroad in particular during ceremonials by the medicine societies. If an attendant at a ceremony faints, the inference is that his or her spirit has gone abroad on witchcraft. When the medicine societies initiate a new member, the witch society feels called upon to initiate one also. After killing a person, the witch society may exhume him to initiate him" (Parsons 1932:242-43).

Such beliefs are comparable to those of the other pueblos. It should also be mentioned that, apparently, persons other than medicine society members had clairvoyant powers, heightened by ingestion of a narcotic substance which enabled them to see great distances.

Reliable information on other ritual groups is scanty. A Warriors Society appears formerly to have existed, consisting of scalp takers. They functioned in leading war parties, at war dances, and, at least initially, in the ritual care of scalps. After taking scalps, a man was required to undergo purification. Female assistants to the town chief apparently took care of the scalp–fetishes the rest of the time–but appear not to have formed a regular women's organization. Whether the members of the Warriors Society assisted in the maintenance of internal affairs and were guardians of ritual is not known. A Hunters Society existed. Its leaders staged an animal ritual to bring game close to the pueblo during the fall and manufactured prayersticks for hunting success. There is no formal Caching organizations at Isleta (except for the Laguna colony). There is, however, a position of leadership (Caching father) and some general beliefs relative to these spirits. No masked dances occur although some without masks may have a connection to such masked dances elsewhere. Similarly, the existence and function of clown societies are not clear in the literature.

Ritual elements at Isleta are comparable to those elsewhere. Prominent were prayersticks, fetishes, altars, medicine water, ritual smoking, dancing, and singing. All ritual groups had their part to play in the calendrical rituals, those of the corn groups at the solstices perhaps being the most important. We can give a brief description of such rites for comparison to Western Pueblo practices.

The corn groups and medicine societies went into retreat for four days. After preliminary activities–prayerstick preparation, vomiting for purification, and rabbit hunting–each leader called down the "sun."

> In the roof of the ceremonial room there is a hole through which at noon the sun shines on to a spot on the floor near where the chief now stands. In front of the chief stand his assistants, then the row of the other men present, and then the row of women present. All turn to face the east, singing to call the sun....
>
> ....
>
> All sing the song of 'pulling down the sun,' while the chief makes the motions of drawing something toward himself. Now the sun drops down on the spot of sunlight on the floor. It is a round object, white as cotton....To this the chief ties the prayer

> feathers, as all sing. All stand and throw pollen toward the sun object. The chief waves the sun object....As the chief waves the sun around his head the sun goes back through the roof hole (Parsons 1932:292-93).

After ritual smoking, the participants rested. Then in the evening, they went outside and offered cornmeal to the moon and stars, and everyone gave thanks for the first day. The second and third days were similar with the addition of drinking water from the river for health and long life.

On the fourth day, medicine water was made, and an altar constructed. The leader chewed a ritual root and danced in the various directions, finally facing the sun as it shines through the roof hole at noon. He repeated the calling down of the sun rite, and special offerings were made. People entered for a drink of the medicine water, bringing food with them. Thanks was given, and they ritually ate. They were given cornmeal to keep for use at the time of spring planting and returned home. The leader and his assistants remained until the next morning.

Data for Taos are even more incomplete. That which we do possess should be treated with extreme caution. The most important groups at this pueblo consisted of kiva groupings. There were six of these divided equally into northside and southside organizations. The choice of kiva membership appears to have been optional, but only males seem to be formally initiated. Beginning at about the age of eight, a one-and-a-half year training period was formally observed, candidates sleeping in the kiva they were joining and learning songs, etc. Apparently, some concluding rite was held during a pilgrimage to a nearby sacred lake. Kivas probably took turns in the training of new members. Girls underwent brief puberty rites at the time of their first menstruation, staying in a room for four days and grinding corn in a manner similar to that of the Hopi. Hair and clothing changes signified the resultant change in status.

The kivas coordinated ceremonial activity, and with each kiva membership group, there appears to have been some "branches" or divisions. Some of these subgroups appear to have associations with more than one kiva. Data are more fragmentary; perhaps at one time they were separate groups that were absorbed or there were members in each kiva. "Each of these groups is small, from four to ten members....The head of the group or 'branch' is the kiva chief, although most of the groups have a special head or chief....All the 'branches' have special functions or ceremonies" (Parsons 1936:75). Of interest is the fact that the head of the Big Earring kiva (Northside) was also the town chief (cacique). He was assisted in such activity by the leaders of the other kiva groups.

Apparently the "branches" correspond to the specialized groups found elsewhere in the pueblo areas, as do some of the regular kiva groupings. For example, the Day kiva leader seems to have also been the hunt chief. The Black Eyes "branch" appear to have functioned as clowns. A second clown group may have been associated with a now defunct kiva which itself, possibly, was the ceremonial chamber of an extinct but remembered Warriors Society. Parsons feels that both clown groups had war functions (as do similar groups among Plain Indians). Data on women's associations is lacking. Curing activities by formal associations appear also to be absent, but individual practitioners exist and cure in typical pueblo fashion. Some of the other groups, however, may have controlled/cured certain illnesses. The Caching organizations, as at Isleta, are absent, but there are maskless dances of a similar nature and a belief in Latsina, "cloud people" who were once human. They are not equated with the ordinary dead, however. The turtle dance may be a maskless Kachina dance.

Tanoan Religion: Towa

Inasmuch as there is only one surviving Towa pueblo, Jemez, it is hard to generalize on what was certainly a widespread variation on the common pueblo themes of supernaturalism. Religious patterns are not unlike those observed for other pueblo groups although some unique structuring may have existed.

> Jemez control is in the hands of a supreme council known as the "Fathers," composed of the leaders of all the religious societies. Among these leaders the two most important are the Cacique and the War Priest....These two men wield more power in the pueblo than any of the other society heads, the War Priest taking the most active part in village affairs...and the Cacique spending more time in the retirement necessary to his "good heart" and the prayerful consideration of his people. That these men should function with aid of the religious

> council is common to the Rio Grande Pueblos, but that the members of the supreme council...all should be selected by the council itself rather than by members of those individual societies is an innovation as peculiar as selection of all the top twelve men of each society by the same general council (Ellis 1953:386-87).

The cacique had a fetish and was a sun watcher, and the war priest was a guardian of custom as well as a war leader.

There were also two general Men's Societies, the Arrow and the Eagle, into which all adult males were initiated. Membership was via father's affiliation, and a whipping initiation seems to have occurred. There appears to be no Kachina organization as such. Initiation into one of the two men's groupings and the consequent whipping are sufficient to allow a person to impersonate Kachina in dances the following spring. The men's groups appear to be the counterpart of the Tewa moiety organizations.

There were a number of other religious societies which included a pair of Medicine groups: the Arrowhead and Fire Societies. In addition to typical curing activities, they also functioned in weather control. As among the Keresans, the stick person generally became a member of society. There are also a pair of Clown groups like the Keresan Koshare and Kwirana, a Hunt Society, a pair of Women's Societies, and other groupings, some of which (i.e. Snake) appear to have counterparts elsewhere. Each society was headed by a group of twelve main men (priests) who were its most active members. As previously stated, these twelve were picked by the council–based upon their presumed qualities of leadership–giving strong centralized theocratic control at Jemez.

Inasmuch as a brief overview of Pueblo religion is presented in the last (comparative) chapter of this book, we can now turn to a consideration of another Southwest Indian system of supernaturalism, that of the Pima and Papago.

PUEBLO BIBLIOGRAPHY AND REFERENCES

Aberle, Sophie D.

1948. The Pueblo Indians of Mexico: their land, economy, and civil organization. *American Anthropological Association Memoir* #70.

Alexander, Hartley Burr.

1916. North American Mythology. The Mythology of All Races. Volume 10. Boston: Marshall Jones

Anderson, Frank G.

1960. Intertribal relations in the Pueblo Kachina Cult. *5th International Congress of Anthropological and Ethnological Sciences*, selected papers, pp. 377-83.

1955. The Pueblo Kachina Cult: a historical reconstruction. *Southwestern Journal of Anthropology* 11:404-19.

Bandelier, Adolph F.

1918. The Delight Makers. New York: Harcourt, Brace, Jovanovich.

Beaglehole, E.

1935. Hopi of the Second Mesa. *American Anthropological Association Memoir* 44:1-65.

Bourke, J. G.

1884. The Snake Dance of the Moquis of Arizona. New York: Charles Scribner's Sons.

Bunzel, R. L.

1930. Introduction to Zuni Ceremonialism. *Bureau of American Ethnology Annual Report* 47:467-544

Curtis, E. S.

1922. The North American Indian. Volume 12:1-291. Norwood: Plimpton Press. (Hopi)

Dockstader, F. J.

1956. The Hopi Kachina Cult. *Tomorrow* 4: #3:57-63.

Dorsey, G. A. and Voth, H. R.

1902. The Mishongnovi Ceremonies of the Snake and Antelope Fraternities. *Field Museum of Natural History Anthropological Series* 3:165-261.

1901. The Oraibi Soyal Ceremony. *Field Museum of Natural History Anthropological Publications* 3: 5-59.

Dozier, Edward P.
1970. The Pueblo Indians of North America. New York: Holt, Rinehart and Winston.

1966. Hano: A Tewa Indian Community in Arizona. New York: Holt, Rinehart and Winston.

Eggan, Dorothy.
1943. The General Problem of Hopi Adjustment. *American Anthropologist* 45:357-73.

Eggan, Fred.
1950. Social Organization of the Western Pueblos. Chicago: University of Chicago Press.

Ellis, Florence Hawley.
1953. Authoritative Control and the Society System in Jemez Pueblo. *Southwestern Journal of Anthropology* 9:385-94.

1951. Patterns of Aggression and the War Cult in Southwestern Pueblos. *Southwestern Journal of Anthropology* 7:177-201.

Fewkes, J. W.
1897. Tusayan Snake Ceremonies. *Bureau of American Ethnology Annual Report* 16:267-312.

1894. The Snake Ceremonials at Walpi *Journal of American Ethnology and Archaeology* 4:3-126.

Fox, Robin.
1967. The Keresan Bridge: A Problem in Pueblo Ethnology. London: Athlone Press.

Goldman, I.
1937. The Zuni Indians of New Mexico. In Margaret Mead (editor), Cooperation and Competition Among Primitive Peoples, pp. 313-53. New York: McGraw-Hill.

Haeberlin, H. K.
1916. The Idea of Fertilization of the Culture of the Pueblo Indians. *American Anthropological Association Memoir.* Volume 3, #1.

Harvey, Byron.
1972. An Overview of Pueblo Religion. In Alfonso Ortiz (editor), New Perspectives on the Pueblos, pp. 197-217. Albuquerque: University of New Mexico Press.

Hoebel, E. A.
1952. Keresan Witchcraft. *American Anthropologist* 54:586-89.

Hough, W.
1915. The Hopi Indians. Cedar Rapids: Torch Press.

Kirk, R. F.
1943. Introduction to Zuni Fetishism. *El Palacio* 50:117-29, 146-59, 183-98, 206-19, 235-45.

Lange, Charles H.
1959. Cochiti. Austin: University of Texas Press.

1958. The Keresan Component of Southwestern Pueblo Culture. *Southwestern Journal of Anthropology* 14:34-50.

1957. Corn Dances of the Rio Grande Pueblo Indians. *Texas Journal of Science* 9:59-74.

Laski, Vera.
1959. Seeking Life. Philadelphia: American Folklore Society Memoir. Volume 50.

Leighton, Dorothea C. and Adair, John.
1966. People of the Middle Place. New Haven: Human Relations Area Files Press.

O'Kane, W. C.
1953. The Hopi. Norman: University of Oklahoma Press.

Ortiz, Alfonso.
1972. New Perspectives on the Pueblos. Albuquerque: University of New Mexico Press.

1969. The World of the Tewa Indians. Chicago: University of Chicago Press.

1965. Dual Organization as an Operational Concept in the Pueblo Southwest. *Ethnology* 4:389-96.

Parsons, Elsie Clews.
1939A.Picuris. *American Anthropologist*, 41:206-22.

1939B.Pueblo Indian Religion. 2 Volumes. Chicago: University of Chicago Press.

1936. Taos Pueblo. Menasha: George Banta Publishing Company.

1933A.Hopi and Zuni Ceremonialism. *American Anthropological Association Memoir* 39:1-108.

1933B.Some Aztec and Pueblo Parallels. *American Anthropologist* 35:611-31.

1932. (1930) Isleta, New Mexico. *Bureau of American Ethnology Annual Report*, 47:197-466.

1929. Ritual Parallels in Pueblo and Plains Cultures. *American Anthropologist*, 31:642-54.

1927. Witchcraft Among the Pueblos: Indian or Spanish? *Man*, 27: 106-12, 125-28.

1925. The Pueblo of Jemez. New Haven: Yale University Press.

1924. The Scalp Ceremonial of Zuni. *American Anthropological Association Memoirs* 31:1-42.

1920. Notes of Ceremonialism at Laguna. *Anthropological Papers of American Museum of Natural History* 19:85-131.

Regan, A. B.
Dances of the Jemez Pueblo Indians. *Transactions of the Kansas Academy of Science* 23:241-72.

Robbins, W. J.
1941. Some Aspects of Pueblo Indian Religion. *Harvard Theological Review* 34:25-49.

Roberts, J. M.
1956. Zuni Daily Life. *Notebook of the Laboratory of Anthropology of the University of Nebraska*: Lincoln.

Simmons, L. W.
1942. Sun Chief. New Haven: Yale University Press.

Stevenson, Matilda Coxe.
1904. The Zuni Indians. *Bureau of American Ethnology Annual Report* 23:13-608.

1894. The Sia. *Bureau of American Ethnology Annual Report* 11:3-157.

Terrell, John Upton.
1973. Pueblos, Gods and Spaniards. New York: Dial Press.

Thompson, L. and Joseph, A.
1945. The Hopi Way. Chicago: University of Chicago Press.

Titiev, M.
1944. Old Oraibi. *Peabody Museum Papers* 22:1-277.

Underhill, Ruth M.
1948. Ceremonial Patterns in the Greater Southwest. *Monograph of the American Ethnological Society* 13:1-62.

Voth, H. R.

1912. The Oraibi Marau Ceremony. *Field Museum of Natural History Anthropological Series* 9:1-88.

1903A. The Oraibi Oaquol Ceremony. *Field Museum of Natural History Anthropological Series* 6:1-46.

1903B. The Oraibi Summer Snake Ceremony. *Field Museum of Natural History Anthropological Series*, 3:262-358.

1901. The Oraibi Powamu Ceremony. *Field Museum of Natural History Anthropological Series* 3:67-158.

White, Leslie A.

1962. The Pueblo of Sia, New Mexico. *Bureau of American Ethnology Bulletin* 184.

1942. The Pueblo of Santa Ana. *American Anthropological Association Memoirs* 60:1-360.

1935. The Pueblo of Santo Domingo. *American Anthropological Association Memoirs* 43:1-210.

1932. The Pueblo of San Felipe. *American Anthropological Association Memoirs* 38:1-69.

1930. The Acoma Indians. *Bureau of American Ethnology Annual Report* 47:17-192.

1928. A Comparative Study of Keresan Medicine Societies. *Proceedings of International Congress of Americanists* 23:604-19.

Whitman, W.

1947. The Pueblo Indians of San Ildefonso. *Columbia University Contribution to Anthropology* 34:1-164.

CHAPTER V

PIMAN RELIGION

The Pima and Papago represent another variant of Southwest Indian religion. More is known of the aboriginal patterns of the Papago since their more isolated geographical position insulated them to a higher degree against the influences of Europeans. This being the case, we will first discuss them and then close this chapter with remarks concerning the Pima. The assumption has traditionally been made that the religion of the two groups was roughly comparable, with that of the Pima being perhaps a little more complex in nature.

Papago Religion

The paraphernalia and ritual activities of the Papago are more than a little reminiscent of those of the Pueblos. The focal point for supernaturalism in each village was a dance area and a ceremonial house. The latter was a simple brush shelter and was under the care and supervision of a ritual official called the smoke keeper. This individual exhibits a priestly character and has charge of fetish objects which gave supernatural power to the village as a whole. He was also the main village leader. Fetishes were brought to the ceremonial house from places of hiding on the occasion of ritual activities; they were, apparently, not permanently located there. Other fetishes were possessed by shamans and other people and were kept in baskets. Shrines were fairly common, the most important for some villages consisted of piles of stones surrounded by a fence-like structure. These had connections to mythological events, and people who passed by them deposited offerings and requested luck and good fortune. Offerings included eagle down, tobacco (smoked in cane cigarettes), beads, cornmeal, and prayersticks, the latter of which may have been borrowed from the Pueblos.

In rituals themselves, there were a number of common elements. Purification was necessary prior to such events, consisting of fasting and abstinence from sex relations. At the close of a ritual, bathing in cold water removed any supernatural influences. Blessing (as among Pueblos) was accomplished by inhaling (breathing in) from ritual objects and blowing smoke over the body. Fetishes were also passed over the body to derive their supernatural benefits. Singing, dancing, and speech recitations were also very common among the Papago in their rituals. Songs and recitations describe the event or thing desired, and their articulation was felt sufficient to attain it. The songs were not really invocations to gods and spirits in most cases. Generally speaking, it was the elders or ritual officers who sang and recited and the younger people who performed the dances. Songs occurred in sets for each ceremony. Some were traditional, but new ones derived from dreams could be added. There were more formal beginning and ending songs in these sets. The middle of a song cycle was the occasion for more improvisation. Dancing, except for one possible borrowed rite, was without special costume although dancers did carry carved effigies of symbolic and natural phenomena. Ritual recitations fell into two classes. Some, like the songs, were to accomplish the purpose of the ritual. These formulas were mumbled in low tones and were not accompanied by gesture, etc. Other speeches had moralizing overtones and were shouted out by the speakers. Most rites seem to have involved the exposure of the appropriate fetish objects.

According to the chief student of Papago religion (on whose accounts the present chapter is heavily based), there were two major types of ritual activities.

> On the one hand was a calendric round of ceremonies conducted by a priestly hierarchy and bringing blessing to the whole community. It was a system of group control, in which the average man made no individual approach to the supernatural and received no individual power....Opposed to

> this was the democratic concept of the guardian spirit, opening the power quest to everyone. Formerly a Papago expected no success in life unless he met some spirit tutelary who had given him a song for use in time of need (Underhill 1939:17).

She goes on to characterize these as the food ceremonies and the power ceremonies. While the modus operandi appears different for both types and the contexts change, they both, nevertheless, had the same ritual goal in common: rain. The former type of rite was a communal public affair based upon a schedule; the latter rites were based upon individual initiative and were prompted by desire for the vision experience. The communal rites were essentially magical repetitions of supernatural means utilized by a mythical culture hero – Iitoi – in the past, and the songs sung are those he used to gain power. The power rites were based upon having gone through an activity fraught with supernatural danger: killing an enemy or an eagle, journeying to the ocean to gather salt, becoming a shaman, or, in the case of females, becoming pubescent. In most cases, such activities required the eventual seclusion of the participant, during which time not only purification but a vision was secured. The vision followed a standard pattern, and the content was, apparently, partially learned from a ceremonial guardian ("made father") who had himself undergone such an experience. Visions also occurred outside of this context. We can now examine the major manifestation of these two major frames of ritualistic activity.

Common Rites (Food Ceremonies)

Like their Pueblo neighbors, the Papago had concerns about their environment. Rain, fertility, and the abundance of the food supply were perhaps chief among these concerns. Rain was an end secured by many rituals, but it also had its own special specific ceremony. Each July, about the beginning of the rainy season, an annual Rain Making Rite was held. Its chief behavior consisted in fermenting and drinking a mildly alcoholic beverage from the juice of the giant cactus. The idea involved was that the saturation of the bodies of the participants magically would produce the saturation of the earth with rain.

The preparation of this rite consisted of women going to the groves of the cactus and collecting quantities of sap. As they did this, old men would recite speeches dealing with the origin of such activities. They would then return to the villages. Certain fetishes were brought to the ceremonial house as aids in proper fermentation, and eagle down was placed there as an offering. A special person or persons would be appointed to preside over the fermentation activities. Special songs were sung, and people would dance to assist in this process. The dancing took place for two successive nights, and during pauses in the dance, shamans were called upon to make rain magic. Some data exists concerning sexual license at this time. While some men apparently kept their wives at home, there were women whose activities in this regard furthered the ends of securing fertility.

At the main rite of consumption of the drink itself, a local village representative plus three guests occupied the four directional positions (sometimes four shamans from the same village). They represented the rain gods of the directions. The guests were invited by messengers who delivered formal speeches of invitation. After everyone had gathered near the ceremonial house and the guests had been seated, more formal recitations were delivered, and cup bearers brought the drink from the house to the main participants. They drank a portion and sang four rain charm songs. They also dripped the drink from their fingertips onto the ground, symbolizing rainfall. Subsequent to this main rite, everyone went to his own house and consumed the drink he had fermented until the supply had been totally depleted. Men went visiting from house to house to aid in this process. During the time of consumption, those who vomited were considered as "throwing up clouds" in keeping with the symbolism of the occasion. After the completion of this rite, rain and crop growth were considered as assured.

Planting occurred in the past after the above rite, and the growing season itself had a number of associated rites and observances. In April or May–prior to the crop cycle–pilgrimages were made by the members of some villages to the stonepile shrines previously mentioned. These were renewed so that winds and floods would not come and destroy the crops. In myth, the children had been sacrificed here to prevent this. Men whittled cactus sticks symbolic of cornstalks and took down the old fence around the shrine and used these to erect a new one. The stones were unpiled, bread offerings were deposited, and then the pile was rebuilt. A special speaker made a recitation to the four directions to ensure good crops and also a plentiful supply of wild plant foods. After their return, the night was spent singing special songs in the ceremonial house. Those villages lacking such special shrines used the village fetish that was in the charge of the smoke keeper, this individual smoking over it and reciting the appropriate formula.

During the actual cycle of plant growth, a great deal of song magic took place. Some villages left this to the individual farmer, others utilized the shaman for this task, some used a community song approach. In all cases, such singing encouraged growth and fertility of crops. Group rituals also occurred. Images were made representing the crops expected. Legends were recited and shamans assisted.

> After four songs the shaman took up one sample of each fruit in succession, blew upon it, held it up, and asked help of the rain houses of east, north, west and south. As the singing proceeded, he looked about, as he would look for a war party, to see if danger threatened the crop from any direction. If he foresaw the coming of the pest, blight, or sorcery, the company sang the songs to avert evil....(Underhill 1939:83).

The images were later placed in the fields to ensure the success of crop growth.

Some villages also appear to have had a green corn festival at the time the ears were forming and the size of the expected harvest could be estimated. Again effigies representing crops were placed in the ceremonial house, and rows of boys and girls danced, and the village fetish was ritually opened. Afterwards, the dancers were subject to various taboos for a period of four days to avoid any danger from the magic of the dance.

After harvest of the crops, still other rituals of the food cycle occurred. "Another ceremony which always took place in the autumn just before the people moved to the winter village was called the deer dance or cleansing ceremony. Its object was to work magic over all the crops which had been gathered and over the first deer of the season to make them safe for eating during the winter" (Underhill 1940:50). A special deer was hunted and killed. It was cooked along with plants from the harvest. Old men sang while the younger men and women danced. The songs made deer easier to kill, and the speeches were made to sanctify the food objects. During the dancing, shamans removed any evil from the foods by sucking it out of them. After the deer meat was distributed to the people, they rubbed it over their bodies to ensure good health.

Supernaturalism also surrounded hunting activities in general. A special society of full-time deer hunters appears to have existed with a hunt chief as its leader. These men hunted on a year-round basis and had in their possession hunting disguises, fetishes, and special song magic. They had the power, via dream divination, to know the whereabouts of game, and their leader performed rituals in collective deer (rabbit?) hunts to draw the game towards the hunters. Young men who joined the hunters society underwent no formal initiation but simply learned the appropriate tasks involved in such activities. Apparently only group hunting involved special ritual.

In the fall, after the harvest, there was also the opportunity to mix ritual with recreational activity. This was a time for villages to compete with each other in race activity. While bets were made, essentially the winning of the race brought luck and rain to a village, and other rites, likewise, aided certain village individuals. A village would challenge another village in the spring. In the fall activities, the challengers sang a series of rain-bringing songs, and the other village reciprocated with food. Dancing accompanied the singing. The dance had been designed beforehand to correlate with the songs, and these represented the visionary experiences of the singer. Elaborate paraphernalia were created to carry out the appropriate theme. Sometimes special songs called "naming songs" were sung which mentioned the names of important men in the village of one's opponents. This resulted in good luck for the individuals so mentioned. The chief event, however, was the race itself, either a relay race or a kickball contest over a considerable distance. Many songs were sung to strengthen one's own runners and weaken those of the opposition. All the able-bodied men took part in the contest, and many individuals wagered on the outcome.

Perhaps the most outstanding Papago ceremony is the prayerstick festival: the Viikita. It is difficult to know exactly the original purpose of this ritual. It was a feast of thanksgiving, it kept the world in order and prevented floods, and it promoted crop growth. Like most of the food ceremonies, it had been instituted by Iitoi in myth. He had placed prayersticks during the legendary migrations of the Papago to show them where to settle, hence the name of the festival. Like many Pueblo rites, it represented a coalescence of a number of motives and elements. Among the northern Papago, it was held during the winter, once every four years. Among the southern Papago, it was held every summer. It was set and organized by a number of hereditary officials; a chief director and four assistants, a head clown and about thirty others, a head cornmeal sprinkler and his assistants were the main people involved. There were other dancers and a number of singers on a more voluntary basis. Masks and special costumes characterized this rite, the performance of which involved the cooperation of a number of villages.

After the official announcement of the date of the ritual by its head director, this individual went into retreat to purify himself, observing a number of taboos. Four days later, in the company of other leaders, he opened a special basket containing a fetish and passed it around. He recited a formula dealing with the coming of clouds and rain. In the dance area, a representation of the fields of all the participating villages was constructed out of sand into which prayersticks from the basket were placed. The basket was then returned to the ceremonial house, and it was announced that the public rite would take place in ten days. The leader now recited a speech dealing with the activities that will occupy this interval of time. A brush shelter was erected (for each village) in which paraphernalia were made and song practice occurred. Because of the sacredness of this rite, women were not permitted to see these preparations. Cornmeal sprinklers placed meal on those who left the enclosure. Prayersticks were manufactured. While such was going on, the clowns, Navitcu, went throughout the host village begging food for those involved in the preparations. They also cured any people at this time, merely by touching them (more a blessing?). "The clowns were supposed to be holy beings from a magic country who spoke a language none could understand. Therefore, they never really talked but gave strange, shrill cries. Certain men in every village had inherited, from their fathers, the right to be clowns and cherished it as a sacred privilege" (Underhill 1940:52).

A large enclosure was constructed near the symbolic fields, and on the tenth morning, the public rites began. A clown gave a special welcoming speech, and the singers went into the enclosure at night and rehearsed their songs. At dawn, the dancing and singing began. Two masked personages representing the sun and the moon walked out first and circled the enclosure as cornmeal was sprinkled upon them. Then the singers circled the dance area for the greater part of the day. Singers from each village had eight songs. They carried images representing the subject matter of these songs, and they came out separately for each song production. Cornmeal sprinklers placed meal on the ground before and after the procession. As they sang and danced, they stopped before the ceremonial house in which special dancers (two young boys and girls representing the mythical flood children) spent the entire day dancing. They are symbolic of meat and vegetable foods. At noon, the clowns, who have been moving in and out of the procession and the audience, put on a special rite in which they imitate rain, planting, and harvesting. After the villages had all sung and danced, the ritual closed with prayersticks being distributed to be placed in actual fields, in storehouses, or rubbed over people's bodies to bring good luck. We can now turn to a consideration of other types of ritual.

Power Ceremonies

More individualistic forms of supernaturalism among the Papago centered upon the visionary experience. Young men hoped that an animal guardian spirit would appear to them and teach them magical songs. On an informal level, such a spirit could appear at any time when a person was by himself. Formally, however, several deliberate activities could promote this process: going to collect salt, killing an eagle, or killing and scalping any enemy in war. After engaging in such activities, a person had to be purified and also had to spend a number of days (usually 16) in seclusion. While so secluded, accompanied by an old man as a guardian, strict taboos had to be observed. Generally, in a dream, the spirit would appear and teach the supplicant the desired song. Generally, after his return, some further rites would occur for purification. Those who had undergone such ordeals were called "ripe men" and were now able to participate in the political life of their villages. We can examine the special occasions of the above activities.

The Salt Pilgrimage to the Gulf of California was usually first made by boys at the age of sixteen, generally prior to their having achieved a power ceremony experience by any of the other means. This journey, which was hazardous due to the inhospitable environment to be traveled, not only was an opportunity for the individuals to gain power but also was thought to bring back rain for the community. They went once a year in the summer, and a person had to go at least four times in his life to avoid the magical danger involved. Each village had a special leader selected for this activity, a person who had been many times, was free from the dangers, and who had learned the route and the practicalities that made a safe trip. For those who were going for the first time, many travel restrictions had to be observed; all of which made the trip an even greater ordeal. Each stage of the journey had its attendant rites. On the second evening of the trip (by a waterhole), the leader recited a long formula which was to prepare the young men for their activities once the ocean had been reached. Prior to reaching it, prayersticks were planted, and the neophytes reached out towards the ocean to gain power.

Once they arrived, they went to the salt beds themselves and gathered the amounts they required. The leader then gave each man cornmeal and a prayerstick, and they waded out into the water, an act requiring bravery inasmuch as they considered this the end of the world and hence fraught with danger. They threw the cornmeal on the waves. They then ran on the beach for a distance of many miles. What the runner "saw" was (omen-like) an indication of his future. Apparently, some men even had visions at this time. They left the next morning after another ritual address to the ocean by the leader to aid in their return. They camped outside the village and returned much like a war party. A public purification followed during which old men who were veterans of the trip sang to purify them and breathed power into them. Cornmeal was also sprinkled on the salt they had brought back with them. Following this, the young men were secluded and received their visions.

Eagle Killing was a second way for an individual to gain power. This was also generally accomplished in summer. While the eagle appeared the most sought after bird, several species of hawk were also considered appropriate. Generally, the bird was shot although trapping was also a possibility. A successful hunter summoned his human guardian (old man) and then plucked the bird in a ritual fashion arranging the feathers in a cross-shape pointing to the four directions. They were then covered by the supplicant, and he began his period of purification. The old man acting as guardian taught the neophyte any songs he himself knew (for purifying others), and the vision experience itself took place, the spirit of the dead bird becoming the guardian spirit. Finally, other old men who had undergone similar experiences came to sing and invoke their blessings on the killer.

The final regular approach by which a male gained personal power was through killing and scalp taking in warfare activities. The Papago treated their Apache enemies as evil magicians who were tainted with supernatural powers. As a result, the killer and scalp taker required great purification. The scalp itself had a supernatural potential which could be harnessed. During warfare as soon as a Papago had killed and scalped an enemy, he retired from the field under the guardianship of an old man who had accompanied the war party for this purpose. Other men were waiting (preselected) back in the village to aid in the same task. From this point on, the scalp taker was secluded from "normal" people as, to a lesser extent, was his wife. The returning war party (followed at a distance by the killers) camped outside the village and entered at dawn with the scalps tied to a long pole. Announcement was made concerning those who were to be segregated and those who had died, and the scalp pole was set up in the dance area. Preparations were made for the purification dance in sixteen days.

During this period of time, the killers were undergoing their visionary experiences accompanied by their guardians who also taught them recitations requisite for the cure of any illnesses resulting from the scalps. Shortly before the end of this period, the scalps were prepared as fetishes. Meanwhile, the other villagers danced around the pole each night, leaping back and forth in a circle and singing a song cycle from myth. On the sixteenth night, this dance was repeated, and the scalp takers were brought in and seated. Former scalp takers took the weapons and purified them in a dance imitating the war battle. Somewhat after midnight, the killers themselves underwent formal purification. Shamans sang songs and blew smoke over them. Near dawn, a basket holding the scalps was brought to the dance area to be exposed to the rays of the sun. This had the purpose of catching the soul of the slain enemy and making it invest the scalp. The baskets were then tied up and given to the slayers who later deposited them in a place in the surrounding countryside. Offerings were placed by them periodically. Seen in its entirety, such rites had both individualistic and communal importance. "Moreover, in the Papago mind, which abhorred emphasis on killing and revenge, their real result was supposed to be a magical one, bringing rain and crops" (Underhill 1939:166). Still other rites were utilized prior to the war actions themselves: to produce power, locate the enemy, and render them defenseless.

A sort of negative and involuntary power ceremony is represented in the Girl's Puberty Dance. This was occasioned by the onset of the first menstrual period. Since menstrual blood/power was seen as harmful to men and their activities, the girl had to go into seclusion in a special hut (as all women did) and undergo purification. The young girl remained in the hut for a period of four days and was in partial seclusion for the time until the next menstrual period, at which time four more days of total seclusion were required. During such times, she was instructed by a female guardian in the role of womanhood and was subject to taboos. She also practiced womanly activities such as gathering wood and grinding corn. During the time between the four-day seclusions, her parents hosted (in keeping with the limits of their food supply) a series of dances. These also helped to purify the pubescent girl. In the dances, which were led by a special song leader, lines of males and females (among which is the girl) held each other by the shoulders and walked back and forth while singing. Apparently, this was another occasion for sexual license. After the second four-day seclusion, the girl was finally purified by the blessings of a shaman.

Shamanism in Papago supernaturalism occupied another dimension of individualistic power.

> The shaman was the only individualist in Papago society. He received genuine pay for his services....But he paid for his eminence with the constant risk of his life. He must guess correctly at the outcome of war and games, for if he failed and had no equivocation ready, he was liable to lynching. If he lost

> too many patients, he must be quick to accuse some other shaman of sorcery and to choose one weaker than himself, lest the accusation rebound and destroy him. Only a bold and astute man could have sustained such a role, and it was, perhaps his unusual character as well as the dread of his power which subjected him to the constant suspicion of sorcery (Underhill 1939:263).

The shaman was not as complete a practitioner as were those found in many other North American Indian groups. While the shaman could cure illness set by sorcerers (an intrusive disease object), at least in the realm of curing he functioned primarily as a diviner. The actual curing of the affliction was often left to other practitioners. In like manner, he could locate game or the whereabouts of the enemy, with actual hunters and warriors being other individuals.

The shaman obtained his special powers via dreams. These might be involuntary, but regular power experiences, especially eagle killing, could also be employed to attain this end. The content of the vision experienced suggested shamanistic practice, but a number of subsequent visions were necessary for the revelation of the specific powers that were to be granted. In addition, long practice was necessary during which time the visions were kept secret. Only after successfully practicing on a family member would a shaman make his powers public. Expectably, most shamans were males; a female pursued such a vocation only when she was past childbearing age. The paraphernalia of the shaman included a gourd rattle, a quartz crystal for divination, and eagle feathers.

In the event of being summoned with cornmeal to divine the nature of an illness, the shaman would arrive at the house of the patient in the evening. He sang songs, went into trance, and determined the cause. He would cleanse the patient by brushing him with feathers and perhaps blow smoke on him. Prior to dawn, he would announce the type of cure required. If the cause were sorcery, he himself would suck out the disease object. If the cause were one of the other two major causes of disease, he would recommend the appropriate person to effect the cure. These other causes were ceremonial lapse (an error or disrespect by the patient in some previous ritual) or the anger of animals. Animals controlled diseases which they could send to those who had displeased them. The ceremonial leader would repeat part of the ritual to cure in the first case, and individuals who had dreamed of animals and had learned the appropriate songs functioned like shamans in the second situation. We have already mentioned that scalp takers handled scalp illnesses. The shaman himself also functioned in communal rites to drive out evil and bring rain. Sometimes a shaman went out to where he dreamed a sorcerer had buried an evil charm which would harm the village, dug it up, and destroyed it. As previously indicated, the powers of the shaman marked him as a potential sorcerer himself, and repeated failures or suspected malpractice marked him for death.

We can conclude the discussion of Papago supernaturalism with a brief discussion of the life cycle. Little ritual surrounded birth. The mother and child were secluded in the menstrual hut for a month, and then a shaman cleansed the parents by brushing them with his eagle feathers. Girls did have a puberty rite, as previously indicated, but boys were not similarly treated. Later on, the males engaged in the power rituals. No real ritual occurred at marriage. Speeches at that time dealt with practical advice and concerns. Death also was not extremely ritualized, although more than for the Pueblos. From the time of death until burial (a short time), ritual wailing took place. The dead were buried with some of their possessions, and a short speech asking the deceased not to return was made by a close relative. Those who died in war (if recovered) were cremated by the scalp takers. After death, the house of the deceased was destroyed, and mourners cut their hair. The souls of the dead were thought to travel through a dangerous gap in the mountains and into the village of the dead. "Dead persons are potential threats to health and good fortune, and care is taken to avoid offending them lest their ghosts return to bring sickness upon their living relatives" (Joseph, Spicer and Chesky 1949:77). It was also felt that the dead might visit the living in dreams. We can now make some very brief comments on Pima supernaturalism.

Pima Religion

As previously suggested, far less data are available on the supernatural beliefs and practices of the Pima. This is especially the case for rites of a communal nature or emphasis. A purity ceremony for girls existed along nearly identical lines to that of the Papago. At the time of first menstruation, the girl was isolated and cared for by a woman guardian. She instructed the young girl in the ways of womanhood. During this four-day period, the girl observed a considerable number of taboos and made a basket to present to her guardian. The "dangerous" condition of the girl was countered by songs. After this period, the parents of the girl hosted a four-day "coming out" dance at which friends and relatives (and the girl) danced, and special puberty songs were sung. Males and females formed parallel lines and moved back and forth all night.

There was also a cactus wine festival and a harvest festival, but little unambiguous information exists concerning these rites. There seems to have been a communal curing ritual performed by clown types of curing practitioners, perhaps functioning in like manner to those of the Papago. Warfare ritual is better known. After the return of a war party, a killer was separated from his companions and remained in seclusion for a period of sixteen days observing taboos. A scalp dance took place in the village dance plaza. Men and women danced around a pole from which the scalp and other body parts were hung. According to some sources, some of these parts were later eaten! If male captives were taken, they were ritually clubbed to death. On the evening of the sixteenth day, the warrior was brought to the dance area. He assumed a prone position on the ground, and a war shaman placed saliva in his mouth and breathed into his nostrils for final purification. The warrior rose and was then congratulated on his achievements. Some ritual apparently preceded the onset of a war expedition. It consisted of dancing by the warriors – for as many nights as the party planned to be absent from their village – and included divining the probable success of the endeavor by the war shamans.

Death rites are also comparable to those of the Papago. After a person died, the female relatives expressed their grief via stylized wailing until burial took place. All except those who had failed in battle were buried, these special deceased persons being cremated to minimize the supernatural dangers they represented. Some grave goods were placed on or near the grave: weapons, supplies, and water. The paraphernalia of shamans were buried with them. Other goods of the deceased were apparently destroyed by some Pima groups. A rite of mourning occurred with relatives cutting their hair. It is asserted by some sources that a widow was required to remain at home for four years, not to wash her hair, and to shout the name of the deceased each day at dawn during this period. The soul, which existed in the center of the chest, was thought to leave the body at death (perhaps becoming an owl) and to go to the land of the dead which existed in the east. It was reached by crossing a large chasm. While life was considered to be quite pleasant there, occasionally a soul would return (or not make it there?) and might possibly harm the living. To counter this ghost, a shaman would go to the grave and order the soul to "be quiet."

Clearly, the most information we possess on the aboriginal Pima concerns their shamanistic practices:

> This component of...Pima life can be regarded as the strongest orientation of their culture. Even in the matter of war, the most elaborate and most assiduously performed ceremony was directed not toward war itself as an end, but toward the prevention or curing of the maleficent effects upon the...Pima warrior arising from contact with an enemy feared because of his supernatural power rather than his military prowess (Ezell 1961:79).

There appears to have been three types of shamans. One type, "examining doctors," seems to have been the most numerous and the most powerful and included a sizeable proportion of women among their numbers. They functioned primarily in the treatment of disease. A second type seems to have functioned in more communally oriented rites and may have been somewhat more priestlike. They had power to deal with weather control, crop growth, and war. They were less numerous than the curers and mostly males. A final type of supernatural practitioner was the herbalist. These people, a small number of males and females, treated the more mundane illnesses, most by more empirical techniques.

One acquired power to perform such tasks in a variety of ways. One could inherit the ability along family lines (especially for the first type), one could be given the power unsought in dream experiences, or one could acquire it "automatically" if one recovered from a snakebite. There does, however, appear to have been a learning component.

> Several informants declared that 'any man who received instruction from a medicine-man and learned to do some little tricks could become a medicine-man.' The process of acquiring power was called...'getting power.'...The novice was tested, either alone or along with one or more fellow aspirants, by the medicine-man, who had the youth kneel before him on all fours, and then threw four sticks, each about 8 inches long, at him. If the novice fell to the ground during the throwing he was 'shot' with the power and could then take the next degree (Russell 1908:257).

This sounds somewhat like Puebloan practices.

Cures took an expectable form. The shaman would sing special songs to aid in the diagnosis and puff cigarette smoke to ascertain the cause of the disease. Disease was caused by animal or bird supernatural agents or witches. Then the cure would take place, involving such techniques as sucking out disease objects, rubbing feathers or fetishes over the body of the patient, and burning or scarifying the skin. In the case of animal-sent disease, appropriate songs were sung. In the case of witchcraft, the shaman, along with four assistants, went to find the charm of an evil shaman who was held responsible. Ashes were apparently rubbed on the body of the patient in all cases as a general blessing.

Shamans that functioned in more communal roles employed other types of predominantly magical techniques.

> To cause an abundance of melons and squashes, the Makai entered the field and took from his mouth – or, as his followers supposed, from the store of magic power in his body – a small melon or squash. The object was partially covered with hardened mud, symbolic of the productive earth. The rite was performed at a time when no melons or squashes had yet appeared and it is supposed that he obtained the "magic" melon by stripping the outer leaves from the growing end of young vines. This was buried at the root of a growing plant to insure a prolific yield (Russell 1908:258).

Shamans in general had great influence in their villages, and some performed feats demonstrating their ability and power; for example, holding hot coals in their mouth. They were also somewhat feared, and they were killed if found guilty of malpractice. We can turn now to another variety of Southwest Indian Religion, that of the Apache and Navaho.

PIMAN BIBLIOGRAPHY AND REFERENCES

Davis, E. H.

1920. The Papago Ceremony of Vikita. *Indian Notes and Monographs – Museum of American Indian* 3:155-77.

DePosa, C. C.

1956. The Upper Pima of San Cayetano del Tumacacori. *Publications of the American Foundation* 7.

1953. The Sobaipuri Indians of the Upper San Pedro River Valley Southeastern Arizona. *Publications of the American Foundation* 12.

Ezell, Paul H.

1961. The Hispanic Acculturation of the Gila River Pimas. *American Anthropological Association Memoirs* 90.

Grossman, F. E.

1873. The Pima Indians of Arizona. *Smithsonian Annual Report for 1871*, pp. 407-19.

Hayden, J. and Steen, C. R.

1937. The Viikita Ceremony of the Papago. *Southwestern Monuments Monthly Reports*, April:263-83.

Johnson, B.

1960. The Wind Ceremony. *El Palacio* 47:28-31.

Joseph, Alice, Spicer, R. and Chesky, J.

1949. The Desert People. Chicago: University of Chicago Press.

Mason, J. A.

1920. The Papago Harvest Festival. *American Anthropologist* 22:13-25.

Parsons, E. C.

1928. Notes on the Pima. *American Anthropologist* 30:445-64.

Russell, Frank.

1908. The Pima Indians. *Bureau of American Ethnology Annual Report* 26:3-390.

Underhill, Ruth M.

1946. Papago Indian Religion. *Columbia University Contributions to Anthropology* 33.

1940. The Papago Indians of Arizona and their Relatives the Pima. *Indian Life and Customs Pamphlets* 3:1-68

1939. Social Organization of the Papago Indians. Columbia University Contributions to Anthropology 30.

1938. Singing for Power: The Song Magic of the Papago Indians. Berkeley: University of California Press.

CHAPTER VI

ATHABASCAN RELIGION

The five Apache groupings together with the Navaho represent the Athabascan variety of Southwest Indian religion. Because of the range of variation among the Apache, we can discuss them first, leaving the Navaho, who are really only a further variation on a common theme, until last. In our discussion of some of the basic features of Apache religion, we will concentrate mostly upon the Chiricahua and the Jicarilla, bringing in data on other groups as applicable.

Apache Religion

The religion of the Apache was in some respects like that of the Papago. There were individual and more communal rituals organized around the concept of the acquisition or use of supernatural power. Perhaps even more so among the Apache was the individualistic nature of such activities. Speaking of the Mescalero and Chiricahua:

> Power is thought of as a mighty force that pervades the universe. Some of it filters through to the hands of man. But to become manifest to man, power must approach him through the medium of certain agencies and channels....The most conspicuous of these agencies are certain natural phenomena such as the lightning or sun and a number of animals....In fact nothing is barred apriori from being a conductor of supernatural power, though the tendency to expect transmission through traditional and well-known channels is strong (Opler 1935:66-67).

Coming into contact and control of such power was very important to the individual, and people looked forward to such time as they would gain some for themselves, come to possess "strength" beyond normal ordinary human capacity! Gaining such power for oneself not only gave the individual the ability to function in some specific way but also provided general protection against misfortunes. Any individual, male or female, at least potentially could acquire such power. Generally such powers were acquired near the time of marriage when their need became most apparent.

Basically one could acquire power in one of two ways. A person might be selected by a power in an unbidden manner in a dream, vision, or via some unusual happening. Among the Chiricahua:

> It seems that these powers select for themselves. Perhaps you want to be a shaman of a certain kind, but the power doesn't speak to you. It seems that before power wants to work through you, you've got to be just so, as in the original time. You've got to believe in things as in the old days and carry everything out....Some hear it, the power speaks to them. Power usually comes in a voice to the one who is getting a ceremony. A person doesn't fast or prepare for it (Opler 1941:202).

While powers that are so offered might be refused by the recipient, such was, apparently, seldom the case. In the event of accepting the "call" by the powers, the individual was given the necessary directions for conducting the appropriate ceremony: prayers, songs, paraphernalia, and the taboos associated with them and with the power source itself. This information was said to be revealed at the home of the power to which the human being was supernaturalistically transported and then returned. Such power could also be gained by learning it from someone else who already controlled it. Here an individual might consciously select some desired power source and ceremony. However, the power source could decide to reject the supplicant. This is generally revealed by the inability of the supplicant to learn the appropriate songs and prayers associated with the given power. If the power approved of the transmission of the ceremony, these were learned easily. It should be mentioned that the learning of a ceremony was a most difficult and time-consuming task. "In addition to mental agility and a tenacious memory, the acquisition of a corpus of chants requires sheer physical strength...when we take into account that it (one chant) can span thirty minutes, and that a full day of practice may involve the singing of at least a dozen chants. It is no wonder that persons acquiring a power sometimes find themselves close to exhaustion" (Basso 1970:44). It should also be mentioned that the possessor of supernatural power must also continually observe the rules set down by the power source. "The person who fails to live up to his part of the power relationship agreement runs the risk of alienating the power and inviting retaliation (Opler 1941:207).

There were a number of functional usages for such supernatural power. As previously mentioned, its ownership gave general protection, functioning somewhat like a guardian spirit. Obviously, the most important was in the diagnosis and treatment of disease. The power to cure was generally limited to specific diseases although more than one power might be effective in any given case. The possessor of supernatural power could also bring success in the activities of life (the counterpart to protection against evil). Hunting, games, warfare, etc., even love thus were rendered more productive. While much of this appears ego-centered, the power could also be used in a more communal manner, not only for the aforementioned curing, but to weaken the enemy, find lost persons or objects, and in weather control. So the use of power was reflected in many channels.

When one attempts to translate these power concepts in actual ritual forms, one encounters classification difficulties. Opler, speaking of the Jicarilla Apache, divided rituals into two types. The first type he calls shamanistic or personal rites. These were based upon obtaining power by the personal dream or vision experience, and it could not be transmitted to another individual. A person controlled only one such rite, and rituals thus acquired were used primarily for curing although they might also be used for such tasks as the location of the enemy in war. "The hallmark of the shamanistic rite is the close personal bond between the shaman and his power. Through his songs and prayers he is thought to be in constant communication with his power" (Opler 1936:214). The other type of ritual he calls the *Traditional* or "long rite" rite. These were rituals which have justification in myth and were taught by persons who already knew them. Here a person might come to know more than one such rite. Most of these rites appeared to have more communal orientations and were not limited to the strict treatment of sickness, although "health" in its broadest definition was probably a feature of almost every Apache ritual. The female puberty ritual, the relay race, and the treatment of widespread illness were examples of this ritual type.

Among the White Mountain Apache (Western) a somewhat similar ritual scheme has been proposed:

> Ceremonies may be divided into three types. The first is purely traditional, to which nothing can be added by any personal experience of the man conducting it. The second is also considered traditional and handed down intact; but it is possible for the possessor of the ceremony to have direct contact with the source of the power...whereby additional power and songs are acquired....In the third kind of ceremony all songs, ceremonial prayers and knowledge of power are gained by actual experience in dream or waking (Goodwin 1938:29).

Such classification fits fairly well with that given for the Jicarilla, and we may assume, although incompletely documented, similar arrangements for other Apache groups. Such divisions seem to rather closely follow the initial distinction made relative to the derivation of power. Against this theoretical background, we may briefly and incompletely sketch a few examples of Apache ritualism.

We can begin this attempt with a review of the life cycle. Among the Chiricahua, little ritual surrounded birth itself, but on the fourth day after there was a "cradle ceremony." A shaman constructed a cradleboard. As he did so, he prayed for the welfare and the long life of the newborn. He marked the infant with pollen, held the cradle to each of the directions, and then placed the infant inside. The significance of this brief rite was to spare the child from evil influences so that it would occupy the cradle in the future. Charms were also placed on the cradleboard to accomplish the same end. Later on, the first steps of the infant were celebrated by the "putting on moccasins" rite. The shaman led the infant on a path of footprints made of pollen, sang songs, and placed moccasins on the feet of the infant. This recreated the path trod by mythical heroes and helped to ensure long life.

The next spring there was a "hair cutting" rite. The shaman placed pollen on the face of the child, cut its hair, and prayed for the health and long life of that individual. This was repeated for the next three springs. After this, hair-cutting was considered, except under special conditions, to bring bad rather than good luck. Young girls, at the time of their first menstrual periods, underwent a puberty rite. Much of the literature on Apache supernaturalism deals with this rite and its variations. The ritual procedures among the Chiricahua ran as follows. Preparations were made in advance of the expected occasion, and a female attendant (guardian) was selected by the girl's family. She was called "she who makes the sound," since during the rite she emitted a special cry of applause, based upon the mythic acts of a culture heroine (White Painted Woman). This guardian had learned her ritual duties as had the shaman who conducted the rite since this is a traditional type of ceremony.

> The most conspicuous ritualist of the ceremony is one who will be called "the singer" because it is his primary task to superintend the erection of the sacred shelter in which the songs of the rite are chanted and to sing the songs. He does not depend on a personal supernatural encounter for obtaining his songs, nor does he believe that he can intercede for the benefit of the girl through impromptu appeals to supernatural forces with which he is in special rapport...the songs are not a personal shamanistic possession but are conceived of as the sacred property of the people as a whole (Opler 1941:85).

Other participants, besides the girl herself, included masked dancers representing the mountain spirits (Gans). A shaman who had the power to make the masks and direct the dancers was also involved since the men who impersonated the spirits had by themselves no power. These dancers functioned as entertainers during much of the rite but served other ends as well.

A special area was reserved for this rite, and beforehand the girl was placed under taboos by her guardian. This woman also dressed the girl and prayed for her well-being. The singer directed the building of a special ritual structure and sang power songs at appropriate stages during its construction. The girl now arrived on the scene. The woman guardian marked the girl with pollen and was marked by her in return. This procedure was also repeated by onlookers since during this rite the girl incorporated curing powers and those who were painted by her were thought to be relieved or protected from illness; she represented White Painted Woman. The guardian then massaged the girl to give her health, strength, and long life. The woman made pollen footprints, and the girl walked these for future blessings. A basket containing ritual objects was placed a short distance away, and the girl ran to it and returned to be assured of long life. This was repeated three more times. When she returned the last time, she took a buckskin (on which she had been standing) and shook it in the directions to send away any evil that might harm her. Her family then distributed food and she retires into the ritual structure.

That afternoon was reserved for social dancing. In the evening, the masked dancers made their appearance along with some of their number who functioned as ceremonial clowns (grey ones). Prior to the beginning, they might also be requested to cure anyone who was sick. The lead dancer blew away the disease while the controlling shaman (masked dancer shaman) sang and prayed. It should again be mentioned that these dancers by themselves had no power and also that they did not actually become the spirits they impersonated. After this curing rite, they then came into the special area and performed their dance. Meanwhile, the leading shaman was inside the ritual structure with the girl. He smoked, prayed, and sang, symbolizing as he did so the passage of the girl through a long and successful life. The girl danced to accompany these songs, and the woman guardian shouted her ritual applause. After a time, these ritualists would take their leave, the masked dancers outside would leave, and social dancing occupied the remainder of the night.

The events of the second and third day were about the same. On the fourth day, however, the activities reached their culmination. The singing and dancing by the shaman and the girl inside the ritual structure went on until about daybreak, and the masked dancers also remained and forced the onlookers to dance the entire night. Outside, in the first rays of the sun, the shaman painted the girl and also the onlookers and sang, and a ritual meal was held. The structure was taken down, and a pollen path made over which the girl was led by the shaman. Four more runs to the basket were made as the last poles of the structure were pushed over. The ritual was concluded.

This rite certainly represented a high point of supernaturalism for the Apache and reveals in its structure a coalescence of a number of ritual elements.

Generally speaking, the Apache Girl's Puberty Rite followed the same approximate ritual format for all groups. There are, however, some significant differences. Among the Jicarilla, for example, the girl was accompanied through her rite not only by a shaman and guardian but also by a young boy who represented a culture hero (Slayer of Monsters), analogous to the symbolic representation of the girl. The boy underwent the same taboos as the girl, did as she did, danced, was painted, and apparently received the same kind of blessing.

> The singer tells them that how they act during the ceremony will decide their natures, that if they are obedient and willing, they will be like that through life. If the girl gets angry and scolds anyone during the four days, it will her disposition during life. And he tells them that if they don't believe in the songs, the ceremony won't do them any good (Opler 1942:32).

Here it would seem that all boys sooner or later were so involved. It may have been an attempt to more specifically distribute strength, health, and long life. It should also be mentioned that the clown masked dancers could serve a bogeyman function, frightening unruly children. They also mimicked the other dancers but for at least some groups did not have the obscene character that occurs elsewhere.

Boys did not undergo a clear-cut puberty ritual. From little up, they were trained to contend with hardships, and as they grew older they spent a great deal of time running and in patterned fighting with each other. At about the age of sixteen, the young boy began to accompany the men on warfare expeditions. They went four times as novices. On these occasions, they had to undergo food and behavioral taboos since their conduct was considered essential to the success of the particular war enterprise they accompanied. Like the pubescent girls, they represented the supernatural. They themselves did not fight on these expeditions. They were taught how to behave properly. "...shamans whose rites center about the location and frustration of the enemy and the granting of invulnerability in battle often prepare the youths for these journeys" (Opler 1941:136). These shamans might also make articles of clothing and charms for the war novices. After four expeditions, unless there has been criticism of their conduct, they were considered as adult men who were now able to participate fully in war.

Warfare itself, as expected, was surrounded by rituals. Among the Chiricahua, a revenge expedition was preceded by a special war dance which was for the warriors involved a pledge to participate and be brave. Two pairs of dancers performed at a time, followed by social dances. War power shamans sang blessing songs. Charms were worn, and shamans were consulted to divine the outcome of the coming battle. Among the Jicarilla, in their dances, the warriors painted their hair white and red to symbolize a scalped and bleeding enemy. Among these people, apparently, not everyone was privileged to take scalps, even though these, as tangible objects of Jicarilla superiority, were greatly desired. Only a leader who had learned to handle the power involved could scalp, and those who had killed enemies were obligated to request his services in this regard.

> When a victorious war party returned home, the first action was to hold a ceremony over the warriors that the ghosts of the enemy might be driven away. The scalps were considered much too dangerous still to entrust to the warriors: instead the scalps and all the possessions taken from the foes were put into the care of old men with the requisite ceremonial knowledge, to be sung over and cleansed. These old men, usually four in number, had complete charge of the scalp dance which was to follow (Opler 1935:211-12).

The format of the scalp dance was as follows. A flat area was prepared, and a central pole erected along with other poles surrounding it in a circle. Scalps were placed on the latter. Those people who had lost relatives in the present or previous hostilities went around this area four times and "mistreated" the scalps. Then the warriors who had taken part related their deeds, each speaker vouching for the authenticity of the narrative of the man who had preceded him until all had so participated. Then the warriors danced around the central pole, eventually being joined by the onlookers. Social dancing took place later in the evening. The dancing took place for four days and nights and was ended by prayers by the old men in charge of the ritual. After four more days, the scalps were given to the warriors responsible for killing the enemy, to keep in their possession. The scalps seem not to have had the same fetish nature as among some of the other Southwestern peoples. Comparable war rites occurred among other Apache groups.

Death among the Apache generated a great deal of fear.

> As soon as a death occurred among the Mescalero Apache...the women of the encampment in which those related to the dead person lived began to wail. As a symbol of grief and despair relatives of both sexes tore the clothing from their bodies and threw them away. During the mourning period they wore only as much clothing as the weather and canons of modesty required, and always were clad in the poorest and most dilapidated garments at hand. Close relatives cut the ends of the hair... (Opler 1946:454).

The rites of burial occurred quickly, in the same day if possible, because of fear of the ghost. The body was taken to an isolated spot and buried, the possessions of the deceased destroyed, the close relatives purified, and the camp moved. Speaking of the Chiricahua, "It is the intention of the members of the burial party and of the close relatives of the deceased to alter so completely the situation with which their dead kinsman was associated that nothing will remind them of him, and nothing they have or do will draw his ghost to them" (Opler 1941:475). Expectably, ghosts could cause sickness by returning to harm the living or by "drawing them" to the abode of the dead, and special shamans had the power to deal with such situations. Generally speaking, the final repose of the dead was an underworld although the exact location is disputed. Life there apparently reflected the world of the living in terms of attributes and activities.

We can now turn to the curing rites and some other supernatural activities. It is probably safe to say that most Apache rituals dealt with the curing of some kind of illness. While some illnesses may be seen to have natural causes, many were considered to be supernaturally induced. Among the Chiricahua, "Ailments which do not yield to ordinary herbal remedies...are thought to have been contracted from unclean animals or from animals or supernaturals capable of sending disease when offended, defied, or instigated by malevolent forces. It is to combat sickness of this kind that the intricate curing ceremonies are reserved" (Opler 1941:224). So some animals and other supernaturals might have functioned not only positively in giving power but also negatively in sending disease. Some animal types were felt to be especially dangerous in this regard: the coyote, snake, owl, and bear. We have previously mentioned the ghost as a source of illness. Extreme cases of sickness, which did not yield to the usual ministrations of shamans, were felt to be caused by witches or sorcerers. We can briefly expand on this latter possibility.

The Apache had well-developed beliefs in practitioners of evil supernatural power. Among the Western Apache, for example, there were sorcerers who cause sickness, property destruction, and death, and "love" witches who could use their powers more for sexual gratification. The sorcerers utilized poison, the power of enchantments or spells, or sent disease objects into the body of their victim.

> Sorcerers have always been and are today far more numerous than love witches. They are also the most dangerous type of witch most feared by the Apache. Both men and women become sorcerers, but male sorcerers are said to be more common. This is explained on the grounds that men experience the emotion...(of hatred)...more intensely than women (Basso 1969:33).

Protection against such evil was generally thought to be effected by the wearing of beads, marking with pollen, and the use of eagle feathers, and sometimes a person who believed himself so attacked would use these only, hoping the sorcerer might shift attention elsewhere. If one chose to have a cure, generally a shaman with bear, snake, or lightning power would be called in for the attempt at relieving the illness. In the past, suspected sorcerers were often killed.

Curing rituals followed a general pattern of activities. The ailing individual picked a shaman who was able to cure the supposed illness, usually one who controlled the power source thought to be involved. The request to cure was made in such a fashion that the shaman could not really refuse. Gifts were given to the shaman, at least some of which were actually employed in the rite and which ensured the beneficial cooperation of the power source. The shaman announced when and where the rite would take place. Rites usually lasted four days, the highlight or public portion beginning after dark and continuing until midnight. The shaman laid out his paraphernalia, blew smoke to the directions, marked and was marked by the patient with pollen (sometimes also the onlookers), and sang and prayed to discover the extent of the illness and whether he would be able to effect a cure. The songs and prayers were divided into sections or verses. The former were standardized, the latter improvised for the specific case that was involved. During these activities, the shaman received information from the power source which might give special instructions at this time. Sometimes a ground painting was employed. After the ritual was over, food and/or behavioral taboos were placed on the patient.

More collective curing rituals could also occur. We have already discussed the functioning of masked dancer shamans at the girl's puberty rite. If it was suspected at any time that disease threatens the community, these people might also be requested to perform for the general public good. In fact, even single individuals could be so cured if they requested the services of such a person. Speaking of such activities among the Chiricahua and Mescalero,

> Ordinarily the clown is not used for curing. But if the cure cannot be effected through the efforts of the other masked dancers, the clown is employed. He is regarded as the most powerful masked dancer, but is to be used in case of dire need or emergency only. Masked dancers are "made" when an epidemic is thought to be on the way (Opler 1938:79).

We may give one example of a specific (group) curing ceremony among the Jicarilla Apache. This is the famous Holiness rite, popularly called the bear dance and performed to relieve sickness caused either by bear or snake. It is a traditional or "long life" rite and so was sanctioned by myth. When a person realized he was suffering from such an ailment, he found others who were similarly afflicted to share in the ritual since it was ordinarily not held for a single patient (usually three or four). These individuals collected paraphernalia and gifts and selected the shamans who would be involved in the rite. The chief shaman determined where and when the rite would occur. Two ritual structures, a corral and a tipi in its western end, were constructed.

On the first night, a ground drawing was made in the back of the tipi by the chief shaman, consisting of a motif of snake representations with bear tracks leading to it. An assistant who would represent the bear was now prepared. The male relatives of the patients sat in the tipi and smoked and prayed. About nine o'clock in the evening, the patients were brought in and seated, after first walking on the bear tracks. The shamans sang four songs, and the bear impersonator came and ran back and forth in front of the patients and then retired. The chief shaman blew smoke on the patients, and they also smoked. The chief shaman massaged the patients, gave them medicine to drink, and rubbed some of it on them. An assistant also gave some to their relatives. The leader sang more songs for the patients who would then leave. Now the relatives made eight fires in the corral, and the shamans erased the ground painting. The patients returned, and all the people went into the tipi. The shamans sang and the women and girls danced outside in the corral, eventually being joined by the men. This helped to make the sick people better and was not a social dance. After twelve songs, the night's activities were concluded. The second and third days are comparable.

The events of the fourth day and night were somewhat different. A more complicated ground drawing was made–one that included representations of many animal and plant types. The patients came in and were seated upon it, and the chief shaman sang forty-four songs that dealt with these representations. The patients then left, and eighteen men were selected to serve as special dancers. "Twelve of them go to the south side, the snake's side. They stand for the wonder workers because these cure snake sickness. The other six line up on the north side, the bear's side. They are going to represent the clowns" (Opler 1943:33). They were not costumed at this time, but went to special tipis outside the corral for this purpose. The fourth night's activities alternated between the regular dances previously performed and four performances by these special dancers. Eventually, they returned and danced without their costumes. At sunrise, the ritual closed with a procession towards the east led by the chief shaman.

We can conclude this brief account of Apache supernaturalism by mentioning another kind of rite apparently unique to the Jicarilla. It reminds us of the borrowing of religious traits that has taken place in the aboriginal southwest. The ritual was the ceremonial relay race. This took place for boys beyond the age of puberty but prior to marriage. They had to run at least once in these autumn events. The race was contested between bands and occasioned bets as to which group would win. It was another ritual justified in myths which ensured an abundance of meat and vegetables for humankind as well as fertility. One side was symbolic of meat and the Sun and the other of wild vegetables and the Moon. The result of the race suggested in a divinatory manner the comparative future abundance of these foods. The leaders of each side were shamans who learned the appropriate ritual techniques and observances. The boys who were selected to run also observed taboos and wore the objects of magic to give them speed and endurance.

The race track ran between two brush corrals which were built on the first day with great ritual. Trial races were held by each side to determine the best runners, who occupied honorary positions in the race. Then each side sang and danced three times along the race track towards each other. On the fourth movement, they passed each other and reached the corral of their opponents where they rested before reversing the activities and returning to their own enclosures. Leaders then sang songs to bring success and ensure long life. On the third day, the runners were decorated, and the leaders made ground drawings. The runners then left the corral, stepping on the ground drawings. After further dancing along the course of the race, four old men ran, making a "path" for the younger men to follow (they represented people who ran the first race in myth). Then the actual race occurred. Opler believed this ritual to have been derived primarily from Tanoan Pueblos but to have been reinterpreted.

> We may suppose that the relay race, with the associations let it in the Pueblo area, was received enthusiastically and developed rapidly and fully by the Jicarilla because it was so appropriate to the needs and nature of Jicarilla culture...but, being primarily hunters and gatherers, they were spurred by a profound interest in a dual food supply, an even-handed interest which the more agricultural Pueblos could not match (Opler 1944:97).

We may now examine some of the rituals of the other Athabascan group, the Navaho.

Navaho Religion

In many respects, in-depth material on Navaho supernaturalism outranks that of other southwestern groups. This is partly due to historic factors in their study and to the fact that the Navaho have been less secretive about communicating mythic and ritual details to outsiders. As a result, we possess fairly complete accounts (see the works of Reichard, Haile, Kluckhohn, and Wyman) of their supernatural practices. Such activities generally seem to parallel those of the Apache except for an increase in their complexity. Because of this complexity and the existence of useful and rather complete summaries elsewhere, only a brief comparative discussion is given in the present chapter.

Navaho rituals brought human beings into a good relationship with the supernatural powers that exist in the world as well as serving to keep them away from or aiding in the removal of evil influences. Disease and especially accidental injury could be dealt with in such a fashion, and, in fact, all rituals had preventive or curative aspects. Rituals and their associated techniques fell into a number of classes. Some rites were possessed by every person and were daily observances; others were more of a taboo or negative nature: not killing coyotes, never combing hair at night, etc. Still others were heavily laced with esoteric knowledge and were in the possession of only special practitioners. Most Navaho rites had an individualistic bias in outcome although other people were often thought to derive some benefit as well. We can examine these more esoteric rites and discuss the various types of practitioners associated with them.

All rituals were based upon myth which states how they originated in the beginning and how they must be carried out. Most specific ritual myths appear to be episodes connected to the major myth of origin itself.

> ...every Navaho chant and rite is based upon a legend descriptive of its origin and of the details of its ritual. Furthermore, a knowledge of this basic legend is not required of the native singer. To successfully qualify as a singer, however, he must become familiar with that part of a given chant ritual of which he plans to be a practitioner. Hence, his so-called religious knowledge may be limited to a minimum. Frequently the only requisite is to memorize certain sets of

> songs and prayers, with one or other minor ceremony...thrown in and he becomes a recognized singer (Haile 1935:84)

Some practitioners, however, did possess greater knowledge than others and as a result were accorded greater respect.

Classification of Navaho ritual practices has been completed from a number of points of view by anthropologists, and no complete consensus exists. Wyman and Kluckhohn (1938) have presented the following ceremonial division, each category of which consists of numbers of ritual types and variations: Blessing Way rituals were mostly for general protection – health, prosperity, and success – and were often performed as a precaution for avoiding danger rather than as a cure. Holy Way ceremonies did have specific curing connections but also have ritual types which secure rain. Life Way varieties existed to cure injuries of an accidental nature. Evil Way ceremonies were basically exorcistic in nature and were used to combat the evil derived from ghosts of Navaho and foreigners as well as evil spirits. Game Way essentially represented hunting rituals relative to the securing of bears and eagles and communal hunting of deer and antelope. War rituals dealt with activities originating out of and relating to warfare.

Other scholars asserted the existence of somewhat different ritual categories. The reason for such differing opinions is that each Navaho ritual or chant was a kind of framework into which many elements or units could be placed. These were used repeatedly in different chants, sometimes only with minor modifications. Such overlap makes discrete classification difficult and has led Reichard (1963) to lump all rituals as basically concerned with the attraction of good or the expulsion of evil, perhaps an overly simplistic dichotomy since both concerns may appear in the same rituals. At any rate, the chants were considered by the Navaho to be effective ways of dealing with the supernatural, but they could become harmful as well if any mistakes were made during their performance.

To obtain a feeling for the quality of such ceremonial practices, we can examine some of the ritual elements employed. Since the term chant is commonly applied to such activities, we can begin with the song involved. Songs accompanied all phases of rituals, and their content fit in with the prayers. Many song syllables, however, appear to have had no meaning, merely helping to fit those that do to the music. There were many distinct songs for each chant–perhaps hundreds. "Some songs are favorites or required and may be heard often; some are appropriate only under unusual circumstances; occasionally one song and no other will do" (Reichard 1963:287). Many times songs would occur in a specific sequence which must be followed in a given ritual, so songs differ, apparently, as to whether they were "stem songs"–which are appropriate and precise and follow in order, and "branch songs"–where the singer had more latitude in use and rendition. Generally, those songs sung early in a rite would be repeated on the last night of a lengthy ritual.

Prayers used in the ceremonies were not sung. Some prayers were given by the singer as he undertook his other activities; other prayers were said by participants, including the patient or person who is the object of the rite. Prayers were often long and had to be intoned without omitting any of the words and without making errors. Some prayers took more than one hour to complete. Especially important were "dialogue" prayers. "...every chant has at least one litany which the patient repeats sentence by sentence after the singer. The supernaturals pertinent to the chant are invoked, often particularly those represented by the figures in the sandpaintings or connected with the offerings. Much attention is given to exactness of wording, even more than in other spoken parts of ceremonials" (Wyman and Kluckhohn 1938:67). In the event of a discovered error in ritual, the part could apparently be repeated to rectify the situation.

Another common ritual element is the use of sandpaintings. Usually every chant had at least one such construction associated with it, the form and content of which may be altered on successive days of the rite. These paintings represented mythic events or supernatural beings and were made on a layer of clean sand or occasionally on a piece of skin.

> When the painting had been completed to the accompaniment of song and prayer, the patient sits upon it in ceremonially dictated fashion and the treatment begins. The Singer gives the patient an infusion of herbs to drink. He touches the feet of a figure in the painting and then the patient's feet saying. 'May his feet be well. His feet restore him.' In turn he presses his hands upon the knees, hands, shoulders....When the treatment is finished and the patient has gone outside, the

> painting is destroyed bit by bit in the order in which it was made....When the last picture has been completed and the patient treated in this fashion, his relatives may walk in ceremonial fashion across the painting, treading where the holy figures have trod. Thus not only the sick man but the family as well have come into close communion with the Holy People, and all those present have seen their power (Kluckhohn and Leighton 1946:154-55).

In addition to songs, prayers, and sandpaintings, there are a great number of other elements distributed in Navaho chants. These included, among other things, the use of herbal, mineral, and animal medicines and prayersticks used as invocatory offerings as well as special ones used in pairs for protection and to make prayers come true; Navaho ritual was very compulsive and mechanistic. Pollen was also extensively employed in chants as well as drums and rattles and noisemakers, special arrows and flints, and fumigants – placed upon hot coals from the fire for purification at the end of the ritual. Many of these items were kept in a bundle by the singer in anticipation of their use, and a singer might or might not keep those used in different rituals in separate bundles. These were ritually laid out at the beginning of rituals. The use of the sweathouse and hair and body washing were also common. A few rituals also had public dances as an associated feature.

There appear to be two main classes of practitioners associated with Navaho rituals. The Diviner was the person who sought to ascertain the cause of illness, as well as to predict the outcome of war and hunting, locate lost objects, and in general to know the future. The ability to perform such tasks was apparently unsought, coming as a gift of the supernatural either while a person was under conditions of solitude or while attending a ritual. The ability, however, appeared to have been concentrated only in certain families. The major techniques of divination included listening to the wind, gazing at the sun or other natural phenomena, chewing a narcotic plant, and, most typical, hand trembling. In this last technique, the way the hand moved as it shook indicated the answer sought. The Singer, on the other hand, was a person who had learned the appropriate rituals. This may be accomplished by formal apprenticeships under a practicing ceremonialist. When judged competent, the novice was initiated to fix his knowledge and protect him against the dangers of possessing such powers. Sometimes a would-be practitioner learned the rites in a more indirect, piecemeal fashion by simply attending the desired rite repeatedly and asking questions. In either case, one came to desire and pursue such knowledge rather late in one's life. Singers were often ranked in terms of how completely they knew these rites. Basically, however, the major distinction is between the diviner who ascertains causes and the singer who effects the cures.

> A rather striking feature of Navaho culture to which attention has never been explicitly drawn is the contrast between the manner in which the practice of hand-trembling divination is begun. The former [singers] falls into the "priestly" tradition–there is formal instruction in a system of abundant lore. The latter falls into the "shamanistic" tradition–there is no formal instruction and a minimum of lore; it is a question of a direct gift (Kluckhohn 1939:66-67).

We can now briefly examine the genesis and structure of rituals.

A curing ritual was undertaken when a person communicates about his trouble to his family (or is injured, etc.). They discussed the possible causes, usually calling in a diviner to confirm their guess interpretation, if the symptoms are definite, or to suggest a possible course of action, if indefinite. Common causes of illness included failure to observe taboos, excess in some activity, improper contact with animals, natural phenomena such as lightning and wind, improper behavior in some past ceremony, witchcraft and sorcery, and contact with ghosts and enemies. If the diagnosis proved to be difficult, a number of chants might be tried until one proved to be successful; sometimes chants were first held in shortened form to ascertain their effectiveness. The selection of the proper singer was conditioned by a number of factors: geographical distance, reputed knowledge, and the closeness of social relation to the patient; a related practitioner charged less for the cure!

The singer who has been chosen was aided by a chief assistant, usually a member of his family or kinship group who was learning the ritual. The family of the patient chose the other assistants who would collect some of the paraphernalia, run errands for the singer, and help in other ways. Such assistants usually had undergone the rite themselves and hence were protected from its power as well as knowing something about it. The family members of the patient were usually in attendance throughout the rite, along with a few close friends. Other spectators could attend at the end (climax).

Reichard (1963) has summarized the "typical" structure of Navaho ritual in the following fashion (the most complete generalized account is found in Wyman and Kluckhohn 1938). Chants lasted from one to nine nights, including the intervening days. On the first night, only simple rituals occurred, along with a few hours of singing. The next four days were spent in invoking the supernaturals involved and exorcising any possible evil. This was accomplished by sweat bath rites for purification each morning and the use of prayersticks over which the dialogue prayer was intoned by singer and patient. Prayersticks were placed to assure the presence of the deities. Prior to sunrise on the fifth day, the singer laid out his bundle objects. These "...are laid out on a mount which forms an altar a few yards from the door of the dwelling in which the ceremony is held. As each piece of ritualistic property is placed, the chanter utters the appropriate sentence of a prayer and the patient...takes hold of the property. The altar is there to announce the preparation of a sandpainting inside the house, to inform the gods that they are expected, to warn persons not concerned that they should stay away" (Reichard 1963:xxxv). On this and the next three days, sandpaintings were constructed to identify the patient with the deities and attract good power to the patient. These rites lasted a longer period of time on each successive day. The hair and body of the patient were washed on the last day. On the second through the eighth nights, the singing lasted for a longer period of time. On the last (climax) night, this singing, and other rites, continued until dawn, and song groups from all previous rites were included "...to summarize all the purification, invocation, attraction of power, and identification of the entire ceremony" (Reichard 1963:xxxvi). We can now turn to a brief discussion of some other aspects of Navaho supernaturalism.

One of the sources of evil that profoundly disturbed the Navaho was that emanating from witches.

> The Navaho Indians...believe there are human wolves; or more especially, that men and women disguised in wolf or mountain lion skins go about practicing witchcraft.

....

> There is myth and tale material about these human wolves; and stories, delusions, hallucinations. Diagnosticians find them to be the cause of sickness and there are songs for protection and songs for cure. Sandpaintings, prayers, herbs, and rituals free the patient and send the harmful influences back upon the witch (Morgan 1936:3).

Witches were generally active at night, and they caused sickness and death in a number of ways. Kluckhohn (1944) had distinguished four basic formats for such evil practices. In Witchery, a preparation was made from the flesh of corpses, and after being ground into a powder, it was placed on people and things. Thus it works by contamination. These people, apparently, were the most typical human-wolves and were believed to meet together to plan and carry out their terrible activities. Sorcery, perhaps a branch practice of the above, gained its end by the method of enchantment by spell, reciting evil words over the possessions of the intended victim and then burying them with materials from a grave. Sorcerers might have special spirit powers to aid them. In Wizardry, the evil activity consisted of projecting a disease object into the victim. This was accomplished by placing it on an animal skin or in a basket and intoning the correct spell to make it travel into the victim. Usually one had to kill a close relative to become a practitioner of the above categories. The last type is Frenzy Witchcraft and involved the use of love magic to gain unfair advantages. This could also be used in trading and gambling.

One gained protection from such evil persons by using charms and by possessing ceremonial knowledge. One could undergo protective rituals. There was also the notion that a strong and well-protected person can cause the evil of such persons to backfire.

> All ceremonial cures, if successful, are believed to cause the death of the witch before long, and various deaths are accounted for in this way. Some Navahos also believe that witches are commonly struck down by lightning. When public feeling is sufficiently aroused, the supposed witch is made to confess, which ensures his 'magical' death within a year or he is actually put to death, sometimes by bloody and brutal means (Kluckhohn and Leighton 1946:129-30).

Certainly the belief in types of witches among the Navaho led to an amount of fear and caution in their daily lives.

A somewhat related supernatural concept is the great fear of ghosts displayed by most Navaho. The ghost was conceived of as a malignant influence which was released at the time of the death of an individual. In actual definition, it seems unclear in conceptualization. Some Navaho characterize it as being an actual spirit, others simply as the embodiment of evil that a person (however unwittingly) possessed during life. In any event, its presence could cause sickness and death in others. Such beliefs help explain the Navaho fear of the dead and anything connected with them. Ghosts were believed to often appear after dark in animal forms and could change their size rapidly. Animal sounds, whistling, or a ball of fire were signs of their presence, and they might chase people or jump on them and then suddenly disappear. In fact, unusual behavior in any natural things could lead to its suspicion of being ghost-connected.

> Ghosts return to earth to avenge some offense. Improper burial of a corpse, holding back belongings of the deceased, failure to kill a horse and a sheep for the use of the deceased, disturbing or taking away from the grave parts of the earthly body or things buried with it...may impel the ghost to return to claim belongings or to locate missing parts....Hence death rites are oriented towards the prevention of such return rather than towards the loss situation (Wyman, Hill and Osanai 1942:23).

Since ghosts might attack anyone, avoidance and circumspection were the proper avenues taken. If a person evidenced typical symptoms, the proper chant (i.e., Evil Way) was performed. Even dreaming of ghosts might lead to a Blessing Way rite for general protection. Some of these practices and beliefs, understandably, seem reminiscent of Apache beliefs. So too was the Girls Puberty Rite and many other supernatural elements. We can turn now to the last component of Southwestern supernaturalism, the Yumans.

ATHABASCAN BIBLIOGRAPHY AND REFERENCES

Basso, Keith H.

1970. The Cibecue Apache. New York: Holt, Rinehart and Winston.

1969. Western Apache Witchcraft. *University of Arizona. Anthropological Papers* #15.

Bourke, J. G.

1892. The Medicine Men of the Apache. *Bureau of American Ethnology Annual Report* 9:451-595.

1891. Notes on the Religion of the Apache Indians. *Fólklore* 2:419-54.

Dutton, B. P.

1941. The Navaho Wind Way Ceremonials. *El Palacio* 48:73-82.

Frisbie, Charlotte J.

1967. Kinaalda: A Study of the Navaho Girl's Puberty Ceremony. Middletown: Wesleyan University Press.

Goddard, P. E.

1909. Gotal – A Mescalero Apache Ceremony. In Franz Boas (editor) *Putnam Anniversary Volume*, pp. 385-94. New York: G. E. Stechert.

Goodwin, G.

1942. The Social Organization of the Western Apache. Chicago: University of Chicago Press.

1938. White Mountain Apache Religion. *American Anthropologist* 40:24-37.

Goodwin, G. and Clyde Kluckhohn.

1945. A Comparison of Navaho and White Mountain Ceremonial Forms and Categories. *Southwestern Journal of Anthropology* 1:498-506.

Haile, B.

1938. Navaho Chantways and Ceremonials. *American Anthropologist* 40:639-52.

1935. Religious Concepts of the Navaho Indians. *Proceedings of the Catholic Philosophical Association* 10:84-98.

Hill, W. W.

1936. Navaho Warfare. *Yale University Publications in Anthropology* 5:1-19.

Kaut, C. R.
1959. Notes on Western Apache Religions and Social Organization. *American Anthropologist* 61:99-102.

Kluckhohn, C.
1944. Navaho Witchcraft. *Peabody Museum Papers* 22:1-149.

1939. Some Personal and Social Aspects of Navaho Ceremonial Practice. *Theological Review* 32:57-82.

Kluckhohn, C. and Leighton, D. C. .
1946. The Navaho. Cambridge: Harvard University Press.

Leighton, A. H. and D. C.
1949. Gregorio, the Hand-Trembler. *Peabody Museum Papers* 40:1-177.

Morgan, W.
1936. Human Wolves Among The Navaho. *Yale University Publications in Anthropology* 11:1-43.

1931. Navaho Treatment of Sickness. *American Anthropologist* 33:390-402.

Nicholas, D.
1939. Mescalero Apaches Girls' Puberty Ceremony. *El Palacio* 46:193-204.

Opler, M. E.
1946A. Chiracahua Apache Material Relating to Sorcery. *Primitive Man* 19:81-92.

1946B. Mountain Spirits of the Chiracahua Apache. *Masterkey* 20:125-31.

1946C. Reaction to Death Among the Mescalero Apache. *Southwestern Journal of Anthropology* 2:455-67.

1946D. The Creative Role of Shamanism in Mescalero Apache Mythology. *Journal of American Folklore* 59:268-81.

1944. The Jicarilla Apache Ceremonial Relay Race. *American Anthropologist* 46:75-96.

1943. The Character and Derivation of Jicarilla Holiness Rites. *University of New Mexico Bulletin Anthropology Series* 4:1-98.

1942. Adolescence Rite of the Jicarilla. *El Palacio* 49:25-38.

1941A. A Jicarilla Apache Expedition and Scalp Dance. *Journal of American Folklore* 44:10-23.

1941B. An Apache Life-Way. Chicago: University of Chicago Press.

1938. The Sacred Clowns of the Chiracahua and Mescalero Indians. *El Palacio* 44:75-79.

1936. A Summary of Jicarilla Apache Culture. *American Anthropologist* 38:202-23.

1935. The Concept of Supernatural Power Among the Chiricahua and Mescalero Apache. *American Anthropologist* 37:65-70.

Regan, A. B.
1904. Apache Medicine Ceremonies. *Proceedings of the Indiana Academy of Science* 14:275-83.

Reichard, G.
1963. Navaho Religion. New York: Pantheon Books.

1945. Distinctive Features of Navaho Religion. *Southwestern Journal of Anthropology* 1:199-220.

1939. Navaho Medicine Man. New York: J. J. Augustin.

Sonnichsen, C. L.
1958. The Mescalero Apache. Norman: University of Oklahoma Press.

Tozzer, A. M.
1909. Notes on Religious Ceremonials of the Navaho. *Putnam Anniversary Volume* pp. 299-343.

Underhill, R. M.
1956. The Navahos. Norman: University of Oklahoma Press.

Wyman, L. C.
1936. The Female Shooting Life Chant. *American Anthropologist* 38:236-46.

Wyman, L. C. and Bailey, F. L.
1946. Navaho Striped Windway, An Injury Way Chant. *Southwestern Journal of Anthropology* 2:213-38.

1943. Navaho Upward Reaching Way. *University of New Mexico Bulletin* 4:1-47.

Wyman, L. C. and Hill, W. W. and Osanai, I.
1942. Navaho Eschatology. *University of New Mexico Bulletin* #377.

Wyman, L. C. and Kluckhohn, C.
1938. Navaho Classification of their Song Ceremonials. *American Anthropological Association Memoir* 50:1-38.

Wyman, L. C. and Hill, W. W. and Osanai, I.
1942. Navaho Eschatology. *University of New Mexico Bulletin* #377.

Wyman, L. C. and Kluckhohn, C.
1938. Navaho Classification of their Song Ceremonials. *American Anthropological Association Memoir* 50:1-38.

CHAPTER VII

YUMAN RELIGION

The Yuman component of Southwestern supernaturalism in some respects represents a transitional phenomenon between the other groupings in this area and societies in Southern California and the Great Basin. Data on religious beliefs and practices are less complete and certain than for most of the other groups we have considered previously in this volume. Hence, appraisal of their true complexity (or lack of it) must necessarily be brief. We can discuss the River Yumans first: the Mohave, Yuma, Cocopa, and Maricopa.

River Yuman Religion

At the basis of the River Yuman supernaturalism was the conception that all supernatural power and the ability to accomplish extraordinary things, as well as knowledge of songs and myths, are gained via dream experiences. For example:

> The Mohave adhere to a belief in dreams as the basis of everything in life....Not only as shamanistic power but most myths and songs, bravery and fortune in war, success with women or in gaming, every special ability, are dreamed. Knowledge is not a thing to be learned, the Mohave declare, but to be acquired by each man according to his dreams (Kroeber 1925:754).

Among the Maricopa, too, those persons who were successful were so because they had dreamed as a prerequisite. The fact that one might learn techniques or songs was considered clearly secondary to the validatory dream experience. Of course, not all persons were favored and "regular" dreams might also occur. Such power or knowledge came involuntarily in special dreams, usually reoccurring over a long period of time. Not until the spirits or beings responsible for the dream experience told the dreamer that his preparations were complete could the powers granted actually be used. At this point, the dreams and their contents were revealed.

Generally speaking, dreams were sent by spirits of various sorts: animal or natural – mountains, lightning – insect, or by a major supernatural being, this last usually in the case of shamanism. Powers or knowledge from particular spirits were different and almost always specific – for war powers, to cure a certain disease, etc. In the dream experience itself, usually a person's soul or spirit was considered to have left the body and to have experienced an adventure, the events of the dream. So important were such dreams to the individual in these groups that the hallucinogenic Jimson Weed was used as a way to increase their frequency. In fact, among the Cocopa, a shaman would administer this to a group of young men on a formal basis to reveal their "aptitude," and they would remain under its influence for a period of some days. However, such practices were not as complex or initiatory in character as similar practices in Southern California.

Scholars have questioned how a person could learn such information as songs, myths, and techniques entirely in dreams, especially since some of these are lengthy and closely identical or comparable for different individuals. Certainly conscious or unconscious learning is involved in such acquisitions. As had been pointed out for the Mohave:

> Although Mohave shamans and singers are supported to acquire their knowledge in dream, they actually learn it in waking life and then have dreams which condense or allude to this body of knowledge. Society accepts these condensations as equivalents of the full text....The power of the songs is not inherent in their letter-perfect wording and reproduction; it is due to the fact that they are accepted as condensed equivalents of the myth....Power dreams and the songs which actualize power are both condensations of the myth, which does not mean that the two...are necessarily the same, although differences between the two versions of a set of songs may be due to the actual dream experienced by the singers (Devereux 1957:1044).

Certainly, as time passes, the conviction of individuals concerning the dream origins of their power and knowledge increases, as does perhaps their conception of the correctness of their own version or rendition.

Granted the individualistic basis of the dream experience, River Yuman supernaturalism in terms of public ceremonies was little developed. Song cycles were perhaps the central ritual element although their basis, complexity, and identification vary somewhat from group to group. Among the Mohave, there were about thirty separate-named cycles of songs, each comprising from 100 to 200 separate songs. All such cycles were identified with rites for various purposes and were based on myths dealing with the adventures of supernatural beings. Little of the myth story, however, appeared in the somewhat distorted words of the songs. Some degree of improvisation occurs. Among the Yuma, "The songs are arranged in groups or series which should be sung as a whole. Each song refers to an incident in a myth on which the series itself is based. The song consists of a few disconnected words taken from the subject matter of the legend and is often meaningless apart from its context" (Forde 1931:127). Some cycles among the Maricopa were less bound to myth and were more confined to the personal experience of the person who had dreamed them. Songs were sung at formal occasions of a ritual nature as well as at social occasions.

On this background of dreaming and singing and power acquisitions, we can briefly sketch a few of the occasions for these and other expressions of supernaturalism among the River Yumans. Expectably, shamanism played a major role in their religious culture, especially surrounding curing activities. Among the Yuma, illness had a number of causes in addition to those injuries of a natural sort. Witchcraft, loss of one's soul, and dream poisoning were common interpretations. This last is a rather interesting variety of object intrusion theory. In it a person consumed some kind of poisonous substance while under the influence of a malevolent spirit. The shaman who was called upon to effect such cures not only had power of a dream-derived nature but his power differed from that of other dreamers in that the spirit encountered in the dreams remained in continuous rapport with him, advising him on treatment and on other matters. The spirit also exacted special obedience from the shaman in turn. Spiritual help consisted mainly in giving strength to the shaman for his performance, but in the case of witchcraft cures, actual possession by the spirit occurred. Common curing techniques included sucking blood, massage, blowing saliva, blowing smoke, and brushing with feathers. Causes and cures among other River Yuman tribes were quite similar. Among the Mohave and perhaps the Cocopa, the shamans appear to have had no private spirit allies but received their powers before birth directly from a creator deity. "The shaman's experiences begin in myth at the world origin and are myth in form. The god Mastambo gave their special powers to all shamans of today..." (Kroeber 1925:775). In all groups, shamans were feared because of their possible malpractice via witchcraft and, if so suspected, might be killed.

Warfare also occasioned ritual activity. As elsewhere in the southwest, the taking of scalps was an important adjunct to war techniques. Among the Mohave, only a special individual who had scalping power from dreams removed a scalp, consisting of most of the head skin. The scalp was feared because of its magical potency. Scalps were only taken from chiefs and outstanding warriors. The scalp taker, killers, and apparently all of the warriors of the war expedition underwent four or eight days of purification. Meanwhile, the scalp was prepared by a special leader into whose permanent possession it would soon pass. This person also had the requisite dream power so as to be safe from harm from it. He placed the scalp on a long pole in the dance ground, and for a period of four days and nights, males sung song cycles and women danced around it. Yuma practice was closely identical to that of the Maricopa and Cocopa although Maricopa practices in purification appear to have been somewhat more formal. Scalps were generally kept in pottery bowls and occasionally were taken along on war expeditions.

War itself was not only for revenge and other secular motives. "Fighting was not justified as a virile pursuit, nor was economic need adduced as a factor; warfare to the Yuma possessed a strong mystical value as the means whereby the spiritual power of the entire tribe was enhanced and at the same time demonstrated" (Forde 1931:162). Generally speaking, war parties were led by people who had special powers from dreams to do so. Possibly the Mohave were the most warlike, and, according to Stewart

(1947), a special group of "brave men" (Kwanamis) were a warrior class whose chief pursuits were always along such lines. They had received dream power for war and were eager to test its applicability! Other groups appear less organized in these respects. There were often special dances prior to leaving for warfare activities, and shamans accompanied war parties to cure wounds as did diviners who would ascertain the whereabouts of the enemy. Among the Maricopa:

> Clairvoyants could reveal the whereabouts of the enemy or forecast his coming. The clairvoyant shaman who accompanied a war party into the mountains, one who dreamed of Buzzard or Coyote, smoked four cigarettes and fell as though dead. His smoking was thought to lift him high into the air. When he recovered he told how Buzzard had taken him to the highest mountain where the location and numbers of the enemy were revealed and how easily they might be slain. The war party then set off following his leadership (Spier 1933:292).

We can conclude this brief account of River Yuman supernaturalism with data relative to some of their life-cycle observances.

A ritual for young girls at puberty occurred among all groups, but in contrast to most of these previously discussed for this culture area, it was a rather simple affair. All groups confined the girl for four or eight days during which time her behavior was supposed to affect her future character and qualities. Taboos were observed, and dreams often interpreted as clues to the future of the girl. The central rite consisted of the girl lying in a depression filled with hot sand. Among the Mohave:

> Each night for four nights the menstruant lies in a pit scooped out of the sand to a depth of six inches or a foot in one corner of the house. The pit is warmed by building a fire in it and scraping out the embers. Warm sand is heaped up around the girl and blankets are placed over her. This 'roasting' is believed to be of therapeutic value and to contribute to the general physiological well-being of the pubescent (Wallace 1948:38).

Among some groups, older women surrounded the girl and sang and advised her as to the conducts expected of women. Among the Yuma, special orations were made. Among most groups, the girl ran some distance for strength and endurance, and among the Maricopa, at least, a special dance involving the girl and parallel lines of males and females occurred. Generally the rite was repeated on the next three successive menstrual periods, after which time the girl was eligible for marriage.

Comparable puberty rituals existing for young boys are dubious. All groups appear to have had tests of manhood. Among the Maricopa, for example, boys between the ages of sixteen and eighteen were taken to a location where a swarm of bees existed and were made to sit on the hive and kill them all one at a time. This represented going to war. Among the Yuma and Cocopa, boys had their nasal septums pierced and ran distances and observed taboos. Among the latter, they were also placed in heated trenches to mold their future character.

Death occasioned grief and ritual but less fear of the ghost than among Athabascans. Generally speaking, the deceased was rather quickly prepared and placed on a funeral pyre and cremated, the ashes being placed in a pit beneath the crematory or in special pits elsewhere. Property belonging to the deceased was also destroyed, as was his home. This functioned both to get rid of any leftover sickness and to keep the dead from returning. A prominent feature of such activities was ritual wailing by relatives, reaching a crescendo at the time of the consumption of the body by the flames. Formal orations speaking of the dead individual and enjoining relatives not to grieve unduly were also widespread. Close relatives cut their hair and observed taboos for four days afterwards in the effort to achieve purification. All groups seem also to have had special mourning rituals for prominent individuals although such rites were more extensive among some groups (Yuma and Cocopa) than others. Among the Yuma, the mourning ritual (Keruk) was a four-day ritual which not only commemorated the recent dead but was also a reenactment of myth–perpetuating a ritual that was given to the first humans by a culture hero deity after the death of the creator god. The deceased individual went to a "land of the dead." In summary, River Yuman religion was based on the dream experience and expressed itself mostly in song cycles of a compulsive and mechanistic sort. Ground paintings, fetishes, prayers, invoking deities, and prayer offerings were lacking. We can now discuss the Upland Yumans: Yavapai, Walapai, and Havasupai.

Upland Yuman Religion

Supernaturalism among Upland Yuman societies was perhaps the least complex of the various groups previously considered. The data we presently possess relative to such beliefs and practices are also meager, making for very incomplete understandings of this aspect of their cultural behavior. "Religious matters occupy but a minor place in Havasupai life. Ceremonialism is meager and interest in the supernatural is neither extensive nor developed in systematic form" (Spier 1928:275). "Yavapai religion was undeveloped on the ritual or ceremonial side" (Gifford 1936:307). Much the same can be said of the Walapai. The focal point of the supernaturalism of this Southwestern unit was shamanism, and we can briefly summarize it and then survey some other aspects of their religion.

The shaman was primarily a medical practitioner although one type seems to have functioned somewhat in weather control. Basically, the power to be a shaman was acquired by the dream experience although there was a tendency toward inheritance–shamanism being confined to certain family lines. Among the Havasupai, one would dream continually, and when one felt competent, one would begin to practice–success being the validation of the dream experience. Among the Yavapai, however, it is maintained that the true vision experience occurred, falling down in a trance and then relating what had been seen in the altered condition. Spirits were felt responsible in any case for the bestowal of powers. The Walapai may have been theologically the most sophisticated in this respect with two somewhat distinct power sources. Each shaman apparently allied himself with the spirit of some feature of nature. After a dream experience, he would go to the proper geographic location and communicate with the spirit that had appeared to him. The shaman also had a second power source, having been asked by the spirit of his father in a dream to take up such practice in the first place. This spirit also gave power and became a supernatural patron. Among the Walapai and the Yavapai, such spirits could possess the shaman and speak through him.

Concepts of disease were poorly developed in contrast to other groups, and sometimes a number of shamans with different specialities would simultaneously engage in the curing of a patient. Some basic disease concepts were evil spirits, breach of taboo, ghosts, and witches, the latter usually being malpracticing shamans although they might be women in some Yavapai groups. The most typical curing performances included singing over the patient, shaking a gourd rattle, and sucking out blood through a cut made in the body. A disease object sometimes was exhibited in the blood. Among the Havasupai:

> The shaman is called in by a relative of the sick man. He performs by night in the camp...singing over the patient, and sucking out the disease which he exhibits. The characteristic attitude while singing is with the clenched knuckles of the left hand held against the forehead, the right hand holding the gourd rattle, while the trunk is slowly twisted from side to side. Relatives and friends gather to shout as the shaman may enjoin them (Spier 1928:279).

Cures usually took place over a four-night period. Shamans in most groups were killed for malpractice, as were women who were accused of witchcraft. Sweatbaths and vomiting were also occasionally used for curing and the former also for general purification.

The Southwestern Yavapai also had a group curing ritual in which masked dancers performed under the control of a shaman. The dancers impersonated spirits called Akoka. The ceremony was held in autumn in a brush enclosure. The shaman summoned the dancers (8) by swinging a noisemaker, and they came into the enclosure, sprinkled pollen on the head of the shaman and his assistant singers, and then treated the patients four times each by placing pollen on parts of their bodies and in their mouths. This rite probably had Apache origins. Among the Northeastern Yavapai, "Sandpaintings were made by shamans to ward off epidemics of measles and smallpox. Men sang, women and some men danced or marched in approaching and retreating lines. This (was) done if the shaman dreamed of heavy wind or rainstorm, which foreboded disease" (Gifford 1936:310).

The Southeastern Yavapai also held dances in the spring to ensure bountiful harvests of wild foods. Prayers to a goddess were part of the songs sung by a group of three or four men who knew this ritual, and two lines of male and female dancers performed. This was, apparently, also an occasion for sexual license among unmarried people. The Havasupai (who had greater dependence upon agriculture) performed a masked dance to make crops grow and for rain, and at the end of August, after the harvest, they held a general prosperity dance interspersed with speeches by the chief. An interesting feature was a masked clown who forced people to dance. This was also a social occasion.

Warfare customs followed those described for other Yuman groups, if less complex. Scalps were taken by the killers. Among the Southwestern Yavapai:

> A victorious raid was followed first by a fast and then a celebration dance at home. Women went to meet the returning warriors and relieved them of plunder and scalps. Prisoners were seldom taken. The warriors and the mastava (chief) went to some creek to wash and there they fasted for two days. Their garments were discarded, but not their weapons. Upon their return to camp they feasted and the mastava delivered a brief speech about the victory....Then there was dancing. The warriors did not boast of their exploits, but told about the fight if asked. Thereafter they might go to another camp to dance in celebration of the victory (Gifford 1932:184).

Sometimes war dances preceded war activities, and taboos were observed while on the warpath.

Puberty for girls occasioned some ritual. Among the Havasupai, the girl was washed with yucca suds and spent four days and nights on a typically Yuman "hot bed" and was harangued by an older woman on her future duties. Among some groups, the girl had to gather wood and food to demonstrate her industry. Formal dances seem not to have occurred. Comparable rites for young boys are lacking. At the end of the life cycle, the dead were cremated accompanied by ritual wailing. Many of the possessions of the dead were also destroyed as was their dwelling. Relatives cut their hair, but there was no real mourning ceremony. Beliefs as to the soul, its possible return as a ghost, and the precise nature of the land of the dead are meager and confusing. We can now make some summary and comparative statements about Southwestern religion.

We have now briefly and incompletely surveyed some of the religious practices and beliefs of the various Southwestern Indian groups. It should again be mentioned that the data we possess on the supernaturalism of this culture area are less than what we might desire. The extinction or near extinction of aboriginal groups and/or practices, secretiveness, and changes due to the process of acculturation to the national society severely hamper understanding of these behaviors. Dislocations and borrowings between tribes in the early historic period may also be responsible for similarities that are not purely aboriginal. For example, many Pueblo peoples lived a considerable time among the Navaho after the revolt of 1680. Interpretative biases and mistakes also lend to confusion and misinterpretation. These statements also apply to all areas covered in these books. We can, however, make a brief summation of religious customs for each group and suggest some comparative notions of a tentative nature.

It can be said of the Western Pueblos, Hopi, Zuni, and less so for Hano, that the main thrust of supernaturalism deals with weather control and the growth cycle of crops. Rites were multipurpose, however, with general blessing and diverse other ends also involved. Ceremonialism was in the hands of specialized practitioners organized into societies where, despite some recruitment options, the emphasis was upon learning a complex series of prayers and ritual maneuvers. Many rites were largely esoteric, being conducted in secret by those who knew them and followed by public exhibitions. Paraphernalia were very complex. A major religious element was the presence of Kachina spirits who are represented in masked dances.

Among the Hopi, major ceremonies included the Soyal/winter solstice rite which among other things aided the sun in its course, the Powamu/bean dance which aided crop growth and which initiated individuals into the Kachina cult, the Snake/Antelope performances for rain and crop fertility and sun reversal, and the Wuwutzim, initiation into the four male tribal societies with their emphasis upon life and death. Girls went through a mild puberty observance involving performance of adult female activities and segregation surrounded by taboos. There were also formal women's groups or societies. A developed war society with a scalp takers subgroup occurred with purifications and a victory dance. A hunt society, clown groups, and curing society were more dubious for the Hopi. The first apparently was not formally organized, the second occurred on an ad hoc basis, and the last was basically individualized. However, other formal groups may have performed set functions in these areas. Death and burial were not greatly emphasized in nature ritual.

Many Hopi supernatural elements were generally duplicated among the Zuni: sun "worship" via solstice rites, initiation into the Kachina cult (although only for males), a concern for weather control, and rituals in the hands of esoteric societies. The Zuni appear to have theologically magnified weather concerns resulting not only in the Kachinas but in the cult of the Kachina Priest Gods and the Uwanami or water spirits. They also, in their cult of animal spirits, had a series of curing societies (also functioning in weather control, etc.). A formal hunters society, clown societies, and a well-developed war-scalp cult with initiation and purification also existed. A generalized cult of ancestors was shared by all Zuni although death and burial were not elaborated.

The Eastern Pueblos represent, as previously indicated, variations on the common Pueblo theme. The emphasis, however, passes from weather control (with water for crops more assured) to curing activities. Among the Keresans, a number of medicine societies existed to cure the sick and especially to fight witchcraft. They also were important in solstice rites and rainmaking activities. Here much ritualism was organized by moiety divisions. A Kachina cult seems well developed with two clown groups. A war society and a hunters group occurred. The existence of formal women's groups is dubious. Some of these latter groups also had curing potential.

The data on the Tewa also exhibit a dual division and a Kachina cult with associated rituals emphasizing fertility and abundance of crops. Possibly two medicine societies, two clown groups and hunt and war organizations are documented. Tiwa data are more incomplete. Isleta appears to have a moiety organization and a number of corn groups which performed solstice retreats and other rites. Medicine societies not only controlled witches and cured the sick but also functioned in weather control. A war society for scalps and purification and a hunter's group also occurred. There are no Kachinas or masked dances, and the existence of clowns is dubious. At Taos, six ritual groupings with subdivisions occurred with specialized ritual functions. These groups may have furnished aid in hunting and in health, as well as had clown functions. There may also have been a warrior's group.

Some individual curers existed. Among the Towa (Jemez), there were two general men's tribal societies, a Kachina cult and clowns, a pair of curing societies, and a hunting and war group. In sum, the various Pueblo groups–not all closely related to each other–do exhibit common basic supernatural patterns, one consisting of variously organized religious groupings pursuing with differing emphases weather control, the growth of crops, curing, hunting, and war along with keeping the world in order. Ritualism was heavily esoteric with most groups exhibiting masked and other kinds of public dances and performances. Calendrically organized rituals with group or community benefit were heavily emphasized. Leaders were very priest-like with their knowledge and techniques learned.

The Pimans (as chiefly known from the Papago) also exhibited calendrical, group-benefit ceremonialism conducted by essentially priestly types of individuals, but individualistic power rituals supplemented these to a large extent, success in life being predicated on powers given by spirit forces. Communally oriented rituals centered on rain and the food cycle and were based on mythic repetition and tradition. They included rainmaking, a crop magic, and dances. A hunt society aided in communal hunts, and at least in the Viikita festival, clowns and dancing of essentially Puebloan varieties existed. Ritual races also existed. The acquisition of personal power and success was stimulated by undertaking hazardous activities such as war or were negatively conceived for girls at puberty. War involved scalp taking, purification, and dancing. The girl's puberty rite was marked by greater ritualism than among the Pueblos, being accompanied by seclusion, taboos, and dances. Curing rituals were conducted by individualistic shamans who obtained special powers via dreams, who specialized, and who possessed a somewhat feared, ambivalent nature. Communal curing also occurred. Death and burial were also quite ritualized with wailing and dwelling destructions. Ghosts were induced not to return and harm the living. Among Pimans, then, there is a split between individualistic and communal ritual concerns to a greater extent than among Puebloans.

Athabascan religion presents still further variation on supernatural themes. For the various Apache groups, individual and communal rituals occurred with perhaps the greater emphasis upon the former. Gaining power gave individuals special success potential. Somewhat like the Pimans, some such power came directly from the spirits while other power was gained by learning. Ritual types reflect this dichotomy. Life-cycle occasions are well emphasized with the girl's puberty rite being perhaps the central rite here and having collective benefits and public aspects. Death and ghosts occasioned great fear. Warfare was similarly marked with rituals before and after combat with a special scalp taker, dances, and purifications. The curing of illness by individualistic shamans in intricate ceremonies was a major feature of Apache ritualism, along with occasional communal curing activities by masked dancers and clowns. Navaho ceremonialism also heavily reflected an individualistic bias although acquisition of power was tied more to learning, all rituals being based upon myth and comprising a very complex series of chants and developed song, maneuver, and paraphernalia. The position of diviner remains one of a more personal-shamanistic nature.

Among the River Yumans, the basis of supernaturalism was the conception that supernatural power is based on dream experiences constructed basically along an involuntary fashion. Song cycles were the religious format, and there were few communally oriented rites. Warfare with a special scalp taker was surrounded with ritual, and at least one group had a warrior's society. The girl's puberty ritual, with somewhat different format than among other Southwestern groups, was an occasion of importance, and death was accompanied by ritual wailing and speech making and by cremation and property destruction. Mourning rituals were common and often complex. Shamanism played the major role in ritualism. Upland Yumans also displayed a shamanistic bias with power derived from dream experiences. Curing ceremonies, war dances, purifications, the puberty ritual for young girls and death rites without formal mourning were the most common expressions of supernaturalism.

In sum, the Yumans and other non-Puebloan groups in the southwest exhibit varying degrees of individualism with respect to the supernatural. Instead of formal community rituals performed by variously composed societies, we discover many more informal aspects of ceremonialism; learning gives way to inspiration. This process appears to be somewhat developed among the Pimans, with a dichotomy between communal and power rituals (but with most occasions for power rites basically standardized). It is also found among the Athabascans where individualism advances perhaps farther (but where learning in various degrees is still required) and appears most opposite to the Pueblos among the various Yuman groups where the vision/dream had fully subordinated learning (at least as a conscious activity). Despite the varying mechanism of expression for supernaturalism in the aboriginal Southwest, many of the formats, elements, and paraphernalia are of fairly wide distribution although specific emphasis, collectivization, and content may be different. Agriculture and weather control figures among many groups in some manner. Hunting also formed a basis for concern, at least in its communal efforts. Warfare along with an emphasis upon scalp taking and purification was a general and remarkable similar trait as was curing the sick of supernaturally induced illnesses. Puberty rites for girls were also a common supernatural trait although their importance varied inversely with the presence of collective concerns of tribal initiation for girls as well as boys among many of the Pueblos. Songs, prayers, orations, altars, ground paintings, smoking, pollen, masked dances, clowns, and a host of other traits also exhibited rather wide and comparable distribution. There is definitely a sense of interconnectedness in the religious varieties of Southwestern Indians.

As indicated in the preface, the purpose of this book is to present descriptively some general introductory data on the religions of Southwest Indians and of other Native American culture areas. As such, developmental and comparative suggestions (beyond that already indicated) and the pursuit of more narrow specializing concerns are not appropriate here. In fact, as previously indicated, their expression is difficult anyway. Clearly one general pattern is discernible.

> ...it would be possible to build up a picture of the development of ceremonial patterns in the Southwest and perhaps in a much wider area. We start with a simple vision experience, among people who have little occasion for communal activity and whose contact with the spirits must be individual and immediate. The elements in such an experience may have been very widely distributed before the coming of agriculture. Its elements where we know of them, seem to be constant and would have formed a kernel from which more elaborate ceremonies developed (Underhill 1948:49).

These elements are the power given by a spirit (in song, technique, etc.), a fetish, and the caring of it and use of it in ritual.

> The same basic elements appear in communal ceremonies, though with many additions and elaborations....The few words 'dictated' by a spirit to one individual could be enlarged by contributions from many others....The verbal part of the ceremony might then become so complicated that no single officiant could assume to have dreamed it. He must learn the procedure....Thus, the original visionary could gradually be turned into a ritualist, while direct revelation from the spirits was relegated to a legendary past....Just as the verbal ceremony into an array of altar decorations....The end of all communal ceremonies is the same as that expected by the vision recipient. The spirits, or their powers, arrive. Whether that power be in the form of a deer, masked dancer, a sandpainting or merely a revelation to the shaman, it must come if the ceremony is truly performed (Underhill 1948:49-50).

The specifics of this development await a synthesis of reconstruction via archaeological data and a better comparative understanding of other religious patterns in aboriginal North and Central America. We do not lack for archaeological possibilities, but we do lack consensus on tribal movements within the Southwest and elsewhere. When these are pinned down more accurately and when we have cast the religious data we possess (and gather more) in a more complete and comparative framework, we should be able to make specific comparative statements. Until then, the religious life of the various Southwestern Indian societies remains an outstanding example of the many ways humans have sought to interact with the world of the supernatural. We can now examine religious patterns found in other Native American Culture Areas.

YUMAN BIBLIOGRAPHY AND REFERENCES

Brown, H.

1906. A Prima-Maricopa Ceremony. *American Anthropologist* 8:688-90.

Devereux, George.

1957. Dream Learning and Ritual Differences in Mohave Shamanism. *American Anthropologist* 59:1036-45.

1949 The Mohave Male Puberty Rite. *Samiksa, Journal of the Psychoanalytic Society.* Calcutta 3:11-25.

1937. Mohave Soul Concepts. *American Anthropologist* 39:417-22.

Dobyns, H. F., et al.

1957. Thematic Changes in Yuman Warfare. In V. F. Ray (editor), Cultural Stability and Culture Change, pp. 46-71. Seattle: University of Washington Press.

Drucker, P.

1941. Yuman-Piman. *Anthropological Records* 6:91-230.

Fathauer, G. H.

1951. Religion in Mohave Social Structure. *Ohio Journal of Science* 51:273-76.

Forde, C. D.

1931. Ethnography of the Yuma Indians. *University of California Publications in American Archaeology and Ethnology* 28:83-278.

Gifford, E. W.

1936. Northeastern and Western Yavapai. *University of California Publications in American Archaeology and Ethnology* 34:247-354.

1933. The Cocopa. *University of California Publications in American Archaeology and Ethnology* 31:257-334.

1932. The Southeastern Yavapai. *University of California Publications in American Archaeology and Ethnology* 19:177-252.

Kelly, W. H.

1949. The Place of Scalps in Cocopa Warfare. *El Palacio* 56:85-91.

Kroeber, A. L. (editor).

1935. Walapai Ethnography. *American Anthropological Association Memoir* 42:1-293.

1925A. Handbook of the Indians of California. *Bureau of American Ethnology Bulletin* 78:726-80.

1925B. Handbook of the Indians of California. *Bureau of American Ethnology Bulletin* 78:(Yuma 781-95).

Peet, S. D.

1894. The Worship of the Rain-God. *American Antiquarian* 16:341-56.

Spier, Leslie.

1936. Cultural Relations of the Gila River and Lower Colorado Tribes. *Yale University Publications in Anthropology* 3:1-22.

1933. Yuman Tribes of the Gila River. Chicago: University of Chicago Press.

1928. Havasupai Ethnography. *Anthropological Papers of the American Museum of Natural History* 29:83-392.

Stewart, K. M.

1947A. An account of the Mohave Mourning Ceremony. *American Anthropologist* 49:146-48.

Stewart, Kenneth M.

1947B. Mohave Warfare. *Southwestern Journal of Anthropology* 3:257-78.

Underhill, Ruth M.

1948. Ceremonial Patterns in the Greater Southwest. NY: Monographs of the American Ethnological Society.

Wallace, William J.

1948. The Girl's Puberty Rite of the Mohave. *Proceedings of the Indiana Academy of Science* 57:37-40.

CHAPTER VIII

WESTERN NORTH AMERICAN CULTURE

The culture area often called Western North America in the literature of Native America encompasses the geographical areas of California, the Plateau, and the Great Basin. All three cultural regions are represented as reflecting marginality in their development. "The native cultures become impressive not so much for what they possess as what they lack" (Spencer, Jennings, et al. 1965:213). Borrowings from adjacent areas also make it difficult to clearly ascertain the baseline of original developments. While there are definite differences in cultural adaptations in these three regions, their being lumped together is primarily an expression of the fact that all three emphasized gathering activities as their basis of subsistence technology. Acorns in California, roots in the Plateau, and seeds in the Great Basin were primary foci for survival. Hunting was practiced in all three with varying results, as was fishing, which was of special importance among some Plateau people. We may now examine some major cultural elements of each area very briefly before proceeding to a more detailed discussion of their supernaturalism.

California

California was among the most densely populated areas of aboriginal North America, especially so along the coastal plain and in the lower parts of river valleys. No doubt, the equable climate played a role in attracting various groups to this area as did the great natural abundance of foods. Such resources permitted a fairly easy style of life for many peoples there. Great linguistic diversity reflected the movement of peoples into California. Major groups were Penutian (Maidu, Yokuts), Hokan (Shasta, Pomo), and Shoshonian (Cahuilla, Serrano) as well as many others. So a real prehistoric crossroads existed here. Generally, California is divided into three climate-cultural regions: North–narrow valleys and high rainfall; Central–rather diverse micro-environments (the classic area); and South–more arid and barren.

Subsistence technology was heavily dependent upon wild plants such as acorns, seeds, fruits, and berries. The types and concentration of these were regionally variable. Fish and shellfish were taken, especially along coastal areas. Elk and deer were among the most important big game animals along with mountain sheep and antelope in some areas. Small game included rabbits, birds, snakes, and insects; in fact, almost everything edible might be utilized. Techniques of food production were absent as elsewhere in Western North America.

Housing varied somewhat from group to group. Quite often it took a dome-shaped form made of poles and covered with bark, earth, or matting materials. Plank dwellings occurred in the North. Sweathouses were utilized. Clothing was extremely simple, women wearing short skirts and men loincloths. Fur blankets or robes of skin sufficed during the winter. Other items of material culture reflect this technological simplicity: simple wooden canoes and poorly made pottery among some peoples. The best craft was basketry, expressed in a number of forms and among the best made in North America. It reflected the need to store and collect wild plant foods.

Californian society varied regionally. Each group seems to have inhabited territory circumscribed by specific and recognized boundaries and often defended these when necessary. The land-owning group was generally small, perhaps fewer than a few hundred people. Population was concentrated in one main village plus (perhaps) a few outlying smaller and temporary ones. The basic nuclear family seems the most important socioeconomic group. Group membership was reckoned patrilineally. Some groups had clans, and among some, dual divisions or moieties for regulation of marriage relations existed. The village itself, however, may have been ultimately more important than descent groups in this area. Each such local group had a headman or chiefly leader. While often based on hereditary notions, the selection of such a person based on his personal character was an equal consideration. The extent of authority of these leaders is difficult to determine; certainly peace keeping in civil affairs, leadership in some technological activities, and, for some, ritual direction. War leaders, in basically hit-run oriented retaliation or defensive aggression, may have been separate. War was often in response to suspected witchcraft activities. Beyond the village, various social relations occurred, such as ritual cooperation. But only the Yokuts appear to have approached anything like a real sense of tribal consciousness.

Plateau

This area is defined as being located between the Rocky Mountains in the east and the Cascade Mountains in the west. It is essentially an elevated region drained by the Columbia and the Frazer river systems. Great natural diversity occurs, and populations were not distributed as heavily as in California. Two main language groupings occurred for most of the aboriginal peoples, although a few were outside this classification. The main groups were Salishan (Sanpoil, Flathead) and Penutian (Nez Perce, Yakima).

Roots were probably the most common subsistence food, especially camas, plus berries, nuts, and seeds. Salmon became a major dietary staple of some groups and were taken by a variety of techniques. Deer, elk, mountain sheep, and rabbits were commonly hunted, as well as bison by more eastern groups during an annual trek into the plains area. This intensified after the introduction of the horse. Housing varied seasonally, simple-pole dwellings covered with bark or mats and more substantial earth dwellings in the winter. Clothing was basically like California but with the addition of leggings and well-made robes of rabbit skin in the winter. Some groups had dugout canoes, but material culture was simple, basketry and mats being the best items of manufacture.

Society was also simple. As in California, the basic social group was a village settlement that owned some resource locations as a unit (especially fishing sites) but who also moved separately to exploit more distant food possibilities. Each village had a leader selected along hereditary lines and/or by the choice of village males based upon his personal abilities. In any case, a village council composed of adult males was a major policy unit. Leaders settled disputes and perhaps occasionally led in war. As in California, aggressive behavior was sporadic and minimal except during the summer buffalo hunt when contact was established with traditionally hostile groups.

Great Basin

The Great Basin culture area extended across Utah and Nevada and adjacent territories. It is surrounded by mountains higher than those within, and since moisture has little outlet, it accumulates in lakes and evaporates into salt. Much of this area, consequently, was barren and scarcely habitable. Population densities were quite low, and groups were small and scattered in their quest for food resources. Most groups spoke languages classified as Shoshonian.

Subsistence technology was heavily dependent upon seeds, roots, nuts, and berries. Almost all wild plants of an edible nature were utilized. Hunting of antelope, mountain sheep, and deer occurred, but the results were often poor. Periodic drives of antelope probably yielded the best returns. Rabbits were also taken through communal effort by driving them into big nets. Grasshoppers, lizards, and prairie dogs were also utilized. Fish were a valuable resource in some regions. Housing generally consisted of temporary lean-tos of poles covered with brush (wickiups). Caves and rock shelters were also occupied. Leggings and rabbit skin robes were added as winter clothing. Loin cloths were worn in summer, a time when people often went nude. Due to the rather constant nomadism, material items were kept to a minimum and were underdeveloped, although basketry was quite adequate.

Social life was extremely simple. As it has been nicely summarized for these people and some of their Plateau linguistic relatives:

A very fundamental feature of Basin-Plateau Shoshonian society is the remarkable absence of any traditional institutions other than nuclear families. There were no men's initiations or secret societies, no marriage-regulating clans, moieties, segments or lineages, no age grade or women's societies, and no ceremonials, recreational activities, or warfare that united all members of what were later called "bands."...The small family cluster based on bilateral principles was the inevitable response to areas of meager resources, low population density, and an annual cycle of nomadism (Steward 1970:115).

CHAPTER IX

CALIFORNIA RELIGION

For purposes of simplification as well as a reflection of genuine differences in emphasis, we can divide aboriginal religions in the culture province of California into three divisions: South, Central and North.

Southern California

The religious life of the various groups of Indians in Southern California was, with very few exceptions, remarkably similar. This is so despite linguistic differences which suggest at least somewhat different origins and arrivals in this area. As will be done for Central and Northern California, basic commonalities will be discussed, and exceptions or variations noted. It should also be mentioned that the disruptive effects of early missionizing in this area make many present-day reconstructions extremely tentative.

Most of all groups in Southern California can be categorized as having had a priest-house-fetish complex. This is to say that special ritual leaders existed who were in charge of sacred ritual paraphernalia kept in a special structure in the community. Sometimes these persons were also leaders in a kinship and/or political sense; sometimes they were simply dance leaders or "chiefs" of religious organizations. Quite often, they also possessed shamanistic powers as well, although other shamans existed in the more usual sense. The sacred paraphernalia usually consisted of a fetish bundle, a number of highly sacred objects wrapped in a strip of fibre matting and charged with supernatural power. This was most often kept hidden away in the house of the leader himself although other paraphernalia might be stored elsewhere. Most of the ritual acts themselves took place in a ceremonial enclosure made with brush walls – to enclose an area for a fire and dancing – and open to the sky. Some rites were performed completely in the open.

We can employ the example of the Cahuilla to suggest the types of typical leaders since rather full descriptions are available for them. One of the main ritual leaders was the chief (Net) of each descent group. This was a position inherited along male lines and included many different kinds of functions.

> The responsibilities of this office pervaded all Cahuilla life. The net, as a ceremonial leader, was responsible for the correct maintenance of ritual and the proper care and maintenance of the ceremonial bundle...and ceremonial house....The net also served as an economic executive determining where and when people would go to gather foods or hunt game. He administered first fruit rites...he collected goods which he stored for future ceremonial use....He was responsible for remembering group boundaries...(Bean 1972:104-05).

This important leader had an assistant who apparently did much of the actual direction of activities as well as coordinating such rituals and punishing any related breaches of custom. He also often led community efforts to secure the foodstuffs necessary to hold such events. With variations this leader assistant pattern was found in all groups in this subarea. Among the Serrano, however, the leader and his assistant were from different descent groups (one with the house and the other possessing the fetish bundle), their respective descent groups forming a larger ritual unit. Among the Luiseno, numbers of groups regularly formed into "religious parties," perhaps due to disruption and population loss after contact times. In all cases, descent groups regularly cooperated in many ritual endeavors.

For the Cahuilla, there was also a ritual singer for each descent group who knew the song cycles appropriate to the rituals and who performed and led in the singing of these. This was probably a hereditary position, and such a person was also charged with teaching these songs to others of his group.

He also exhorted novices during initiation rites relative to proper adult behavior. Such a position was also found among the Serrano. Comparable functions were discharged among other Southern California groups, but the definition of the position in the literature appears less certain, old men or shamans often accomplishing these tasks. In some cases, the leader's assistant seems to have had this responsibility. Formal dancers also occurred among the Cahuilla, apparently chosen for the promise of skill during the initiation rites and specially trained for their positions. Whether selection of dancers among other groups followed such set procedures is not entirely clear. Certainly numbers of men and women danced in various contexts, especially older members of the community. The general impression for most groups is that beyond the leader/assistant category much of ritual responsibility depended upon a temporary selection basis and on possession of the requisite knowledge.

Shamans occurred among all groups in this subarea, although the data on this topic is mixed and incomplete. Among the Cahuilla, shamanism was based upon possession of supernatural power. "Power was acquired by one of several means: an individual could be born with the power, it could be passed on to an individual by another...or it could be given to him by a spirit being. The power often came to a child or man in dreams" (Bean 1972:109). This dream experience, in which an animal familiar appears and teaches songs, dances, and other esoteric knowledge, appears to have been most common. Of considerable interest is the notion that the visionary had to be interviewed by the chief and his assistant (who were themselves usually shamans) on the genuineness of his experience. He also had to publicly demonstrate his new-found powers. Curing disease was probably the most usual specialized shamanistic function, dealing with witchcraft, breach of taboo, and soul loss. The normal technique involved sucking out disease objects and blowing away evil with tobacco smoke. Songs usually accompanied such endeavors. Some shamans apparently attempted to use their powers to aid in control of the food supply and control of weather. They also, as a group, functioned to keep ghosts and evil spirits away during major rituals. A few shamans also had the special power to transform themselves into animal forms (an inborn power?), especially the bear. These seem to have been greatly feared.

Shamans among groups other than the Cahuilla are less understood. Everywhere, apparently, the dream call was the major avenue towards the acquisition of such powers. Possession of physical or mental disabilities is also mentioned in this connection for many groups. Public demonstration/validation was also common. Sucking disease objects or blood, blowing smoke, and brushing with feathers as remedies in curing appear universal. Among the Gabrielino, for example,

> The removal of disease was by sucking blood and perhaps the disease object. Smoking, manipulation, and singing preceded. The words of the songs appear to have been descriptive of the practices applied....It may be conjectured that the doctor sang not so much of what he was doing as of what had been done to a god in the far past, or what he in a dream had seen a deity or animal perform (Kroeber 1953:627).

Many, perhaps all groups, had special wands which symbolized the powers of the shamans. The ultimate source of such power, however, for all of these groups is not really definite. The idea of a special teaching and helping spirit is not specifically indicated for the Luiseno and some others in this subarea either by implication or lack of data. Very possibly, shamanistic power was of degree rather than kind, the shaman not really being greatly different from other ritual performers who did gain a measure of power by undergoing initiation. Among the southern Diegueno, for example, "The reasons for the lack of distinction may be that there is no clearly defined mode of becoming a shaman...and (by) acquisition of analogous knowledge by all who pass through to toloache initiation" (Spier 1923:312). In fact, this may well be the key to understanding the typical shaman in most of this subarea. It appears entirely possible that such experiences were originally structured as part of the initiation experience where all novices were expected to dream and possibly receive power. Those who had unusual natures and received special dream instructions were the persons who became shamans. Something along these lines is specifically suggested by Benedict for the Serrano.

> It seems that...the boys' toloache ceremony...was not a tribal initiation into the status of manhood. Only the sons of chiefs and pahas (assistants) and all boys who were different went through the ceremony. Afterwards, not all boys who had the drink would be smart enough to practice as shamans, but it was always a possibility. Some informants thought that it was at this time that the future shaman got his medicine....One would never know for certain, however, for no shaman ever told his medicine or the circumstances under which it came to him (Benedict 1924:383).

This is a problem that may not be amenable to solution at the present time. We can turn now to a discussion of major ritual activities.

Perhaps the most characteristic rite in Southern California is the boys' initiation or Toloache ceremony. We can describe its basic features for the Diegueno and then give additional comparative and theoretical comments. Among the Diegueno, young boys at puberty (probably all boys and only once in their lives) underwent an initiation rite during the course of which they drank an infusion of Jimson Weed to obtain visions of the supernatural. For them, this seems to have permitted taking part in other rites as well as receiving shamanistic or other powers. "There exist a number of tricks, such as dancing on the fire or killing an eagle by witchcraft, which are passed along to other initiates. Those who have undergone the ceremony may almost be said to be bound into a fraternity by the possession of these secrets" (Waterman 1910:293). In this rite, the boys were taken to a special location where the Jimson Weed was ritually crushed in special stone mortars and water added to it. Those in charge seem to have been assistant chiefs. The boys drank directly from the mortar while their heads were held by the leaders. They were then taken to the brush enclosure (dance area) where a fire had been built. When they arrived, old men acting as their sponsors took charge of the boys. They held them under their armpits and swayed them back and forth while marching around the fire to the accompaniment of songs. In a short while, the boys passed out from the effects of the drink, and they were carried out of the enclosure and taken somewhere to sleep off its effects. During this time, they were expected to have a dream of some animal which would be important for their future lives. While a sacred song was "learned" during these dreams, their actual content and the types of power or blessings received appear vague; perhaps they requested some kind of favor or protection from danger. While the boys dreamed, other people continued dancing in the brush enclosure until dawn.

The next morning the boys were purified by drinking water and by bathing. They were painted symbolically at this time and entered into a six day-fasting period. Beginning on the second of these days, they crawled on their hands and knees to the brush enclosure, and after this procession, their sponsors taught them dancing all night (and possibly other ritual knowledge). After the sixth day, their fast was partly broken, and people from other villages came and taught them their dances. At the end of a month, a ritual foot race occurred, the winner apparently being considered as an especially promising person. For the next month, the first half of each night was given over to dancing activity. At the end of this time, the leaders constructed a ground painting which represented the world in conventional symbols and the creatures associated with a special supernatural being–called Chingishnish among neighboring people. Among the Diegueno, who apparently received this addition to the toloache rites fairly late, there was no belief (as elsewhere) in this being as a god who sent personal punishments. We can return to this conception shortly. At any rate, the meaning of the ground painting was explained to the young boys who finally spat lumps of sage seeds and salt into a hole in its middle to ensure long lives for themselves. On the next day, a large pit was dug, and the outline of a human figure made out of nettle fibre was placed into it. Small flat stones were placed on the figure.

> One by one the boys are placed in the pit, their feet resting on the first stone. Each boys sponsor stands behind him and takes him under the armpits....The boy jumps on to the next stone...and so on. Should he miss landing fairly on one of the stones his relatives all begin to wail, in the belief that he will die before long...the boys and their sponsors push the dirt in from all sides, filling the trench and burying the netting figure (Waterman 1910:305).

An all-night dance concluded the rite with the stomping out of the fire by dawn.

Before passing on to such rites among other groups, we can comment on the added aspect of the Chingishnish being. This notion may have developed among the Juaneno and may have been a prophet who became a god. Chingishnish "...watched the deeds of the people. He knew their thoughts and sent poisonous beasts...as well as calamities and death, to punish those who disobeyed his teachings and laws" (Moriarty 1969:14). Regardless of origin, this conception was grafted onto the earlier toloache initiation rites throughout much of southern California, as well as on many other earlier rites as well. The presence of these elements obviously makes our understanding of the initiation rites themselves more difficult, as well as the whole problem of shamanism mentioned earlier. Alfred Kroeber (1923) considers the evolution of this institution as developing from shaman's societies initiating selected members to more general initiation after the Chingishnish elements were added, considering perhaps the more popular appearance of the latter beliefs. My own view, based on the fact that many groups appeared to limit membership, is that initiation originally included all boys. Then the obtaining of shamanistic power led to an emphasis on and self-perpetuation of this in more exclusive rites. Such tendencies possibly become intensified with the spread of the Chingishnish ideas. Speaking again of the Juaneno in this connection: "Only the chiefs and certain of the shamans knew these mysteries...these men taught their sons, and only those sons who were going to succeed them in their practices" (Moriarity 1969:14). It seems as reasonable to assume a narrowing as a widening of such activities. At the time of the contact, they may well have been in the process of contracting into specialized groups among some peoples. Certainly the basic initiation rite procedures are comparable among those groups for which we possess full information. Among the Luiseno, they were nearly identical, with the addition of ordeals such as boys being placed on beds of stinging ants and whisking these off with nettles. Along similar lines, the Cahuilla tattooed boys at this time and pierced ears and nasal septums. Among the Serrano, the boy who won the race was selected to be trained for a special dance. The fact that the time frame for these activities differs for some groups may be merely a reflection of the necessity to foreshorten them in the interests of some food-getting activity. We can now turn to a second common southern rite.

Another ritual of universal distribution was the girl's puberty rite. For most groups this seems to have occurred about once each year and involved more than a single young girl. While at least one girl perhaps had to be near the time of her first menstrual period, the others apparently were not so restricted. Sources indicated that all young girls went through the rite, although for the Serrano it is specifically mentioned that the rite was more public and elaborate for the daughters of chiefs and their assistants to make them into especially smart women. We can briefly describe this rite for the Luiseno.

The names of the girls were publicly announced, and food and presents for guests accumulated. A pit was excavated and lined with stones. A fire was made to heat the stones, removed, and the warmed pit was lined with brush. Prior to the girls being placed in the pit, men sang the appropriate songs, and older female relatives of the girls held their heads and gave them advice. The girls were then obliged to swallow balls of tobacco with water, possibly as a kind of ordeal. They were then placed in the pit and covered with grass and sand. According to some accounts, warm stones were also placed on their abdomens to insure childbirth potential. Such stones were also placed between the legs of Diegueno girls for this purpose, but most other groups seem not to have added this magical procedure. At any rate, a basket was placed over the girl's head, and they attempted to remain as immobile as possible. They left the pit every so often (every 24 hours?) while the pit was reheated. They appear to have remained in the pit for three days and nights, leaving it for good on the morning of the fourth day. "After three days of constant singing and dancing day and night by men and women, the girl is taken out and the wife of the chief paints her face" (DuBois 1908:97).

At this point, the girls were subject to a month of food taboos on salt and meat. At the end of this time, a sand painting was constructed (another penetration of the Chingishnish cult on earlier custom). It was explained to the girls, and they were given sage weed and salt to spit into a hole in its middle as in the boy's rite. Missing the hole was regarded as a bad omen. Sermons on good conduct were also given at this time. Now a race was held by the girls, as well as by some of the women. "They run to the appointed hill, where the wife of the chief paints the girls' faces...and scraping some of the paint from their faces uses it to paint the rock in certain designs (DuBois

1917:97). Mention is made in this connection of diamond-shaped designs which may have had phallic significance. This ended the rite although the race may perhaps have been repeated three or four times over ensuing months. The girls may also have been tattooed. The entire sequence of rites apparently helped to induce long life. Rites among other groups displayed no major differences although some groups like the Juaneno lacked the ground painting.

Along with boy's and girl's rites which reflect life-stage transition, another universal ritual was the mourning rite for those descent group members who had died during the preceding year. When a person died, the body was prepared; clothes washed, etc. A pit was dug, the firewood and brush placed within it. Singing and dancing took place all night to banish the spirit of the deceased. The dead person was then taken to the pit for cremation. Some of the clothes of the dead person were burned, and among at least a few groups, some of the property of that person as well. Close relatives cut their hair and painted their faces black as a sign of morning. An interesting comment on the Luiseno by Strong (1929) suggests that some of the ashes of the deceased may have been mixed with water and drunk by relatives. We can discuss the actual later mourning ritual itself with references to the Serrano.

Among these people, the ritual occurred over a six-day period. It is hard to escape the impression that it was a sort of amalgamation of rites which at one time may have been separate entities. On the first days, Monday through Wednesday, food and paraphernalia were collected. The chief's assistant led a rabbit hunt, and the chief himself spent time in isolation with the ritual bundle. On Wednesday night, the bundle was ceremonially opened by the chief, and feathers from it were hung in the ceremonial house while the assembled people danced. On Thursday, all the children born in the preceding year were named. They were carried about by the assistant and given their names by the chief. Singing and dancing occupied the rest of the day. On Friday, the eagle-killing rite occurred. In it, an eagle–captured previously–was killed, and its feathers were used to decorate images made that same day to represent the recent dead. Since this rite may also have occurred in other contexts, it will be more fully described later. On Saturday, the eagle dance took place. Using an eagle feather dance skirt, it was performed in a whirling fashion by the boy who had won the race during the toloache rite. That night the descent groups that had assembled danced until morning, and at that time, the images of the dead were ritually destroyed.

> About an hour before sunrise gifts are distributed to the invited clans....Then the various images of the dead are brought out, usually by a clanswoman of the deceased....They dance with the images for about half an hour and then place them on the fire which has been kindled outside the ceremonial house. Formerly, a male relative of the deceased danced with the image, while the...(assistant)...shot...at him with a bow and arrow. The dancer dodged the arrows....At the time of the dance with the death images the bereaved families distribute many presents by throwing them up in the air for the guests to catch (Strong 1929:34).

All this apparently gave final release to the souls of the dead and enabled them to enter into the afterlife.

Among most groups, property and clothing of the deceased were also burned at this time. The Diegueno even had a special building in which the images were placed and which was burned along with them. While all groups devoted much time to singing, we are not certain of the content of many of the songs interspersed throughout this rite. Among the Cahuilla, they are specifically said to deal with the universe, the saga of the creator god Mukat, and the place of the Cahuilla in the general scheme of things. Among some groups, numbers of men participated in the eagle dance, and there were other minor differences from group to group. Overall, however, most procedures were shared in common, and the rite did occupy a central place in ritual activity. A recent observation (1952) of a surviving form of this rite for the Luiseno has been described and reinforces its general nature and function. "...the spirits of Luiseno dead are...reluctant to leave the region of their lifetime attachments. The clothes burning ceremony serves to make the spirits happy and less reluctant to depart by restoring to them belongings made inaccessible by death" (White 1953:569).

We can also briefly elaborate on the idea of the eagle-killing portion of this rite. For some groups, it was believed that the eagle was a kind of supernatural that permitted itself to be killed so that people were assured of life after death. This certainly fit in with the theme of the mourning for chiefs or dance leaders and perhaps their relatives. At any rate, the proceedings among the Diegueno went as follows. The eagle was captured previously and kept until the time of the rite. A leader opened the proceedings by giving an exhortation on the antiquity of this rite, explaining also that due to its special nature the eagle would have to be "witched" to death. Then a line of dancers appeared with one of their number holding the eagle. Other participants then joined the line and all marched around the fire. The daughter or close relative of the person being mourned then threw cloth over the bird, and many songs were sung relating to the eagle. A man (shaman?) then held the eagle at arm's length while another aimed a special stick at it. As this stick quivered, the eagle died, apparently from pressure exerted on its heart. Wailing took place followed by more dances and songs while old men took turns carrying the body of the eagle. It was then buried after removing its longest feathers for other ritual uses.

Beyond these rites, girl's puberty, the toloache, death and mourning, and shamanism, the distribution of other activities and descriptions of them are most vague for this portion of California. Certainly first-fruit rites were held at the beginning of the gathering season for each plant species, giving thanks to the supernatural to ensure plant fertility. Rites also were associated with the killing of big game animals, especially deer. Rites accompanied the installation of ritual chiefs. There are also tantalizing references to certain destructive rites. Among the Gabrieleno, for example, a shaman might stand on a ground painting holding strings radiating out to assistants. When he shook these, the earth was supposed to quake and bring sickness to whomever he had in mind. Likewise, a most interesting fragment on the Juaneno mentions a person called coyote or "Eater" who devoured small portions of the flesh of deceased toloache initiates. Unfortunately, not enough data exists to substantiate these possible aspects of Southern Californian religion. Before making final comment on those aspects we are fairly certain of, we can pass on to the central area customs.

Central California

The religious beliefs and behaviors of the Native American Peoples of Central California were most complex, and there is substantial contradiction in early anthropological accounts that concern them. It is very possible that we will never be able to reconstruct their practices with any real degree of accuracy and completeness. It is clear that the tribal groups of this subarea varied considerably in their religious customs as did more local units within them. To present some of the general features involved, the present chapter uses the expedient of highlighting two somewhat contrasting societies to intimate the range for such differences. The central cult activity in this region of California was the Kuksu Cult, a system of god-impersonating dances. While different in character from the Southern Toloache Cults, it occupied a comparable position of religious importance. All scholars seem in agreement on the notion that the Kuksu cults fall into a western and eastern variety. The latter was found among such groups as the Patwin and Maidu; the former is indicated for such groups as the Pomo and Yuki. As Kroeber has summarized the major cult differences:

> The western form of Kuksu cult everywhere has two initiating societies. One of these...contains Kuksu and his companion Shalnis, sometimes one or two other impersonations. The other society impersonates a class of spirits more or less identified with ghosts of the dead....The total number of impersonated spirits...is relatively small; and mostly ceremonies are also few.
>
> ....
>
> The cults of the eastern tribes vary from one to three in the number of their societies. The socially basic society is the one that makes a great spectacular dance ceremony...into which a varied array of spirits enter.... Other societies are either merged into this...society, or exist alongside it as separate organizations of restricted...membership...(Kroeber 1932:255-56).

To explore these differences and add comment on other aspects of ritual and its organization, we can discuss the Maidu and the Pomo as examples of tribes possessing the eastern and western Kuksu cult forms respectively.

The Maidu

The Maidu were divided dialectically into Northeast, Northwest, and Southern divisions. As in Southern California, definite ritual leaders existed. Generally speaking, in the South the chief of each village was both a political and a ritual leader, living in the dance house and exercising great authority over both aspects of life. Among more Northern Maidu, however, a division of function occurred. There was a secular chief who belonged to the dance society but was not too important in its functioning. He had an assistant who did train young boys in dancing for the society. The main ritualist was the Yokbe or spirit medium who was the director of the dance society as well as the chief shaman of one class of "doctors." Finally, there were one or more ritual clowns in each village. In addition to their clowning activities, they also served as interpreters for the Yokbe during his periodic seances and as helpers to training boys for ritual practices. Drummers, singers, and dancers also occurred.

Shamanistic practitioners mostly seem to have attained their status due to their relations to helping spirits called Kakeni. These were sometimes thought to be animals, place spirits, or possibly even spirits impersonated in dances. Among hill peoples, these spirits might have been the ghosts of ancestors since there was a tendency for shamanism to be of a hereditary nature. Quite often, the vision involved imparting of knowledge and power. In the South, among the Maidu known as the Nisenan, the acquisition of shamanistic power is less clear. Here, apparently, a person became a shaman more by learning how to use medicine having supernatural effects rather than by contact with spirits. "There was nothing most shamans did which an ordinary man might not do if he learned the necessary medicines and observed the proper taboos. While many of the things some shamans did were undoubtedly supernatural, their power to do them was not caused by any direct contact with the supernatural world through...visions" (Beals 1933:386). In all Maidu cases, some form of training at the hands of practicing shamans was necessary for the novice to develop his full powers, either to learn proper use of medicines or to come to complete terms with the spirits themselves. In more extreme Northern cases, the contact itself resulted in a sickness requiring shamanistic curing.

It appears that, at least for more Northern groups, at least two basic classes of shamans existed. These were sucking shamans and singing shamans. They differed in several respects. The sucking type was usually in contact with only one spirit. They wore porcupine quills in their noses and could cause sickness by "throwing" these. They cured illness by sucking out disease objects such as bits of wood or stone and also blew smoke over the patient. The singing type was in contact with a variety of spirits and possessed clairvoyant powers, holding frequent seances and talking to their spirits in a special language interpreted by a clown. Most questions dealt with immediate situations such as hunting or the cause of group sickness. Apparently, they made no attempts to predict the remote future. Singing shamans also worked with those of the sucking type with their patients as diagnosticians, dreaming regarding methods of curing.

Sucking shamans also engaged in annual public competitions to discover who possessed the greatest powers. This event for some groups seems to have been combined with initiating recently trained novices and/or to send disease back to shamans in other villages who were thought to have caused it. Briefly, these contests involved shooting supernatural power back and forth; being hit was revealed by nasal bleeding and seizures. Less powerful victims were cured, and the activities continued until only one participant was left. Among the Nisenan:

> When shooting the shaman makes a hole in the ground with his heel, raising a little mound of earth by turning his heel in the soil. He takes the poison between the thumb and finger of his right hand. Then he points at his victim with his left hand, stooping and striking the pile of dust as he throws his poison with an underhand motion of his right arm. Sometimes the intended victim, if he is a good shaman, catches the poison as it flies toward him (Gifford 1927:244).

After this, rites of purification occurred. Other special types of shamans are said to have existed among the Maidu. While only fragmentary information is available on these, they include rain or weather shamans, rattlesnake shamans, and grizzly bear shamans. Some confusion exists as to whether this last type merely impersonated bears or were thought to actually transform themselves into this animal. We can now examine ritual activities.

Many life-cycle observances were held. Among these, a girl's puberty rite was featured, but it varied in elaborateness among Maidu divisions. We can discuss an intermediate case, the Northwest Hill Maidu. Among these people, a girl was symbolically painted at the time of her first menstrual period, and these designs were periodically removed during the course of the rite. The girl was isolated in a special hut, but prior to this she and a younger girl had their heads covered with crude deerskin masks and were placed in the center of a ring made of pine needles. Men and women then set this ring on fire, and the girls jumped out and ran a distance from it. The pubescent girl then retired to the hut where she observed numerous taboos and was instructed by her mother on adult responsibilities and tribal lore. On each of four nights, a special dance was held involving the girl and older women. At the conclusion of these, the girl had her ears pierced and a feast occurred. In the spring, a feast was also held for all the girls who had undergone the puberty rite the preceding year.

Other life-cycle activities focused on death and mourning. Originally, when a person died, relatives congregated; the body was prepared and either buried or cremated amidst wailing. Among many groups, wailing even preceded death. The possessions of the deceased were given away or destroyed. If the death occurred in the house, it too was burned. In any event, the family moved a distance from the place of the death. Among more Northern Maidu, an annual mourning rite followed under the supervision of a special director. Mourners visited the graves, cried, and sprinkled meal on them. Poles were placed in an open bush enclosure, erected or repaired at this time, and material goods were hung from them. An oration was given by the director, and crying and singing lasted until dawn. Eventually, the hung objects were taken down and then thrown into a fire as a sacrifice to the dead. Other goods were traded at this time. In the case of a secret society member (Yeponi), special images were made to represent them. These were maneuvered to the fire and also burned. "It was believed that the dead Yeponi's spirit occupied his image from the moment that work commenced on it" (Loeb 1933:154). The burning of this image may have released the spirit from its last earthly constraints. Among the Southern Maidu, this mourning rite was not an annual affair but was held shortly after the actual death.

Many other rituals of the Maidu dealt with relations to the food supply and can perhaps best be classified as first fruit rites, increase rites, or "good relations" rites. We can briefly mention examples of these. Among some groups, rites surrounding salmon took place. A shaman ritually caught the first fish of the season, prepared and cooked it, and gave portions of it to village members. This opened the fishing season and assured abundant catches. Other types of food resources probably were similarly treated. An acorn rite was held to increase the supply of this basic staple.

> A special ceremony...was enacted every April for the purpose of increasing the crop: first the medium sang for three or four nights in his ceremonial house. Then the members of the society...went to all black acorn trees and left feather wands.... Finally the medium went out and collected the sticks, singing the while to the trees and imploring them to yield an abundant supply of nuts....The clown accompanied the medium, both for the sake of interpreting the songs and the reply of the trees and to give his moral support to the medium....(Loeb 1933:141).

Finally, bears (and perhaps other animals) when killed were given special treatment. This included offerings and prayers apologizing for engaging in killing and eating it. We may now examine the Kuksu rites.

As a beginning, the basic features of this cult may be mentioned. These included the existence of a male secret society and a set of rites performed by its initiates. At least some of these members, in the course of their activities, wore concealing devices: face paintings, feather headdresses, etc., although actual masks seem to be absent. These men impersonated various spirits and may have been interpreted as being these spirits by younger uninitiated people. Such rituals focused in or around a large sod-covered house or ritual chamber containing a large hollowed log drum inverted over a trench, the foot drum. Members may have belonged to several classes since very young boys seem to pass through rites and then repeated these when they were older. Among some Central Californians, it is probable that there were degrees of knowledge corresponding to the various impersonations. Unfortunately, the mechanics of status in membership is not clear from the literature. Nor are the motives underlying the cult fully understandable. "The purpose of the initiation is generally stated to be to make the boys healthy, long-lived, hardy, swift, strong, and enduring....In much the same way the specific cycle of dances was thought to bring rains, nourish the earth, and produce a bountiful natural crop; perhaps also to ward off epidemics, floods, earthquakes, and other disasters (Kroeber 1953:383-84). Another confusion in our understanding of the cult revolves around distinctions apparently drawn between the names of impersonations, dances, and the rites themselves. This, coupled with the fact that different groups as well as villages differed in the cycle of impersonations and ranking of them, makes any general statement inconclusive. We can elaborate on some of the above features.

The pattern of actual initiation has been reported in some detail for several Maidu groups. Among the Yuba River Maidu, for example, young boys about ten years of age were "caught" in the fall by the leader of the society and taken to the ceremonial house. Here they were sequestered and instructed by a member. Discipline occurred – carrying wood and water – and a slow learner might be whipped. The novices remained in the house all winter, but the most stringent taboos lasted only for the first month. The novices received new names during their stay: these being the names of deceased relatives who had been former cult members. In the spring, a special dance terminated the period of initiation. The boys were tied up and repeatedly passed close to the fire and finally were thrown out of the smokehole. Their mothers waiting outside tossed water on them to symbolically restore them to life. We can now turn to the dances and impersonations themselves and give some very brief examples.

Among the Maidu, the following were major impersonated spirits. Highest in rank was Moki ("insane?"). His impersonator wore a complete feather cloke. This spirit appeared in the Hesi, Duck, and Aki ceremonies. In the important Hesi, two such impersonators were directors, and, apparently, a person was selected to do so rather than learning it in the same way as other impersonators. The second highest spirit character was Yati, represented in apparel by a special headdress and a bow. This spirit was also impersonated in the aforementioned three rites and was the cloud spirit. Sili was third in rank, and its impersonation was carried out with a net of feathers from the crown of the head down over the face. It appeared just in the Hesi rite. The Yohyo impersonator, who is equivalent to Kuksu in other groups, wears the typical "big head" headdress – a large ball joined by many feathered sticks. This spirit also appears in the Hesi, Duck, and Aki rites. Du, who may also appear in these rites, represents women and has apparel consisting of a diamond shaped headstrap to which woodpecker scalps fringed with raven feathers are attached. Oleli, represented in impersonation by a feather cape and a coyote head, appears in the coyote ceremony, and the Hesi and two other spirits, Pano-bear and Sumi-deer, appear only in rites with these names.

As is evident by the number of spirit impersonations associated with each of these ceremonies, the various dances of the Kuksu dance cycle differed greatly in the spirits represented in them. For example, in the Hesi, almost all spirits were represented, Duck and Aki had many appear, and Bear and Deer only one. Still other dances, "common dances," had no spirit impersonations at all. The spirit impersonation dances followed a yearly sequence among the Maidu, and the common dances were interspersed among these (see Kroeber 1953:435). Description of these complicated rites is impossible in the context of the present volume as each is complex and differs in significant routines from the others. Nor can we with certainty determine their order of development although all writers seem in agreement as to the Hesi being the highest and latest development. For the Southern Maidu, specifically, Gifford (1927:214-57), we can see three strata of dances. An original set of rites only a few of which had spirit impersonations, a second set derived from the North and having spirit impersonations but not involving secret instructions or initiations, and a later introduced set (from the South after 1872) which were older dances reconstructed under the influence of the Ghost Dance and which did entail confinement and instruction. While other scholars feel Gifford is in some error regarding these, there must certainly have been profound influence on many Central Californian groups by the Ghost Dance and attempts to communicate with spirits of past human generations. Resolution of this and related problems awaits detailed analysis by a student of Californian culture if such is at all possible at this point. We may now examine an example of the Western manifestation of the Kuksu cult.

We may use the Pomo as a somewhat typical example of this variety of ritual practices. Shamanism was well developed among these people. There appears to have been two basic types, although a given individual might have been both. First, there was the "outfit doctor." The powers of this practitioner tended to be hereditary in families. One would begin to learn in childhood by observing a teacher, later becoming this man's assistant and inheriting his paraphernalia. The outfit was a deerskin bag containing many objects: cocoon rattle, obsidian blade, unusual rocks, a sharpened stick covered with rattlesnake skin, stone pestle, herbs, and other medicines and the like. The real abilities of this type of shaman stemmed from his possession of this object. "The chief power...was concentrated in the outfit. It was kept when not in use close under the rafters of the house where no shadow of a profane person could fall upon it" (Freeland 1923:61). Among some Pomo groups, these shamans were also secret society members (yomta), and each day they addressed prayers to spirits associated with it.

Outfit doctors were called upon to cure all types of illness. Treatment commonly involved the use of medicinal herbs and other substances combined in various ways and ground up to drink, burn on the fire, or made into a paste and rubbed on the patient. They might also sweat a patient over a bed of hot coals. In the case of spirit intrusion, this shaman type might impersonate various spirits and note the reaction of the patient. If violent, then it was considered a diagnosis of the spirit involved, and the practitioner would then sing and pray to make the spirit leave. Among Coast Central Pomo:

> An outfit was used for counteracting poison in the following manner. The yomta tied the outfit on a string and placed it over the head of the patient. Then while the yomta sang, he pulled the string and made the objects rattle....The patient was treated for four days and if he did not recover he was then treated by Kuksu doctoring....Sometimes only one man came dressed as Kuksu, and sometimes four....The Kuksu pried the patient up with a stick, first under the knees and the waist on one side and then going around to the other side he repeated the process. While he was doing this he danced and blew on his whistle. When he was finished he made a prayer....(Loeb 1926:321).

The head of the secret society would also sing over the patient and wash him with water to terminate this curing rite.

The other shamanistic type was the "sucking doctor." This practitioner was an older man who usually received his special nature via a vision which occurred during sickness. The spirit involved was an anthropomorphic type sent by Marumda, the creator god. In the vision experience, healing songs and procedures were taught to the prospective shaman. As a result of this spirit contact, very little equipment was employed. General techniques included feeling or sucking on the skin to discover the cause of illness and then the singing of healing songs. Sucking doctors were consulted in crises of sudden onset of illness or to serve as diagnosticians for the other type.

Bear doctors were apparently also common among most Pomo groups. They might be both males and females, and their power was derived from a bear skin costume rather than from the bear itself. Techniques were usually learned from an older practitioner who then bequeathed his costume to his protégé. Sometimes a person was caught by a bear shaman and had such knowledge forced upon him. The costume itself was very complex, consisting of a basket device with openings for eyes and nose and mouth and worn on the head. Over this went the bear head and skin. Belts of shell beads were also wrapped around the body. These shamans carried daggers and were said to keep baskets of water on their persons to swish like the viscera of the bear. Elaborate rites accompanied the act of dressing in this costume which apparently was kept hidden in the mountains. Certain supernatural beings were considered patrons of such persons or were dealt with by them, especially one associated with the sun.

> He sang to and invoked particularly Sun-man because he was an all-seeing deity and knew everything that happened all over the earth, and more particularly because as Sun-man rises with the sun each morning he comes with his bow and arrow drawn and ready to shoot on sight any wrongdoer. Unless, therefore, Sun-man was propitiated and previously informed of the bear doctor's intentions, he was likely to shoot him just as the sun appeared above the horizon (Barrett 1917:460).

Bear shamans were considered very dangerous to human beings as they roamed the hills looking for people to kill, although the village chief and his family seem to have been immune from attack.

Another category of supernatural practitioner, one apparently without special qualifications, was the "poison man." Such individuals were not shamans since they were felt not to engage in malpractice. When such a person wished to harm his enemy, he engaged in the following activities. He would spend the summer in collecting all types of poisons (from snakes, spiders, plants, etc.). Then he and four associates would go to a secret place in the woods, and, after fasting and other ritual preparations, he would grind the poisons with a pestle into a paste. Prayers were made to the spirits of these poisons. Then a little image of the intended victim was constructed. "Something of the victim should be built into it: a hair, nail paring, perhaps a bit of dance costume....Then the figure is touched with some of the new-made poison and the men enact the death. They dig a grave, cremate the figure, bury its ashes, and hold a crying" (Freeland 1923:70). The men then took some of the poison back to the village and surreptitiously tried to touch their victim with it or place it in close proximity to him.

Major dances among the Pomo fell into two classes: Kuksu and Ghost rites. These included many officials: a master of ceremonies who acted under the general direction of the village chief, a head singer who planned the sequence of songs and dances and who initiated them, fire tenders, other singers, drummers, and the chief impersonators themselves. Rites generally lasted for four days and were made up of a varying number of dances. They took the name of the dance that was the special feature of the rite. Each rite consisted of an introductory proceeding, the dance series, exhortation by ritual leaders, final purification and feasting. We can briefly indicate the nature of these two classes of dances.

The Ghost class was held in the spring, possibly in a newly constructed dance house each time. The underlying motive may have been to atone for mythic offenses against the dead; at least the dancers impersonated spirits of the dead. Paraphernalia was guarded by shamans between rites, and they also helped the dancers dress for their impersonations. Two general types of impersonators existed: ghost dancers and ash ghosts (or fire eaters). The latter functioned as clowns but also had their own dramatic portion of rites. In a typical rite, the dancers stayed in the hills and were called by the leader. They came to the dance house and were met by the singers and others with much ritual maneuvering before entering the chamber. Rites inside excluded women and uninitiated persons. The chief ghost dancer gave a speech relating to the removal of sickness and gaining strength, and the dance performance began and was repeated a number of times. After each series, the dancer would disrobe, go to the hills, dress differently, and return. On the first day this occurred four times; during the ensuing three days, any number of times during the day. The ash ghosts served as clowns and enforcers of discipline during these dances and also engaged in their own special rite.

> Fire-eating was restricted...to the ash-devils, and while sometimes practiced during intermissions in the regular ghost dance, it was usually held as a separate ceremony in the evening....When this special ceremony commenced, the ash-devils became supreme and took precedence over everybody....Immediately upon entering the dance-house the main group...took up a position at the foot of the center pole....The actual dancing lasted for perhaps half an hour, after which the ash-devils sat down and began to "eat fire," jump into it, and perform other miraculous feats with it.
>
> ....
>
> During this ceremony, and apparently as an initiation of novices, little boys were thrown by the ash-devils back and forth a number of times through the blaze of a large fire. Finally...they sat down and became ordinary persons once more (Barrett 1917:418-20).

On the fourth night, near dawn, a special dance of purification occurred followed by a feast and the imposition of taboos for some time afterwards.

The Kuksu class of dances were also performed by the members of a secret society, and their rites were most elaborate among inland Pomo groups. Membership included both men and women. A rather limited number of impersonations occurred. Most common were Kuksu, who was impersonated by a number of dancers, and Calnis, a god thought to reside with Kuksu in the south. There was a head chief of this society and a chief woman member who was privy to all ritual knowledge and could instruct a new leader in the event of sudden death of a current chief. The rites themselves apparently took place in the open rather than in a ritual house.

The ritual cycle itself lasted four days (or more?) and opened with the pole ceremony–getting a pole and placing it in the dance area with great ritual. Rites optional at the discretion of the chief occurred over the next day–bear impersonations, etc. Sometimes even common dances were held. At least one or two Kuksu impersonations occurred on each day of the cycle which always ended with the xaidaxal or closing ceremony. On the fourth evening, a cutting rite occurred to bring good fortune and health to all the children of the group who were newly pubescent. These lay on the ground around the pole, naked except for a skin blanket, and the chief entered.

> During the entire ceremony he kept up a continuous praying in the secret language. Beginning at the east and circling counterclockwise, the yomta drew the blanket off each child and gave a scratch in the small of the back...covering each child again before passing on. The cut was usually deep enough to draw blood, although the informant claimed that this was not necessary. The children were not supposed to cry out under the ordeal (Loeb 1926:383).

Those more select boys and girls who would actually become society members were carefully prepared from earliest childhood. Actual initiation occurred at the occasion to the first dance cycle to which they were admitted accompanied by a sponsoring relative. Initiates were purified, swore oaths of secrecy, and swallowed medicine while the chief rubbed other substances on their bodies. No payments were required for initiation.

We can conclude this abbreviated account of Pomo ritualism with mention of the girl's puberty rite and procedures at death. At the time of the first menstrual period, the girl was segregated in a small hut connected to the main house. Here she lay on a "hot bed" and observed some taboos. She then bathed and ground up a small basket of acorns into meal and made food for her family and close friends. No dance occurred in this relatively small affair designed to keep the unclean girl removed from normal activities and to demonstrate the responsibilities of womanhood.

As elsewhere in Central California, crying might precede the death of an individual. After death gifts were heaped on the body by relatives and friends and, after a few days, the deceased was carried a short distance from the village and cremated. Mournful chants and dances accompanied these proceedings. While people cried, many acted as mad and threw their possessions into the fire (after stripping them from their bodies). Return presents had to be given for these "fits of grief." Leftover bones were buried. The widow and perhaps other close relatives cut their hair and smeared pitch and ashes on their foreheads. Seed or acorn meal was sprinkled over places the dead person had frequented for about one year afterward. Evidently, there was no subsequent major mourning rite. We can now turn to supernatural experiences in Northern California.

Northern California

The most outstanding ritual expressions of a collective nature in this region of aboriginal California were found among such groups as the Yurok, Karok, and Hupa. These rites, which consisted of a number of somewhat differing local expressions, are generally designated as World Renewal Cults. As such, they offer effective comparisons to the Kuksu and Toloache Cults of the Central and Southern areas. In point of fact, however, this northern expression seems to the present writer to be less a unified cult and more an anthropological convenience in designating ritual activities. Nonetheless, we can present here the more standard interpretation. According to many writers, these World Renewal Cults are characterized by the following traits. "The esoteric magic and avowed purpose of the focal ceremonies comprising the system include the re-establishment or forming of the earth, first fruits observances, new fire, prevention of disease and calamity for another year or biennium" (Kroeber & Gifford 1949:1). This purpose was accomplished by certain ritual recitations and activities performed at a series of special locations by priest-like practitioners who have been purified in advance for such tasks. The actions of these leaders imitated comparable behavior by supernatural beings who also did them but who had departed or transformed themselves after the creation of humanity. The words and actions thus repeated operations performed at the beginning of time. They may, in fact, have been mythic recitations which merely dealt with the acts of these beings. Priests often had one or more assistants, often female, and there were structures sacred to such performances. These might be made special or could be a sweathouse or even a regular structure made temporarily sacred.

The activities of the leader differed depending upon the content of the rite, as will presently be demonstrated. Finally, special dances, basically unique to this region, often accompanied or terminated the more priestly esoteric proceedings. Since such dances could only be performed at special locations, this means that more than one group became involved in their performance.

Since the dances were perhaps the most universal aspect of such ritual activities, they deserve more detailed general comment. They were called the Jumping Dance and the Deerskin Dance. They were put on as a privilege of wealthy individuals who could provide the food requisite to holding them and who could supply the costly paraphernalia employed by the dancers. Speaking specifically of the Hupa White Deerskin Dance:

> ...the persons of prestige and wealth are in control because they give the dance....There are two sides or camps. The entire ceremony consists of individual dances put on by each alternately....Each leader, besides providing all the dance paraphernalia he owns or can muster for the occasion, also establishes a fire...at which his wife cooks food for anyone, dancer or onlooker, who wishes to be his guest. We have then a ceremonial division into two groups and subdivisions of these according to the number of responsible men of wealth interested in presenting the dance (Goldschmidt and Driver 1940:106).

Certainly a by-product of such endeavors was to display wealth, reinforce prestige, and to make public one's social status.

The Jumping and Deerskin Dances sometimes were performed at the same rite, but more often it appears they were associated with different occasions in the ceremonial system. Dancers in either were usually younger, poorer men who performed for the pleasure of participation. Special singers accompanied them and were chosen with great care, especially for their voice quality. Dancers were costumed differently. In the Jumping Dance, headbands with attached woodpecker scalps and dance baskets were used; in the Deerskin Dance, albino and other deerskins plus long flint blades were employed. Other regalia also differed as did the songs and the dance steps themselves. The dance costumes were regarded as treasures. The dance consisted of a slow series of steps and ritual maneuvers to melodic (wordless) songs sung by some of the dancers. Each performance lasted about three minutes, but each performing group made a number of appearances each of which had a number of different song performances. Thus, a number of days might be taken up with such activities. Generally speaking, as the dance series progressed, the number of the dancers increased as did the complexity and wealth of the costumes themselves. While such dances were occasions for wealth displays as well as social contact between usually dispersed groups, they, nevertheless, did follow the greater theme of the ritual system. Speaking again of the Hupa: "The very purpose of the dance is to wipe out the evil brought into the world by members of the society who have broken taboos...only the White Deerskin Dance wipes away the evil brought on by those who have spoiled the world" (Goldschmidt and Driver 1940:121).

Most scholars appear to suggest that there were twelve or thirteen "centers" of this cult which ranged over the territory of the various tribal groups concerned. Rites of the above nature (although highly variable) were performed in a series, and visiting took place between different groups on such occasions. To indicate some notion of the different kinds of performance involved, we can very briefly describe a couple of such activities and then turn to other aspects of ritual in this northern area. As a first example, mention can be made of a ritual at the Kepal Fish Dam in Yurok territory.

This site was a wooden weir of poles and stakes constructed early every summer to trap salmon in their annual upstream run. Fish were collected in it and then removed with hand nets. The construction of this dam was surrounded with rituals and taboos. As with other locations in this cult, the Yurok believed the spirits to have originally chosen this location. Modern leaders duplicated spirit activities "...the general superintendent of the fish-dam enterprise...obtained his office...because he possessed the necessary medicine. The medicine is a mythical tale which recounts in elaborate detail how the first dam was built by the...immortals" (Waterman and Kroeber 1938:51). After removing a taboo on salmon eating, this individual then came to the dam area, visiting several other sacred locations along the way. Shortly thereafter, he visited throughout the locality, apparently reciting the myth. He also took ritual steps along the banks where the dam was to be constructed. Then, along with an assistant, he manufactured special building stakes. The following day many people began manufacturing the materials required for the dam, and for some days while such preparations continued, the leader and his assistant remained in seclusion. Only ten days were permitted in the building of the dam, and only ten days of use before it was dismantled. Boat dances attended its construction, restrained dancing in canoes accompanied by singing when the work was concluded each evening. On the last day, a special rite removed restrictions on behavior that applied to the workers. A tall pole was erected near one end of the completed dam, and a party of women danced nearby. One of these then ran partly around the pole and looked at the men gathered on the other side of the dam. Her glance apparently symbolically removed them from their sacred construction condition.

The ritual leader was also taken out in a canoe paddled by two other men who then capsized the boat and swam ashore. Soon after, those who had worked on the dam brought long poles specially decorated and noisily knocked these together eventually dropping them on the now crouching leader. While no interpretation is given for this rite, it might be assumed that this rite freed the leader from his own ritual obligations – the knocking of the poles representing the dam building and their dropping suggesting the work as having been successfully completed. After a few days of rest, a series of deerskin dances were held which attracted tribesmen from many surrounding groups.

As a somewhat contrasting variation in the cult series were rituals performed among the Hupa near the village of Takimilding. These (among others) involved a first salmon rite in late spring, a series of White Deerskin Dances in August or September in alternate years, and an acorn rite and jumping dance series in late fall. We may briefly indicate the nature of these proceedings. A priest purified himself for ten days in a sweathouse to prepare for the salmon rite. He then went to the river, caught a salmon, killed it with a special stick, removed it without touching the skin, and cut it open with a stone flake.

> This was done to secure an abundance of good salmon for the year and to so bless food of all kinds that man, bird, and beast might be satisfied with a small quantity. When the salmon had been caught a long formula is repeated. This recites the making of the first salmon....It tells of the killing, cooking and

> eating of the first salmon and sets forth all the laws to be observed in connection with fishing and salmon. The priest puts incense root in the fire and prays for plenty of salmon. He cuts the salmon in a ceremonial manner, cooks it in the fire, and eats it (Goddard 1903:78-79).

The priest then fished for ten days more. A feast occurred, and the fishing season was officially opened, but the officiant was himself under a taboo on eating salmon until the fall and had to refrain from sex for an entire year.

The acorn rite was likewise in the nature of a first fruits endeavor. In more recent times, it was led by a woman officiant. She moved to a sacred house and took with her quantities of newly fallen acorns. She fasted and prayed to the god of vegetation for plenty of acorns and to prevent sickness. The acorns were then ground up, and the meal placed in the baskets. The next morning she took this to a feasting place and built a special fire and cooked the meal over it accompanied by prayers. Salmon were also cooked at that time and a feast followed.

> When the men are through eating, they go away....Women...rebuild the fire, pick up the remnants of salmon and acorns and burn them in the blazing fire, and pray for many acorns. Acorns will be plentiful on these mountains in our district. There will be no sickness. People will gather acorns happily. If a man eats little, he will feel as though he has eaten much. Birds, and other animals' stomachs will be upset, they will not eat much; similarly insects of all kinds (Kroeber & Gifford 1949:58).

Similar although specifically varied rites occurred at other locations throughout the area of this ritual system. Perhaps originally, each ritual endeavor was limited to merely first fruits concerns, but it appears as though over time the focus came to transcend this more specific intent, leading to control over the food supply in general as well as human health and the condition of the earth. The fact that such rites are mostly concentrated among three rather small groups also may suggest the relatively recent development of this cult. We can not turn to some other aspects of supernatural behavior.

Shamanism was also an important aspect of supernaturalism in Northern California although it had a number of distinct variations. Among World Renewal rite adherents, the shaman shared his or her leadership position with the leaders of those rites, the priests or formulists. This latter type of practitioner also functioned in the curing process although in somewhat different contexts.

> Shamans and formulists may collectively be described as semi-specialists in ritual, among whom some differentiation had taken place. The shaman is a diagnostician and doctor who, by a rite of passage, treats most personal ailments which are not directly associated with a...transition in an individual's status. The formulist functions in all other rites...that require ritual direction by someone outside the family which is concerned.... In more serious cases the shaman may supplement his or her own therapy by prescribing a purificatory rite...which must be conducted by a formulist who possesses the relevant formula... (also)...ailments of individuals are properly the concern of a shaman, whereas even mild ailments which affect a family or a village require the services of a formulist after a shamanistic diagnosis has been made (Posinsky 1965:227-28).

As partially indicated previously, the formulist had effective power because he knew a long ritual formula. In its application to curing, such a recitation consisted essentially of a description of a spirit being's affliction and the attempt by that spirit to search for relief. The power of the words had some intrinsic strength which was enhanced or decreased by the purifications attempted by the formulist himself. Among groups such as the Yurok, both males and females might be formulists either by inheriting the formulas or by purchasing them. Those leading the more significant renewal rites of course were men.

Among the Yurok, shamans were generally women, and their functions apparently included both diagnosis of disease as well as its cure. Such a woman indicated her future potential by prolonged sleeping, unusual dreams, and nausea or vomiting. Some of the things may have been deliberate rather than unsought manifestations. Eventually the would-be shaman dreamed of a deceased shaman (or animal?) who put a "pain" into the body of the novice. Possessing such a pain which was manifested as a tangible object on occasion was the most important part and prerequisite of shamanistic practice, "the emphasis...is wholly on the pain. The spirit enters into belief only to bestow the first pain and seems not to be considered active thereafter" (Kroeber 1953:63). Such a person then had to undergo anywhere from a few months to several years of preparations under the direction of older shamans. A special dance was held during which the novice removed the pain from her body, exhibited it, and then reswallowed it to demonstrate her control over this source of power. In many cases, after more practice, a final rite was held at which a formulist presided, possibly to sanction the new specialist in the eyes of the community. The shaman danced around a large fire to "cook" the pain and make it more amenable to her will. The possession of one or more of these pains permitted the shaman to extract, by sucking, those of a similar nature from her patients.

Comparable shamanistic behaviors occurred among other World Renewal peoples. Among the Hupa, the tasks of diagnosis and cure appear to have been subdivided between dancing doctors and sucking doctors. The first type had clairvoyant powers. In dancing by the patient, he could determine the ailment and the appropriate cure. This type was also able to recover lost objects. The sucking doctor, who might on occasion also diagnose, was able to remove the cause of the illness. He "applies his lips to the part affected and sucks with great power acquired by practice. After the sucking, he vomits, continuing to bring up secretions until he produces the required pain..." (Goddard 1903:66). Formulists among the Hupa also applied herbs in the curing practice, and in the event of chronic sickness or to safeguard a child, a special performance called the Brush Dance was held. In it, dances and recitations occurred, and the patient was bathed with medicine.

Among other groups in Northern California, the helping spirit aspects of shamanism were more pronounced. As an example of this variety, we may cite the Modoc. Among these people:

> Power derived from spirits was the possession of shamans exclusively. It was received through a series of experiences which uniquely linked the dreams and the quest; neither, alone, was efficacious. Properly, the initiative rested with the spirits rather than with man. The latter, in his eagerness to acquire power, sometimes assumed the initiative but failure was certain unless the spirits were particularly well disposed towards him (Ray 1963:31).

During maturity, a man would have a dream in which a number of spirits appeared. These dreams were rather vague and would continue, and the would-be shaman would then engage in a five day quest to seek personal contact, visiting sacred locations and sleeping there. At this point, the dreams took on sharper clarity, and a special overall spirit controller would appear and give a song to the visionary. After a brief wait at home while observing taboos, the novice received instruction from a number of specific helping spirits. After this, a rather lengthy initiation process occurred during which the shaman displayed some of his newly acquired powers.

Curing rituals themselves were fairly complex, perhaps as compensation for the lack of renewal rites, and involved several people who acted as assistant to the shamans. Chief of these was an invoker who would summon the shaman's spirits and a spokesman to interpret the spirit voices that emanated from the shaman. The essential aspects of the rite proceeded about as follows. The shaman lighted his pipe and placed his hands on the patient to ease the pain. He spoke briefly to the spirits and summoned them to the side of the patient. The invoker requested the spirits to obey this summons. The shaman then became the voices of the spirits, and these were interpreted to the audience by the spokesman. The spirit voice argued over and resolved the cause of the illness. A recess followed after these diagnostic procedures, and then the shaman effected his cure. He began to suck on the patient while the audience sang. The intensity of the sucking increased (choking and gasping). Finally the shaman jerked his head backwards and extracted the disease object from his mouth and disposed of it by swallowing or burying it. He then sucked out any "contaminating matter" and also disposed of this. Some curing activities among the Modoc were also performed by a different sort of practitioner, the dream doctor, who merely placed his hands on the patient to cure minor illnesses. Such a person had no spirit helpers or assistants and was apparently more noted for his clairvoyant abilities to predict the future. We can now briefly examine some other forms of ritual activity in Northern California.

Notice-taking of girl's puberty occurred among all groups in this area. Most groups associated dance activities at these times. For example, among the Karok the girl danced back and forth before a line of men which included a special singer. This was followed by a round dance around the pubescent girl involving circles of men and women. Each of the men also took turns dancing with her. This dancing occurred at night to keep the girl awake, and for ten days, observance of taboos plus other activities designed to prepare her for womanhood were part of her transition. The Hupa and Modoc made similar observances. Among the latter, the dance was also performed to keep the girl from dreaming since dreams at this time were thought to harm her later. The dance lasted five nights followed by a purifying sweat bath for the girl and then five more nights of taboos. The Yorok, on the other hand, appear to have observed no dancing activities in this connection. Among these people, the girl merely remained at home under restrictions for ten days. Periodically, she went outside to gather firewood – a common task at this time among all groups – as well as bathing a ritual number of times each evening.

Death rites were also events of importance in Northern California. Among the Hupa, wailing began at the time of death, and the closest male relative to the deceased prepared the body and dug a grave near the village. The body was removed through the side of the dwelling while being ritually addressed not to return as a ghost to disturb the living. The body was placed in the grave along with personal possessions, and if the deceased were an important leader, money and dance paraphernalia were also destroyed and buried with him. After filling in the grave, a fence-like structure was erected on it, and objects were placed there to accompany the deceased to the next life (clothes, dishes, etc.). Loud wailing accompanied this entire rite by all in attendance. The close relatives then retired to the dwelling and were purified by recitations intoned by a formulist, as usual telling of original death practices. This man then rubbed medicine on the persons to be purified. The close relative had additional ritual chores to perform and more purifications. Near relatives cut their hair short as a sign of mourning and wore necklaces of braided grass to prevent their dreaming of the deceased. The dead were thought to go to an underworld in the west of a rather undesirable nature. Fairly comparable rites occurred among other groups although groups such as the Modoc cremated the body. Apparently, anniversary mourning rites were either absent or of little consequence in this area of California.

We have now very briefly surveyed major ritual features among some typical societies in Southern, Central, and Northern California. Much has been omitted. Yet any less concentrated an account would have resulted in a lengthy document which would work against the stated purpose of the present volume: to indicate the general flavor of aboriginal religion in various Native American culture areas. Some very general features have been suggested which fall into three major dimensions. First and most uniquely Californian in their structure are the various cult activities: Toloache, Kuksu, and World Renewal. In the first two cases, we observe somewhat communal organizations heavily committed to the initiation of at least some members of their societies. Kuksu, in its eastern and western forms, also went beyond this with a series of dance activities. The more northern World Renewal rites had no cult organizations per se, but certainly in their performances they served communal purposes. Were these cultic features indigenous to the Californian culture area? Possibly they were not, although the forms taken remain comparatively distinct. Certainly, the World Renewal Rites build upon the presence of "first fruits" rites generally in North America and "first salmon" and other rites more specifically in the North West Coast area. Derivation from both sources is probable but the degree of elaboration is somewhat unique. Perhaps a simple form came into California with the first inhabitants and was stimulated to develop from the north. The Kuksu Cult shows many general resemblances to both Northwest Coast spirit impersonations and to the very complex Southwest Puebloan practices. In the latter case, there is a territorial gap in such god impersonations; perhaps both the Southwest and Californian practices were ultimately derived from Mexican sources.

A second major Californian feature was shamanism, a phenomenon of universal distribution in North America. California does display considerable uniformity in such practices despite its other regional differences. The main shaman function seems to have been to cure disease, and this was usually caused by a disease object which was sucked out of the body of the patient. Singing, blowing tobacco smoke, and dancing were also often employed as part of curing techniques. Major differences in attaining such powers occurred, and the classic North American Guardian Spirit supernatural helper aspects were not always found in California. Likewise, some distinctions between diagnosticians or diviners and sucking shamans occurred in many groups as did those between shamans as such and those who (like formulists or society members) had more priestly functions. The presence of "bear doctors" throughout California suggests the antiquity of this shaman type. The general fact of shamanistic involvement in cult societies was a fairly general Native American phenomenon.

The last major aspect of Californian Religion was the emphasis upon life-cycle observances, especially those relative to girl's puberty and to death. In the first case, we witness a widespread North American trait, although substantial variations occur in California – between types of segregation for the girl, in the presence of dances and their degree of elaboration and significance, and the hot pit rites in the Southern subarea. Certainly such rites are to be counted among the rituals of the first settlers of this culture area. Death rites, likewise, were important and original everywhere, but only in the south did subsequent rituals (mourning rites) become so complex as to loom more important than the original activities at death. While the above rituals – cults, shamanism, and life-cycle observances – were not the only native Californian supernatural practices, they are those on which most of our data exists. It must again be pointed out that much of even this data is either incomplete or contradictory. Many developmental and distributional problems remain to be resolved by area specialists. This chapter has attempted to set forth for comparative purposes some of the major ritual features of the three major subareas of aboriginal California.

CALIFORNIA BIBLIOGRAPHY AND REFERENCES

Barrett, S. A.

1919. The Wintun Hesi Ceremony. *University of California Publications in American Archaeology and Ethnology* 14:437-88.

1917A. Ceremonies of the Pomo Indians. *University of California Publications in American Archaeology and Ethnology* 12:397-441.

1917B. Pomo Bear Doctors. *University of California Publications in American Archaeology and Ethnology* 12:433-65.

Beals, R. L.

1933. Ethnology of the Niseanan (S. Maidu). *University of California Publications in American Archaeology and Ethnology* 31:335-410.

Bean, L. J.

1972. Muktat's People. Berkeley: University of California Press.

Benedict, Ruth.

1924. A Brief Sketch of Serrano Culture. *American Anthropologist* 26:366-92.

Dixon, R. B.

1907. The Shasta. *American Museum of Natural History Bulletin* 17:381-498.

1905. The Northern Maidu. *American Museum of Natural History Bulletin* 17:119-346.

Driver, H. E.

1936. Wappo Ethnography. *University of California Publications in American Archaeology and Ethnology* 36:179-220.

Drucker, Philip.

1936. The Tolowa and Their Southwest Oregon Kin. *University of California Publications in American Archaeology and Ethnology* 36:221-230.

DuBois, Constance.

1935. Wintu Ethnography. *University of California Publications in American Archaeology and Ethnology* 36:1-148.

1908. The Religion of the Luiseno Indians. *University of California Publications in American Archaeology and Ethnology* 8:69-186.

Foster, G. M.
1944. A Summary of Yuki Culture. *Anthropological Records* 5:155-244.

Freeland, L. S.
1923. Pomo Doctors and Poisoners. *University of California Publications in American Archaeology and Ethnology* 20: 57-73.

Gayton, A. H.
1930. Yokuts-Mono Chiefs and Shamans. *University of California Publications in American Archaeology and Ethnology* 24:361-420.

Gifford, E. W.
1955. Central Miwok Ceremonies. *Anthropological Records* 14:261-318.

1927. Southern Maidu Religious Ceremonies. *American Anthropologist* 29:214-57.

Goddard, P. E.
1903. Life and Culture of the Hupa. *University of California Publications in American Archaeology and Ethnology* 1:1-88.

Goldschmidt, W. R. & Driver, H. E.
1940. The Hupa White Deerskin Dance. *University of California Publications in American Archaeology and Ethnology* 35:103-42.

Kroeber, A. L.
1953. Handbook of the Indians of California. Berkeley: California Book Company.

1932. The Patwin and Their Neighbors. *University of California Publications in American Archaeology and Ethnology* 29:255-423.

1923. The History of Native Culture in *California. University of California Publications in American Archaeology and Ethnology* 20:125-42.

Kroeber, A. L. and Gifford, E. W.
1949. World Renewal: A Cult System of Native Northwest California. *Anthropological Records* 13:1-155.

Loeb, E. M.
1933. The Eastern Kuksu Cult. *University of California Publications in American Archaeology and Ethnology* 33:140-206.

1932. The Western Kuksu Cult. *University of California Publications in American Archaeology and Ethnology* 33:55-72.

1926. Pomo Folkways. *University of California Publications in American Archaeology and Ethnology* 19:149-405.

Mason, J. A.
1912. The Ethnology of the Salinan Indians. *University of California Publications in American Archaeology and Ethnology* 10:97-240.

Moriarty, J. R.
1969. Chinigchinix: An Indigenous California Religion. Los Angeles: Southwest Museum.

Posinsky, Sollie H.
1965. Yurok Shamanism. *Psychiatric Quarterly* 39:227-43.

Ray, V. F.
1963. Primitive Pragmatists. Seattle: University of Washington Press.

Spier, Leslie.
1923. Southern Diegueno Customs. *University of California Publications in American Archaeology and Ethnology* 20:297-358.

Strong, W. D.
1929. Aboriginal Society in Southern California. *University of California Publications in American Archaeology and Ethnology* 26:1-349.

Waterman, T. T.
1910. The Religious Practices of the Diegueno Indians. *University of California Publications in American Archaeology and Ethnology* 8:271-358.

Waterman, T. T. and Kroeber, A. L.
1938. The Kepel Fish Dam. *University of California Publications in American Archaeology and Ethnology* 35:49-80.

White, R. C.
1953. Two Surviving Luiseno Ceremonies. *American Anthropologist* 55:569-78.

CHAPTER X

PLATEAU-GREAT BASIN RELIGION

It has been seen in the previous chapter that supernatural beliefs and behaviors in California attained a rather sophisticated level of development, at least in some regions. This was due to abundant natural resources which provided both the time to devote to ritual endeavors and the sufficient concentration of population to give a group flavor to them. While other areas of Western North America were much like California in some respects, the less rich resource base precluded the richness of religion previously described. This was especially true with respect to communal activities. In the present chapter we first discuss the Plateau and then the Great Basin.

Plateau

We can discuss the major religious practices of Plateau peoples under four main perspectives: the vision quest, shamanism, the Midwinter festival and related rituals, and life-cycle rites. We will conclude with a few additional remarks. Generally speaking, a fair degree of uniformity existed in this area with regard to such aspects of supernaturalism.

As elsewhere in North America, the vision quest at puberty to obtain a guardian spirit was a highlight of supernatural practice. In the Plateau, apparently both males and females attempted to obtain such powers generally early in childhood. This occurred among most groups between ages six and twelve. There is some evidence to indicate that boys, for whom it was necessary in life, were more successful in such endeavors than girls. Among the Sanpoil, only about a third of female seekers succeeded in obtaining a guardian. Among all groups, the quest was preceded by a period of training. This included instruction and advice by older men or women, less often by an experienced shaman. The would-be seekers were told where likely spots for such encounters might be found as well as how to behave once there. Fasting and bathing might accompany such preparations.

When preparations were deemed adequate, the child went off on the quest and apparently made several such attempts if the first proved to be unsuccessful. For the Nez Perce the method of keeping the sacred vigil was as follows:

> The child (boy or girl) went up into the mountains usually ascending to one of the highest peaks. Here he built up a heap of stones and then sat down beside it with his mind steadfastly fixed on the purpose of his vigil. He took no food or drink, and kept awake as long as possible. After three or four days of fasting and vigil he fell into a troubled sleep, during which the animal or object appeared gave him a name, and taught him a sacred song (Spinden 1908:248).

There were some tribal variations in terms of whether the spirit was thought to appear when the visionary was asleep or awake, although the spirits themselves may have differed along these lines. Likewise, it seems possible to have gained more than one such spirit helper. Generally speaking, such guardians were thought to be intimately associated with the future lives of those to whom they appeared. They served to protect one from danger as well as bestowing certain special powers or skills such as in war, hunting, or for mystical insight. The precise nature of such gifts depended upon the nature of the spirits themselves.

Spirits appeared to be of animal nature, for example bear or rattlesnake, although some groups had dwarf spirits or anthropomorphic types. In some groups, perhaps most, transformation occurred. Among the Tenino:

> Upon revealing itself to the child in human form, the spirit uttered its characteristic animal cry, sang its special spirit song, explained the specific power it was conferring and how to evoke it, and finally resumed its animal form and disappeared.
>
> ......

> A power could not be rejected or revealed to others on penalty of punishment or its loss (Murdock 1965:166,167).

Among most groups, the powers so acquired seem to have declined with age. Along with a special song as a tangible result of such a visitation, quite often a special object or objects were ordered to be kept on one's person. There might also be, as among the Nez Perce, restrictions on interaction with the living animal species.

The results of such quests were usually not disclosed. Among the Sanpoil, for example, the experience was "forgotten" until sometime after adulthood had been reached. At this point, spirit illness would afflict the past seeker, and a shaman would be called in to remove the guardian. Rather than follow the usual curing sequence, however, the shaman would blow the extracted spirit back into the patient who, after some following days of singing, recovered and had solidified his relationship to his spirit. Among all groups, successful seekers would hint at the nature of their supernatural guardians during winter dance activities, and, of course, their special successes in life were interpreted in such terms. Under some circumstances, such acquired powers might be temporarily or permanently transferred to another person.

The difference between Shamans and other power holders seems to have chiefly been one of degree, the extra ability to help others in addition to oneself. In some groups, such as the Tenino, it was also a question of obtaining extra spirits who had been guardians of deceased persons and who were eager for a new master or of special types of spirits. Among the Nez Perce, the guardians were of a higher order than those disposed to appear to ordinary people. Among these people, shamanism was also partly hereditary, an older shaman selecting his successor and teaching the appropriate songs and techniques.

Generally speaking, some sort of "coming out rite" was necessary for a person thought to have shaman power. Among the Wishram, if a boy had obtained shamanistic power, he revealed this to his relatives. They then prepared a dance platform made of tanned elkskin stretched over a wood frame. The boy danced on this while holding onto a pole positioned at the side for support. When he finished, his relatives also danced and sang their spirit songs to help the boy. They then called upon a shaman to complete the inaugural rite.

> The shaman danced and gave presents away, he danced for a long time. Then they helped the lad onto the shaman's back who then danced with him and sang to make him strong. The boy became unconscious and stiff as a board. He was laid beside the elkskin, where the shaman blew over him until the boy began to sing. Then he rose again, reascended the elkskin platform, and danced once more. Now he was strong (Spier and Sapir 1930:241).

After this, the boy demonstrated his powers, probably on the last of five nights of such activities. He sucked sickness out from someone who was ill and swallowed it to feed his spirit. In a more formal sense, a novice shaman among the Tenino was required to be certified by a group of practicing shamans who deliberated his overall fitness for his craft.

Shamanistic practice included divination, performances at death rites, and other activities at the winter spirit dance. Their primary function, however, was in the curing of sickness. Typical difficulties along such lines included those symptomatic of breach of taboo, bewitching, soul loss (or spirit illness), and disease object intrusion. Cures involved both diagnosis – shamans in some groups had special spirits for just this task – and therapeutic manipulations.

Among the Sanpoil, the shaman smoked for a short time, washed his hands in a basket of water for purity, sat beside the patient, and ran his hands over the unfortunate's body to discover the nature of the illness. He then described this to all present. The shaman then went to work while the audience sang.

> Drawing out of the cause of the sickness consisted in the shaman moving his hands, one on each side of the patient's body but not touching it, from the feet to the head. While doing this he made repeated explosive sounds with his lips. This movement was repeated several times before the object was eliminated. When finally drawn out at the top of the head the patient sighed heavily and the shaman clasped his hands together. The assistant, who stood in readiness for this act, immediately grasped the shamans wrists and carried his hands to the basket of water (Ray 1932:205).

After the object had been neutralized in the water, it could then be harmlessly blown away. Finally, water was rubbed all over the patient's body for purification.

Among the Kutenai, the most powerful shaman type was the Blanket shaman who practiced divination of the future and the locating of lost objects in addition to his curing. A typical activity of such a person can be described as follows. Part of a dwelling was walled off with blankets. The shaman sat and began to drum while singing his spirit songs and blowing his whistle. One or more spirits came to take up a position behind the blankets, the shaking of these being a sign of arrival. The shaman retired behind the screen, soon to emerge tied up in some way (by the spirits). He then returned to whistle until more spirits arrived. The shaman was then believed to fly off with one spirit, leaving the others behind in the empty space to converse with the audience.

> When this stage of the seance is reached, the people bring their pipes to the blanket to pray. An official sits on the left side of the blanket's face to light the pipes for the people. He hands a pipe back of the blanket, where a spirit takes it and smokes. After the spirit has blown a few puffs, he hands it back....The supernatural who has smoked then advises his client. It is often very hard to understand the spirits since they mumble far more often than they shriek (Turney-High 1941:175).

The voices of the spirits were interpreted and relayed to the audience. When the conversation is over, the shaman returns and rolls or walks from behind the blankets in a dazed condition. After smoking, he recovers from his experience. This whole behavior is a variety of conjuring which is described in part two.

Among the Kutenai, there also seems to have been an incipient shaman's society, unusual for this area. If an illness refused to yield to individual treatment, the group of shamans would meet to discuss it under the leadership of one of their number. Then each sang and examined the patient in turn, treating that disease aspect he was best prepared to do. The cause of illness was then removed by the leader and nullified by juniper smoke. For these people, there also existed a woman's group, the Crazy Owl society, which functioned to ward off epidemics caused by disobeying the spirits. They sang and danced and engaged in ritual maneuvers. Both groups were most likely a result of Plains influences and contrasts.

While shamans in the Plateau were not ordinarily feared by more common people, they do seem occasionally to have been guilty of malpractice, often being induced to kill an enemy for some client. There were also special types of shamans who will be treated later in the context of the winter rites. In sum, shamanism and the basic acquisition of personal power to varying degrees seem to have been the primary focus of supernaturalism in this area. We can now turn to a third recurrent feature (and closely related activity).

The Winter Spirit Dance was the high point of ritual endeavors in the Plateau. It went on for as long as two months during the winter, and economic pursuits were generally suspended for its duration. We can describe these activities among the Sanpoil as generally representative. It was at this point of the year that relations to guardian spirits were most pervasive. As among North West Coast peoples, life was in the realm of the sacred at this time of the year. Impersonation of spirits in dance was the major ritual element. Such dances were usually held in a special structure or very large house and were usually sponsored by shamans and by initiates – those dancing for the first time. A fir tree was cut and fixed in the center of the dance area and other poles placed nearby, the latter to hang gifts on. The shaman was thought to put his own guardian on top of the tree to protect the dancers from harm. Along these lines, among the Sanpoil, as in most other groups, there were also other guards, people who had Blue Jay power. These individuals apparently reverted to their guardians in actual behavior. Speaking of the Plateau in general:

> With the approach of the winter period given over to guardian spirit dances...these individuals removed all clothing except the breechcloth, and blackened the face, hands, and feet. For the two months of the dances they donned no clothing despite rigors of weather. They shunned human beings and avoided conversation, even among themselves. Further they ate apart, became scavengers of refuse from meals, and stale food....During the dances they acted as sentries, patrolling the grounds outside the dance house or perching on the rafter supports inside the building. From the latter vantage point they observed intently the actions of those below to detect any breach of the formal rules of conduct (Ray 1937:595).

Such practices also demonstrate Northwest Coast influences as well as reminding one of the sacred clowns among Pueblo peoples.

In the actual dances, a shaman would help a novice in his first attempts. The shaman remained by the tree, and the novice walked to him. The shaman sang the latter's song to draw that person's guardian spirit to the outside of the dance house. The fires were then doused with water, and the shaman began to sing his own songs. The audience (other persons possessing guardians) also joined in singing and dancing. The fires were rekindled, and the shaman, continuing to sing, placed his hands on the head of the novice to give him possession of his power. The guardian had arrived. This was then drawn into the shaman's hands. If the novice did not become ill, it was then blown back into him and he began to sing his own song. The shaman grasped the tree and directed the dance in which the audience formed lines at each side of the initiate, moving to and away from him. At its conclusions, the novice held equal place with the other dancers. "Exclusive of initiation ceremonies each dance consisted of individual guardian spirit songs...and dances, (in which others joined after the song had been started by its owner), shamanistic tricks and the stealing of spirits, and giving of presents" (Ray 1932:194). The initial part of each evening consisted of the dances, each person being permitted only one such expression until all had taken their turns. Like the shaman, each participant held the fir tree and danced clockwise around it. The other dancers moved around it in any direction. The dances involved simple up-down step sequences except when particular guardians were being impersonated.

Sometime after midnight, shamans performed, having visions, stealing the spirits from other people, and performing tricks of various sorts, such as pushing sticks into the hard ground of the dance floor. Such activities lasted until dawn with the following day given over chiefly to resting up for the next night's activities. After the last night of dancing, the leader shaman distributed the gifts which had been tied to the poles, the most valuable ones being given to those who were judged to have performed best. Some individual gift giving also seems to have occurred. When the winter dances ended, it was also necessary to capture the Blue Jay people (shamans?) to transform them back to a normal existence since they were apparently incapable of doing so by themselves. They were caught and held over a smoky fire and so restored. It must also be remarked that among some groups men might have a small piece of flesh cut from their arms as they impersonated their guardians. This they would then eat, another imitation of North West Coast practice. If we can trust the sources, among some eastern groups – Kutenai, Flathead, and Nez Perce – the flow of activities of the winter spirit dances were in the process of fragmenting into a series of more sharply demarcated individual segments not all held at the same time.

Although our overall data are less secure, there appears to have been a number of other annual ritual endeavors, most of which were connected in some way to food supply concerns. These generally treated the first plant or animal of each species taken seasonally in a special manner. For example:

> The Coeur d'Alene...had first fruits or harvest ceremonies. When the first important berries, such as service berries, were gathered, before any were eaten the chief of each band who had supervision over the berry and root crops of his territory, called his people together, and in their presence offered a long prayer to Amo'tquen, thanking him for the berry crop....After this the people often danced for a short time, and after that they had a feast of the berries. Exactly the same kind of ceremony was performed when the first important root crop was gathered, such as camas (Teit 1930:185).

Perhaps the most elaborate of such rites among people who lived in proximity to rivers were in reference to salmon, another reflection of Northwest Coast practices. Among the Sanpoil, this ritual was under the direction of a special leader, the Salmon Chief, a man who generally had the salmon as his guardian spirit. Among all such groups, the first salmon was specially caught and was taken to the village, and no further fishing took place until the proper ritual maneuver had been carried out. A shaman or power person cut up the fish in a most precise manner and cooked it. A feast then occurred at which, among other foods, small pieces of the fish were eaten by older (and perhaps other) persons. Afterwards, fishing commenced in earnest. Such symbolic procedures insured that the salmon run would be plentiful for that year.

Among more eastern groups, first bison rites might occur (after introduction of the horse made possible seasonal migrations out onto the great plains). Among the Flathead, for example, the first few taken would be cooked and distributed among the people, and the chief or leader of the hunting group would pray for future success. Along these lines, if there was difficulty in locating the herds, shamans would engage in a ritual designed to lure them to the hunters. A special structure would be built, and the shamans would sing and dance surrounded by a ring of people. This was repeated a second night with the added feature that a special woman would lead the dancers. She covered herself with a bison-skin robe and imitated that animal as she danced. All this was supposed to make bad weather force the animals to the hunters. It was very similar to some ritual procedures among Plains peoples.

Among the Plateau peoples, then, first fruits rites were connected with hunting and gathering procedures to help gain and/or maintain control over the food supply. In addition to the overt purposes involved, other features also occurred among some groups. Among the Flathead, it has been remarked that,

> The Camas Dance was always considered a riotous tension release feast. All bars of dignity went down. A person was entitled to make all manner of fun of his neighbor. The butt of ridicule was not supposed to resent these jibes....These names by which people were called at this time are ordinarily so completely and descriptively salacious that even the most case-hardened are embarrassed upon hearing them mentioned at any other time (Turney-High 1937:38).

Sometimes these rites took forms only indirectly related to the specific foods. Among the Kutenai, the so-called Grizzly Bear Dance was really a device to ensure that berries would be plentiful during their season – since these were a favorite food of bears as well as humans. A shaman (or shamans) with bear power would have a tent erected, a dance area demarcated, and would set up an earth alter. A bear skull was placed behind the alter and facing the door. The ritual itself involved the shaman singing and talking to his guardian spirit. An adult audience would enter, and the shaman would sing again, passing a special rattle to other persons who also had the bear as their guardian. Other men and women danced at this time. Finally the shaman offered a pipe to the bear skull, lighted it, puffed smoke, and then passed it to others (or to a special man?) who prayed for a plentiful supply of berries and for the special protection of the bear spirit. Such activities concluded on the fourth night with a feast.

Other periodic rituals occurred among Plateau peoples. While many groups in this area appeared basically pacifist, some, generally those invading the plains for buffalo, had war and/or scalp dances to gain extra aid or celebrate relative to these activities. Among the Nez Perce, for example, war dances were performed by men just prior to leaving for the annual buffalo hunt or before an actual battle. In each dwelling in the camp, they sang and danced, reflecting their guardian spirits. They also displayed war trophies at this time and gave details of their acquisition. The scalp dance among these people was more of an intertribal affair, held when victory had been achieved over a common enemy. It was performed early in the evening for four or five days. The rite involved singing and dancing which referred to the taking of scalps and to female captives. Speeches were made during breaks in these activities. If male captives had been secured, they might be tortured at this time. Such procedures show Plains influence as does the presence of the Sun Dance among many of these same people (not, however, the Nez Perce). Since this rite is more obviously of recent outside introduction, it will not be discussed here.

We may conclude this summary with a brief description of major life-cycle rituals. There were many taboos on the behavior of a husband and wife before, during, and after the birth of a child. Among the Sanpoil, it was believed that the acts of parents, especially the mother-to-be, prior to birth could determine the character of the child. Food taboos were very heavy. For example, rabbits should not be eaten lest the child have weak legs. Pregnant women also underwent a special program of physical exercise. Birth took place in a special hut or area of the regular dwelling and "certain post-natal observances were incumbent upon the father if the welfare of the child were to be protected" (Ray 1932:126). Any illness on the part of the child was traceable to failure to follow such procedures.

Among the Flathead (and others), after a few weeks, a naming feast was held, the name given to the child being that of a special ancestor or reflecting the war honors of distinguished people. Prayers were offered so that the child would have success in living up to its name. Children were also protected with charms at this time, ointments made from the hearts of animals being rubbed on their bodies. It was typical among most peoples for the first successful economic efforts of children to be the occasion of small feasts. A few relatives were invited to eat the game or fish, roots or fruit, in the case of boys and girls respectively. Older persons would speak to the child involved at this point relative to the merits of hard work.

At puberty, girls were isolated, generally in a small hut away from the village. Here they were covered by many taboos and had to undertake special exercises at dawn and dusk when no one was around. They might also have to collect firewood or fetch water. Meals were brought to them by relatives, and sermons on adulthood themes were provided by older women. Some groups painted the girl's body. This was, apparently, also a chance for the girl to obtain a guardian spirit. At the end of her confinement, the girl put on new clothes (or her best) and returned to the camp. Notice-taking of boys at puberty was much less formal. When their voices changed, their economic training intensified, and they might be given special physical exercises. There might also be a small feast. If a guardian spirit had not already been obtained, efforts in such a direction would become a preoccupation at this time.

Death rituals occurred at the end of the life cycle. Among the Sanpoil when a person became very ill, he confessed any misdeeds to an old man so that his ghost would not return after death. At the time of death, the corpse was quickly prepared, taken from the house, and buried as quickly possible. Some groups were less hasty in these regards. Quickness was for the prevention of any bad influences from the deceased person. Only relatives and close friends (and at least one shaman) attended the burial activities. Generally, burial took place in a sandbank so that the corpse could be covered up more quickly. Upon arrival at the chosen site, an older man spoke about the inevitability of death and mentioned aspects of the life of the deceased. The shaman, using branches of a rose bush, brushed the corpse to rid it of any invading evil spirits. The body was then placed in the grave.

> With the body were deposited the person's keepsakes, fetishes, and ornaments....No time was lost in covering the body for every moment that elapsed gave further opportunities for spirits to enter. Flat rocks were laid on the corpse, then smaller rocks, gravel or sand....

....

> Occasionally a short speech of consolation to the bereaved followed the interment. It was delivered by someone who had not previously talked. Upon its conclusion the mourners returned to the village (Ray 1932:151).

A feast then followed at the dwelling of the deceased, and at least some of his property was distributed. Recipients wrapped such items with rose bush branches to prevent evil spirits from establishing connections to them. The chief mourner and all who had touched the corpse then purified themselves for a lengthy period of time, wearing old clothes, and mourning the deceased until relieved from this obligation by their relatives-in-law. Comparable rites occurred among other Plateau peoples.

In sum, the religious experience among Plateau Peoples can be seen as relatively underdeveloped in contrast to most other culture areas in North America. It appears especially meager with respect to such nearby areas as the Northwest Coast, the Southwest, and portions of California. In the Plateau, the quest for and exhibition of personal power were the foci of beliefs and practices. While the Winter Spirit Dance was a ritual mechanism for bringing people together in a supernatural context, it was not truly a collective rite but essentially exhibited an individualistic flavor. Overtly group-oriented rites were at best indicated by the first fruits ceremonies. Shamanism too was less elaborate and dramatic in this area. Such a remark can also be applied to life-cycle observances. We can now turn to a consideration of such behaviors among Great Basin Peoples who have been traditionally characterized as even more marginal in their expressions of supernaturalism.

Great Basin

It is clear for this culture province of Western North America that shamanism and the obtaining of other sorts of spirit-given were the central focus of supernatural belief and behavior. In fact, with the exception of relatively undeveloped life-cycle observances, these came close to being the only avenues of approach to this facet of human existence. We can discuss such endeavors principally among two groups from this area to give an indication of their scope: various Paiute peoples and the Washo.

Among the Paviotso (Northern Paiute), many individuals were thought to possess supernatural power. This would aid them in hunting, gambling, and similar activities. The shamans, however, who were in contact with especially powerful spirits, had the ability to cure sick persons in their group. The spirits thought to be the origin of such power were of plants, animals (probably the whole species rather than an individual), natural phenomena, ghosts (in some cases), dwarfs or water babies, and water serpents. Such spirits were only visible to those to whom they had appeared; even later during curing rites only the shaman could discern their physical presence. As is generally the case in North America, both males and females might obtain such powers, but males were more likely to do so and had the greater abilities to cure.

Shamanistic power was obtained in three major ways. Most people gained it through dreams, that is to say in an unsought manner. Less frequently, one could actively seek its possession by means of a voluntary quest. In such cases, one would spend a period of time in the mountains or in some other likely power location. Here the dream experience was actively sought. In some cases, such powers might be transferred along family lines in a hereditary manner. However, this still required dream validation. In such cases, the ghost of the deceased shaman appears, followed by the more usual animal which actually bestowed the gifts of healing.

As previously mentioned, it was the unsought dream experience which were most typical.

> The first few dreams in which supernatural spirits appear can be safely disregarded. But shortly, if the instructions received in the dream are not followed, it is necessary to call a shaman to doctor the patient. In the course of curing, the shaman tells the patient to do as he had been told in his dreams. Then, if the summons is obeyed, recovery is assured. Usually a person is reluctant to become a shaman... (Park 1938:26).

It seems fairly typical throughout the area that the shaman might come to have more than one helping spirit and that, as in the above quote, one rejected such selection as a "power person" at great danger to oneself. The actual mechanics of selection are largely unknown, but Beatrice Whiting (1950) has suggested that, in fact, such power was gained in one of three ways. In some people, cases of nervousness and/or sickness were interpreted by shamans as a sign of failure to recognize power dreams. In the case of other people, they might simply begin to cure and being successful would then seek a confirming dream after the fact. In the case of supposed inheritance, she suggests that they simply observed a relative who was a shaman and consciously or unconsciously learned the requisite techniques. Their father or other relative then convinced them to dream, and this was reinforced by the wider community who accepted the general idea of hereditary transmission.

The paraphernalia of the Great Basin shaman was rather limited. For the Paviotso, rattles, bird tail feathers, beads, pipes and tobacco, and a few other items were kept in an animal skin bag. While such objects were simple, nonetheless the loss of any of them cause great danger to the shaman. Rationale for such objects was provided by the visionary dream as well as the appropriate curing songs and other curing techniques. It is difficult to determine if formal apprenticeship to an established shaman occurred to perfect these spirit-given abilities. Certainly no Plateau-like public initiation seems to have occurred, but the novice might receive aid on a first curing attempt. Here the established shaman performed the first half of the cure which would then be finished off by the novice.

The cause of shaman-cured illnesses differed only slightly throughout the Great Basin. Speaking of the Washo:

> Illness might come from three sources. A ghost, angry because some piece of his property was being used by the living, might make the user sick. A Sorcerer might cause illness by using magic to "shoot" a foreign body into his victim. Or a person might become ill because he had violated some taboo such as mistreating pine nuts or pinon trees (Downs 1966:56).

Among most groups, apparently, the sorcerer was apt to be an angry or malpracticing shaman. Some confusion over types of illness occurs in the literature. Object intrusion and soul loss are common but might emanate from ghosts, shamans, sorcerers or spirits. Evil thoughts by a shaman might alone be a sufficient cause for sickness. Even dreams themselves were dangerous in that experiences in them were likely to come true, such as being mauled by a bear or falling off a cliff. And, of course, for the power holder himself, any breach of a taboo imposed by the helping spirit could cause misfortune. For a few groups, deterioration of the blood is listed among supernatural maladies.

Among some Basin groups, there appears to have been only a couple of basic types of shamans, perhaps a general practitioner and one with rattlesnake power. For most, however, the spirit power flowed along more specialized lines. The Shivwits Paiute are an excellent case in point. Among them there was a class of ordinary shamans plus more than half a dozen other varieties. Rattlesnake shamans dreamed this power, were bitten, and cured themselves as a prerequisite for helping others. Spider doctors were similar. Rock shamans dreamed of climbing steep cliffs, and while their powers were not felt to be exceptionally strong, they could cure those who had fallen from anything. Arrow doctors dreamed of arrows and cured those who had received wounds in warfare, and weather shamans were able to talk to the rain and influence many varieties of weather due to their dream experiences. Some people also had the ability to find lost objects, although they might not have been recognized as bona fide shamans. A last type among the Shivwits may also have been a kind of general practitioner but of greater powers.

> When ordinary shamans failed, recourse was had to the Datura doctor, who supposedly possessed stronger power. A prospective Datura shaman first drank a liquid in which he had soaked the seeds, after which he gathered those roots of the plant which grew eastward from the stalk. There also he soaked, then drank the fluid from a small basket painted white around the rim. The double dose of seeds and roots was potent.... (Kelly 1917:156).

In the dreams that followed, this plant then gave him its power. We can now discuss some varieties in the format of actual curing activities.

Among the Paviotso, cures were effected at the home of the patient. When relatives of the afflicted individual requested a shaman to cure, the latter directed preparation of a wooden staff about four feet in length. The shaman then placed a feather and a bead on the top. The staff was then taken and placed in the ground near the head of the patient. The shaman arrived after dark with a special interpreter – a man who always assisted him by repeating the usually inaudible words and songs to the audience. The shaman sat beside the patient, laid out his paraphernalia, and smoked his pipe. He than began to sing to summon his spirit helper, and the song was continued by the audience to the accompaniment of the shaman's rattle. After a time, the shaman walked or hopped clockwise around the fire then sat and passed his pipe for all the audience to smoke. This completed the preliminaries.

The shaman then went into trance to diagnose the cause of the illness. In the event of soul loss, he would go to retrieve it. In the case of disease object intrusion, the shaman attempted its extraction. First he sucked out blood (sometimes with the use of a bone tube) and spat it into a hole in the ground. Then he circled the fire as before. He then began sucking again, eventually displaying a disease object (stone, worm) to the audience. This was spat into the same hole where apparently it was neutralized. Singing and smoking involving the audience now continued until about sunrise after which time the shaman departed after leaving instructions for the continued care of the patient. The staff was deposited somewhere – usually under cool water – by a relative of the now cured individual. It should be mentioned that among some Basin groups the shaman placed the body of the sick person across his own while the sucking procedures went on.

If the diagnosis suggested a sorcerer or evil shaman as responsible, attempts were made to discover his identity. Among the Chemeheuvi (Southern Paiute):

> Be the illness caused by intrusion or by soul loss, the tutelary informed the curing shaman which sorcerer was responsible. The malefactor was summoned. Sometimes he would confess, sometimes not. Then the curing shaman would speak to him privately...to retract the evil influence by singing. Sometimes the sorcerer acquiesced and sang, pretending to cure....If such deceit were detected the perpetrator would be dispatched promptly.... (Kelly 1936:133).

Other groups cured along somewhat similar lines.

Among the Washo, curing rites took place over a period of nights. After the requisite paraphernalia was laid out and sprinkled with water for purification, the shaman sang and shook his rattle and ran his hands over the patient. He spoke to the illness within the patient. He then sucked out the disease object, which had tangible form. Among these people, the evil power often had to be struggled with as it went into the shaman's body. Often he fell into the fire in the process of bringing it under control or needed the services of a second shaman. He might also fall to the ground rigid and stiff. He would soon recover. "But then they begin to shake a little and that rattle begins to go you can pick them up. If he can, the doctor will vomit out the sickness. When it's out he puts it in his hand and rubs it with dirt and throws it away towards the north; that kills it" (Downs 1961:370). We can turn now to some other aspects of Great Basin supernatural beliefs and practices.

Life-cycle observances from birth to death in this portion of Western North America generally were very simple affairs. Apparently, there were few special behaviors associated with conception although groups such as the Washo did use the afterbirth as a way to prevent or encourage having children in the future. It was wrapped in a deerhide and buried, rightside up if one desired future children and upside down if not. The act of giving birth and the recovery afterwards took place in a shallow pit filled with warm ashes. At this time, a great number of taboos had to be observed by both parents. Some of these were of value to the child. For example, they could not eat salt until the umbilical cord dropped off. This was hung on the right side of the cradle board so that the child would be right handed. Other acts and prohibitions among the Washo and other basin groups at this point were more for the parent's benefit, for example, food taboos to prevent the father from becoming sick. Among the Northern and Gosiute Shoshone:

> Ritual treatment of both parents was primarily for their own, not for the child's benefit. Weasel skins and other things rubbed on the mother's stomach were for easy delivery. Food taboos, use of the scratching stick, painting, and new clothes were for her subsequent health. Treatment of the father largely paralleled that of the mother... (Steward 1943:280).

Among most groups, a month or so after birth the child had a haircut (often the mother as well), and taboos were removed from the parents.

Rites for boys at puberty were not elaborate and usually coincided with voice changes and emphasized their now greater role as hunters. Instruction along these lines was then intensified as was their program of physical conditioning. The one event that marked this transition was the first kill of a big game animal, usually a deer. Among the Washo at this time, the boy, assisted by his father, crawled under the antlers of the animal and was then ritually bathed. From this point on, the results of the boy's hunting, previously taboo to his family, could be consumed.

Puberty observances for girls were hardly more involved than for boys. Steward's comments on the Nevada Shoshone are probably an apt summary for the whole area. "Girl's puberty rites were always for individuals. Group rites, like those for some Southwestern and California tribes, were generally impossible because of the sparse and scattered population" (Julian Steward 1941:255). Among the Washo, a dance was sponsored by the girl's parents at this time. The girl seems not to have been specially isolated, although this was common in other groups. For a period of four days, the girl had to work hard, actually running from task to task so that she would not be lazy later in life. She also had to give away the products of her labors and refrain from eating foods, perhaps to fast for the entire time. After this, the dance was held. During it, the girl carried a special stick which later was taken by a relative and hidden in an upright position in the hills to insure her good posture and strength. At the conclusion of the dance, she was taken to a nearby stream or lake and dusted with ashes and bathed to ensure her of various benefits in adult life. Among groups which sequestered the girl at the time of her first menses, beliefs and practices followed other areal customs: lectures on adulthood by older women, taboo observances, and fear of contamination. The period of confinement lasted up to one month.

Ritual endeavors at the time of death were limited to the family of the deceased and perhaps near relatives and neighbors. While cremation occurred occasionally, the usual method of disposal of the body of the deceased was by burial or by placing it in a crack or fissure in the mountains. A short speech or prayer was generally offered at this time, and mourning rites applied only to the closest family members. While some of the possessions of the deceased were given away, most, apparently, were placed with the dead person or destroyed. Likewise, the house of the deceased was abandoned or destroyed, and survivors moved to a new location (only if the death occurred inside?). "The Washo viewed this destruction of a house occupied by a dead person as simply preventing his spirit from bothering the living" (Downs 1961:377). In fact, fear of ghosts–usually appearing in the form of whirlwinds–was general for the whole area. Rather curiously, accounts on some groups such as the Ute make mention of the custom of sacrificing a stranger or captive when a group leader or other notable person died. We can now examine some other general ritual forms.

The religious marginality of Great Basin peoples is most overtly represented in their lack of major group rites. "Both in number and complexity of ceremonials...they...are noticeably inferior to the Plains and Pueblo Indians, and even of the slender stock of performances known to them in modern times some are demonstrably due to recent borrowing" (Lowie 1924:298). Chief among such borrowing is the sun dance. Clearly a number of mostly recreational or social dances occurred at the various times of seasonal plenty. How developed supernatural notions were with respect to these and how integrated into such proceedings are perhaps impossible to reconstruct at present. Two brief examples may be given.

Among the Washo, there was a pine nut dance each fall to celebrate the abundance of this crop so important for winter survival. This rite was a first fruits celebration. A leader (shaman?) would dream that the rite be held and all people in the area were summoned to come together.

> During the four-day period the leader who had called the meeting fasted, drinking only cold water and eating small amounts of cooked pinon nuts. During his fast he prayed for the success of the pinon harvest and good luck for the hunters. Each night the people danced the shuffling and monotonous round dance....
>
> ....
>
> At the end of four days...the food gathered and hunted was pooled, and a respected elder chosen to divide it equably....During the feast which followed, respected leaders prayed and exhorted the people to behave properly....At the end of the feast the people all took a ritual bath (Downs 1966:23).

Comparable rites were held among most Great Basin peoples.

It should also be mentioned in connection with food rites that various other supernatural endeavors were practiced. These ranged from simple hunting magic to shamanistic attempts at luring game to hunters. Among the Chemhuevi, for example, a hunter would fill a small cane with honey. He would then ritually bathe and observe various food taboos for a period of four days prior to hunting. When he eventually sighted game, he would place the cane on the tracks of the animal to magically slow it down and make its legs weak. Among the Paviotso (with variations in other groups), a man with antelope power directed the building of a corral in which to impound these animals. Then a dance was held at which he sang his special songs to charm the antelope and make them docile when driven into the trap. He also had the right to impose certain success-inducing taboos on those involved in the hunt and in the group as a whole.

A second example of ceremonial is the bear dance which apparently was earliest among the Ute and spread to some other Basin groups. This was held in the early spring near the time of the breakup of winter camps and the migratory search for new food resources. It is not entirely clear what the original function may have been. Certainly, as among the Kutenai of the Plateau, it must have been performed to placate the bear. It may have gone beyond this however.

> As the Utes consider that they are a higher order of beings than the bears, one of the purposes of the dance is to assist the bears to recover from hibernation, to find food, to choose mates, and to cast the film of blindness from their eyes. Some of the other motives of the ceremonies are to charm the dancers from the danger of death from bears, to enable the Indians to send messages to their dead friends who dwell in the land of immortality, and one or two minor ceremonies are performed usually for the purpose of healing certain forms of sickness (Reed 1896:238).

The rite itself was held in an enclosure newly constructed each year and went on for four or more days. Lines of male and female dancers faced each other, at first dancing as a unit but eventually separating as couples and dancing independently. Possibly each day of the dance helped the bears through the stages of their annual recovery from hibernation. Each dance lasted only a brief period of time. At sunrise of the final day, a man and woman impersonated bears and danced together. "The ceremony was brought to a close by some dancer falling to the ground, and a feast ensued"

(Schaeffer 1966:29). In more modern times, this rite became more purely an opportunity for socializing.

In summary, this brief account indicates an even greater lack of supernatural complexity among Great Basin people in the aboriginal past than that found in the Plateau. As there, shamanism and the desire to obtain power were the primary characters. Such practices in general seem less complex and perhaps less actively pursued. Life crises rites at birth, puberty, and death were roughly comparable and group ritualistic endeavors much less numerous and complex. It could, in fact, be argued that Great Basin patterns come close to representing the original baseline of Native North American supernaturalism prior to more complex developments.

PLATEAU BIBLIOGRAPHY AND REFERENCES

Coale, G. L.

1958. Notes on the guardian spirit concept among the Nez Perce. *Internationales Archive for Ethnographie* 48:135-48.

DuBois, Cora.

1938. The feather cult of the middle Columbia. *General Series in Anthropology.* Menasha 7:1-45.

Haines, Francis D.

1955. The Nez Perce. Norman: University of Oklahoma Press.

Murdock, George P.

1965. Tenino Shamanism. *Ethnology* 4:165-71.

Ray, Verne F.

1941. Historic background of the conjuring complex in the Plateau and Plains. In Language, culture and society; essay in honor of E. Sapir. Menasha, pp. 204-16.

1937. The bluejay character in the Plateau spirit dance. *American Anthropologist* 39:593-601.

1932. The Sanpoil and Nespelem. *University of Washington Publications in Anthropology* 5:1-237.

Spier, Leslie and Sapir, Edward.

1930. Wishram Ethnography. *University of Washington Publications in Anthropology* 3:151-300.

Spinden, Herbert J.

1908. The Nez Perce Indians. *American Anthropological Association Memoirs* 2:165-274.

Steward, Julian H.

1970. The foundations of basin-plateau Shoshonian society. In Earl H. Swanson (editor), Languages and Cultures of Western North America, pp. 113-51. Pocatello: University of Idaho Press.

Teit, J. A.

1930. The Salishan tribes of the Western Plateaus. *Bureau of American Ethnology Annual Report* 44:37-197.

1909. The Shuswap. *American Museum of Natural History Memoirs* 4:447-758.

1906. The Lillooet Indians. *American Museum of Natural History Memoirs* 4:193-300.

1900. The Thompson Indians. *American Museum of Natural History Memoirs* 2:163-392.

Turney-High, H. H.

1941. Ethnography of the Kutenai. *American Anthropological Association Memoirs* 51:1-202.

1937. The Flathead Indians of Montana. *American Anthropological Association Memoirs* 48:1-161.

1933. The Blue Jay Dance. *American Anthropologist* 35:103-07.

Walker, Deward E., Jr.

1966. The Nez Perce Sweatbath Complex: An acculturational analysis. *Southwest Journal of Anthropology* 22:133-71.

GREAT BASIN BIBLIOGRAPHY AND REFERENCES

Barrett, S. A.

1917. The Washo Indians. *Bulletin of the Public Museum of the City of Milwaukee* 2:1-52.

Cortwright, W. D

1955. A Washo Girl's Puberty Ceremony. *International Congress of Americanists* 30:136-42.

D'Azevedo, Warren L. (editor).

1963. The Washo Indians of California and Nevada. *University of Utah Anthropology Papers* #67.

Downs, James F.

1966. The Two Worlds of the Washo. New York: Holt, Rinehart and Winston.

1961. Washo Religion. *Anthropological Records of the University of California* 9:365-85.

Driver, Harold E.

1941. Girl's Puberty Rites in Western North America. *Anthropological Records of the University of California* 6:21-90.

Handelman, Don.

1967. Transcultural Shamanic Healing: A Washo Example. *Ethnos* 32:149-66.

Hutkrantz, Ake.

1961. The Masters of the Animals among Wind River Shoshone. *Ethnos* 26:198-218.

1956. Configurations of Religious Belief Among Wind River Shoshone. *Ethnos* 21:194-215.

1951. The Concept of the Soul Held by the Wind River Shoshone. *Ethnos* 16:18-44.

Kelly, Isabelle T.

1964. Southern Paiute Ethnography. *University of Utah Anthropology Papers*.

1936. Chemehuevi Shamanism. In *Essays in Anthropology presented to A.L. Kroeber*, pp. 129-42.

1932. Ethnography of the Surprise Valley Paiute. *University of California Publications in American Archaeology and Ethnology* 31:67-210.

1917. Southern Paiute Shamanism. *University of California Anthropology Records* 2:151-67.

Lowie, Robert H.
1924. Notes on Shoshonian Ethnography. *American Museum of Natural History Anthropology Publications* 20:185-314.

1908. The Northern Shoshone. *American Museum of Natural History Anthropology Publications* 2:169-306.

Park, Willard Z.
1938. Shamanism in Western North America. *Northwestern University Studies in the Social Sciences* 2:1-166.

1934. Paviotso Shamanism. *American Anthropologist* 36:98-113.

Reed, V. Z.
1898. The Ute Bear Dance. *American Anthropologist* (old series) 9:237-44.

Schaeffer, Claude E.
1966. Bear ceremonialism among the Kutenai Indians. Washington: Indian Arts and Crafts Board–*Studies in Plains Anthropology and History* #4.

1965. The Kutenai Female Berdache. *Ethnohistory* 12:193-236.

Shimkin, D. B.
1947. Wind River Shoshone Ethnography. *University of California Anthropology Records* 5:245-88.

Steward, Julian H.
1943. Northern and Gosiute Shoshoni. *University of California Anthropology Records* 8:263-392.

1941. Nevada Shoshone. *University of California Anthropology Records* 4:209-59.

1938. Basin-Plateau socio-political groups. *Bureau of American Ethnology Bulletin* 120:1-346.

Steward, Omer C.
1941. Northern Paiute. *University of California Anthropology Records* 4:361-446.

Whiting, Beatrice B.
1950. Paiute Sorcery. *Viking Fund Publications in Anthropology* 15.

PART II

CENTRAL, EAST AND NORTHWEST

CHAPTER XI

THE PLAINS CULTURE AREA AND PLAINS RELIGION

The Plains culture area covered the great heartland of North America, approximately between the Mississippi River in the East and the Rocky Mountains in the West. North to South, it stretched from the Saskatchewan River basin to Central Texas. The many people who lived there are often taken as typical Indians; as a stereotype of the way things were prior to European contact. Yet many cultural traits such as horses were European introductions and many groups were very recent migrants into the area. For centuries the peoples who lived in this area were rather settled farmers like many of their Eastern brethren. By the time of extensive European contact two cultural variations existed: semi-agricultural peoples with fairly permanent villages who also engaged in hunting practices and horse-mounted nomadic peoples who were more heavily dependent upon hunting, especially the buffalo. These latter peoples generally lacked agriculture and are the basis for the stereotype alluded to above.

Language affiliations in this area are many, indicating the mix of peoples. Many were driven west from eastern areas or were motivated by the lure of buffalo made more available due to the possession of horses. At least three major linguistic groupings are heavily represented with speakers of others represented by a few tribes. Siouan speakers included such as the Crow, Mandan, and Dakota. Algonkian is represented by the Blackfoot and Cheyenne, and Caddoan by the Pawnee and Arikara. Shoshonian speakers were present in the Comanche and Athabascan speakers are also found.

Such a mix of language groups and people as well as the great amounts of cultural borrowing that occurred between them makes the characterization of the general culture and the religion of this area considerably more difficult than for most of those previously described in this book.

Technology varied in the Plains. Big game animals such as elk, deer, antelope, and especially buffalo formed a great part of the diet of nomadic peoples and were a supplement for villagers. Buffalo were hunted from horseback either by surrounding a herd or riding next to it. Previous to the horse, herds were driven over cliffs in annual tribal hunts, stalked by solitary hunters in disguise, and hunted on snowshoes in winter. The buffalo furnished many useful resources such as hides, bone, and fuel, in addition to their food value. Fish were used in times of scarcity. Wild plants were collected by both nomads and farmers and included berries, turnips, and chokecherries. An important food product was pemmican: sun dried slices of meat pounded with a mixture of fat, marrow and cherry paste. This was a food for the trail since it kept indefinitely. Agricultural village people grew corn, beans, squash, pumpkins and sunflowers; often in the fertile bottom lands along rivers.

The nomads lived year-round in portable tipi dwellings consisting of about sixteen poles leaned together and covered with skins. Such tents were about thirty feet high and typically fourteen feet in diameter and could be quickly dismantled and rebuilt when on the move. Farmers employed such structures during summer buffalo hunts or in other activities but generally lived in earth lodges. These were circular, dome-shaped buildings of branches, grass and earth laid over a wood foundation. These might hold up to forty or more people plus their possessions and could be ten feet high and fifty feet in diameter. They represented the greater sedentariness of such people. As an aid in movement the travois or pole drag pulled by dogs or horses was used to enhance mobility even though personal property was kept to a minimum.

Social life in the Plains culture area was basically on the same level for most constituent tribes although great variation existed with respect to specific practices. Marriage was an important institution and polygyny was more common here than in most other areas since men often died in war activities or hunting. Marriage helped form alliances that held tribal groups together although some secondary wives were obtained by capturing them from unfriendly neighbors. Residence rules varied although usually some extended family developed, usually based on some unilocal rule. The Cheyenne were matrilocal, the Blackfoot patrilocal, still others indifferent. Such family groups exhibited a high degree of solidarity. Groupings beyond the family level also occurred. Clans usually existed on a non-residential basis to help unite the various bands that composed tribal groups. Some traced affiliation through the father's side, others through that of the mother. Dual divisions – earth/sky, summer/winter – existed in some groups to help regulate exogamous marriage and for games and rituals.

In most Plains groups, societies or clubs mostly for males also occurred. These groups had recreational functions as well as coordination of group hunting activities; also functions as camp police and military aspects. Since ritual endeavors were also dealt with, we can reserve discussion of such societies for later. Larger groupings occurred. Among nomads these were more evident during the summer when the various bands that had split apart for winter reconvened for collective hunting, warfare, and ritual activities. The Kiowa, for example, were usually split into about fifteen bands of over one hundred people each who then came together and camped in one large circle. At least at this time of year tribal identity and common concerns were clearly developed. Among village peoples the collection of earth lodges was a residential unit of identification much of the time although these people too often combined in larger, temporary units.

Warfare and systems of rank partially based upon it were also hallmarks of Plains society; especially after the introduction of horses. Most groups confined war hostilities to groups outside their own tribe. Raiding expeditions involved a small number of warriors and remained in the field until their goal – usually stealing horses – was achieved. Revenge expeditions were often tribal in scope and were short-term affairs to redress some major grievance or "even the score." A major aspect of all war throughout the area was the counting of Coup – touching a live enemy or one that was dead with the hand or with a special stick. This was to show bravery and was incorporated into a whole series of bravery/credit-bearing deeds which included such acts as charging the enemy, rescuing a fallen comrade, fighting on foot, success in stealing horses, and many others. After a battle it would be reconstructed by the participants and the attested exploits would be assigned and publicized.

Rank and status were partly based on such exploits. Among the Kiowa, distinguished persons had many war exploits, wealth in horses, and were generous. "Second Bests" were wealthy and generous but lacked sufficient war honor. "Propertyless" persons were those who were trying but had little honor or wealth as yet. A "Useless" category was reserved for non-tryers as well as war captives and outsiders. Possession of religious powers and/or prerogatives modified this ideal system somewhat as did political leadership.

Political positions were largely informal. Headmen of families, clans, societies, and bands had some degree of influence or even control over their respective group members. Somewhat more formal "chiefs" were chosen to represent their bands in the summer camps. These functioned mainly as peacekeepers and overall coordinators of group activities. Some groups were in the process of developing even more formal political authority. The Cheyenne, for example, had a tribal council consisting of forty-four peace chiefs believed to have access to supernatural powers. Five of these were very sacred and led some major group benefit rites. This group made decisions on migration, had judicial powers, and ordered the police functions of the societies. Other groups had somewhat different arrangements. With this brief cultural summary as a background we can now turn to a treatment of some of the major patterns of religious behavior.

The Indians of the Plains are difficult to characterize religiously due to the many different influences on their culture. As a result the present chapter will merely discuss some rather generally shared features and then highlight some of the more specific behaviors. As a way to begin we can give a list of such behaviors drawn from one group, the Oglala (Dakota, Sioux). We can use them as an entry point into the data. Among these people seven basic rituals were central to their religious life and aspects of these are fairly common among many Plains peoples. These rites were: the sweat lodge rite to renew people spiritually and physically, the vision quest to gain supernatural power or aid; rituals at the death of a person (ghost keeping); the sun dance; a rite to band different persons together like blood brothers; a girl's puberty rite; and a "throwing of the ball" ritual reenacting cosmic events and deities. Several of these rites are found in all groups.

The vision quest is found among most North American Indian groups in the past and we have described it for some in previous chapters. Among Plains tribes it seems to have attained a central role in religious culture. Far from being just a task to accomplish at puberty it was an activity often engaged in by mature men on any number of occasions. The purpose of this ritual is not always easy to determine. Sometimes it was to obtain a guardian spirit, as elsewhere. The Plains vision quest, however, was a more general search for power or spirit contact since such acts might accompany war preliminaries, sickness relief, mourning customs, as well as initiation into certain societies or clubs. It could also be a part of major rites. Ruth Benedict has offered a distinction between a primary or "great vision" to secure a guardian spirit and those of a more secondary nature in which "...the seeker ordinarily received his power or commands directly, without specifically acquiring a guardian spirit" (Benedict 1922:12).

Among the Oglala the quest was called "crying for a vision" or "lamenting." As a rite it was usually performed for the first time when in adolescence and then many times thereafter to gain power, seek understanding of other unsought visions, or divine the outcome of hunting and war acts. "But perhaps the most important reason for lamenting is that it helps us realize our oneness with all things...and then on behalf of all things we pray to Wakantanka (the great spirit) that he may give us knowledge of Him" (Brown 1971:46). If one wished to go on such a quest one first sought out a sacred person, someone with special religious knowledge and power, to be his guide. Preliminary instruction and purification occurred such as the sweatlodge rite and the seeker was taken to a hill or mountain. A pit was dug and covered over with brush and in this the vision seeker stayed for two to four days, emerging from time to time to pray and perform other ritual maneuvers. During this time no water or food was permitted. In periodic intervals of sleep, visions might come from various supernatural beings;

birds, animals, or from the Great Spirit himself. An older seeker might believe himself to be carried away physically and then returned.

After a predetermined time the spiritual guide came and brought the seeker back to camp where, after further purifications, the visions were interpreted as to their meanings and significance. In many cases this might be the limits of one's supernatural experience, but if the vision was considered as one of great potency the visionary generally became more involved in mystical activities; eventually becoming a sacred (Wakan) person himself. This was accomplished by apprenticeship to a mentor and learning secret knowledge and ritual techniques with which to aid "common" people. After a time of assisting, one came to perform rites by oneself and to cooperate with others in the performance of major or tribal ceremonies as well as to serve as advisor to newer seekers. The specialist also periodically renewed his own powers by fresh vision quests. "The more frequently he sought visions, the more power he maintained" (Powers 1977:63). Ultimately, in old age, one lost such powers or perhaps transmitted such as were left to a successor prior to death. It can be also mentioned that those who failed repeatedly in securing a primary vision did have the possibility of buying one from a more fortunate seeker. Such powers apparently could be transmitted once obtained.

Vision practices among other Plains tribes conform in general to this description. We can turn to the Crow for a second example. Among these people youths eagerly sought visions because they realized that such were a basic means of controlling life and were a general way to gain recognition if successful. Later in life the vision quest was engaged in for more specific supernatural aid. The seeker went to a mountain peak, made a circle of rocks, covered himself with a skin robe, and waited for a vision. Self-torture was often used to enhance this process. Typically a seeker would chop off a finger joint and offer it to the Sun while requesting supernatural favors or just general good fortune. Other techniques were also employed.

> ...a man might prefer other austerities. On the eve of his trial he might plant a forked stick on a hill and go there the following morning with an old man who was to pray on his behalf. This mentor painted the faster with white clay, invoked the Sun, and pierced his ward's breast or back. By this

> perforation, he fastened the visionary to the crotched pole and went home, while the younger man began to run around his post. When tired, he was allowed to sit down, then he would resume his running. Some tore through the flesh, others failed to do so. Then in the evening, the old man returned, cut at the edge of the dry flesh, showed it to the sun with another prayer, and once more withdrew. The visionary slept there for the night, and might then receive a revelation (Lowie 1956:240).

One could, however, attain a vision without such austerities and, in fact, visions or the bestowal of power or aid could occur as a windfall without even a quest. As among the Oglala, spirit visitors common to the Crow seeker were the Sun/Great Spirit, various animals, and the eagle/Thunderbird. Powers might be gained from several different supernatural beings.

As among some other groups the Crow saw the result of the vision experience as a kind of patron/protégé relation. The supernatural visitant taught the seeker a special power song, special taboos relative to diet and dress and other injunctions on behavior. In addition the recipient of a supernatural vision might also "...on the strength of successive visions assemble the ingredients to build up a medicine bundle, a wrapper containing a set of sacred objects indicated by the spirit" (Lowie 1963:174). Such bundles were regarded as sacred, high-power objects and provided a focus for individual as well as group rituals.

We can use the Cheyenne as a last specific example of visions. Among them a man who wished personal supernatural power from the high spirits (Maiyun) would "...fast in a lonely place and beg the spirits for indulgence and aid. If favored by a spirit (one) receives a blessing along with how to prepare specific amulets and how to paint himself and what to sing to evoke the power" (Hoebel 1978:91). Self-torture might be an accompaniment of such activities or the vision might be obtained without it. Here too visions might come to a person unsought, during a time of distress, and visions were also obtained in the context of other ritual acts such as the sun dance; as they also were elsewhere. We will presently pursue this point.

The vision experience was indeed a central feature in Plains religion although perhaps more developed among some groups than others. Likewise, the activity of self-torture as an indication of the earnestness of the seeker's intentions is more developed among some peoples. Such austerities appear most developed among the Dakota, Mandan, and Hidatsa and related peoples. For tribes such as the Blackfoot such practices were less developed in the vision quest and in other connections. In still others self-torture may be a recent development since accounts do not appear in the older myths. One last idea is worthy of mention. It has often been maintained that due to the centrality of the vision quest on the Plains that a man was, in effect, his own supernatural expert; that the distinction between shaman and lay person was almost nonexistent. This is, of course, logical if anyone can gain power through such experiences. While this may indeed be true among some groups such as the Arapaho, for many a fairly clear break does occur. In the Oglala case cited above it will be remembered that to be truly Wakan requires further training and repeated spiritual endeavors. It may also require, where self-torture is a feature, even greater austerities. Such is also common elsewhere. Where more priestlike functionaries exist, and in groups with tribal bundle ceremonies, the dividing line between leader and follower is also rather well marked. We can now turn to a second major ritual, the Sun Dance, since it is tied in some ways to the vision quest.

The Sun Dance was among the most visible group ritual activities in the Plains culture area and all but a few tribal groups practiced it. Most of the latter, however, did take up the rite in the late 1800's. It was most highly developed among the Dakota, Cheyenne, and Arapaho. Sun Dance is the popular English name applied to it based upon Dakota practice but it has a different designation and somewhat different functions elsewhere. In all events, however, it is what might be called an omni-ritual; several different and not always integrated elements and functions are involved. Power and world renewal were common aims.

The time period for holding this rite was generally late spring or summer; a time when the various bands or villages congregated in more tribal assemblies. Although the rite was calendrical in nature its performance usually depended upon a pledge or vow by some person to organize the proceedings. The rite lasted approximately one week and self torture was common although of a voluntary nature. We can describe two examples of this rite.

Among the Cheyenne this rite was called the New Life Lodge and its occurrence was believed to recreate and reanimate the world of plants and animals. Its performance resulted from the vow or pledge of an individual called the Lodge Maker or Reproducer who has done this as a way to escape from danger or solve some other personal problem. Ultimately, however, the rite transcended this person.

> The object of the ceremony is to make the whole world over again, and from the time the Lodge-maker makes his vow everything is supposed to begin to take on new life for the Medicine-Spirit (Maiyun), having heard the prayer of the pledger, begins at once to answer it. When the man makes the vow, he does it not so much for himself or his family, as for the whole tribe (Dorsey 1905:186).

The pledger wears special paint until the end of the rite and observes many taboos. He asks the assistance of his own Military society in its direction as well as appointing a woman to provide special aid to him. He also had to secure the direction and assistance of a person who had been a past pledger of the rite, selecting as such an instructor one who had not filled this role very often in the past so his store of supernatural power would not be used up in this respect. Other leaders were also selected from the ranks of past pledgers. It should be mentioned that more than one person could pledge the same ritual and hence more than one society be involved in it. Members of these societies were expected to dance as were other individuals on a more voluntary basis.

The first few days of the ritual were given over to building the ceremonial structure, secret rites, and other preparations. The last days involved more public acts. On the first day a tipi was selected and carried a short distance by women. It was called the priest's tipi and the organizers met to select a chief priest who would enact the role of the Great Spirit. A tree was also selected to become the center pole of the Sun Dance Lodge itself. This was "discovered" by a warrior of suitable rank who counted coup upon it as well as selecting a place in the camp circle where it would eventually be placed. On the initial day the pledger also had a sacred bundle transferred to him from the pledger of the previous year.

On the second day the pledger and his society fasted to prepare themselves for the coming ritual activities, as did the special woman. The chief priest received a sacred pipe as notification of his official appointment and authority. Other officials were also selected. Women carried a tipi into the camp circle and this was now known as the Lone Tipi and the pledger, chief priest, and others went in and smoked. A great amount of ritual activity then followed. For example, the chief priest chewed roots and spit on the pledger's hands repeatedly in various directions to ensure long life and related blessings. A small area was cleared called an "earth" and rites performed to make the world new. This was repeated on successive days until five earths were made.

> The days in the Lone Tipi are replete with symbolic imagery and actions portraying earth renewal and continuance. Five separate earths are successively smoothed out on the ground. A buffalo skull is ritually consecrated through the insertion of balls of water grass in its eye sockets and nostrils. Many special pipe cleaners – sticks with a wad of buffalo hair – represent the life-sustaining buffalo and must be changed after the rituals at each earth, because they would carry away some of the power of growth of the earth if moved from one to another....The Lone Tipi rites...end with a ritual, purificatory sweat bath for the priests (Hoebel 1978:20-21).

While these and other rites occurred in the Lone Tipi – including breaking an arrow to ensure defeat of enemies – other acts were also taking place. Members of societies were practicing their songs and poles were being brought in for the main lodge construction. Feasting and present exchanges occurred as well as recreational dancing. A happy, social atmosphere prevailed. Eventually a public announcement terminated secular activities, usually on the fourth day. Chiefs went to the center pole tree and prayed to it as a symbol of the world and as the sun. It was cut and brought back to camp with ritual halts and five complete circles of the lodge to equal the number of earths made previously. Symbols representing day and night were painted on it and it was raised in the center to complete the framework of the ritual structure. The sacred bundle was placed beside it.

The lodge was dedicated, the chief sang songs, warriors danced outside and as many people as could crowded inside. A great deal of drumming and singing now followed. Priests chanted sacred songs which recounted the mythic origins of the rite. These also were believed to have the potency to bring new life as well as freedom from famine and disease. The chief priest made sacrifices to the Sun and other spirits. More songs and prayers followed and after the fifth series dancers placed eagle-bone whistles in their mouths and moved around the center pole while raising and lowering their arms; giving thanks to the spirits. These acts were repeated later on following days. The chief priest and the special woman went outside to pray. On this day, too, before the regular dances began, the chief priest and the wife of the pledger purified themselves with incense and covered themselves with a buffalo robe and engaged in sexual intercourse. This had the effect of insuring that the regeneration of all things would take place.

On the fifth day what perhaps was the highlight of the rite took place. First an altar was constructed by the lodge center pole. It included the buffalo skull used earlier in the rite, bushes to represent vegetation, symbols of various spirits, a sand painting representing the morning star and the road of the buffalo, sticks representing traditional enemies, rain, and the bands of the Cheyenne themselves. "The altar symbolized the fifth earth made in the priest's rituals; it is the completed and realized earth toward which the whole ceremony is directed – an earth replete with green life and buffalo, sunrise and rainbows, beneficent spirits, healthy Cheyennes and defeated enemies. It is the supreme hope" (Hoebel 1978:22). Dancing now continued along the lines previously described and extended over several more days to the point of exhaustion.

The torture rite also usually occurred on this day. It might involve some of the dancers or it might include other persons who were doing this as the result of some vow. In either case such acts were individual and were not done for tribal welfare or earth renewal. Typical of such acts were piercing the skin with skewers, tying thongs to them and to the center pole, and dancing all night. If these had not torn free by morning the skin was cut to release the exhausted participant. Another possibility was to attach the thongs to a number of buffalo skulls and drag these around the camp circle. In either case the sufferer sought blessings or power from the supernatural and as such this was a kind of vision quest activity.

On the sixth day or somewhat later on, the chief priest and the pledger engaged in a special dance and gave thanks to the appropriate spirits. A final general dance occurred, going into and out of the lodge and these dancers then drank water to vomit and took a sweat bath for final purification. As a last act the pledger and chief priest smoked the sacred pipe and the lodge was then deserted and was allowed to eventually decay. Certainly as a tribal rite and one accompanied by a number of both group and individual endeavors, the Sun Dance was one of the most conspicuous ritual structures of the Cheyenne and was often the central ritual highlight for many such groups. We can now look more briefly at a second example.

Among the Mandan the ceremony closest to the "Sun Dance" was the Okipa. "The Okipa ceremony was an elaborate and complicated affair. It was a dramatization of the creation of the earth, its people, plants, and animals together with the struggles the Mandan endured to attain their present positions" (Bowers 1973:111). The rite was given each summer to insure good fortune in general and an abundance of buffaloes in particular. It took place in a permanent ceremonial lodge with a flat front which faced a circle reserved for ritual activities. In the center of this area was a cedar post surrounded by a plank wall. This post symbolically represented the body of the main tribal deity (Lone Man). The lodge also represented a deity and both figured prominently in mythical events of tribal significance.

This ritual was performed by a group of men who formed a religious society consisting of past and present leaders. These would impersonate the supernaturals involved; especially Lone Man who was the tribal deity who established major religious customs, and Speckled Eagle (Hoita) who was the director of the rite. Besides the current pledger or Maker, special singers and drummers also occurred as officers and the group as a whole possessed a very sacred bundle. Such individuals would meet in council to select qualified individuals to give the rite in a specific year.

> The desire to give the ceremony was the result of a vision experience wherein one had seen buffaloes singing the Okipa songs. The vision recipient would then have a feast prepared in his lodge, to which he invited the Okipa Religious Society. After the feast he would relate his vision experience and ask for an interpretation....A young man having such a dream would tell his parents of his supernatural experience. They

> would know the qualities one must possess to go through the ordeals of the ceremony....It was necessary to eliminate some candidates. Even then, there were two or three performances in each village every summer as a rule. Sons of former Okipa makers received preference, as young men were expected to maintain their fathers' record (Bowers 1973:121-22).

While a person offering to perform the rite did not have to learn too much, being somewhat acquainted with songs, prayers, and dances beforehand, wealth was required since feasts and presents had to be given to the society. A number of taboos, such as not killing or butchering buffalo, also had to be observed.

When the ritual was about to begin the villagers were notified and the Lone Man impersonator entered the village, explaining his identity to members of a society who act as police during the rite. He went to the ritual lodge and recited a myth of the origin of the ceremony to headmen assembled there. Women and children remained inside their lodges while this man walked through the village reciting their parts of Mandan legend; especially that dealing with Mandan origins. He also collected knives from the homes of young men who would later undergo torture and gave each of them food. The actual ceremony began that evening. The Maker brought in paraphernalia, followed by officers and those who would be fasting during the ritual; boys to middle-aged men. Each of these latter was naked and painted for the occasion. Each carried a buffalo skull for a pillow and sagebrush to lay on. The officers then transferred the ritual pipe to the Maker. Dancing began and moved so that it was performed in each of the four directions. This ended at midnight but fasters were expected to "cry" all night.

At daybreak the fasters covered themselves with buffalo robes, imitating buffalo. The Maker left the lodge and walked to the sacred cedar post and asked Lone Man to hear his request to bring buffalo to the villages and to keep misfortune away. The fasters now came out and imitated a herd of buffalo as they danced towards the post. They then returned to the lodge, emerging again prior to noon, at mid-afternoon, and before sunset; making four appearances in all. Some men and many of the boys left at the end of this day, perhaps thirty or more remaining with the intention of staying the whole four days of the rite. They would continue to fast and would undergo self-torture. At sunset the Lone Man impersonator left to bring back special drums used on succeeding days.

On the second day special Bull Dancers performed eight times before the sacred post. They were elaborately painted and their dances were said to be the most colorful of the whole rite. "The Bulls danced directly towards the sacred cedar and formed a circle around it, then formed in pairs to mark out the four cardinal points, and, finally separated to mark the eight directions" (Bowers 1973:134). Also on this day the fasters were prepared for self-torture. A special helper cut holes through the skin and inserted skewers on the chest or back. The visionary would then be hung in midair from the top of the lodge and buffalo skulls were hung from skewers placed in his legs. When a person became unconscious he was lowered to the ground and left alone to hopefully receive his supernatural vision.

The third day was referred to as "everything comes back day." At this time dances symbolized the return of all the mythic creatures that had been on earth when the gods lived among the Mandan. There were twelve sets of dances and in them impersonations were made both of animals–buffalo, eagles, bears, snakes, beavers, etc., and other beings–night, day, Coyote (as the first creator), and a being called the Foolish One. This latter deity represented persons who did not respect sacred things; the forces of chaos. In a very symbolic dance he matched his powers against the Lone Man impersonator and retreated before him while the audience sang songs of victory. After some "clown" activity his staff, the badge of his powers, was broken and he was driven from the village. This assured the welfare of the Mandan people. More self-torture acts also occurred on this day. Most such persons usually left the lodge that evening.

On the fourth day a special dance occurred with four Bull Dancers performing once for each clan and reciting those names as they danced. On this day the Okipa Maker and any remaining fasters underwent self-torture. Sometimes only the Maker was left. The four Bull Dancers then performed in each direction, representing the buffalo herds that would be available at different seasons. The remaining fasters emerged from the lodge dragging buffalo skulls from skewers in their backs and circled the sacred post until becoming unconscious. Paraphernalia was then removed and a sweat lodge for leaders and some others completed the ceremony. As we saw in the previous Cheyenne case, this rite too was a multifaceted endeavor: to give personal benefit to some, to maintain and renew the world for all, and to bring closer together the worlds of spirits and human beings. We can now turn to a consideration of the organization of other ritual activities.

A third major feature found among Plains peoples was the presence of "societies." These are often called military societies in the literature due to their functions in battle. There may have been anywhere from a few such organizations per tribe to more than a dozen with members set apart not only by name but in their behavior in battle or elsewhere. They differed also in their regalia: costume, painting, lances, and other paraphernalia. Lists of the functions of such groups show a variety of useful activities performed by members in addition to their military role. These included preserving order in camp, during migrations, and in hunting; guarding against surprise attack; serving as scouts; providing social recreation for members; serving as keepers of tribal traditions and acting in rites, as well as in other things. The difficulty in discussing such Plains institutions is not just correlating a particular group (Kit Foxes) from one tribe to another, since functions were not identical, but due to the fact that the societies themselves differed in their emphasis. And they differed in emphasis in ways scholars still do not fully understand.

Thomas Mails (1973), in a popularized account of such groups, has suggested a classification into four types as follows. First, the warrior societies per se. These were organized into age-graded and non-age-graded forms. In the former all young men of a tribe entered the lowest such society and then at fairly regular intervals as a group they bought membership and privileges in the next highest society as its members passed on into the one above them. For non-graded types a man would generally join, by choice or invitation, any society and remain there for life. Second, were the religious societies which "...consisted of certain older men who had survived their battle years and...now banded together...to serve the people as influential holy men and counselors" (Mails 1973:37). Women's societies were a third type which divided into groups accompanying warriors, craft guilds, and more religious groups who performed rites or assisted in them relative to buffalo hunting and agriculture. Lastly there were cult societies whose membership was based upon persons who had received comparable visions and whose ties were hence largely religious. Ultimately all such groups based their authority for existence on either mythic or visionary experiences.

It is hard to apply this classification equally to all Plains tribes. It is also true that military types could have religious aspects and activities. Moreover, the trait of age-grading itself is suspect for many groups since men often retained membership in societies they had joined earlier in their lives and young men could, it appears, join older groups. What we may be seeing here are originally clear-cut systems that deteriorated in structure during contact times. At any rate, the reader can at least be aware of the differing emphasis characterizing such groups. Robert Lowie, in his classic historical and comparative summary of such societies, remarks that "The tendency to form societies at all exists in North America as the correlate of a certain complexity of social and religious culture. A particular type of military organization developed in the...Plains...and co-existed with quite different types, sometimes in the very same tribe" (Lowie 1916:953). As such the present book will simply present a few examples of these societies to show organizational type and complexity. We will follow the classifications of individual authors in this presentation and leave out discussion of groups that were purely shamanistic in nature, taking these into consideration later.

We can begin our account with the societies of the Pawnee, as these were fairly clear cut in organization. They had three different sets of such groups; those deriving their authority from sacred tribal bundles, those deriving from the visionary experiences of private individuals, and those which essentially contained shamans. The Pawnee consisted of four main tribes of which the Skidi was the largest, being composed of thirteen villages. Each village had a sacred bundle whose powers came from the West, the home of the thunder spirits. Hence, at the first sound of thunder in the Spring these had to be ritually opened and receive offerings. Most villages of the Skidi were confederated into a common governmental and religious scheme. Four main bundles were of supreme authority: the yellow star, white star, red star and black star bundles. These were each associated with a pole in a special ritual enclosure and reflected the supernatural powers of the four directions in the world as well as the four seasons. Chiefs represented the village bundles as a tribal council but the highest authority belonged to the priests of these four main bundles. Such positions were hereditary in kinship groups. Each priest took a turn as having the responsibility for tribal welfare for one year (spring to fall). It was to him final appeal was made and it was his bundle that aided the success in the buffalo hunt. He selected a bundle society to act as police during this hunt and he was in all respects the supreme authority. In the event of problems with the hunt all four bundles would be appealed to, uniting them through the use of a fifth bundle, the red calf bundle, firesticks from which would be used in a special rite.

The various Pawnee bundles served as a basis for a series of societies that Murie (1914) calls bundle societies. Membership in these was for life, although a given individual might belong to more than one of them. They were non-graded and a strong tendency existed for them to be hereditary in nature. "The number of members was not fixed and so the leaders kept watch over the young men to note candidates of promise...a solemn ceremony of installation was performed in which they were subjected to tests. If one failed he was ejected and forever disqualified" (Murie 1914:558). Among the Skidi tribe specifically, the following bundle societies existed: Horse, Brave Raven Lance, Red Lance, Thunderbird, and Crow Lance or Those Coming Behind. Some other name groups were found in other Pawnee tribes; for example, Fighting Lance, Wolf, and Black Heads. Some were found in more than one tribe.

These groups were seen by the Pawnee as being clubs or fraternities for the pleasure and social aid of their respective members. They did, however, more overtly provide public functions for war and hunting either as single or dual activities, the Brave Raven Lance and Black Head societies performing either function. "In time of need the chief may call upon one or more of the war societies to lead in the line of battle or support the regular camp police in domestic troubles. When setting out upon a buffalo hunt the priest in charge appoints one of the hunting societies to take entire charge of the hunt" (Murie 1914:558). Ritual activities occurred after the Spring tribal bundle renewals. These societies renewed their lances at this time, discarding old ones and making new sets. After this endeavor was completed and followed by a feast, society members danced through the village, returning to their special lodges and placed the new lances outside. Members admonished people to protect these lances since they ultimately guarded all the people and brought in the buffalo. A parade was also held by all societies together at this time. Near the approach of winter another rite was held, stripping the decorations from the lances and keeping such material for the following spring. In at least some societies special lances were highest in rank and significance. Those society members who bore them in battle had to be the last to retreat. In general all lance bearers were required to be at the front of battle and to place their lances in the ground as rallying points for all combatants. Such lances were only used in major war activities and such usages were widespread among Plains peoples with other society schemes.

The other variety of society among the Pawnee was based upon private visionary experiences. If a man had such encounters he might attempt to organize a new society and attract members generally from among the ranks of men who did not belong to the traditional bundle groups. Such membership may have been an alternative way to obtain some social status. While such groups imitated the more established societies and were even rivals to them they still contributed valuable functions to the Pawnee tribes. "As individuals, or even as volunteer organizations, they could carry their standards into the line of battle and win renown" (Murie 1914:579). Such groups, however, did not have formal public functions or even recognition. And they were short-lived. The charisma of the original visionary was the cement that held them together and they seem to have come into and out of existence rather quickly.

Among the Skidi tribe this type of group included the Crazy Dogs, Children of the Iruska, Wonderful Ravens, Crows, Roach Heads, and Young Dogs. We can comment on a couple of these organizations in a little detail for their comparative value. The Crazy Dogs were found in all Pawnee tribes. They copied typical bundle group decoration and some members carried lances. In rituals such as the Okipa they often danced nude, tying feathers to their penises. Some members may have tied their penis to a stake in battle and remained there unless released by someone else, miming some of the lance bearers in the more traditional organizations. They engaged in none of the renewal rites of publicly sanctioned groups but might dance after such groups had concluded their rites in the spring. The Children of the Iruska were a very small group in terms of members but analogous to groups among many Plains peoples. They did things by contraries or in reverse orders. When told not to attack an enemy, they did. If their village was attacked they would play games, not participating in its defense. It appears that they never married and it is possible that such a group – at least among these people – was a refuge for maladjusted youths. There may have been no women's societies as such among the Pawnee. We can turn now to a second example of general societies.

The Crow also had a series of societies although their numbers seems to have fluctuated over time. Some passed out of at least functional existence with their surviving members being absorbed by surviving groups. At times new societies were imported from other groups, principally the Hidatsa. Lowie (1913) designates these groups as "military" societies but is quick to point out that:

> It is true that military duties devolved on some officers in each of the better-known societies, that marital regalia were employed, and that the idea of marital glory was very prominent. Nevertheless...there is...(no)...evidence that war parties were even composed of members of a single society...the origin accounts are meager and trivial, and the dances seem to have been performed solely for amusement" (Lowie 1913:149-150).

He concludes that their social functions were most important.

Members joined these groups primarily by the expedient of taking the place of a relative who had been a member but who had died or been killed by the enemy. Often presents would be offered to a prospective member to induce membership. Less commonly one might join due to having a living relative as a member or simply because they liked the songs and dances. Sometimes a man might hold membership in more than one society and they appear to be basically non-graded. We can discuss some of the basic Crow societies, especially those having equivalents elsewhere.

The two most prominent groups during traditional culture times were the Foxes and the Lumpwoods, each having more than one hundred members. They were also rivals, at least during the Summer season. The Fox group was based on a vision experience of its founder, although accounts of this event differ. Members were divided internally by age, although all apparently had the same privileges and dress. Officers were elected on a yearly basis and were accorded special privileges denied to the rank and file, for example eating first at feats. Such honors were countered by their responsibilities in war. These officers were expected to place their staffs in the ground in battle and remain by them unless removed by someone else. Only then might they retreat–a widespread Plains behavior we have previously noted. Four such officers had staffs and there may have been others with similar obligations. All members wore fox skins as part of their regalia and special body paint designs. A Fox or Kit Fox group was found in many Plains groups.

The Lumpwood society also had legendary origins, one of which suggested that it was named after a knobbed war club. This group certainly had war functions. Religious functions are less certain although this group among the Hidatsa had the ability to lure buffalo in hunting and prayed to the buffalo for general good fortune. The Crow Lumpwoods also had internal age groups like the Foxes as well as officers with special war responsibilities. As mentioned previously a rivalry existed between them and the Fox society. This was expressed in two ways. In warfare each attempted to have one of its members be the first to count coup against the enemy. If successful they could sing the songs of the other group, normally considered an affront. The losing group could then not sing their own songs until redeeming themselves in a future battle. On a different competitive level, members of these two societies endeavored to steal one another's wives. This took place during a relatively short special time period and could only be done if the kidnapper had previously been on intimate terms with the woman in question. Such acts may have occurred with the connivance of some women and the husband was not permitted to offer any resistance lest he bring shame on his society. "If a man expected his wife to be kidnapped, he generally stayed away from his lodge....Should he, however, be in the lodge at the time...the ideal mode of conduct for him was to assume an air of bravado and order his wife to go with her former lover" (Lowie 1913:171). The stolen woman was displayed publicly in a very ritual fashion. Such acts generally preceded the warfare season and all rivalry ceased with the coming of winter.

The Big Dog society was supposedly borrowed from the Hidatsa and differed from most other Crow groups in that each member carried a special stick from which rattles were suspended. The Big Dogs served often as tribal police during the communal hunts and were permitted to whip individuals not acting properly. This society was preeminently a military society and its officers were apparently expected to lead all warriors in battle and to strike the first coup and take initiative in emergency situations. Several of its officers, those wearing bear skin belts, were expected to walk up to any enemy and to never retreat. Such men were certain to be killed and had special privileges granted to them. The Big Dogs danced regularly throughout the summer as did other societies. As a rule most of their members were older men.

We have less information on some of the other Crow societies. The Muddy Hands society had age classes and reorganized itself each spring but seems to have danced infrequently. It did assume police functions and its leaders also were committed to acts of bravery and often certain death in war. This group eventually merged with the Foxes. The Hammer society appears to have been a young boys' organization and, though organized along the lines of other societies, it was a sort of training group; engaging in sham fights and counting coup on wild animals. They did occasionally engage in actual war. They were named for a stone club with a very long handle. They may have been given license to steal food as part of their training. When members grew older they joined other societies. The Bull society was composed of older men, perhaps fifty years or more, and had officers including two men who wore buffalo head masks in rituals. These impersonated blind buffalo and were supposed to be exceptionally fierce. This whole society took part in war and police functions and put on dance performances in which they pretended to be a herd of buffalo. They were able to call the buffalo and improve hunting success through such rites.

A number of other such societies occurred, each with dances and officers. These included the Crazy Dogs, Little Dogs, and Ravens. Mention should also be made of an unorganized group, the Crazy-Dogs-Wishing-To-Die. Like the officers of more formal societies these people, whose number varied from year to year, pledged themselves to die in combat.

> When a man for some reason became tired of life, he announced himself a Crazy Dog. This implied that he must thenceforth 'talk crosswide'...that is, express the opposite of his real intentions and do the opposite of what he was bidden. His most essential duty, however, was to rush into danger and deliberately seek death. This obligation, curiously enough was limited to one season. If at the end of this period he had by chance escaped death, the Crazy Dog was absolved from his pledge... (Lowie 1913:194).

We see here some of the contrary behavior associated with societies in many Plains tribes. We can examine one last brief general example of societies and then deal with some more specific behaviors along these lines.

The Oglala appear to have had several basic forms of societies. Military societies included Kit Foxes, Crows, Strong Hearts, Badgers, Bare Lance Owners, and the White Marked society. Such groups had sacred pipes or medicine rattles, lances, and other paraphernalia and performed much like societies of this nature elsewhere. There were perhaps a greater number of Dream societies. These groups brought together people who had experienced similar visions. Such organizations differed from the Military Societies in that the latter had set numbers of officers, traditional rules, and specific war and police functions. The Dream societies, often called cults in the literature, were more informal; members often performed as private individuals and some also had shamanistic functions. Members were Wakan people and they "...attended to the everyday needs of the common people: they interceded with the sacred to ensure a fair day for hunting and ceremonies; they sought out the buffalo by mystical means, and predicted the outcome of war journeys by divination" (Powers 1977:57). Such people also directed tribal rites and made special medicines to aid the warriors. A number of groups formed by such people existed and we can note some of these briefly.

The Heyoka were people who had received visions from Thunder beings. They appear to have functioned as clowns in some rituals and to have acted in a "contrary" manner; wearing heavy clothing in summer and going naked in winter. Members may have been able to deal with sky spirits in influencing weather. At times members also retrieved bits of dog meat from boiling pots of water–a behavior found in one society or another among many other Plains tribes. There they were usually called the Hot Dance society. The Wolf society dreamed of wolves and wore wolf skins over much of their bodies. Wolf masks were also employed in their rites. They seem to have been highly regarded for their abilities to remove arrows from warriors wounded in combat. The Elks also dressed in animal costumes representing the source of their dream experiences and they were thought to have special powers over women; perhaps in imitation of the bull elk. They may have had the right to appropriate women as desired. They used medicinal herbs of various types. This society may also have contained a division of Deer dreamers who had the power to kill other people by glance alone or by looking at them through a special sacred hoop. At least some members of the Elks/Deers had the ability to deflect evil influences. Along these lines there was also a Mountain Sheep cult which had the powers to make strong war medicines.

The Buffalo society consisted of dreamers receiving power from that animal. In a dance, members impersonated buffalo by wearing buffalo horn headdresses and carrying specially painted shields. They called the buffalo close to the village to increase general hunting success and also demonstrated their abilities in a rite in which Wolf and Thunder dreamers also participated. Its highlight was the killing and then restoration to life of one of the dancers. The Bear society dreamed of bears and wore costumes of bear skin. Such individuals often mimed bear behavior, growling and walking like them, and their ability to gain the power of this animal was often given to warriors before a battle. This involved a ritual bear hunt prior to such hostilities. Bear society members were considered as potent curers and often performed as a group to relieve persons in such distress.

Other dream societies or cults existed. Men who dreamed of a sacred woman or a certain animal became Berdaches and were especially valued in naming (protecting?) children. A Double-Woman group existed consisting of men who had dreamed of a female deity, Anukite. Some of these members may also have become Berdaches; women members gained the powers to seduce men. Finally, among others, we may mention the Sacred Bow society. This group overlapped to some extent with those of a military nature. It had named officers, four of whom carried large bows with lance points at one end. These bows were sacred objects with their own store of supernatural power and were carried in battle. Public rites occurred, in one of which a ritual race was run from a lodge in the center of the camp circle to posts representing the four directions. Its overall function was to aid in warfare.

> The main spiritual and supernatural forces invoked symbolically in the Sacred Bow rite were all capable of killing men: the lightning, the wind and the hail. The snake and the bear were also invoked, but they were considered intermediaries rather than powers from Above. The swift-winged creatures of the air were also called upon by the aid of two feathers worn in the hair in an unusual fashion, the quill base protruding foreword over the forehead....Their use was in reality a prayer that the warrior might, like them, be swift in flight and hard to hit (Mails 1973:265).

We have now surveyed a rather confusing series of groups for three Plains societies. To illustrate more of the range of such organizations, and more specific types, without duplicating previous examples we can now look at a series of individual forms.

Among the Crow, as elsewhere in the plains, tobacco was considered as a sacred plant and medicine. The preparation and planting of tobacco seeds was a ritual task and to do so one had to be a member of a special organization, the Bacusua. This society was much like other Crow groups previously discussed. "The founder adopted novices, precisely as any visionary became ceremonial father to those who craved a share in his supernatural blessings. But newcomers might have independent visions supplementing the primary revolutions...thus branches sprang up...with distinctive songs and emblems as defined in the vision" (Lowie 1956:274). These branches were in reality all part of the same basic society. Only members of this group could obtain the necessary sacred seed and plant it, although non-members did have access to the special tobacco gardens and they might use the prayers of the society for their own success in war and in related activities. Generally speaking, new initiates into the tobacco society included husbands and wives together and originally one joined on the basis of a vow; for example, if successful in war or relieved of illness. Overall membership in traditional times was relatively low.

Candidates were instructed in the rites during the winter and were initiated in the spring at the time of planting. This initiation was at least semi-public and took place in a special, large structure containing an altar representing a tobacco garden. A willow twig was planted in the altar to invoke spiritual protection for the initiate who was painted and given a tobacco seed bag. Dances occurred, drums and rattles were used to imitate thunder, sacred tobacco was smoked, and other ritual maneuvers occurred. Each novice was required to dance with all those who had given instruction. Ultimately a sweat bath finished off these rites. The actual planting came next and for this the members of the society needed their seeds to be mixed with water and other medicines. This was accomplished by a special officer. This man, the Mixer, also determined the site for the garden in any particular year. Eventually members set off for the gardens, often accompanied by the whole camp. The procession made a number of rest stops with rites along the way, the fourth stop being only a short distance from the garden. A race occurred to stakes that had been previously set up to mark individual plots. Grass was then pulled up and burned over to prepare the site and the plots further marked off. The Mixer made symbolic holes in each, women made actual holes and their husbands placed the seeds. This was followed by a dance and society members often slept in the gardens that night in hopes of securing a vision. Between planting and harvest time the members observed various taboos to insure the success of the crop. Four inspection trips with associated dances were also made to these gardens. Four harvesting trips apparently were made and it may have been that the actual harvesting was not a prerogative of all members. Overall, "The Crow firmly believed that it was necessary to plant tobacco in order to ensure the continued welfare of the people..." (Lowie 1956:295). Tobacco may have been identified with the stars as well as having supernatural power in its own right.

The Pawnee offer us a second example of a special ritual. In this case it involved a special bundle object like those previously mentioned for these people. This bundle was in the keeping of one group but its use was initiated by someone outside the society. It involved a sacrifice to the Morning Star. This rite occurred in a short form each December by members of the group singing and making offerings to the Morning Star bundle. In years when Mars was the morning star a more involved procedure occurred. This deity might appear to someone in a dream or vision revealing that he desired the full rite to be performed. The deity would give instructions to capture a girl for sacrifice. "The dreamer went to the keeper of the Morning Star bundle and received from him the warrior's costume kept in it. He then set out...and made a night attack on an enemy village. As soon as a girl of suitable age was captured the attack ceased and the war party returned" (Linton 1926:457). Prior to the attack itself a rite was held by the warriors who sang songs relative to the mythic origins of the rite. After capture the girl was placed in the charge of a chief and she was treated with kindness.

As soon as possible the rite of sacrifice took place. It lasted five days with the killing of the girl occurring on the fifth morning. Representatives from all thirteen villages attended. The first three days consisted of singing songs relative to the exploits of the Morning Star and of making offerings to the bundle. Priests of other bundles assisted. The girl was purified with smoke, painted red and dressed in a costume taken from the bundle. The captor also wore a special costume; he and his captive representing the Morning and the Evening stars. A sacred fire was kept burning throughout all of this time with the ends of four logs pointing out to the four directions. On the fourth night leaders sent a work party to fetch timbers for building a scaffold for the sacrifice. All spectators were dismissed from the ritual tipi and circles were drawn symbolic of the four quarters of the world. Spectators returned and the priests sang songs relative to the journey of the Morning Star while one danced with a war club and obliterated these designs. Priests then sang other songs, placing down a tally stick after the completion of each. This symbolized a game in which the girl was being "won" by the deity. The girl was undressed and painted red and black. Eventually four priests representing the directions each took a log and they pointed their blazing ends at the girl's armpits and groin. She was then covered with a blanket.

In the morning participants set off for the place of sacrifice where the scaffold had been built. The scaffold itself was very symbolic. Two upright stakes stood for the night and day. Four lower bars across its bottom were the directions and a top crosspiece was the sky. It was constructed in a rectangular excavation representing the earth (a mythic garden) and this, lined with eagle feathers, was seen as the source of all plant and animal life. Even up to the time of the sacrifice the girl was kept ignorant of her fate. She was made to climb the lower bars of the scaffold, stand on the top one, and have her hands tied to the upper crosspiece. Her clothes had been removed and two priests came with blazing sticks as the Morning Star appeared in the sky. They touched her lightly in the armpits and groin. Four other men also touched her with war clubs and then her captor shot her in the heart with an arrow taken from the sacred bundle. The main priest opened her chest and smeared his face with her blood while the captor caught the rest on dried meat which was burned as an offering to all the gods. Other participants also shot the dead girl and circled the scaffold four times before leaving. The priests remained and one removed the arrows and placed the body on the ground. Final songs described how the body would be eaten by animals and finally turned to earth. The purpose of this rather remarkable rite was group benefit. "...its real significance lies in the fact that the appeasing of this deity not only prevents the consumption of the earth through the fire of the sun, but causes the life of the earth to be renewed; even the earth itself is conceived of as being reborn" (Dorsey 1907:70). Rites of human sacrifice such as this must have been extremely rare among Plains peoples as indeed they were in general north of Mexico.

A somewhat more common Plains ritual was that of Eagle Trapping, a supernatural activity shared with many groups in the Southwest culture area and elsewhere. The technique seems to have been essentially the same for most groups and we will take the Mandan as a typical example. The right to engage in this behavior was based upon possession of a sacred bundle and was built, as so many rites were, upon mythic origins. One also gained general ownership of a lodge and special pits for capturing the eagles. Such rites in traditional times were apparently passed on to a man from his mother's brother although closeness of residence and other factors played a part. "The actual transfer of the bundle was a public event....Each legitimate participant at the transfer received payment for his attendance and prayed for the success of the purchaser. Instruction was received from the seller privately..." (Bowers 1973:231). Such acts were typical of bundle ownership in general.

In this ritual activity a bundle owner organized a trapping expedition and he and his party left the village for a remote location. This generally occurred in the fall. The main motive was to secure feathers for other ritual uses, much like the tobacco growing acts previously described for the Crow. Mandan apparently also hunted game for meat and hides at this time since the eagle trapping areas were not normally a focus of regular food exploitation. Even if one returned without feathers the hunting prospects made this endeavor worthwhile.

Once arriving in a proper area where one had the right to trap, the special lodge was erected or repaired. It was accompanied by a sweat lodge and tipis for women. A fireplace in the main structure was symbolic of the trapping pit and rites over the bundle occurred seeking to gain luck in the activity. Officers were selected like those of other societies and specific pits were assigned to members of the group. These pits were shallow depressions in the ground in which the trapper could lay covered over with sticks and brush. Bait was placed on top. When eagles landed they were seized by a leg and pulled in to be tied up. Evenings at the camp were spent in the recitation of myths and stories and the trappers themselves generally underwent some forms of self-torture, although some considered reclining in the pits all day to be enough suffering. This was called "suffering for the birds." Actual self-torture included pulling buffalo skulls by thongs attached to the body or hanging over a cliff tied up in the same way. Ordinarily only younger members were involved in these activities unless bad luck in eagle trapping required suffering as an offering to the birds themselves. The leader did not have a pit of his own but remained in camp as the director and main ritualist. The activity ended with a brief closing ritual at the first appearance of ice on the edges of streams and the party then returned to the village.

The Cheyenne give us an example of yet another rite, one which has equivalencies among other peoples. It was a bundle rite and for the Cheyenne specifically it was on the same level of importance as the Sun Dance. It was the Arrow Renewal Ceremony. Among these people this was a tribal bundle on which collective welfare was based. It was made out of fox skin and contained four sacred arrows; Medicine arrows. These had been given to the Cheyenne (in myth) by their culture hero deity, Sweet Medicine, who had himself received them from the highest creator god. Two of these arrows were thought to have power over buffalo and hence improved the hunting success relative to that animal. The other two arrows provided the Cheyenne with similar advantages over tribal enemies in battle. In both cases the arrows caused confusion and permitted easier killing. Thus the possession of this bundle and its periodic renewals assured these people of ultimate success in two important endeavors. "The Arrows are the Cheyennes greatest resource against their most besetting manifest anxieties: failure of the food supply and extermination by enemies. The Arrows, as the supernaturals' great gift to the Cheyennes, are their central insurance for survival" (Hoebel 1978:16). We can appreciate the centrality of this rite in their belief system.

The Medicine Arrow ceremony was held generally as an alternative to the Sun Dance on an every-other-year basis. It originated in the vow of an individual pledger along the same lines as the Sun Dance and this individual undertook to notify all the constituted bands of the tribe as to its time and location. As bands arrived together they pitched their tents in a great crescent opening towards the sun which was now at the summer solstice position. The forces generating and preserving life were believed to be at their highest at this time. The rite lasted four days. On the first day a special offering lodge was erected by the wife of the pledger. Its function was to serve as a collection point for offerings to the creator deity. Such gifts were hung from a pole outside. On this day too an especially large tipi was erected, the Medicine Arrow lodge itself. This was built by men of honor in the tribe. When erected, this tipi was then entered by the priests of the

Arrow bundle who prepared the usual altar and other associated paraphernalia. On the second day the priests again assembled. The pledger and other men ensured that the offering gifts were brought in and placed next to the altar. The pledger and three other men then went to a third structure – the tipi of the actual keeper of the sacred bundle. He gave this to them and they then ritually returned with it to the main lodge. The Arrow bundle was then opened by the priests and the arrows examined and refurbished if necessary.

The ceremony continued on the third day as sticks representing each Cheyenne family were collected and then placed near the altar. These were then individually purified in an incense fire to bring blessings upon all tribal members. On the last day of the ritual the sacred arrows themselves were exposed to the sun. The pledger placed them on a special pole and took this outside the tipi. The offerings were also brought out at this time to be placed beside them. At this point women and children were to remain sequestered in their tipis while all the males of the tribe, young and old alike, marched by the arrows to derive supernatural benefit from them. The main lodge was then taken apart, expanded, and rebuilt over the arrows. The new lodge represented the culture hero, Sweet Medicine. The arrows were now repacked in their container and returned to their keeper. That evening the highest chief of the Cheyenne, representing the culture hero, entered the structure along with all the tribal shamans and they sang four songs related to the associated myth. They finished these at daybreak and concluded the ceremony with a purifying sweat bath. These days were also occasions for shamans to renew their own power bundles or medicine artifacts. Like the Sun Dance, this Arrow renewal activity was an excellent device for also re-establishing a sense of tribal unity and common purpose. We can turn now to a somewhat more limited type of society and rite, one found equally developed among all Plains peoples. This was the woman's type of society.

Among the Mandan and Hidatsa seven such groups formerly existed, although this was the result of fusion between them. Originally the Mandan had a Gun society, River, Hay Woman and White Buffalo societies. The Hidatsa included the Skunk, Enemy, and Wild Goose groups. All of these were apparently joined by purchasing membership and rites and they may have been somewhat related to age groupings. Members assisted each other if necessary in women's daily tasks and some mutual recreation may have occurred. They were known chiefly however for their contribution of ritual acts for more public benefit. The Skunk, Gun, and Enemy societies aided in warfare. They had officers like men's groups and they may have been linked to specific male war societies. The Enemy women society, for example, performed to commemorate warriors who had fallen in battle and sang victory songs. They danced at the lodges of honored warriors and received presents from them. The River, Wild Goose, and White Buffalo groupings were more sacred in character and had to terminate their performances with special purification rites. They were "...associated with securing food through magical-religious means" (Lowie 1913:324). The Goose society specifically performed to aid the growth of corn and helped to attract buffalo herds in the fall. The White Buffalo society had a leader who was wrapped in the skin of a white buffalo cow. This was the sacred power object of the group. They functioned especially in the event of famine during the winter and were believed to be able to make the buffalo draw near the camp. They were called on to perform on the basis of a dream by a village member and danced for four nights. In the case of dire emergency they might dance every other night for a month. This may have been the most sacred of all women's groups and the membership may have been mostly composed of elderly women.

We can finish off this section on general ritual types in the Plains by mentioning one rite which had almost omnipresent existence among these peoples. This was the Sweat Lodge rite.

> Such a sweat bath is employed for its curative properties in cases of illness, and there is little doubt that it does possess such curative properties if properly used. However, a far greater ceremonial use is found for it among most tribes...a man is not considered fit to participate in certain of the major ceremonies, until he has undergone this ceremonial sweat, which is presumed to purify him spiritually, as well as cleanse him bodily. The entire ceremony is performed with a devout religious feeling... (Barnett 1921:80).

We can briefly note this practice among the Blackfoot.

The lodge itself was built of a dome-shaped framework of saplings about seven feet across. It was ordinarily employed many times, being covered with animal skins when used. A fire pit was built in its center as a kind of altar. An owner/priest brought a pipe and tobacco and his assistants heated stones and brought water. The priest sat opposite the door, facing east, and other participants entered. The leader made a prayer to the sun to ensure good luck. He might also waft incense over himself and the others. The pipe was lighted and its smoke blown towards the sun and to the earth. Other participants might also smoke and when all were finished the pipe ashes were scraped and placed in the center and on the four sides of the pit. Five hot stones were then placed near the ashes and then other stones piled in next to them. The priest would begin to sing an initial set of songs and then ladled water on the hot stones to obtain steam. Participants perspired heavily. As they became used to the intense heat larger amounts of water were added. More songs and prayers to the sun occurred and finally the covers would be raised and the nude participants would cool off and then leave the structure. We can now examine three remaining supernatural topics for the Indians of the Plains: life-cycle observances, shamanism and curing, and the nature of supernatural beings and objects.

The various rituals associated with the transition from birth to death differed considerably between the various tribes of Plains Indians. We can discuss a small number of very restricted examples to give some indication of these types of behaviors. Birth occasioned some ritual endeavors. Among the Crow, special women who "owned" herbal mixtures gave the mother an infusion to drink during childbirth to help this process and the husband and all males had to remain away so that their presence would not slow up the delivery. After the birth the mother was given some pemmican with fat and then several taboos covered her subsequent behavior for a short period. Part of the navel cord of the baby was kept and fastened to the cradleboard in which the child was placed, apparently in the effort to ensure good influences. When a child was born among the Omaha it was merely a living thing until it went through special rites giving it a location in the social space of these people and in the world as a whole. On the eighth day after birth a holy man came to the tipi of the child and offered a prayer to all the powers of the universe that the child would pass safely through the four stages of the life cycle; through the "hills of life." This placed the child in the world in general.

When the child was able to walk by itself it passed through a rite placing it in the context of the tribe. It walked into a special tipi and its feet were set on a stone. Here the child was again related to cosmic forces–wind for life and health, earth for wisdom, and fire for life-giving power. All was ultimately related to the tribe. As the child left the tipi it was given a new adult name and new moccasins. It was now a full member of the social group. If the child was female she then joined her mother, if it was male he now underwent a supplemental rite to make him into a warrior. This was called the Webashna rite–"to cut the hair." A priest would cut a tuft of hair from the boy's head and place it in a skin bag while singing a song that explained the ritual. "The severing of the lock was an act that implied the consecration of the life of the boy to the symbol of power that controlled the life and death of the warrior..." (Fletcher and LaFlesche 1972:122). He would now die in life as the will of the gods decreed. This rite generally occurred in the spring. Equivalent rites rook place among most Plains groups indicating a rather greater concern over supernaturally shaping the child in early life than at the time of actual birth.

The next stage for boys was generally the vision quest, the mechanics of which have already been discussed. For girls, the next equivalent stage occurred with the onset of menstruation and took the general form of a puberty ritual. Among the Oglala "They are important because it is at this time that a young girl becomes a woman, and she must understand the meaning of this change and must be instructed in the duties which she is now to fulfill" (Brown 1971:116). This was conceived of as a social change not only since she would now be able to bear children but because her "power" also needed control for fear it would disturb the powers of priests and others. Soon after the event of menstruation occurred the father of the girl requested a Wakan person to perform the requisite ceremony. Very briefly, a new tipi was constructed with an altar inside and many sacred objects. The priest dressed like a buffalo since deities related to that animal were thought to guard over young women. A crowd of observers entered the tipi. After a number of ritual maneuvers including smoking a sacred pipe, the priest instructed the girl in her role as a woman, how to be of benefit to the tribe, and to avoid all evil influences. He then played the role of a bull buffalo and she imitated a cow. While others sang he feigned mating with her in an animal fashion. She then drank special medicine water. She was given new clothing, a hairdo, and face painting symbolic of her new maturity. After this a feast was put on in her honor.

Prior to this "coming out" rite she was apparently secluded, as were older women during subsequent menstrual periods. Other groups might not elaborate on girl's puberty to this degree, a simple notice of the event being considered sufficient. All, however, did seclude women at such times either in the family tipi after removal of sacred objects or, if this was impractical, in a small shelter nearby. Among the Crow, "Such women...abstained from meat for four days, their sustenance being wild roots. When they recovered, they bathed, got new clothes, smoked them over a fire of evergreen leaves, put them on and returned to their homes" (Lowie 1956:45). Other groups enforced similar taboos. Cheyenne women, for example, had to eat only roasted meat and ride a mare rather than a horse if the camp was on the move.

At the end of the life cycle death also occasioned ritual activities. Among the Cheyenne close relatives of the deceased would prepare his body for burial, dressing it in good clothing and wrapping it up in buffalo skin robes. This bundle was then removed from the camp and disposed of by placing it either in a tree or on a wooden scaffold; the most common Plains forms. Less often, graves were used or the body was placed in a cave. A favorite horse was often sacrificed nearby but most other property was usually given away to friends and relatives. In fact, the whole camp gathered at the tipi of the deceased at the time of death and a close relative threw things from it. Eventually even the tipi itself was dismantled and disposed of. Those persons close to the deceased "...cut their hair short, gashed their heads, and sometimes the calves of their legs, with knives. Sometimes they cut off a finger" (Grinnell 1972:161). Much wailing also occurred at the site of disposal. Inflicting injuries and crying were common Plains death elements. For the Cheyenne, all these procedures were done rather hurriedly due to the fear of the ghost which might harm the living; especially small children. Ultimately the soul or spirit of the dead person traveled the Milky Way to an afterlife or camp of the dead among the stars. This also was a common belief among Plains peoples. Among the Omaha, for example, there were seven spirit worlds beyond the Milky Way and the deceased apparently lived for a time in each. The Omaha and some other tribes also kept a fire burning near the body for nights to cheer the soul as it traveled to the next life. Some groups went immediately on the warpath to relieve the grief occasioned by death.

At least some groups did not have the ghost fear of the Cheyenne. The Oglala, it will be remembered, had a Ghost Keeping rite as one of their basic ceremonies. If a favorite son died, his family might elect to perform this rite so that his soul would not travel to the sky but remain near the camp for a few years. A family wishing such a state of affairs would engage a Wakan person who would cut off a lock of hair from the deceased person prior to the disposal of the body. The father then had to observe many taboos to avoid the danger inherent in this situation. These included living separately from his wife and family and not fighting in war. A special tipi was erected for the ghost and the hair lock was put in a special bag which was eventually placed inside this structure. The ghost bundle then required constant care. It was fed ritually and the bundle placed in the sun on warm days. A special horse was used to carry it when the camp moved. All during this time the family involved made a collection of articles to be eventually given away. And they continued to mourn the deceased. Presently a Wakan person was selected to make a special spirit post to represent the dead person. This was erected inside the special tipi and a crowd gathered. The post was embraced, the spirit was released and the collected possessions of the family were given away. So death necessitated various ritual activities. As it was seldom welcomed other ritual endeavors were practiced in the attempt to prevent or circumvent it. Since these involve shamanism and curing we can now turn to those topics.

Shamans as a type of supernatural practitioner or "technician of the sacred" occurred in the Plains as elsewhere even though many people did possess types of power. "At the opposite pole from those unable to gain a personal vision were the Indians who, as demonstrated by their conspicuous success, had obtained exceptional power from the spirits....The services rendered to tribesmen included curing the sick, discovering the whereabouts of the enemy, and helping to recover lost or stolen property" (Lowie 1963:175-76). So they functioned in this culture area as they did elsewhere in North America. In most Plains groups such exceptional individuals formed themselves into societies based either on the similarity of power-giving vision experiences or on desire to receive comparable instruction and training. Because this chapter has discussed a number of types of groups or societies and they may merge together in the mind of the reader, we will confine the shaman's example to one tribe.

The Omaha had five or more societies that specialized in curing the sick and related activities. Reo Fortune (1932) and others have characterized these along the following lines. In these societies the leaders generally had the most powers in the group and many members were apparently simply taught the original vision of the founder and the associated songs, ritual movements, and herbs, and given a medicine bundle. A strong tendency may have existed for such privileges to be passed on to relatives along family lines. One such grouping was called the Grizzly Bear-Rattlesnake society after the two supernatural patrons who gave power to the members. They may originally have been separate groups who either merged due to declining membership in historic times or due to similarities in the techniques of their curing and range of illnesses treated. In both cases some kind of "liquid" was believed to be responsible for the problems and its removal by some form of sucking effected the cure.

In the Bear division of this society the physical symptoms involved swollen limbs, pains in them, rheumatism, and related difficulties. Three or four shamans worked together in treatment by bleeding the patient by sucking blood into a buffalo horn by placing the tip against the affected part. In addition to curing, the Bears did a public dance mimicking bears and they performed many tricks by slight of hand, for example thrusting wands down their throats. The Snake division of this society cured stomach disorders by sucking "snake" poison from the patient's stomach and then spitting it away. Such poison was believed to originate either in the air itself or from an actual snake if a person had passed too closely to it. Both types of shamans were somewhat feared as possibly responsible for the difficulties they cured. Women may also have been members of this society.

A second main group was the Buffalo society. Both males and females belonged to this group and it is possible that persons belonging to other societies might also hold membership here. These shamans treated open wounds primarily through their knowledge of plant medicines; primarily ground up roots mixed with water. Members would take such a mixture in their mouths and then blow it onto their patient's wounds. They might also dance to assure speedy recovery. This society also might have performed for more public benefit. If the corn lacked necessary rain for growth they would fill a vessel with medicine water and dance around it. One member would drink some, spit it in the air, and then knock over the container. The others would drink off the ground and spit that in the air as well to cause rain.

A third group was the Ghost society. The supernatural patrons of these shamans were ghosts and the members treated patients who evidenced unconsciousness, paralysis, delirium, or insanity; all problems resulting from ghost contact. Treatment involved sprinkling hot water to the sides of the tipi door of the patient, hanging cornhusks there, stroking the ill person, and rubbing him with medicine water. Much of this was apparently intended to deflect such ghostly influence. Members were also thought to be able to foretell future events, especially death. Disagreement occurs as to whether this society was derived from outside the tribe, possibly from the Ponca, and if women were formerly permitted membership.

Most of the other illnesses treated by Omaha shamans fell to the Water Monster society, a group with a large membership made up of people from other groups and a core of people who may have belonged to it alone. The extraction of disease objects was the principle technique here and ultimate power was derived from the water monster, Wakandagi. A great deal of confusion concerns the actual organization of this group. This society may ultimately be derived from the outside introduction of a Midewiwin type of group (see Chapter 16) from the Sauk and Fox. The Omaha split this curing society into two groups, the shell and pebble societies. The supernatural patron of both was the same, the water monster who gave power to inject sea shells and pebbles into other persons and to extract them and both groups had dances, the public parts of which involved shooting objects into other members and their removal. This dramatized their powers.

The shell group however may have been an organization of chiefs and their kin, perhaps five separate circles of leaders and followers being involved. The actual shamans may have been limited to the pebble group. Only the latter could cure persons who were not society members. In either society membership seems to have been by purchase or by taking the place of a deceased member. The shells and other objects owned by the members were kept in special skin bags and ultimately represented a metaphysical arrow inside one's stomach. One could project this through the medium of a shell or pebble in a kind of sorcery fashion and extract it from oneself and in some cases from others.

Most Plains tribes had curing societies of one sort or another, a few also had an activity also found to the north and east of this area called the shaking tent rite. We can conclude the ritual aspects of this chapter with a brief description of it. This shamanistic behavior occurred among the Gros Ventre (as well as the Blackfoot and Assiniboine). For the former group, to be a shaman practicing the shaking tent rite one had to have a ghost as a guardian spirit, a Tsatsawa. Rather than obtaining such a helper in the vision quest, the ghost of a relative would be drawn to a descendant who kept a memento of the deceased. The ghost would appear and give knowledge to the shaman. "No one lacking a ghost helper could conduct the shaking tent rite, no matter how great power he had received by fasting and crying, and no matter what guardian spirit or spirits he had acquired" (Cooper 1944:62). Such power might not be transferred, unlike regular vision quest power. The function of the ghost helper was primarily divinatory, to give knowledge of past, present, and future and in the diagnosis of illness.

If a person wished to avail himself of such knowledge he sought out this type of shaman and offered him a pipe as a request for aid. The rite occurred at night in the performer's lodge. The shaman remained behind a blanket hung up to partition off a special stage within it. The shaman was bound up with thongs in a very secure manner and was also rolled up in a blanket. He then sang a song to call his ghost helper and a whistling sound would be heard signaling its arrival. As the ghost entered the lodge it would shake. The ghost then blew away the bonds of the shaman; the ropes being put into a tight ball and then thrown out to the others in the lodge. The voice of the ghost would be heard inquiring as to the information desired by the client. The ghost might give an immediate answer or have to travel for a time to obtain it. Answers were given in either a normal language form or in "whistle talk." A food offering was made to it and the ghost left, the tent again shaking upon its exit. The shaman would then emerge from behind his closed off area, pray, and eat the food offering left from the ghost. We can turn now to one last element in Plains religion.

We can conclude this chapter by making some general observations on the nature of supernatural beings and objects beyond those previously discussed. It has been pointed out earlier that the religion of the Plains Indians was highly individualistic. As a result of the variety of personal vision experiences, the number of supernatural beings and objects were both ill-defined and infinite. Sacredness encompassed a wide range of phenomena and was connected to individual persons in different ways. We can discuss briefly three examples of supernatural beings and one of objects.

Among the Crow Indians the Sun was perhaps the closest deity to a supreme being. This god was also the oldest such conception among these people and most other Plains tribes. For the Crow specifically, the Sun was at least partially merged for creative purposes with Old Man Coyote, a culture hero from whom most human institutions were thought to have been derived.

> Old-Man-Coyote, apart from his mythical exploits and pranks, is as indefinite a being as the Sun, with whom he is so frequently identified. In mythology it is important to note that he is not represented as a coyote...most commonly he appears as a human character and is occasionally called by the...designation of First-worker, which of course has no animal suggestions (Lowie 1922:320).

The Sun was generally addressed as Uncle and was often appealed to in vision quests although its remoteness apparently generally precluded its appearance to such seekers. Nonetheless this deity received more offerings than others. The sweat lodge was often held in its honor, prayers before war activities, and even entreaties for hunting. White buffalo calves were also killed and their skin ritually offered, accompanied by requests for coups and horses or freedom from illness. Desires for longevity were also frequent requests.

There are other deities mentioned in the literature. The Moon, addressed as grandmother, appears frequently in myth and did appear in visions. The Morning Star was considered a deity as was the Dipper. The former was associated specifically with the Tobacco society and the latter was originally seven brothers who were unhappy with earthly things and became a being that could last forever. The Dipper made frequent appearances in visions. The Four Winds were another set of natural phenomena considered divine, as was the Thunder, associated as elsewhere with the eagle (Thunderbird). Other beings also existed.

In addition to the individualization of theology making such beings difficult to precisely identify among the Crow, there is the notion of supernatural power or efficacy in general. The Crow term for this is Maxpe, which is generally equivalent to Wakan among the Dakota. The above-mentioned gods have this power but it applies to persons and objects as well. Deities are merely more personified, concrete manifestations of Maxpe but it is such a diffuse entity that these merge with more shadowy entities that often appear in visions and with objects. Maxpe refers to qualities that transcend the ordinary, particularly the power to accomplish extraordinary things. Clearly, as we have seen, humans, in the vision quest, can attain such power. So for the Crow the dividing line between deity and human being is often impossible to draw. We will see similar definitional difficulties when we discuss supernatural objects among these people.

As a second brief example of deities we can turn to the Omaha and Ponca as reported on by George Dorsey (1890). Among these peoples a number of beings were the objects of prayers. Such activities were often formal and involved raising the arms with the palms facing the deity or power, presenting a pipe with the mouthpiece in the same direction, using pipe smoke or incense, mentioning the name of the deity in question, wailing or crying, and the use of offerings. The most ideal locations for such acts were high bluffs and mountains. The list of deities so worshipped was much like that of the Crow, ranging from those clearly personified to more unclear types.

> The ancestors of the Omaha and Ponka believed that there was a Supreme Being, whom they called Wakanda....They did not know where He was, nor did they undertake to say how He existed. There was no...general assembly for the purpose of offering Him worship and prayer. Each person thought in his heart that Wakanda existed. Some addressed the sun as Wakanda, though many did not so regard him....Some worshipped the Thunder-being under this name....They say they have never seen Wakanda, so they cannot pretend to personify Him... (Dorsey 1890:372).

We witness here the same theological uncertainty seen elsewhere.

Sometimes for these people seven "great" Wakandas were suggested as foremost in importance: Darkness, Warmth/the upper world, Ground, the Thunder being, the Sun, the Moon, and the Morning Star. Other stars were also worshipped, along with the winds. The Omaha and Ponca also believed in a number of water monsters with long bodies and horns on their heads. These dwelled beneath the cliffs underground and in the Missouri River. These could cause harm to unwary humans by trapping them and making them insane. There were also numbers of similar beings in forests. Among these peoples the Thunder being was very important and was invoked in the spring for general benefit as well as in warfare. It should also be mentioned here that if the Moon appeared to a vision seeker the possibility was very great that he would be tricked into receiving the wrong kind of power/destiny and would thereafter have to become a berdache – a person who had to act and dress like a woman. So even "great" powers may have had less beneficial aspects.

Among the Oglala the universe was also defined as being controlled by the supernatural. Beings and powers abound, some benevolent and others more evil in intention towards humans. As Powers (1977) describes them, these people saw in their concept of Wakantanka the collective sum of supernatural power that existed. They called this "great mystery." Aspects of this embodiment might be more specifically personified, as elsewhere, into concrete beings or powers. Apparently some sixteen major expressions formerly existed plus a great number of additional lesser types. Some of these were the objects of formal worship and of vision quests, others were of more purely mythic significance. The main expressions were grouped into a hierarchy consisting of four sets of four: Superior Wakan, associates of these, Lesser Wakan, and those similar to them. In the first category was such as the Sun, Sky, and Earth; associates of these included the Moon, Wind, and the Thunder being. Lesser types are illustrated by the Buffalo and Bear. Those similar included Life or Breath itself, showing again the diffuseness of Plains conceptions of the supernatural. A great many other spirit conceptions also existed. Some were identified with specific locations – water, forests, and in the dwellings themselves. Others, such as Inktomi, the spider, are culture hero/trickster types who transcend geography. "Together, the supernaturals abide in the universe, and specialists may call upon them so that the common people may live in harmony with that which is otherwise inexplicable" (Powers 1977:54). We may now briefly consider supernatural objects.

There were a great number of objects considered as sacred by the Crow. Since most deserved this characterization, as we have seen, from the vision experience, their number was almost unlimited. The concepts involved, however, differed from person to person in terms of the immediacy of content. To the vision seeker, his medicine bundle was a gift from the supernatural as were other categories of objects to those who originally made or discovered them. To other individuals the true sacredness of such items came secondhand. If an object brought success to its owner then it was considered a genuine article and might be purchased or perhaps borrowed in times of emergency, for example as in the case of a war bundle. Copies could also be made of some of these objects. In such cases the original owner could make and transfer up to four copies – along with taboos and associated ritual – before his own rights and the original efficacy was lost.

Some of these objects were more important than others but it is hard to place them in specific categories. Such an attempt is as elusive as with the supernatural beings themselves. "In a certain sense it seems artificial to segregate one class of Crow Medicines as 'bundles.' Literally all medicines are bundles, i.e., wrapped up aggregations of sacred objects...on the other hand...from a comparative point of view it seems proper to separate those medicines which are not only physically more complex but have greater dignity and even tribal significance" (Lowie 1922:391). Such would include the Sun Dance bundle, a Medicine Arrow bundle, and certain tobacco society medicines. Of lesser scope than these would be the bundles created by vision seekers for more personal success, although visions were probably associated with the creation of tribal bundles as well. On a somewhat different level were "medicine rocks." These were stones that had in their appearance some suggestions of an animal, particularly the head. They were usually simply discovered by a person and were considered, due to their shape, as being powerful in their own right, although there is some suggestion that they may have been considered as part of a primordial earth spirit. Such stones were wrapped up in bundles along with other objects and were prayed to for wealth and long life. They were generally not sold like vision bundles but were passed on to descendants.

Another class of Crow sacred objects was the designs painted on tipis. These involved various patterns and designs but their function was essentially the same.

> Painted tipis were of course revealed in visions. Returning from his experience, the visionary would have some men gather, had the buffalo-skin cover spread out and the paint lying about ready for use. Then he would say, 'I saw this fasting on a mountain,' and would give a full description of his vision. He would close with some such words as 'I am painting this tent on behalf of the Crow. You will fare well, horses and scalps will come into our camp from everywhere (Lowie 1922:401).

Along the same lines were the shields used in warfare and as status symbols; since their designs were also revealed in visions. Their prime function was the protection of the user and a person might borrow one to take into combat; promising the owner a gift if successful. They were generally made of buffalo-hide and, in addition to painted designs, feathers and other objects might be attached to them. These also were usually inherited by kin.

Despite great variations in manifestation, supernatural objects and beings or powers were clearly as impressive to the Crow as they were to other Plains groups. Their possession and propitiation were clearly necessary to ensure success in life.

This chapter has examined several of the main features of Plains Indians religion. These have included the Vision Quest, the Sun Dance, rituals connected to sacred bundles, societies having mystical aspects, shamanism, and the life-cycle observances. We have also briefly noted data on supernatural beings and objects. It becomes clear that compared to some other culture areas there was a profound content of individualism found in Plains religious patterns. Plains peoples, especially males, were highly desirous of obtaining and supplementing a store of supernatural power; to gain abilities taking them beyond a normal human range in hunting, warfare, and in other activities. That they might use these powers for the benefit of other persons as shamans and in luring buffalo, or in war, does not alter the situation of a desire for personal benefit. Even in more public rites, those having a context of group benefit or value, opportunities were provided for the pursuit of more purely personal ends. We have seen cases of this in the Sun Dance and in Eagle Trapping rites, among others.

Another major emphasis was on the renewal of the earth and its plants and animals. Major rites such as the Sacred Arrow ceremony of the Cheyenne, the Sun Dance everywhere, and the Pawnee Morning Star sacrifice reflected this. On a more specific level the renewal of lances and other paraphernalia by military and related societies also suggest the desire for humans to gain at least a degree of control over environmental concerns. So such procedures carried over into the refurbishing of sacred power objects themselves. A third major element was the formation of societies which on one level at least functioned as a corrective for the more individualistic aspects of supernatural life. These groups, which seem hyperdeveloped in the Plains, provided a collective approach to the supernatural which not only gave unity of sacred functions, for example in growing sacred tobacco, but often carried over into more secular affairs as well; witness the bundle scheme of the Mandan providing governmental stability.

Lastly, we may remark on the diffuseness of supernatural belief itself; on the lack of formally defined and agreed upon deities or powers. This was certainly a reflection of the strong individualistic tendency commented on bove and surely provoked the very commonly held notion of the existence of generalized power–Wakan, Maxpe–which might be found in all things, including humans. Other aspects of Plains behavior do not seem exceptional when compared to other parts of North America, although we will discuss some comparative aspects in a later chapter. We can turn now to a pair of culture areas where religious beliefs and behaviors were somewhat simpler and the diversity of tribal groups less confusing; the Arctic and Subarctic.

PLAINS BIBLIOGRAPHY AND REFERENCES

Barnett, S. A.

1921. The Blackfoot Sweat Lodge. *Yearbook of the Public Museum of the City of Milwaukee* 1:73-80.

Beckworth, M. W.

1938. Mandan-Hidatsa Myths and Ceremonies. *Memoirs of the American Folklore Society* 32:1-320.

Benedict, Ruth F.

1922. The Vision in Plains Culture. *American Anthropologist* 24:1-23.

Bowers, A. W.

1973. Mandan Social and Ceremonial Organization. Chicago: University of Chicago Press.

Brown, Joseph Epes.

1971. The Sacred Pipe. Baltimore: Penguin Books.

Cooper, John M.

1956. The Gros Ventres of Montana, #2 Religion and Ritual. *Catholic University of America Anthropology Series* 16.

1944. The Shaking Tent Rite Among Plains and Forest Algonquians. *Primitive Man* 17:60-84.

Dorsey, G. A.

1907. The Skidi Rite of Human Sacrifice. *International Congress of Americanists* 15:65-70.

1905. The Cheyenne. *Field Museum of Natural History Anthropological Series*. Volume 9.

1903. The Arapaho Sun Dance. *Field Museum of Natural History Anthropological Series* 4:1-228.

Dorsey, D. O.

1890. A Study of Siouan Cults. *Bureau of American Ethnology*, Annual Report 11:361-422.

1882. Omaha Sociology. *Bureau of American Ethnology*, Annual Report 3:205-370.

Ewers, John C.

1958. The Blackfoot. Norman: University of Oklahoma Press.

1955. The Bear Cult Among the Assinibone and Their Neighbors of the Northern Plains. *Southwestern Journal of Anthropology* 11:1-14.

Fletcher, Alice C.
1904. The Hako: A Pawnee Ceremony. *Bureau of American Ethnology, Annual Report* 22:13-368.

Fletcher, Alice C. and La Flesche, Francis.
1972. The Omaha Tribe. (2 Volumes.) Lincoln: University of Nebraska Press.

Fortune, R. F.
1932. Omaha Secret Societies. *Columbia University Contributions to Anthropology* 14:1-193.

Gilmore, M. R.
1931. The Sacred Bundles of the Arikara. *Papers of the Michigan Academy of Science, Arts, and Letters* 16:33-50.

Grinnell, George B.
1972. The Cheyenne Indians. (2 Volumes.) Lincoln: University of Nebraska Press.

1910. The Great Mysteries of the Cheyenne. *American Anthropologist* 12:542-75.

Hoebel, E. A.
1978. The Cheyennes. New York: Holt, Rinehart and Winston.

Hoebel, E. A. and Wallace E.
1952. The Comanches. Norman: University of Oklahoma Press.

Kroeber, A. L.
1902. The Arapaho. *Bulletin of the American Museum of Natural History* 18:1-279, 299-454.

Linton, Ralph.
1935. The Comanche Sun Dance. *American Anthropologist* 37:420-28.

1926. The Origin of the Skidi Pawnee Sacrifice to the Morning Star. *American Anthropologist* 28:457-66.

Lowie, Robert
1963. Indians of the Plains. Garden City: Natural Press.

1956. The Crow Indians. New York: Holt, Rinehart and Winston.

1922. The Religion of the Crow Indians. *Anthropology Publications of the American Museum of Natural History* 25:309-444.

1916. Plains Indian Age Societies. *Anthropology Publications of the American Museum of Natural History* 16:877-992.

1915. The Sun Dance of the Crow Indians. *Anthropology Publications of the American Museum of Natural History* 16:1-50.

1913. Military Societies of the Crow Indians. *Anthropology Publications of the American Museum of Natural History* 11:143-217.

Mails, Thomas E.
1973. Dog Soldiers, Bearmen and Buffalo Women. Englewood Cliffs: Prentice-Hall.

McClintock, Walter.
1937-1938. Blackfoot Warrior Societies. *Masterkey* 11:148-58, 198 204; 12:11-23.

Murie, J. R.
1914. Pawnee Indian Societies. *Anthropology Publications of the American Museum of Natural History* 11:543-644.

Parsons, E. C.
1941. Notes of the Caddy. *Memoirs of the American Anthropological Association* 57:1-76.

Powers, William K.
1977. Oglala Religion. Lincoln: University of Nebraska Press.

Spier, Leslie.
1921. The Sun Dance of the Plain Indians. *Anthropology Publications of the American Museum of Natural History* 16:451-527.

Walker, J. R.
1917. The Sun Dance and Other Ceremonies of the Oglala. *Anthropology Publications of the American Museum of Natural History* 16:51-221.

Weltfish, Gene.
1965. The Lost Universe. New York: Basic Books.

Will, G. F.
1934. Notes on the Arikara and Their Ceremonies. Denver: Old West Series 3:5-48.

Will, G. F. and Spinden, H. J.
1906. The Mandans. Harvard Peabody Museum Papers 3:81-219.

Wissler, Clark.
1918. The Sun Dance of the Blackfoot Indians. *Anthropology Publications of the American Museum of Natural History* 16:223-70.

1913. Societies and Dance Associations of the Blackfoot Indians. *Anthropology Publications of the American Museum of Natural History* 11:359-460.

1912. Societies and Ceremonial Associations in the Oglala Division of the Teton Dakota. *Anthropology Publications of the American Museum of Natural History* 11:1-97.

CHAPTER XII

THE ARCTIC AND SUBARCTIC CULTURE AREAS

The Arctic and Subarctic culture areas occupied the northern regions of North America and offered difficult environments for human adaptation. That the native inhabitants were so successful at survival there is a testimony not only to their physical stamina and courage but also to their keen understanding of environmental potentials and the technological "know-how" of these peoples. We can discuss each of these areas in turn to gain a partial understanding of their cultures.

The Arctic culture area included the Aleutian Islands, almost all of the Alaskan coast, the Canadian Arctic (only inland a short distance in some cases), and restricted parts of Greenland. The native peoples who lived there were the Eskimo of various types and the Aleut who were a slightly different people. Both groups were latecomers into the New World and they had developed specialized hunting cultures. Only one language family, Eskimoan, exists in this lengthy area. It is divided into two divisions: Eskimo and Aleut, which diverged from each other several thousand years ago. Eskimo itself is divided into western and eastern branches.

The Eskimo environment was a cold "desert." Usually treeless and barren, the Arctic has long, cold winters and short summers during which the tundra (due to the permafrost) becomes boggy and difficult to traverse. There is little drinking water and the seasonal contrasts of light and darkness add to difficulties in summer and winter. Raw materials for tools and other technological items often were limited to bone and driftwood. Resources in general were richer in the west, especially in south and west Alaska, and population density, never very high, was greater there. Throughout the area the Eskimo depended upon wild animals as the basis for their existence, plants being few and short in season or inedible by humans. Game included seals of many species, whale, walrus, caribou, musk ox, fish, and various wild birds including the ptarmigan. Polar bears and others, foxes, wolves, and the like, were also killed; not always for their food value. Not all resources were available to all groups in the same proportions.

While a few groups specialized on marine or on land food resources most groups planned nomadic itineraries so that most available animals might be used for food. The Netsilik, for example, spent the winter on the frozen sea ice hunting seals and sea birds. In the spring they moved to dry land to fish for salmon and lake trout from stone weirs and to repair summer equipment. They then moved deeper inland for more fish and to anticipate the arrival of large herds of caribou which became their late summer staple food as well as being useful for hides. These were taken by a variety of techniques. In late fall musk ox were hunted. Stored fish and caribou meat contributed to the diet at this time and winter equipment was made or repaired. By November they were moving back to the ice for sealing once again.

Eskimo dwellings differed by area and by season. Cold, windy winters demanded substantial heat retaining structures. Most typical were domeshaped houses made of driftwood, whale bones, or stones covered with sod and with entrance passages. In Canadian areas or when traveling, the famous snow house or igloo, often lined with animal skins, was the usual type. Summer dwellings were mostly tents. Ritual structures were also made. House furniture was meager; an earth or snow bench covered with moss or skins; a stone lamp with oil for light and a little heat were most common. Clothing, usually of caribou skin with tailored arms and legs and worn in layers with the inner fur towards the body and the outer fur outside, surely helped these people cope with their winter environment. Waterproof suits of seal intestine also occurred. Other items of material culture included thirty-foot, open-skin boats called umiaks, used when traveling or whaling, and a short, ten-foot, covered skin boat; the kayak. The latter was used by individual hunters in both summer and winter. A dog sled also aided transport. It was made of driftwood ingeniously fastened together, with runners of bone or wood and was drawn by a small team of dogs. The driver walked behind this and his wife often broke trail.

Eskimo social organization was based on the family and on other small groups modified in size by the seasonal demands of their hunting style of life. Kinship was traced through both the father's and mother's sides cognatically. The basic family unit was the nuclear type based on monogamy in marriage. Girls generally married about age fourteen, boys somewhat later after mastering the difficult skills connected to hunting. Because of the one-sidedness of the food contributions of men, female infanticide was often practiced. It should be added that old age was also a difficult stage and "senilicide" was often practiced when, at the end of the life cycle, the elderly were no longer capable of making sufficient contributions to the group. Marriage partners were chosen on the basis of technological abilities and no formal rites existed. Divorce was correspondingly easy. Types of extended families, with sons or a son-in-law remaining with one set of parents, existed as the usual summertime exploiting group. Such was the basic food-sharing unit. One might also depend upon those relatives who lived close enough to give aid. In the winter a band formed out of those who camped together. This maximal unit would change membership somewhat from year to year. Individual men might also have one or two non-kin who were special sharing partners for food or task cooperation. Such relations helped provide integration to keep a band together. Special joking partners who exchanged wives also occurred in some groups as well as trading partners in other groups.

In all these Eskimo groups leadership was most informal, being on a headman/respected person level. People listened to their leaders due to their knowledge; out of a sense of their own best interest. Often such men were simply family elders. Among the values they donated to their groups was their ability to reconcile differences among quarreling individuals whom they requested to settle such problems for the common good. Such quarrels were infrequent and arose from mockery, jealousy, or wife stealing. If the entreaties of such leaders were insufficient, the parties involved might engage in a fist fight or try to shame each other in song contests. A real public nuisance might be killed if a consensus developed to sanction this extreme of behavior. If a "crime" had any supernatural aspects the spirits were thought to be involved in punishment. Perhaps most quarrels were dealt with by the expedient of one party simply joining up with a different group. Warfare was generally limited, being mostly of a defensive nature against non-Eskimo neighbors.

The Eskimo, who called themselves the Innuit–"people"–were the best known of Arctic culture area peoples. The Aleut, who lived in the Aleutian Islands portion of it, are less well represented in the literature. They too thought of themselves as "the people" (Unangan) and shared many traits with their Eskimo neighbors in Alaska. Their islands, some one hundred or more, are washed by the Japan Current making their Arctic niche one of rain, fog, and little sun, but seasonally warm. They lived in villages located along the coasts of islands where access to fresh water and a lookout point for hunting and to prevent surprise attacks was considered essential. Each village consisted of one or more large semi-underground communal houses called Barabaras. These were covered with sod roofs and each family had its own compartment inside. Up to one hundred fifty people might comprise such a population.

Some of their food resources were equivalent to those of the Eskimo and they secured these by making trips out from their permanent villages. Seals and whales were important as well as the sea otter. A greater variety of fish were taken including many that appeared in seasonal runs. Shellfish were very abundant and were a dietary staple as were a variety of bird species: ducks, geese, puffins, ptarmigans, and others. The Aleut also foraged for the eggs of birds as well as having berries, bulbs, and roots available at certain seasons. Both open and covered skin boats were used and their skill in handling kayaks was apparently exceptional. Clothing was often made of bird skins. No dogs or sleds existed and many hunting techniques differed from those of the Eskimo. Their social organization was focused on the village level where members were often cognatic kinsmen. Leaders were skilled older men and there may have been informal councils to organize the quest for food, maintain law and order, and to protect the group against enemies. Aboriginal Aleut culture disappeared rather early in contact times. We can turn now to the Subarctic culture areas.

The Subarctic region crosses North America south of the Arctic culture area. It spreads from the interior of Alaska to the Atlantic Coast and represents a very harsh environment. The winters are long and cold, often colder than the Arctic, and the summers are short and masses of blackflies and other insects make this season difficult to tolerate. Throughout this vast hinterland tribal culture was very simple, based on the hunting and gathering of local resources. The area is divided linguistically at Hudson's Bay. Peoples in the West spoke Athabascan languages and perhaps represent rather recent arrivals into the New World. Some of these people were pressing south in historic times; escaping this forbidding area. In the East, Algonkian languages were spoken. These people had been in North America for a long time and had been pushed into the Subarctic by related groups to the south. Many of these groups were extinct in contact times while those more to the west survived due to their greater isolation from European pressure.

A number of animal species occurred in various places throughout this area. Moose, elk, musk ox, and caribou (mostly of the woodland variety) were big game along with deer and bear. Beaver, rabbits, and other small game, often taken with ingenious traps and snares, helped round out the diet. Wild fowl of various types existed. Fish were a variable resource. They were a supplement for some groups and for those in the West who were fortunate to live along salmon-filled streams they were a seasonal bonanza. A few berries and other wild plants also contributed to the diet. Overall, however, famine may have been more common here than elsewhere in North America. Dwellings differed in this culture area. Perhaps most common was a pole tipi structure covered with skin, bark, or mats of vegetation and heaped-up snow during the winter. Despite appearing rather insubstantial these were made fairly warm due to the abundance of forests used for firewood, the collecting of which was an unending job for women. Some peoples who settled more permanently had small log cabins. Tailored clothing occurred. Transport was primarily by snowshoes in winter and bark canoes in summer. Simple toboggans were found among some groups. Containers of bark and skin were also used.

Social life in the Subarctic focused on the family and on the quest for food. As in the Arctic there was no real sense of tribal identity or cohesion. The largest groups were bands that wandered over hunting territories. Some of these groups were unrestricted in the sense that not all the members ever came together; merely wandering erratically as families or local groups on a seasonal focus. Other groups did have a central base and spent part of the year together. In difficult times a man might even go off by himself for weeks to secure food. In times of stress, cannibalism did occur. The family was basically of the nuclear type although a very successful and admired hunter might be polygynous at any one time and the appropriating of other men's wives was common for some groups. Couples usually resided in either local group of their parents except in the West where a tendency towards matrilocal residence occurred.

Children had to grow up quickly in this area and life was often difficult for all, especially women, who had many tasks assigned, to them and the aged, who were often treated poorly. Leadership was on an informal level with headmen who functioned to keep the peace and to direct any group hunting procedures. Such men were usually outstanding hunters or they were thought to have supernatural abilities. Their positions lasted only as long as they maintained a sense of respect for their abilities. Warfare on a rather limited level occurred for most groups. Revenge for trespass of hunting territory was a common motive as was the appropriation of women. No honor or rank system existed such as was noted for the Plains area. We can turn now to consideration of religious beliefs and behaviors for the Arctic and Subarctic culture areas.

CHAPTER XIII

ESKIMO-ALEUT RELIGION

Eskimo religion has been rather adequately reported upon in a great many publications. Since the Aleut are known only poorly, the bulk of this chapter has been devoted to the beliefs and rituals of the former peoples. If one were to assess the basic tenor of Eskimo behavior with a brief characterization one might say that, positively, they attempted to control the security of their food supply by engaging in hunting rituals and magic and that, negatively, they attempted to avoid the supernatural danger they believed so clearly to be manifested in their hostile physical environment. Indeed, many writers have emphasized this negative aspect to their faith. "The evil spirits, which are instrumental in the misfortunes of life, command the Eskimo's most serious consideration. He seeks an escape from his blank fear of these spirits...he may be able to forestall their designs, at least partially by conciliation and exorcism. This philosophy lies at the root of the whole religious cult of the Eskimos" (Weyer 1969:235-36). While the influences of such evil spirits certainly differed in emphasis from group to group they were an important factor in Eskimo belief and so this chapter begins with an overall treatment of types of supernatural forces; beings and powers including those of an evil nature. We then turn to ritual aspects and to shamanism which, taken together, are the three main focal points for understanding their religion.

Gordon H. Marsh (1954) has suggested that five categories of supernatural beings and powers existed throughout this wide area. On perhaps the lowest level were physical and other objects that might be classified in general terms as charms. Generally these were physical amulets and ranged from quartz crystals and other rocks to objects made from parts of animals, objects once a part of humans, such as the navel cord or teeth from a corpse, and other items. Even objects owned by or associated with some successful hunter might be kept after his death. All of these were kept to be used to provide hunting luck and good fortune in other endeavors; for example, the bone from the flipper of a seal to aid in killing that animal. The power inherent in these might be thought to derive from the essence of the animal or person so connected (especially in Alaska) or it might be conceived of as being inherent in the object itself; perhaps due to its peculiar appearance. In either event, numbers of these were worn by people suspended around their necks or tied to their clothing. Each person's collection was derived either from personal acquisition or by gifts and inheritance from others. While providing some personal security against many of the dangers of life and aiding in task success, sometimes special forms of amulet charms might become a center around which more group ceremonies occurred. Even personal charms might be lent to others.

Along with charm objects like amulets another type of charm existed in the form of special magical formulas or songs. Here the unique words, the verbal utterances, were believed to generate power or bring good fortune and avoid evil or danger. Among the North Alaskan Eskimo such word devices were primarily used to influence hunting and climate conditions, to attract game and bring good weather, although among these people to over-use them was considered dangerous. For them, "A song could take the place of an amulet or charm and was often associated with an amulet. This suggests that these were personal songs which had the general effect of promoting the well-being of the individual" (Spencer 1959:279). It should also be mentioned that taboos on behavior were often associated with either charm types.

The second category of supernatural essences concerns souls which are part of humans and, in some cases, other things as well. Some confusion in the literature exists as to the number and functions of such souls. Edward Weyer (1969), for example, concludes that Eskimo postulated three sorts of souls. These include an immortal spirit that leaves the body at death and goes to some kind of afterlife, one which is the basic animating principal of the body and ceases to exist at death, and a third connected to a person's name. This last also persists after death and rather reflects the personality of the person. This name soul is passed on by the custom of naming the newborn after deceased group members. It does not, as a concept, apply the same way to all Eskimo groups. Gordon Marsh, on the other hand, states that:

> Souls belong only to men and animals and are immortal and imperishable. Humans and dogs possess two kinds of souls, a breath-soul and a name-soul. All other animals have only the breath soul. The various terms designating the breath-soul contain the notion of either breath, life, image, shadow, or appearance. This soul is what gives life...(and)...in subsequent reincarnations they are at will or through the action of other powers interchangeable between animals and people....They are invisible except to certain shamans, and have the power to come and go from the body while the latter is still alive (Marsh 1954:146).

This breath-soul sounds like Weyer's animating principal yet Marsh suggests that it does continue to exist.

The name-soul mentioned in the above quote is seen by Marsh as the other spiritual essence – encompassing personality as well as providing protection to its person throughout life. This name-soul he feels is not immortal and by not using a name its associated essence disappears. This does seem to somewhat match Weyer's conception. What may partially explain this discrepancy in soul substances is a consideration of specific Eskimo views of the aspects of a person. We can take the Nunamiut of North Alaska as a case in point.

Among these people a human being has three essences. One of these is the Inua, his spiritual aspect. It is the life force of the person and comes with the first breath (breath soul). It has no specific location in the body. It lives forever, only "suffering" if a person commits suicide or shamans try to harm it. It is thought not only to give and perpetuate life but it may also bring luck in hunting or ward off sickness. There is also the suggestion that it may descend along kinship lines. Some people considered it associated with the name. This spiritual entity is different from the Ishuma, the person's intellectual capacity or "mind" which develops around the age of five and may be lost just before death. It loses its awareness after the death of a person and even before that may leave the body and be a cause of illness. To complicate the issue the Nunamiut also believe in the existence of the Taganinga, or shadow, which they see as a kind of vague second self. It resembles the person but is insubstantial and "When it leaves the body, the person, in addition to the loss of the Ishuma and Inua, is truly dead" (Gubser 1965:212).

Other Eskimo groups also have slightly different recognition of the essences of a human being so perhaps the one key soul concept is that of the Inua or animating principal. Humans have it and also have other spiritual qualities not given to most other creatures. Further, the Inua also reside in animals as well as in other phenomena; even what would otherwise be seen as lifeless things like lakes, mountains, and even the wind. Possession of an Inua gives these things a certain "personhood" and links them to human beings.

A third category of supernatural beings and powers involves a varied group of spirit beings generally called "persons" or lesser spirit beings. These were perhaps partially an outgrowth of the Inua concept though they do differ from souls. They help explain why things happen–hard luck, the disappearance of hunters and the like–because they were thought to have some powers to cause events or influence them. While lesser spirits as nature beings might inhabit various locations or be in objects, in Alaska they were part of a much richer cosmology than in Central and Eastern areas. In the West every species of animal had such a "person" or lesser spirit which controlled its behavior and ordered its existence. This required special activities of worship on the part of humans to induce such beings to provide game for the hunters. Such "masters of animals" were apparently not found much beyond Alaska. Likewise, in the richer Western Eskimo areas, individual guardian spirits, usually animals, were more common and less limited to shaman types than elsewhere. In Central and Eastern areas guardian spirits and animal masters were replaced by a greater reliance upon protection and aid given by one or another soul essence and on the use of charms which were more extensive there. In these areas, too, a kind of substitute "spirit" occurred; one that perhaps helped to explain the greater number of misfortunes experienced in their even more difficult area. This was the Tupilak, an animal-like creature constructed by sorcerers out of many different animal parts to work harm on other humans. It was brought to life by a spell and would then seek out the intended victim. Among the Netsilik Eskimo such creatures were "Round in shape and filled with blood under considerable pressure, they could cause terrible sickness" (Balikci 1970:226). These stimulated great fear.

Throughout the Arctic culture area other supernatural entities belonging to a category or level approximately equal to "persons" also occurred: giants, dwarfs, who hunted tiny prey, half humans and animals, and other strange creatures. Many of these were of purely legendary significance. These are often called Demonic spirits. "The fourth set of spirit-powers in the Eskimo-Aleut cosmology are the demonic spirits or daemons. These inhabit all parts of the world away from human habitations and, although entirely non-corporeal, are mobile and live in bands like humans, hunting, marrying and reproducing. They are conceived as monstrous and grotesque people and animals" (Marsh 1954:152). These were usually called Tunraq in general and among the Netsilik they included, among other specific types, "Big bellies" who are like man but very gluttonous, being able to eat a caribou with one gulp, "Stone beings" who have human figures but can disappear into stone if seen by people as well as eating stones for subsistence, and a type of "crawlers" having no lower legs who crawl after people in the attempt to kill and eat them. Of the many varieties of Eskimo Tunraq some were particularly dangerous to humans, others were apparently indifferent. Some even became the helping spirits of shamans who often were the only humans thought capable of "seeing" these spirits.

The fifth and last category of supernatural beings and powers are "Persons of the Universe"; spirit powers who control the overall forces of nature. These correspond to the major gods of other culture areas. These varied among Eskimo groups. In Alaska the main such deity is masculine as is the case also in Labrador and Greenland in the East. The Central area is the province of a major female deity. There was also a tendency for gods of the air and sky to be masculine and those of land and sea to be of a feminine nature. We can briefly consider a few specific examples of this type. Perhaps the most "famous" of all was Sedna, the goddess of the sea. In the Central area, and to a limited extent in Greenland, she was considered the special protectress of sea animals like seals and walrus. She was believed to dwell on the bottom of the ocean and might cause storms to protect her creatures from being killed. Many ceremonies were devoted to her in this context, to win her favor; ceremonies that elsewhere were directed to different major gods or to masters of animals. Her cult was surely based on a widespread myth in which parts of her body became the animals in question. Forms of Sedna even occurred among inland groups such as the Caribou Eskimo where as "Pinga" she was thought to watch over human activities as they related to animals killed in hunting; this even though she lived somewhere in space rather than in the sea. In all cases she was the originator of the numerous taboos placed on Eskimo behavior in the quest for food and in its preparation.

Another important deity is the Moon Spirit which had special prime rank in West Alaska. It was a male god and in that area had control over animals as a functional replacement for Sedna. The Moon Man was an object of ritual endeavors which attempted to encourage his beneficence with regards to the food supply. He had expanded functions as well. He was considered a source of disease, especially those of epidemic levels, and eclipses of the moon were considered as a signal of hard times in the future. He was also thought to control human reproduction; regulating menstruation, fertility, and pregnancy in women. This attribute was based on a rather widespread myth in which a moon-brother had sexual relations with a sun-sister as the basis for the creation of these entities of nature. The Sun, however, as the female counterpart to the moon, had much less significance and was of more purely mythic value. "Can it be that the very failure of the sun to furnish light in the depth of winter lends an added significance to the moon, which shines sometimes even where the sun is absent?" (Weyer 1969:388).

A last deity of general occurrence we can examine was Sila, the spirit or personification of the Air. Sila was usually ascribed masculine qualities but he was less anthropomorphized than the other types of deities on this level. He was often conceived of as merely the potentials of weather and as pervading the world, not localized in place. His specific character differed from group to group. Among the Netsilik he was called Narssuk and was a giant baby, orphaned in myth and often angry with humans and behaving against their interests. He was the master of wind, rain, and snow and was wrapped in caribou skins and thongs. Shamans, in the attempt to induce good weather, would "fly" into the air and fight with him; hoping to tighten the thongs binding him which would stop winds and storms that could hinder hunting and other activities. Having examined various categories of supernatural beings and powers we can turn now to a consideration of ritual activities.

Ritual activities among the Eskimo can be divided as a matter of convenience into two basic types. A great number of rites concerned the food supply or things relating to the population in general, others were tied more specifically to the life cycles of individuals. We can discuss each type generally using the Alaskan data for illustrations since Eskimo ritual was much more complex there. A number of cults–long sequences of supernatural actions–occurred with respect to major animals, other rites were briefer affairs. "The most important communal religious festivals were those associated with whaling on the coasts and with caribou drives in the interior...the two major religious patterns were in essence group activities which brought forth all the attitudes which apply in the realm of Eskimo religion" (Spencer 1959:331). And, of course, such rites reinforced group solidarity as well. We can examine rituals connected with the whale cult.

Whale rites went on over a long period of time even though actual whale hunting might be limited to as little as two weeks. During the winter the members of traditional whaling crews spent time together in a ritual structure (Kargi). Their leader made or repaired charms while his men recreated, all the while giving thought to their hunting duties. The charms were thought to have the power to bring the whale close to the boat and easier to harpoon as well as restricting it from writhing about after being hit and thus fouling the lines. By March crews were totally involved in such preparations. New clothes for the act were made by wives and the wife of the leader, herself a ritualist later on, organized the making of a new cover for the whaling boat. A feast followed to celebrate their readiness for the hunt. Then a four day period of solemnity followed with taboos on sex and certain foods. Generally a shaman imposed these, or at least someone possessed of special whaling charm songs. He would sing these to attract the whales. The leader's wife also performed rites by the boat, singing her own songs, putting a special harpoon float in the boat, and other things to ensure success. The leader also gave away all the old whale meat left from the past season.

The group then left for a whaling camp out on the ice. There the boat was launched and paddled to the north, the direction whales passed. The leader sang more attracting songs and the crew observed many restrictions. The wife of the leader sat quietly in her house with a taboo on any work lest her activities harm the outcome of the men's whaling; for example, were she active the whale would also be active and more difficult to kill. When a crew was successful and the whale was dragged up on the ice a runner was dispatched to her house carrying a flipper tip. The woman and the runner each ate a piece of it and she then went to the whale to assist in rituals of greeting. She cut off the snout portion and this was then stood upright. She then poured fresh water from a special container into the boat and onto the whale's snout thanking it for having allowed itself to be caught. The leader also did this, invoking the whale to return again the next year. The whale was then butchered and every member of the community received some portions, as much as they could carry away with them. More formal and complete distribution took place later. A successful leader was also obliged to feast the community. It should also be mentioned that when each whale was killed the crew would retire briefly to the Kargi to dance and dramatize their successful endeavors. The whaling season ended with a final Spring festival of dancing and eating. The Caribou Cult followed along essentially the same lines but it was less elaborate. In both cases care should be taken not to offend animals who gave themselves to humans for food.

Turning from a series of hunting cult rites we can highlight one specific ritual event often involved in such activities. This was the Bladder Festival.

> It is in Alaska that the concept of sacrificing a portion of the carcass of the slain animal in order to maintain a balanced relationship with the animal spirits is observed in its most advanced development. Here...the Eskimos exemplify their beliefs concerning the souls of animals in an elaborate ceremony of a sacrificial nature known as the Bladder Festival. The salient feature...is the offering of a year's accumulated bladders of slain animals in expiation and in appeal for future success in hunting. This cult practice is...towards the spirits of the animals themselves or toward unnamed supernatural forces controlling their propagation (Weyer 1969:340).

On Nunivak Island this rite lasted about five days and was preceded by a sweat bath and a feast dance. Taboos on sex and other observances lasted throughout it. A wooden seal figure was placed inside the Kargi, carved by a shaman. Shamans also sang songs for seals and good weather, men brought new clothing and other paraphernalia inside which included dishes painted with designs illustrating successful hunt activities. New songs were composed and dancing took place. Women brought in seal bladders (and others) saved from the past hunting season. These were inflated and would eventually be painted. Subsequent to all of these acts the ritual proper began, during it a light was kept burning, restrictions of behavior occurred so as not to frighten the animal's souls, and someone was always in attendance. Each day singing went on as well as dances which mimed hunting activities. On the fourth day a shaman went through a hole in the ice into the sea to "open" the link between the worlds of men and seals. The next day various small models of hunting gear were attached to the bladders which in turn were tied to harpoons. A grass fire was set burning on the shore. Then "They went on to the holes in the ice where the bladders were punctured with a drumstick and pushed down under the ice into the water. When these were all dispatched, they gathered into family groups to sing their inherited hunting songs" (Lantis 1947:57). A sweat bath and a feast eventually concluded the activities.

In addition to the major rituals that related to the quest for food, more minor rituals also took place. A number of "first-time" observances might relate to subsistence or to other technological activities. Often the first animal of its kind taken each year was distributed in a ritual manner as was also a boy's first kill celebrated. Minor rites were also conducted when constructing boats and ritual houses and to ensure good weather. Rites were also held on the occasion of more purely social feast activities. We can now examine some activities connected to the life cycle.

A great number of observances were connected with the transition from birth to death. These varied somewhat from group to group. Magical songs might be used to prevent or encourage conception and in the former case a belt sung over by a barren woman might also be employed. Generally, however, children were desired and during pregnancy many taboos were incumbent upon the mother-to-be to prevent harm to the child. For example, she might not sleep or rest except at bedtime lest the child be born lazy. Among most Eskimo birth took place in a special small structure, since the woman was considered dangerous at that time. At birth the husband was usually absent although he himself was not normally under many taboos. Taboos did apply to his wife. Among the central Eskimo, "After the birth of her child the mother must observe a great number of regulations, referring particularly to food and work. She is not allowed for a whole year to eat raw meat...two months after delivery she must make a call at every hut while before this she is not allowed to enter any but her own. At the end of this period she must also throw away her old clothing" (Boas 1964:203). Because of the supernatural status of the woman, shamans were seldom involved lest they lose their power.

Puberty was generally not ritually elaborated. For girls it was tied to first menstruation, at which time they were subject to various restrictions since this was a critical event, much more so than later such events in her life; the girl was dangerous to herself and to her community. Taboos might be applied to the girl at this time and she was generally secluded for about four days; her circumspect behavior, as elsewhere in North America, helping to determine her subsequent career as a mature woman. Taboos included such prohibitions as not touching a weapon since then it would no longer kill game. Among boys no formal initiation rite occurred as they often did elsewhere although changes of clothing were provided to signal maturity and, in some areas, such as North Alaska, the lower lip would be pierced and a plug (labret) representing adult status was inserted. "When a boy donned the labrets, it was a sign that his childhood and adolescence were passed. He could now marry" (Spencer 1959:242). Whether any more elaborate observances occurred in the past has not been determined.

Eskimo attitudes towards death varied widely. Some peoples feared death while others were said to have little of such beliefs. Perhaps this confusion results form the lack of discrimination in the reports of such observers. Among the Labrador Eskimo, for example, there was "...little fear of death itself, which the hunter braves many times a day on the shifting ice....But they do have a superstitious fear of a corpse, owing to the malignant influence it is supposed to exert, and they are very much afraid of ghosts" (Hawkes 1916:118). To this we may add fear of the part a shaman might play in causing death and of evil spirits. Tied to such beliefs it was a fairly widespread custom to remove an ailing person from the regular shelter and place that person in isolation in a small structure so that he might not die in the company of others. Methods of disposing of the body differed from group to group and by season. If on the move it might simply be abandoned as the group moved on. A body might often be buried on the ground–covered with rocks or other materials–placed in a cave or in the sea. Only seldom was a body cremated or actually buried in the ground. The body itself was often bound up in a flexed position to counter the ghost which was also placated in various ways. These included taboos on mentioning the name of the deceased unless given to a newborn, on certain types of activities, and on foods. More positively, food offerings might be made to the deceased and personal articles placed with the corpse as well as more formal ritual activities.

While some confusion exists in the literature, two main ritual efforts served to place Eskimos in good relations with the spirits of their deceased. These were a general Mortuary Feast and a Great Feast of the Dead; the latter occurring rather infrequently. Among Bering Strait Eskimo, the Mortuary Feast was held in late November or early December. "It is given for the sole purpose of making offerings of food, water, and clothing to the shades of those recently deceased, and of offerings to the dead who have not yet been honored by one of the great festivals. The makers of this feast are the nearest relatives of those who have died during the preceding year, joined by all others of the village who have not given a great feast to their dead"

(Nelson 1899:363). Prior to this rite special offerings were placed at the "grave" of the deceased to notify the dead of the coming activities and lure such spirits to the grave. When the living assembled in the Kargi an opening song of invitation was sung and the spirits of the deceased were believed to arrive and enter into the bodies of their namesakes so as to directly partake of the feast that followed. Lamps might also be burned in their honor. Food offerings might also be poured on the floor to provide for the wants of the deceased in the next life. Further songs as well as dances occurred along with the feasting and then the spirits were dismissed.

The Great Feast of the Dead occurred approximately every ten years. Over much of Alaska, in a year this was to be held, the dead were notified of it in the regular Mortuary Feast. This rite generally lasted five days and it was an elaboration of the regular observances. Guests were invited from other villages and were hosted by families wishing to honor their own deceased. These people had collected food and presents requisite to carry out the ritual. During the first few days of this ceremony guests ritually presented themselves and the feast-givers dressed up to represent their dead relatives. Eventually lamps were lighted in the ritual house and were kept burning to honor the dead. Songs of invitation were addressed to the deceased and dances acting out routines of daily life were followed by purifications. Food was then sprinkled on the floor to nourish the spirits and a gift of food was made to all guests; an act repeated later on. Gifts of other material items were also distributed. These were often tied together in long strings and were pulled through the roof hole in a very dramatic fashion. Pantomime dances might also occur, highlighting the achievements of the deceased. The namesakes of the dead were dressed up in fine clothing, which in reality went to the spirits, and much feasting occurred. On the last night dances took place and were followed by a sweat bath to conclude this rite.

We can now examine shamanism as the third major element in Eskimo religious beliefs and behaviors. Shamans occupied important positions in their groups as technicians of the sacred, as people who possessed supernatural powers. As such, these people functioned much like shamans did in other culture areas. They cured the sick, divined the future, and engaged in contests with each other. They were respected and were also feared lest they use their often considerable powers in an antisocial manner. As elsewhere, Eskimo shamans differed in their abilities and in the sources of their powers. We can give one main example of them here as a more-or-less typical indication of the variety and range of shamanism in the Arctic culture area.

The Netsilik of Canada had a main type of shaman which they called an Angatkok and who practiced with a helping spirit that would possess or enter into his body while in a trance state. Such people thus had direct intercourse with supernatural beings. One became such a shaman in the following manner. "The Angatkoks were in the habit of observing the behavior of boys, to discover if some bright young man had received the call. Once selection had been made, the formal training started" (Balikci 1970:225). Such a call was often evidenced in unusual behavior exhibited by the youth. Usually such a novice lived with a practicing shaman during this training period, having to observe many taboos and often going without sleep. This was intended to assist him in obtaining visions from spirits. He would also learn various shamanistic techniques during this time, gain the necessary paraphernalia and eventually he would have a protective spirit from the Tunraq class presented to him. He would originally be controlled by this spirit until his training and skill permitted him to become its master. Once he was fully in control and was competent to begin his practice he would continue to acquire still other spirits all of which were thought to always be close to "their" shaman. Such aspects were common elsewhere. Among the Copper Eskimo, for example, "As a rule the shaman's spirits are nameless....As their attachment to their owners is voluntary, so they can desert them at will. If the shaman for example should break the food prohibitions his familiars have enjoined on him they will leave him immediately" (Jenness 1922:192). Shamans were part-time practitioners having to hunt and engage in other normal male activities.

Curing the sick and related phenomena were primary shamanic responsibilities for Netsilik practitioners although they also controlled the weather, called animals and did other things. In the case of illness which was caused by evil ghosts and spirits, a shaman would be summoned to chase them from the body of the patient. To do so he would come to the house of the ill person, cover himself with an animal skin and have the lamps extinguished. He would summon his spirit which, having entered his body, spoke while the shaman was in a trance state. This was usually enough to frighten the evil spirit from the patient's body and outside the house. The shaman then sent his helping spirit after the evil one to drive it back inside where (in the dark) he could kill it with a knife. When light was restored the blood from the evil spirit was on the shaman's hands.

Some men also cured by a lesser technique not involving a trance state or even special training although one did relate to the spirit world in it. This was called "head-lifting" and was common among the Netsilik and elsewhere. Such a person had only weak helping spirits; not Tunraqs. A head-lifter was usually assisted by his wife around whose head a special thong was tied. When such a person cured, the technique consisted of asking his helping spirit if the patient had broken some taboo eliciting a supernatural punishment; the evil spirit in his body. The practitioner held the thong while asking such questions and "...an easy answering pull meant a negative answer from the spirits, a heavy pull the contrary" (Balikci 1963:196). Once the nature of the broken taboo was ascertained then the evil spirit was thought to leave the body. The patient might then perform some sort of penance. Still other "lesser shaman" types also were helped but not possessed by weak spirits. These men simply sat near the patient, eventually declaring that they saw the evil spirit leaving and encouraging the patient to recover on his own.

While shamans were thought to be capable of turning against people and harming rather than helping them there was a class of people who were solely evil in intent, practicing a technique called ilisiniq.

> It is probable that numerous persons could engage in this evil art in order to bring calamity, paralysis, or death to a secret enemy or to a person disliked or envied. Many manipulative techniques were known, most of them based upon connecting something associated with the enemy to the dead or to menstrual blood; animal bones brought in by the enemy might be stolen and placed in a graveyard; the enemy might be touched with the mitt of a dead man....It was essential for all such acts to be accompanied by mental wishes specifying the evil aim desired (Balikci 1963:197).

Of course many activities of actual shamans (Angatkoks) were designed purely to enhance their own position in society. Contests between shamans were fairly common, each trying to display greater skills, slight of hand, or even attempting to bring about death. Sometimes a shaman would simply impress an audience by manipulations of his own body; piercing it with spears and yet leaving no wound, as well as other feats of magic. This gave an immense amount of prestige to shamans within their groups. In keeping with such rivalry it should be mentioned that shamans functioned as individuals, there were no societies as among Plains and other peoples.

Shamanistic techniques elsewhere in the Arctic were comparable. In Alaska, for example, on Saint Lawrence Island, Jane Murphy gives the following details on behaviors which continue at the present time. Among these people shamans also become religious professionals on the basis of a call; their "initiation" involving a period of wandering about alone, going without food and undertaking other privations. As a result they gained a helping spirit who possessed them as they perform supernatural activities. Some apprenticeship to older shamans also occurred. Curing was and is the major focal point of such shamanism and the seance nature of it was well marked, a highlight coming when the shaman would "...fall unconscious to the floor and would rise after a time, with changed visage and possessed by his spirit-familiar, to carry on the drama" (Murphy 1964:59). Common causes of disease were soul loss, sorcery, and spirit and object intrusion, with the first the most basic malady. In that case the shaman sent his helping spirit to search for the lost soul of his patient. Various levels of shaman types also existed among these people.

We can add some very brief comments on the nature of Aleut religion to the above discussion of Eskimo supernatural beliefs and behaviors. Because Aleut traditions along such lines were eradicated early on in the contact period we have very little accurate information on them. Much of what we do know has been gleaned from surviving fragments of mythology and by archaeologists from finds of artifacts in caves. Their religious customs have also been said to parallel those of the Eskimo which may or may not be entirely accurate. For example, "As with other Eskimoid peoples, shamans held important positions and practiced curing, prediction, and witchcraft...both the vision quest and apprenticeship could lead to shamanism, and animal-human transformations and communications were common" (Granburn and Strong 1973:128). Perhaps the use of hunting charms and magic procedures may also be inferred as well as taboos and rites to win the favor of animals or animal spirits. We do know that each communal house had a carved figurine representing a deity that was suspended from a ceiling beam and that this was "talked to" before and after hunting expeditions.

There does seem to have been a well-defined belief in the existence of spiritual power that resided within the human body. This power was expressed and dealt with in three main ways. First of all it had to be controlled or regulated during certain periods in the life of an individual lest it bring harm to that person or the community itself. The main manifestations of this occurred at puberty in the case of young girls and later in life at the death of spouses. When a young girl had her first menstrual period she was isolated in a special hut for a period of about forty days followed by a briefer length of time during which she had to observe certain taboos. Some of these may have lasted even longer. During her actual confinement "Each joint of the girl, ankle, knee, wrist, elbow, and shoulder was bound...a special sewn cloth belt was worn, the neck was bound, and the hair was tied at the back of the head" (Laughlin 1980:104). Along with taboos she also practiced womanly tasks such as weaving baskets to make her productive in later life.

The joint-binding and restrictions kept the power of the girl in check, a power that had curative aspects to it as well as being harmful; it might stop game animals from nearing the village and hence ruin the hunting activities of men. In terms of its curing potential, if any person suffered from seasickness – a common Aleut problem – he might bring food to the girl at this time and she would warm it in her hands and feed it to him as a cure as well as rubbing saliva on his body to relieve any pain. Even later on the special belt she had worn might be used in curing. She might also weave a special "charm" belt a man could use to ensure his safety. A widow or widower was likewise restricted and for the surviving wife, joint-binding and special period of isolation followed with her belt also having powers. "It appears that the belt worn by the girl menstruating for the first time and the widow derived their curative powers from the body at the two times they had been used to regulate and retain the power in their bodies" (Laughlin 1980:105).

A second way to deal with power in the body was to let it out, to remove it from its human receptacle. When an enemy was killed or a dangerous person within the group was eliminated, such individuals were chopped into pieces by cutting off arms and legs and then hacking them apart at the joints. If the powers within were not so dispersed they might continue to be a source of harm to the living even though the body itself was dead. Destroying the body further negated this danger. The third and most elaborate manipulation of the power in human bodies was expressed at the time of the death of regular group members. Their bodies were made into "mummies" in the attempt to preserve their power for group benefits in the future.

When such a person died some of their internal organs were removed through a slit in the lower abdomen and grass was then stuffed in to take their place. The body was tightly flexed into as small a bundle as possible and then wrapped up in a number of layers of seal skins and mats. It was then tied with wrappings of sinew cord. Thus prepared, the body bundle was then removed to a cave where it was placed next to others on a scaffolding of planks. There it could be kept dry and safe to continue human-like activities in the next life with its powers intact. Many objects were placed with it. These caves could be visited by the living to request aid from the departed by placing gifts by the mummies. Relatives might also request "answers" relative to the future prospects of hunting or other endeavors. It should also be mentioned that a finger joint or some other part of the deceased person might be carried as a good luck charm in hunting. Such behaviors suggest a rather well-developed system of supernaturalism and belie the meagerness of the surviving data. We can turn now to a consideration of religion among Subarctic peoples.

CHAPTER XIV

SUBARCTIC RELIGION

In many respects the religion of the Subarctic peoples was like that of the Eskimo, reflecting many of the same technological and environmental concerns. Like peoples of the Arctic, religion was not elaborate or formal except in a couple of subareas and every male at least was expected to have some power; to be in some respects his own shaman. As such, Subarctic religion is a bit difficult to characterize. John Honigmann, in an overview article on this topic, suggests that supernatural power, shamanism, and sorcery were central elements throughout the area. "From the Indian's point of view, many things a man successfully accomplished revealed that he held power granted by non-human helpers who attended him" (Honigmann 1981:718). Shamans and sorcerers were just more potent, positively and negatively, along such lines and such was certainly a base level for Native American religion in general. Ceremonies ranged from simple avoidance and taboos to more formal procedures, although these were rare given the dispersed nature of many peoples in this culture area. A widespread focus centered on respect for animals; hunting them being a religious act requiring proper killing, butchering, distribution of meat, and ultimate gratitude expressed to the spirits or supernatural forces involved. Still another communality surrounded what Honigmann calls biological symbolism. By this he chiefly means childbirth and menstruation in women and male coming of age, the latter usually attended to in less obligatory fashion. Lastly, death occasioned observances of various types. In illustrating these and other concerns the present brief chapter will focus mostly on the Eastern Subarctic, describing some of the more typical aspects there, and then make a few comparative remarks on the Western, Athabascan-speaking area.

We can deal mainly with the topic of supernatural power and shamanism or shamanistic-like practices since these were the most basic ritual forms in this culture area. As a main example we can describe the Naskapi, since an excellent literature is available on these people. Among them, as among Algonkian speakers elsewhere, a concept of general supernatural power existed called Mantu or Manitou. It was equivalent to the Wakan concept described in chapter eleven. Mantu existed in all things, some of which were more personified than others. Tcetcimantu was the greatest power as a creator and controller of the universe itself; a kind of deity of deities although remote and not usually the object of worship. More firmly in the minds of the Naskapi was Tsuabec, a culture-hero type widespread in this area who slayed monsters and transformed the earth for human habitation. Wind spirits existed, as did forces behind other natural phenomena. Animal spirits, controllers especially of caribou, bear, and beaver, were very important and a host of forest and water spirits existed. Many of these, like Witigo, were cannibalistic in nature and harmful towards humans.

On a level intermediate among all these manifestations was the soul concept which among the Naskapi rose to a central and spirit-like position in supernatural belief and behavior. As elsewhere the soul was the animating principle of the body. Located in the heart it gave life and could survive the death of the body. It was often thought to be the reincarnation of an ancestor after spending some time in the heavens as a star. In its spiritual state, however, the soul was called the Mistapeo, the "Great Man," and it could provide guidance to a person in all aspects of life; especially in how to deal with the spirits of game animals in hunting.

> The Great Man reveals itself in dreams. Every individual has one, and in consequence has dreams. Those who respond to their dreams by giving them serious attention, by thinking about them, by trying to interpret their meaning in secret and testing out their truth, can cultivate deeper communication with the Great Man. He then favors such a person with more dreams, and these better in quality. The next obligation is for

> the individual to follow instructions given him in dreams, and to memorialize them in representations of art. We encounter the warning against neglect of dreams, against indifference to their vague suggestion lest the Great Man of the individual cease to appear to him (Speck 1935:35-36).

As such the Mistapeo functioned like a guardian spirit elsewhere and every man was more or less his own shaman, functioning for himself and his family with such aid.

Having a personal helper however was not enough to bring success in life's endeavors; more active efforts were also required. To motivate the all-important dream communication one would also sing and dance. The songs came mostly from dream suggestions and pleased the soul as well as exerting an influence upon game animals. Dancing also invoked spiritual forces. It helped to awaken the soul and, by sweating in it, to develop strength. Along these lines the sweat bath described for other areas was also employed. Drumming was crucial to such activities. Its vibrations could reach the ears of animals and spirit entities alike. All these practices also helped the practitioner accomplish his desires through the application of "wish power," a type of magic widespread in this area. One simply concentrated on one's desire and waited for the soul to make it a reality. While any man might be able to accomplish such things, some became special. "The practice of individual spirit control may mount to the level of a profession. One who...has cultivated such a high degree of power...is a professional conjurer....He is thought to have succeeded in cultivating almost complete harmony with his Great Man" (Speck 1924:272). The Penobscot (Abnaki) offer a good example of this more visible performer.

Among the Penobscot the shaman was called the Mudeolinu – the "drum sound person" – from the use of the drum in his practice. Here the spirit helper was apparently extrinsic to the soul in a more typical shamanistic practice. Each such person "...had his helper which seems to have been an animal's body into which he could transfer his state of being at will. The helper was virtually a disguise" (Speck 1919:249). This helper was called a Baohigan – "instrument of mystery" – and was basically acquired by going into the woods, singing to it until it drew near, and then stroking it to make it into a supernatural servant. Such an animal spirit was sent on supernatural errands by its master while in a trance state. If the spirit/disguise was harmed a similar fate would befall the human. The chief activities of this practitioner were closely connected to the needs of his own kinship group: protecting their hunting areas against trespass, curing illnesses, aiding in hunting, and related things. It should be mentioned that for the Penobscot another type of specialist existed, the Kiugwasowino or "dreamer." This man, reminiscent of Eskimo notions, had no spirit helper but did have a special ability to discover the future or hidden knowledge in dreams for hunting and war. Such dreams, apparently, had no revelatory nature for others among these people. Perhaps as power specializes common people become detached from it.

The Micmac shaman seems closely identical in attributes and functions. He was called the Buowin–"mystery man." Such a practitioner obtained his power through dreams from spirit helpers which, as in the Naskapi case, he could send on missions although not taking up such a disguise himself. He possessed a special medicine bag which contained among other objects pieces of bone carved into animal shapes which represented these spirit helpers. "His power motivates an animal represented in bone. The animal fulfills the desires of the shaman" (Johnson 1943:69). The Micmac shaman perhaps did not use the drum so common elsewhere but he did make use of wish magic as well as shooting disease objects into enemies. He was also a prophet, curer, and used his power to aid in the quest for food and in other activities.

Actual curing practices differed. For many groups much of the relief of illness was accomplished by the use of medicines made from plants. Generally these were prepared and administered in a common-sense, non-shamanistic manner. "The practical use of herbs is a fundamentally primitive idea that has survived in this region devoid of the complexities of ritual. It seems to me that a ritual associated with the practice of herb medicines denotes a higher stage in the development of folklore thought" (Speck 1915:303). Usually single herbs were used by women primarily and they reflected a suspected relationship between the quality of the plant and the symptoms of the disease. For more serious situations however, the shaman would have to be called in. One treatment among the Micmac went as follows. If a patient failed to respond to herbal remedies the Buowin would examine him to see where the evil spirit or disease object might be lodged. He then blew over the body of the patient and sucked at the afflicted part, accompanying these manipulations with incantations. Hopefully this alone would expel the cause of the problem. If this did not happen then force was used. "The medicine man dug a deep hole and within it buried a stick tied to a protruding cord. He chanted, danced, and howled over the hole and, alternately, over the sick man who lay nearby. He then entered into active combat with the evil, slashing about so furiously or pulling so hard at the rope that he broke out in sweat" (Wallis and Wallis 1955:135). The audience then pulled at the rope and eventually the stick was torn out of the ground. On its end were objects that represented the evil. The shaman then divined by dreaming to see if success had been achieved or if the evil had merely gone a short distance away. In the latter case he would predict death in a certain number of days and the patient was given up on by his family.

A major aspect of shamanism and the use of supernatural power was divination. In fact, Frank Speck remarks that Naskapi religion was almost wholly a religion of divination so that one would know where and when to hunt, what the weather might be like, the cause of sickness, and other personal concerns. Many techniques were available among these people. A person might, for example, gaze at a pool of water and concentrate until an image appeared giving the information desired. This answer may have been supplied from the soul. Fish bones (lower jaws) might be tossed in the air and if they fell with the teeth up the answer was considered affirmative. One might take a beaver pelvis and pass it over one's head with one hand, bringing it to the extended index finger of the other. If this digit entered the hole the answer was positive for some questions or contemplated activity. Perhaps the most common ordinary technique, and certainly the most famous in the literature, was that of scapulimancy; divining with the shoulder blade of an animal. This was generally taken from a caribou. After the meat had been removed from it and it had been allowed to dry, a small piece of wood was split and used as a handle. The bone was then held over hot coals for a short period of time and it then began to crack in various directions. These cracks and burnt spots were then "read" in terms of pre-established meanings.

More professional divining techniques existed among the Naskapi and other groups and here the most common one was conjuring, or the "shaking tent" method, which as has been noted also extended into other culture areas. Among the Salutes (Ojibwa) it formed a focus of supernatural activity and perhaps twenty percent of the male population was thought to possess skills along these lines. At least one such person existed in every winter group since the need for spiritual assistance along divinatory lines was greatest at this time. The basis of this technique was to build a small lodge, enter it, summon various spirits, and then the audience could question these beings as to the future and other desired information. The conjurer apparently did not enter into a trance state and he acquired his abilities during a puberty fast. In a vision at this time a special "master" spirit of conjuring appeared and during four dreams/visions it bestowed knowledge and power upon the seeker. Certain other basic spirits, such as the great turtle (Mikinak), also appeared at this time plus others which made the abilities of each such conjurer a little bit different. All such practitioners had the same basic repertoire of skills and activities.

> With the aid of his spiritual tutelaries a conjurer is able to secure news about people who are hundreds of miles away, or learn of events that are taking place in another part of the country. He can discover what is going to happen in the future and he can find out a great deal about the past lives of his fellows. As occasion demands he may recover lost or stolen articles for their owners or discover the hidden cause of some puzzling malady. On the other hand, with malevolent ends in view, he can abduct the souls of human beings, causing sickness, mental disorder or even death, if this vital animating agency is not returned to them (Hallowell 1942:12).

Such powers apparently set the conjurer off from other types of shamans.

A typical divinatory seance went about as follows. After the lodge was built the conjurer would enter after sunset and kneel, concealed from his audience. As he entered the structure would shake due to the presence of wind spirits. Tobacco supplied by the questioners would be distributed to the audience by the shaman's helper and the onlookers would smoke it in honor of the various spirit entities. A performance might last up to three hours and many spirit voices would be heard. These were usually unintelligible save for that of the Great Turtle who was the real intermediary involved and who spoke in a manner that all could understand as well as actually making the journeys for obtaining the desired information. Shortly after the rite was concluded the structure would be dismantled and the poles placed under a taboo on any other use. As Hallowell (1934) has also pointed out, such dramatic performances, along with dreams, were major proofs of the reality of the world of the supernatural. We can now very briefly mention some other aspects of religious beliefs and practices.

As previously mentioned it was important for hunters to treat animals in a ritualized fashion to impress them and their spirit owners with proper respect and consideration. All tribal groups had a great number of observances along these lines and we can describe in some detail those of one group, the Cree, who lived near Lake Mistassini, west of the Naskapi area. These people carry on many of these behaviors in their hunting at the present time. Various human-animal relations were thought to exist. There was a kind of male-female aspect in which, in myth and dreams, the animal was likened to a female victim of the male hunter who dominates as in social relations. There was a sense of "animal friendship" too in which a particular hunter over a period of time would develop a special relation of privilege to a species. This was based on a reputation for successful killing and usually characterized an older individual who might no longer kill the animal in question but who would help younger men in such endeavors. When such a man died it was believed he would be mourned by that species and care was taken during his funeral to request that he not take his animal friends out of the area with him. Of course animal masters also existed who controlled each species and looked after them and good relations between hunters and these entities were carefully encouraged.

There were many ritual aspects involved in the killing of animals. Hunters, as among the Eskimo to the north, wore various types of charms. Some of these were made from the bones of animals or were peculiar natural objects. These could be kept near one's head at night to induce divinatory dreams, displayed in camp to please the spirits, and worn during the hunt itself to show respect and give power to the hunter. Other charms were made of decorative materials like beads and were applied to weapons and clothing. These were based on dreams although they employed a rather limited range of design elements. They made great use of color symbolism. For many animals most magic was apparently focused at the time of actual killing.

> But in the case of the beaver there are two critical moments: first, when the hunter finds the beaver colony, and second, when the animal is caught in his trap...when a beaver lodge is found the hunter selects pieces of wood from the lodge which have clear impressions of beavers teeth marks on them....One such stick is usually brought back to camp...and placed at the wall where the hunter's head rests at night in order to promote dreams that will give the hunter power...the hunter would be able to kill all the beavers in the lodge (Tanner 1979:144).

This was also thought to please the controlling spirit. After actual killing, the beaver was dragged back to camp with a special drag rope or harness. Bears were also accorded special treatment. The hunter "talked to" this animal prior to killing and afterwards placed tobacco on its body and then smoked this. During bear-hunting expeditions the hunter's wife had to keep the camp neat lest the animal be offended and refuse to allow itself to be caught. It should also be mentioned that other spirits were taken into account during hunting. Negatively, for example, a hunter must not let blood get on the snow without covering it up. Failure here would result in the spirit of the North Wind becoming angry and sending a snowstorm. Positively, one should pay attention to other spirits who lived in the bush and woods since they might well be inclined to give useful advice to the hunter.

After a successful kill the hunter returned to camp for further rites. These seem to have all been intended to express the hope of gaining similar good fortune in the future as well as expressing gratitude in general. They all involved treating the carcass of the animal in a proper fashion. When game was brought to camp, or some token of it, little was said; the hunter had to reveal his luck non-verbally to old people first. The kill was then displayed inside the tent facing towards the door so the game might "see" how the hunter had left for the hunt. The meat was then distributed to others in the camp. In subsequent meals food offerings were placed in the fire by the family head prior to consumption. In distribution and eating special portions were reserved for respected persons to honor them; for example, the head was given to a good hunter. Different parts were also considered appropriate for men and women. Special feasts also occurred at various times during the life cycle such as after the birth of a child; after the conclusion of a particularly successful hunt; or in timing with natural cycles. A case of this last opportunity would be at the start of winter when a new camp was made.

> All members of a camp attended such feasts and offerings of food are always made to spiritual entities at feasts. A little of each kind of food served is put into the fire. The recipients may be identified as the spirits of living or dead persons with kin ties to the group; more often they are the spirits who aid in hunting, or game animals such as the bear. Other offerings, apart from feast food and tobacco, include drumming, songs addressed to particular spirits, and dancing. These latter performances take place after the feast meal is finished... (Tanner 1979:165).

On such occasions the cooking was done by men as supernatural leaders rather than women and extraordinary care was taken to preserve the shape of the animal during preparation and to account for all the food. None of it was wasted or given as scraps to the dogs and leftovers were carefully wrapped up to be taken away. In all cases of consumption, non-edible remains were also ritually treated. Bones were carefully disposed of so that dogs could not get at them and the camp would be left clear and "natural." Some parts such as hides, skulls, or antlers might also be prepared as trophies for use in display to the spirits; to give them further honor or bring good luck. Such rites of respect consumed much time but cemented relations between the human and animal worlds, bringing them together in one sphere. We can now examine a few other Subarctic supernatural beliefs and behaviors.

Life-cycle observances were relatively underdeveloped among Algonkian speakers and this was especially so in the case of birth. Among the Micmac, for example, this event usually occurred outside the family dwelling and the mother resumed normal activities very soon afterward. The newborn was washed in a cold stream and had to swallow grease from an animal. Among some groups such as the Western Cree, if twins were born one was killed, apparently due to the impracticality of raising two children at the same time. Naming was not highlighted apart from possibly a feast given by the father on that occasion. Minor "first time" rites were held for boys. At puberty girls were often covered by taboos and were secluded as in other culture areas. Among the Attawapiskat Swampy Cree, "Because women were dangerous during menstruation...precautions surrounded these processes. A menstruant...observed seclusion in a small shelter located close to the regular dwellings. Nobody used the dish from which the girl ate at this time and later it was burned" (Honigmann 1956:70). Girls at this time or women in this condition had to be extremely careful in following the rules laid down for the respect of game animals.

Prior to full adulthood, as had been implied earlier, a dream or vision quest might occur. It was limited to boys in many groups but some also gave girls this opportunity Among the above-mentioned Cree, boys spent up to a month in solitude and while they had to restrict eating and go without fires, they usually went only a short distance from the camp. Girls spent a shorter period of time. In order for a successful dream experience to reach its full potency its details had to remain a secret until a feast was given in a boy's honor. Even then some years would pass before the abilities or powers granted by the spirits would be tried out.

At the end of the life cycle, death occasioned grief. Among the Micmac, mourners put charcoal on their faces to blacken them and then cried for three days. Among some Cree groups, a wife might go into seclusion in a special hut for three or four days to cry and observe food taboos. In most groups, apparently, a wife might not remarry for a year or more and both men and women might cut their hair short or treat it in some other symbolic manner. The body was generally washed and dressed in good clothing. Disposal varied. Burial in the ground may have been the most common means but the use of mounds and scaffolds were not uncommon and cremation also occurred. Some of the personal possessions of the deceased were placed with the body to accompany the soul into the next life and mourners often added a few items of their own. Often a few observances occurred to guard against the return of the soul of the deceased. "Although nobody feared the soul, seeing ghosts represented a frightening experience, chiefly because it foretold death. Ghostly apparitions might be encountered in any place and not merely around burial sites" (Honigmann 1956:80). Death itself was believed to be due to accident, evil spirits or sorcerers, and often was met with resignation; the dying person making many of his own arrangements and distributing some of his possessions to survivors as mementoes.

We can now make a very few, brief, comments on the nature of religion among the Western Subarctic peoples where such beliefs and behaviors, in most cases, were very similar to what we have already discussed. In characterizing this region, James Van Stone has said that the most significant feature was the "...reciprocal relationship that existed between men and the animals on which they were dependent for their livelihood....Another characteristic feature of traditional Northern Athapascan religion was its individualism...this meant that a great deal of emphasis was placed on individual rituals rather than on community rites" (Van Stone 1974:59). Also, as in the East, many different spirit entities existed. Spirits of animals or controllers of them were very important as were a host of spirits that animated various elements of nature. A shadowy supreme being was widespread but was usually given less mythic and ritual attention than culture-hero types. Among the Kaska, for example, "Several culture heroes were assumed to have existed at an earlier time. Klictata invented the bow, the snowshoe, and taught the people to make fish nets from willow-bark line" (Honigmann 1954:103). Such beings also fought with monsters and in other ways aided humans.

Human souls also existed as spirit entities with animating and immortal qualities but specific beliefs in the afterlife are confusing and often vague as in the East. Evil spirits and creatures abounded, many of which were like the Windigo concept previously mentioned. Among the Tanaina, a very typical expression of this was Nakani, a human-like being who was thought to run away with women and children and who could be heard whistling in the woods. The Nakani usually was thought to insert sleep-causing medicines in the mouth of its victim and then to put the person in a bag and carry him away over his shoulder. Along these lines there was a well-developed fear of ghosts. Partially to keep danger away and for use in hunting endeavors, charms of various sorts were used. These were much like eastern types. Among the Kaska, "...a man with strong power etched the image of an animal on a small piece of caribou bone. The hunter took this amulet on his journey and returned it when it had served its purpose"

(Honigmann 1954:110). Among the Tanaina a common magic object was a small stone originally discovered under peculiar conditions. The colors of such stones indicated the various aspects of their usefulness and they were generally kept in a skin bag. Songs and taboos were also common and applied in a similar fashion to those already described.

Shamanism was the central ritual focus and such powers were generally gained as the result of an encounter of some type with an animal helper or spirit. Such individuals could prevent or cure disease and sometimes were believed to cause it. Cures often consisted of blowing on a patient or spitting medicine on him and then sucking out a disease object. Shamans also could lure game animals to hunters or divine their whereabouts; often through the use of forms like scapulimancy. They could also divine the future and were an aid in war like some of their Eastern counterparts. We can give one specific example here to demonstrate the level of complexity of such practices.

Among the Tanaina the outfits of shamans set them apart from ordinary people. These included a parka of claws and beaks which rattled during their dances. Hand rattles or noisemakers were also carried and masks were employed both by shamans and their assistants and were limited in use in this society to them. The purpose of the mask apparently was to give the shaman the vision (and other powers?) of his spirit helper. Shamans also carried a long stick with the head end carved in the shape of the animal spirit of the practitioner and used a small figurine during their curing activities. These special objects in recent times were called the "devil stick" and the "devil doll" in a reflection of their use in driving out evil spirits thought to be responsible for illness or misfortune.

Shamans could divine the nature of an illness by sleeping on a piece of the sick person's clothing. In the event that the evil could be treated it might be sucked out but more dramatic performances employed the special objects mentioned above.

> The devil dolls are one of the most important means of extracting the evil spirit from an afflicted person. When a shaman is called upon to save a patient in serious condition, he darkens the room and begins to dance to the accompaniment of a drum, holding the doll close to his breast. At the very

> height of the ceremony, when the drumming is deafening and the shaman ecstatic with emotion, he suddenly thrusts the devil doll at the patient. When the noise had died away and the shaman sinks in exhaustion to the ground, the devil doll has disappeared. It can have gone no place, it is said, but into the body of the one for whom the performance was being made (Osgood 1937:179).

The shaman returns the next night and repeats his manipulations and ends up with the figurine back in his possession. The power from the object while in the patient was thought to drive the evil from that person. As in the East, contests between shamans existed in which they could augment their reputations. They also performed various supernatural tricks for the amazement and amusement of group members. Few other activities brought the members of groups together. Only in the extreme Western region (Alaska) were true ceremonial performances common. Cornelius Osgood (1958, 1959) discussed seven such occasions for the Ingalik involving singing, dancing, feasting, and other activities. Most such rites had as their major aims the increase of food supplies and one memorialized the dead. Such events were doubtless influenced by the adjacent Eskimo and since comparable rites have already been described for them we will not discuss this topic in the present chapter.

We can conclude with some remarks about the life cycle. Little ritual attention focused on childbirth save that the pregnant woman observed various taboos and should give birth apart from men in isolation in a special structure. Otherwise hunting and other male activities would be negatively affected. Taboos extended for a short period of time after birth to ensure a healthy child. Naming seems not to have been a very important occasion. Girls were isolated at puberty for up to a month in some groups with many restrictions on behavior, especially the avoidance of men. No formal male puberty rites occurred beyond mild forms of the vision quest for the seeking of spirit helpers. Death customs were also comparable to Algonkian-speaking groups with cremation being perhaps the most often used means of disposal, along with burial or placing in trees. The body was specially dressed and accompanied by some personal possessions or gifts and fear of the ghost occasioned leaving the area immediately. Among the Taniana:

> At death the breath goes up into the sky but the shadow-spirit lingers for about forty days before going underground. The explanation for the lingering is that the shadow-spirit may be loath to leave living friends or at least wish for a last farewell. Also the desire to revenge an injury in life may influence the spirit and the period of potential contact is considered dangerous (Osgood 1937:170).

We can now turn to the consideration of a much more complex set of beliefs and practices, those found in the Eastern Woodlands.

ARCTIC AND SUBARCTIC BIBLIOGRAPHY AND REFERENCES

A. Arctic

Balikci, Asen.

1970. The Netsilik Eskimo. New York: Natural History Press.

1963. Shamanistic Behavior Among the Netsilik Eskimo. *Southwestern Journal of Anthropology* 19:380-96.

Birket-Smith, K.

1929. The Caribou Eskimo. *Report of the Fifth Thule Expedition* 5:1-725.

Boas, Frank

1964. The Central Eskimo. Lincoln: University of Nebraska Press.

1901-1907. The Eskimo of Baffin Land and Hudson Bay. *American Museum of Natural History Bulletin* 15:1-570.

1900. Religious Beliefs of the Central Eskimo. *Popular Science Monthly* 57:624-31.

Carpenter, E. S.

1953. Witch fear among the Aivilik Eskimos. *American Journal of Psychiatry* 110: 194-99.

Fitzhugh, William and Kaplan, Susan A.

1982. Inua: Spirit World of the Bering Sea Eskimos. Washington: Smithsonian Institution Press.

Granburn, Nelson and Strong, Stephen.

1973. Circumpolar Peoples: An Anthropological Perspective. Pacific Palisades: Goodyear Publishing Company.

Gubser, Nicholas.

1965. The Nunamiut Eskimos: Hunters of Caribou. New Haven: Yale University Press.

Hawkes, M. W.

1916. The Labrador Eskimo. *Canada Department of Mines Geological Survey* #1637.

Jenness, Diamond.

1922. The Life of the Copper Eskimo. *Report of the Canadian Arctic Expedition* 12:1-277.

Juel, E.

1945. Notes on Seal-hunting Ceremonialism in the Arctic. *Ethnos* 10:143-64.

Lantis, M.

1950. The Religion of the Eskimos. In V. Ferm (editor), Forgotten Religions, pp. 309-40. New York: Doubleday.

1947. Alaskan Eskimo Ceremonialism. *American Ethnological Memoirs* 11:1-127.

1938. The Alaskan Whale Cult and its Affinities. *American Anthropologist* 40:438-64.

Laughlin, William S.

1980. Aleuts: Survivors of the Bering Land Bridge. New York: Holt, Rinehart and Winston.

Marsh, Gordon H.

1954. A Comparative Study of Eskimo-Aleut Religion. *University of Alaska Anthropological Papers* 3:21-36.

Murphy, Jane M.

1964. Psychotherapeutic Aspects of Shamanism on St. Lawrence Island, Alaska. In Ari Kiev (editor), Magic, Faith and Healing, pp. 53-83. Glencoe: Free Press.

Nelson, E. W.

1899. The Eskimo about Bering Strait. *Bureau of American Ethnology Anthropology Report* 18:3-518.

Oswalt, Wendall H.

1967. Alaskan Eskimos. San Francisco: Chandler Publishing Company.

Rasmussen, K.

1932. Intellectual Culture of the Copper Eskimo. *Report of the Canadian Arctic Expedition* 9:1-350.

1931. The Netsilik Eskimos. *Report of the Fifth Thule Expedition* 8:1-542.

1930. Observations on the intellectual culture of the Caribou Eskimos. *Report of the Fifth Thule Expedition* 7:1-114.

1929. Intellectual Culture of the Iglulik Eskimos. *Report of the Fifth Thule Expedition* 6:1-304.

Shade, C. I.

1951. The Girls' Puberty Ceremony of Umnak, Aleutian Islands. *American Anthropologist* 53:145-48.

Spencer, Robert F.
1959. The North Alaskan Eskimo. *Bureau of American Ethnology Bulletin* 171.

Stefansson, V.
1913. Religious Beliefs of the Eskimo. *Harper's Monthly Magazine* 127:869-78.

Thalbitzer, W.
1926. The Cultic deities of the Innuit. *International Congress of Americanists Proceedings* 22:367-93.

1924. Cultic games and festivals in Greenland. *International Congress of Americanists Proceedings* 21:236-55.

Wardle, H. W.
1900. The Sedna Cycle. *American Anthropologist* 2:568-80.

Weyer, Edward M.
1969. The Eskimos. New Haven: Yale University Press.

B. Subarctic

Birket-Smith, K.
1930. Contributions to Chipewayan Ethnology. *Report of the Fifth Thule Expedition* 5:1-114.

Cooper, John M.
1946. The Culture of the Northeastern Indian Hunters. *Papers of the Peabody Foundation of Archaeology* 3:372-405.

1934. The Northern Algonquian Supreme Being. *Catholic University of America Anthropological Series* 2:1-78.

Flannery, Regina.
1939. An Analysis of Coastal Algonquian Culture. *Catholic University of American Anthropological Series* 7:1-219.

Goddard, Pliny E.
1916. The Beaver Indians. *American Museum of Natural History Anthropology Papers* 10:201-93.

Hallowell, A. Irving.
1942. The Role of Conjuring in Saulteaux Society. *Philadelphia Anthropological Society Papers* 2:1-96.

1940. The Spirits of the dead in Saulteaux life and thought. *Journal of the Royal Anthropological Institute* 70:29-51.

1934. Some empirical aspects of Northern Saulteaux Religion. *American Anthropologist* 36:389-404.

Honigmann, John J.

1981. Expressive Aspects of the Subarctic Indian Culture. In Handbook of North American Indians, *Subarctic*, June Helm (editor), pp. 718-38. Washington: Smithsonian Institution Press.

1956. The Attawapiskat Swampy Cree. *University of Alaska Anthropology Papers* 5:23-82.

1954. The Kaska Indians. *Yale University Publications in Anthropology* 51:1-163.

1945. Northern and Southern Athapascan Eschatology. *American Anthropologist* 47:467-69.

Jenness, Diamond.

1955. The Indians of Canada. *National Museum of Canada Bulletin* 65.

1943. The Carrier Indians of the Buckley River. *Bureau of American Ethnology Bulletin* 133:469-586.

1938. The Sarcee Indians of Alberta. *Bulletin of the Canada Department of Mines* 90:1-98.

Jette, J.

1907. On the Medicine-Men of the Ten'a. *Journal of the Royal Anthropological Institute* 37:157-88.

Johnson, F.

1943. Notes on Micmac Shamanism. *Primitive Man* 16:53-80.

McKenna, R. A.

1959. The Upper Tanana Indians. *Yale University Publications in Anthropology* 55:1-223.

Osgood, Cornelius.

1959. Ingalik Mental Culture. *Yale University Publications in Anthropology* 56:1-195.

1958. Ingalik Social Culture. *Yale University Publications in Anthropology* 53:1-289.

1937. The Ethnography of the Tanaina. *Yale University Publications in Anthropology* 16:1-229.

1936. Contributions to the Ethnography of the Kutchin. *Yale University Publications in Anthropology* 14:1-189.

Skinner, A.
1911. Notes on the Eastern Cree and Northern Saulteaux. *American Museum of Natural History Anthropology Papers* 9:1-116.

Speck, Frank G.
1950. Concerning Iconology and the Masking Complex in Eastern North America. *University of Pennsylvania Museum Bulletin* 15:6-57.

1940. Penobscot Man. Philadelphia: University of Pennsylvania Press.

1935. Naskapi. Norman: University of Oklahoma Press.

1924. Spiritual beliefs among Labrador Indians. *International Congress of Americanists* 21:266-75.

1919. Penobscot Shamanism. *American Anthropological Association Memoirs* 6:237-88.

1915. Medicine Practices Among the Northeastern Algonkians. *International Congress of Americanists Proceedings* 19:303-21.

Tanner, Adrian.
1979. Bringing Home Animals. New York: St. Martin's Press.

Van Stone, James W.
1974. Athapascan Adaptations. Chicago: Aldine Publishing Company.

Wallis, Wilson D. and R. S.
1955. The Micmac Indians of Eastern Canada. Minneapolis: University of Minnesota Press.

CHAPTER XV

THE EASTERN CULTURE AREA

The Eastern culture area extends from the Great Lakes, Southern Canada, and part of New England in the north (excluding the Subarctic) to the Gulf of Mexico in the south. East to west it includes peoples who lived along the Atlantic Coast across to the lower Mississippi River. It is a large and culturally diverse area and is traditionally divided by anthropologists into a number of subareas. The Northeast portion includes the northern Iroquoian speakers. These were the Huron tribes and peoples in New York State called *the* Iroquois: Seneca, Cayuga, Onondaga, Oneida, and Mohawk; as well as others about which much less information is available. It also included a great number of Algonkian-speaking peoples related to those of the Subarctic. These latter peoples lived both along the Atlantic Coast and in the Great Lakes region, forming a kind of circle around those of Iroquoian stock. These groups included such as the Shawnee and Delaware and the Sauk, Fox, Kickapoo, Menomini, Potawatomi, and Ojibwa. Groups such as the Winnebago spoke Siouan. The other major subarea is that of the Southeast which runs from about Tennessee and Virginia south to the Gulf. It was the home of many, often populous, tribes representing a number of different language families. Many groups, such as the Creek (a number of tribes), Choctaw, and Chickasaw, spoke languages in the Muskogean family. Others spoke Iroquoian, among these being the Cherokee and the Yuchi. Algonkian speakers had spread along the Atlantic Coast. The Natchez were in yet another language grouping and still others had affiliations to the Plains and to Northern Mexico. For purposes of simplification, this chapter and those that follow will look at the Northern Iroquoians, the Algonkians, and the Southeast as a unit.

In the Northeast area, Iroquoian culture is fairly well known, the New York State groups being among the most "famous" of Eastern peoples. They were agricultural peoples, slashing and burning the forest near their villages to plant corn, beans, and squash. Wild plant foods collected by women were also important: roots, berries, nuts, and the like. Hunting was crucial to their survival and special camps were set up to pursue it intensively. Deer, bear, and small mammals were common as well as migrating birds such as the passenger pigeon. Turkeys and partridge occurred in some parts of this area. Fishing was also an important part of subsistence. Life revolved around settled villages with populations ranging from one hundred or so persons to over a thousand. Men did the hunting and fishing which, along with war, made the forest their domain. Women did most of the farming which somewhat gave them "domination" over the village and the clearings about it.

Villages were usually surrounded by palisade fences and often ditches for defensive purposes and contained communal long houses made of poles usually covered with elm bark. These structures were 25 feet wide and perhaps 80 to 100 feet long on average and contained a number of families in compartments along both sides of a central row of fires. Sleeping platforms lined the walls and storage areas existed at both ends. Such villages moved a short distance every decade or so as the local soil lost its agricultural potential and firewood became scarce. Political leaders often had villages named after them and their long houses had extra compartments for guests and served as council houses. Snowshoes and bark canoes, often poorly made in comparison to elsewhere, and deerskin clothing were common. Baskets were used for carrying and for storage. Crude pottery also existed. The use of wampum, strings of beads made from shells, was originally a part of personal decoration but more importantly became an aspect of social and political behavior. Woodcarving, especially in making masks, was well developed. Technology among other Iroquoians was comparable to this description.

Social and political life among the New York State Iroquoians was rather complex. The simplest social unit was that of the fireside group or simple family living in a long house compartment. This was the nuclear family of husband, wife, and children. These were combined, based on matrilocal patterns of residence, into an extended family grouping as occupants of the entire long house structure – mothers and their daughters, sisters and nieces, with their in-marrying husbands and children. The senior woman organized the details of social living and collective work in the fields. Descent was matrilineal and two or more extended families formed a clan whose members had ties of mutual aid in economics and war, who shared the rights to a political position, and who were usually exogamous. Husbands, of course, belonged to their own clans. Normally there were eight such descent groups in each tribe and in the west and perhaps throughout the region they were grouped in turn into larger matrilineal units or moieties. These were dual divisions with mainly ceremonial functions; to console and bury each other's dead and to carry out some other religious activities. As we will see presently the five tribes in question were united in a political league and here too "moieties" existed with the Mohawk, Onondaga, and Seneca lumped together in one and the Oneida and Cayuga in the other. At least on the tribal level clan and moiety members regarded one another as family members. Again, Huron and other Iroquoian groups appear to have been generally comparable.

Iroquois political organization, as suggested, was highly developed with the five New York State tribes having formed a league or confederacy; perhaps to avoid previous fighting among themselves. It operated under a council composed of fifty super-chiefs or Sachems who represented the constituent tribes – rather like summer Plains leaders often represented their bands or villages. Clan chiefs operated at the local level. The Sachemships were not evenly distributed through the groups involved. The Onondaga, for example, had fourteen and the Seneca only eight. Each such position did have a special name and passed along matrilineal clan lines, members choosing successors with women forming a kind of nominating committee and the clan confirming a person as worthwhile. When a new occupant was placed in a Sachem position a special condolence council was held in which men of the opposite league moiety consoled the survivors and formally installed the new person in the position. That man would drop his own name and take that of the office. Apparently each Sachem also had some specific duties to perform, for example, keeping wampum records of various transactions. Sachems dealt mainly with external affairs pertaining to the league itself, holding both civil councils in which to do this and some religious ones as well.

Matters of public interest could be taken to the Sachem of one's clan who would take them to the council itself. Here much discussion would occur with each officeholder having the right to present his opinion on it. Discussion often occurred on a small group level and these would have spokesmen pass back and forth between them to compare opinions. Apparently total consensus had to form on a matter before it was raised to the level of a formal, public vote. Failing this the matter would be set aside. Politics operated very much like this at the local level as well. Besides these civil chiefs there were other leaders whose offices were based on achievement and were not hereditary. The most basic of these was gained by prowess in warfare and had the designation, Pine Tree Chiefs. These men, after war intensified following the formation of the league, the fur trade, and other factors, came to rival the formally constituted Sachems in power and eventually to intimidate them. In war, fighting might result from council decisions, in which case special Seneca war chiefs might be chosen to lead or coordinate it, or it might stem from the ambitious desires of individuals. The elder matron of long houses also played a role in stimulating or discouraging such endeavors.

War was a common activity for the Iroquois, being perhaps "the" male activity. It led in formal cases to the virtual extinction of some other Iroquoian-speaking groups such as the Erie, and to severe depopulation among those initiating it as well. As war was fairly constant, battles were often hit-and-run affairs and were highly motivated by the desire to take prisoners who would either be adopted to replace lost group members or tortured and killed. The latter alternative apparently was in the nature of an offering to the chief war god or the sun and might involve cannibalistic use of the remains. Simple killing and scalping were also the results of war activities. The Huron had a similar type of political organization with tribal confederacies and major chiefs. The typical war complex was also found among them and in fact was distributed even among some Algonkians and in the Southeast subarea as a rather old culture trait. We can turn now to a second variety of Eastern culture.

The Algonkian-speaking groups of the Northeast were primarily hunting, fishing, and gathering peoples with agriculture possessed by most as a secondary strategy of subsistence. Corn, beans and squash were the usual basic crops. In some areas wild rice harvested on lakes from canoes constituted a crop of equal value. In the Great Lakes region many groups lived in semi-permanent villages which were moved in a seasonal cycle from maple sugar collecting camps in the Spring, to Summer camps where agricultural activities were undertaken, and then Winter quarters in protected areas. Throughout the year hunting and fishing occurred. Deer, bear, moose, and small game were taken by the stalking technique and by traps. Fresh-water fish were obtained by hook and line as well as by nets. wild plants were abundant as they were throughout most of the Northeast with species of berries, cherries, acorns and other nuts, and grapes in some regions. Among the Coastal Algonkians the staple crops were also corn, along with beans and squash. Wild plants were also collected. Hunting, either as a year-round occupation or seasonally, was very important; especially in late fall. Drives were common as were fire surrounds. Among these peoples fish and shellfish taken along the coast added greatly to subsistence and a more sedentary existence.

Housing in the Great Lakes area commonly included the wigwam, a dome-shaped structure of poles covered by mats and/or bark, as well as more gabled bark houses. Along the coast very often bark long house-like structures occurred as multiple family dwellings. They were often clustered within stockades for protection among peoples near to Iroquois tribes. Simpler huts were also employed. In more northerly regions a narrow toboggan and snowshoes were employed for transportation and throughout the area bark canoes and dugouts were found. Many baskets and bark containers existed and most groups apparently had simple pottery. Wampum was widespread and, in style and functions, it was like that of the Iroquois.

Some groups had quill work – dyed porcupine quill pieces sewn to some material in a pattern – as an excellent craft. Clothing varied from winter to summer but consisted basically of sleeveless dresses for women and loincloths and leggings for men.

In the Great Lakes region the nuclear family was the smallest social unit and was generally organized for economic purposes into matrilocal extended families. This was a basic technological unit for agriculture, hunting, and other activities. As among Iroquoians marriage was mostly monogamous. People also belonged to clans which usually reckoned a member's affiliation through the father's side; patrilineally. These were exogamous in marriage, often owned sacred bundles in common with which to secure their collective welfare, and owed the usual support to those within the unit. Such clans were often organized into moieties which also functioned to regulate marriage and to bury the dead of opposite groups and to compete in games. A number of extended families with cross-cutting clans made up a village and these generally had a leader or at least a representative selected on a hereditary basis from a certain clan. His duties fell chiefly under the headings of keeping peace and internal order along with some technological coordinations. The associated authority was largely informal and very often based upon oratorical skills more than anything else. Very comparable social units occurred along the Coast although there – due to European stimulus – small groups may have allied themselves and functioned on larger political levels. Certainly the village was a basic unit and both matrilineal and patrilineal descent existed. Here too, chiefs were simply first among equals although some did organize confederacies; many in historic times.

Warfare was developed as elsewhere in the East. In the region of the Great Lakes it was often led by warriors who felt called to do so based upon some vision experience or dream. Motives included revenge and the gaining of some personal honor as an enhancement of prestige. While war generally took the form of hit-and-run attacks by a few men, occasionally villages might temporarily join together and precipitate larger "battles." Scalping was common. along the Atlantic Coast scalping was also a culture trait and was often involved with the Iroquoian patterns of capturing individuals for adoption or torture.

The Southeast subarea of the Eastern culture province is difficult to adequately characterize because of a marked difference in levels of cultural development. This fact is perhaps tied to the spread of the Mississippian Formative influence in prehistoric times. Thus tribal groups differed in technology from those practicing intensive agriculture with irrigation down to simple shellfish collectors. Social and religious differences followed the same lines. Since most groups did tend towards complexity we will focus on them in this very brief account. These peoples lived in farming villages, had leaders with real political power, and formed confederacies like some of the northern groups. Unfortunately many of these tribes either became extinct in early Colonial times or were removed to "Indian Territory" further west and so our understanding of these cultures is not very complete. Almost all groups also took on aspects of European culture very early.

As indicated above, most groups led a settled farming way of life based on the cultivation of corn, beans, squash, melons, and other plants along with a reliance upon many wild varieties; roots, berries, and grapes. Deer and bear were big game animals and, along with small game, there were various wild fowl such as turkeys. Fish were a variable resource, more important in some regions than others. Dugout canoes and occasionally rafts served as transportation devices used along the many rivers in this area. Villages were basically permanent and consisted of great numbers of houses clustered inside stockades. Among many groups dwellings were high, domed frames of poles covered by grass, thatch, or mud plaster, although along the Gulf coast they tended to be simple sun shades without walls. Quite frequently villages contained special structures of political and religious significance, for example, thatch temples built on mounds in the Mississippian style. Among the Creek three such special structures existed. A council house was raised up on a low mound at one end of the village. It was built of sod and clay on heavy wooden posts with a roof of bark raised in a pyramid shape. It was called a "hot house" and served for political deliberations. A flat area enclosed by low mounds along its sides served as a place for games and the torturing of prisoners captured in war and there was also a public square. This consisted of four square buildings raised up on another low mound. They were open in front, faced the center where a sacred fire was kept burning, and had sitting places inside on three tiers to accommodate persons of different social status. Public meetings as well as war rites and religious performances took place there. In contrast to architecture, clothing was extremely simple and, when the weather was hot, people went nearly nude. Pottery, which disappeared early in contact times, was probably the most outstanding craft.

We have a great deal of incompleteness in our knowledge of aboriginal social life. Many groups, certainly, had matrilocal extended families as techno-economic units and traced their descent for membership in clans and other descent groups along matrilineal lines. Marriages were mostly monogamous except for some upper class persons. Unlike many groups elsewhere in North America some important status differences occurred based upon political and military as well as religious considerations. These differed from group to group. Among the Natchez, for example, there appear to have been four main ranks of people. The Suns were a power elite at the top level and were considered as being descended from the Sun God. They monopolized political as well as religious authority. Nobles ranked second and had functions related to trade. Honoreds formed a third, military group, and the bulk of the population was composed of commoners (Stinkards) who performed the subsistence and other tasks related to survival. These were not completely exclusive groups. Mobility between them was possible due to kinship aspects and a practice of higher groups marrying into the commoner class.

The Creek offer another variation on the theme of status and rank. Each village had a dual civil and military hierarchy. The main government was in the hands of a chief, the Miko, who directed the town council. while he gained this position by virtue of membership in a special clan, the power did come from the office itself. He represented his village in a confederacy much like the Iroquois Sachem and made local civil decisions as well as coordinating economic activity. An assistant Miko and other government officials also existed. Paralleling them was a main war chief who directed military endeavors and who may have had absolute powers during war, unit leaders who actually led in battle, and elder warriors. These latter, who had held other military positions but who were too old for active hostilities, functioned as general advisors as well as helping to govern religious observances. War itself was generally like that of the Northeast; surprise attacks, close infighting, and the extermination of some groups. Scalps were taken and the adoption or torture and sacrifice complex was common. We can now turn to a consideration of religious beliefs and behaviors in the East.

CHAPTER XVI

NORTHEAST RELIGION

This chapter deals with the religious beliefs and behaviors of the Iroquoian- and Algonkian-speaking peoples of the Northeast subarea of the Eastern culture area. It also includes a few remarks on other groups such as the Siouan-speaking Winnebago. We can begin with the Iroquoians, specifically focusing on those who lived in what is now New York State since a great deal of the available data deals with them. The second part of the chapter then treats such elements of culture among Algonkians, peoples who surrounded the Iroquois in this region. It should be mentioned at the outset that reconstructing Iroquoian beliefs and rituals is very difficult. This is due to the influence of a revitalization movement – the Handsome Lake Cult (see chapter 19) – which forbade some older practices and may have changed or differently emphasized others. This is especially true of rites relating to agriculture. As a result, much of the following descriptions may reflect rather modernized tendencies.

The New York State Iroquois had a series of periodic festivals or ceremonies that had as a central core within them the endeavor to give thanks to the various supernatural beings that existed as well as, on some occasions, human beings. These rituals of thanksgiving also involved, as they did among the Huron tribes, the distribution of food to those participating. They were, as well, social events. Other ritual activities had more to do with disease and death. As one scholar puts these emphases in psychological terms: "In general, these ways can be analytically separated into rituals of thanksgiving and hope and rituals of fear and mourning. The former...worked to provide reassurance of continued protection and support from supernaturals....The latter–notably witchcraft, the masked medicine ceremonies, and the condolence rituals–attempted to cope with the consequences of loss..." (Wallace 1970:50). Most priest-like ritualists may have been largely responsible for conducting the thanksgiving rites; shamanistic-oriented types, as elsewhere, were involved in curing and more direct applications of supernatural power. The priestly types were called Keepers of the Faith and occupied elective but hereditary positions within clans, functioning rather like religious Sachems. In similar fashion they took the name of the office and acted as moral and religious guardians. It was also "...their duty to designate the times for holding the periodical festivals, to make the necessary arrangements for their celebration, and to conduct the ceremonies. Certain ones of their number...made the opening speech and the thanksgiving address...and also delivered religious discourses whenever they were deemed advisable" (Morgan 1962:185-86). Both males and females had such responsibilities. Modern Iroquois Faithkeepers have probably lost some of the former functions connected to such positions. We will discuss the shaman type of practitioner later.

A number of periodic festivals of thanksgiving occurred, all having essentially the same format. They involved morning-long series of ritual activities. If a rite was more than one day in length the regular format took up the first day with additions occurring on subsequent days. Rites were held in a long house. A speech would be given relative to the safe arrival of participants and, perhaps, a report on the general condition of the village. Then a special thanksgiving speech or prayer was recited. In it various supernatural beings and other entities were mentioned beginning with those on earth and close to the village and then moving outward to include those more distant and located in the heavens. People themselves were included here. Things mentioned included water, grass, the forest, animals, and agricultural products such as corn, beans, and squash. Other supernatural beings comprised a list of entities the definition of which is not entirely clear in the literature. Female spirits of agriculture, called "our life supporters," were important, as were those of wind, thunder and rain. The sun, moon, and other celestial phenomena were also made into religious conceptions as was a rather active creator type of being, variously named. In myth he was thought to be responsible for many aspects of the natural world and, unlike such deities we have mentioned for some other culture areas, he seems to have kept an active interest in the control of the world and human affairs. He did receive prayers, as suggested above, and had special rites devoted to him. In myth he was also pitted against an evil-minded brother who was responsible for many of the bad things encountered in life; their struggles accounting for the way things were in the world. These appear to have been pre-Christian concepts; notions also found in the Southeast area. At any rate, the creator was mentioned in the general thanksgiving prayer in periodic rituals as are today, also, deities associated with the Handsome Lake Cult. The prayer was followed by whatever specific ritual maneuvers were appropriate for that occasion and then a short form of it was repeated, followed by a feast or food distribution. Special dances and songs also occurred in the context of these rites of thanksgiving and in some cases tobacco was also burned, depending upon the main spirits invoked. Confession of sins, which accompanies such ceremonies today, is a modern embellishment.

We can examine some of these period rites against the general structural background provided above. Many of them were tied to some natural cycle.

> A number of these ceremonies recognize the appearance of the item mentioned in the Thanksgiving Speech and are so timed. For example, the Maple ceremony is held when the sap begins to flow in the maple trees; the Strawberry ceremony, when the berries hang on the bushes; the Thunder ceremony when the Thunderers are first heard in the west in the spring or when it is wished that thunder will be heard and rain fall; the Sun ceremony when the Sun begins to feel warm in the spring; the Bean ceremony when the green beans are mature; the Green Corn ceremony, when the first corn is ripe (Tooker 1978B:458-59).

The Maple ritual was a one-day rite and occurred in the spring as the first festival. It was an attempt to give thanks to the spirit of the maple tree as well as to the creator deity for having originally created it for the benefit of humans. As on other ritual occasions, shamanistic elements might also intrude. In the evening the Chanters For The Dead Society would sing special songs for persons who had been troubled by dreams of dead relatives or friends. We will presently discuss this rite and the role of dreams among the Iroquois. The Planting festival was also a one-day rite, held to coincide with the return of that season. It thanked the creator for it as well as seeking to invoke his blessings upon the seeds themselves; to assure their potential in the fields. Seeds were taken to the long house to be soaked in water at this time and the rain spirits and the sun were requested to aid in their germination and fruition. This rite, as in the case of others, also afforded opportunities for the request of other favors. From a recorded thanksgiving address given at a planting festival we have the following:

> Great Spirit, who dwellest alone, listen now to the words of thy people here assembled. The smoke of our offering arises. Give kind attention to our words, as they arise to thee in the smoke. We thank thee for this return of the planting season. Give to us a good season, that our crops may be plentiful.
>
> ....
>
> Continue to listen, for the smoke yet arises....Preserve us from all pestilential diseases. Give strength to us that we may not fall. Preserve our old men among us, and protect the young. Help us to celebrate with feeling the ceremonies of this season. Guide the minds of thy people, that they may remember thee in all their actions (Morgan 1962:196).

Shortly after this if rain had not fallen a special Thunder ceremony would be held to rectify that situation.

A Berry festival was held a bit later on, coinciding with the ripening of strawberries, the first wild fruits to become available. The invocation and thanks on this ritual occasion were extended to include all foodstuffs of this nature and it concluded with a feast of strawberries. In the past, other specific first-fruit rites may also have occurred. About this same time a day of general exorcism related to disease and witchcraft took place. Different sorts of spirits were invoked, along with the Thunderers and Winds, to keep disasters away from the fields and the village. In addition, two groups of performers went through the village. Starting at opposite ends of it they removed evil by rubbing and brushing the long houses and the furniture within them.

Towards Fall a rather more involved ceremony took place, The Green Corn festival. This was similar to comparable rites in the Southeast and in fact it is likely that many Iroquoian rituals had originated from that region. "When the corn was ready for eating, sometime late in August or early September, the community gathered at the council house to give thanks for the ripening of the crops for another year. The festival required four days" (Wallace 1970:57-58). The first day was much like that of the Maple festival and other one-day rites. On the second day a special thanksgiving dance was held during which speeches were given thanking all of nature's objects, apparently with a song and dance for each. Feasting followed as it did on each day of the rite. Something like this was repeated on the third day, including thanks to other humans for their achievements and past favors. This was perhaps also a time to recite war exploits. It may also have included a special sacrifice of a white dog to the creator since it marked a half-year period of time. The last day was given over to the playing of a game, the Bowl game, which has taken on more religious elements, symbolizing the struggle of the creator deity against his enemy. It is played today with six peach stones colored black on one side. These are placed in a bowl which is struck against the ground to shake the contents. One has to have five or six of the same color to score points, moieties playing against each other until one has secured the proper total to win. At any rate, this ritual surely represented the culmination of a number of rites dealing with both cultivated and uncultivated crops. It was intended to express the desire that "...this good fortune may extend into the future and that winter will not arrive until the crops are in" (Whitthoft 1949:22).

After the Green Corn festival was held the actual harvest was taken in and prepared for winter storage. When this was complete and prior to the annual fall hunt and war activities, a Harvest festival was held to again thank the creator and various other deities for the agricultural bounty of that year. It may also have lasted four days and was a kind of copy of the Green Corn rite. The major ritual effort of the year took place in late January or early February. It was the Midwinter or New Year's rite and lasted at least a week, often longer. Part of it recapitulated religious activities performed in other rites, some actions in it were symbolic of renewal, and still others were related to the Iroquois dream complex. We may briefly mention some aspects of this latter concept at this point since it was also found among the Hurons.

Much like the Algonkians of the Eastern Subarctic, Iroquoians believed that dreams could be used as information devices. Not only might one gain a spirit protector in such a fashion but dreams could reveal to the dreamer the innermost wishes or desires of his own soul. "Looking over the material on Iroquois dreams, it is apparent that there were two major types of dreams....These two types may be called symptomatic and visitation dreams" (Wallace 1958:241). The first type reflected a desire on the part of the soul itself, one that had to be acted upon lest the dreamer suffer harmful consequences. He would have to react to that dream in real action. The second type of dream was inspired by some supernatural being working through the soul or speaking directly to the dreamer; giving him information of greater importance to himself or to his wider community. It was important in both types to know what the dream thus signified and to act upon it. The Midwinter festival, and probably other occasions as well, provided opportunities for this to occur. Since dreams were often symbolic, their true content might be guessed by others at this time; if not, then the dreamer might propound a riddle, the true meaning of which could be discovered. We can turn now to a consideration of this ceremony.

The general, overt, purpose of the Midwinter rite was to begin a new year and to give thanks to the creator deity for the benefits of that past period of time and to pray for similar blessings to accompany the next one. "In this ritual man's essential relationship to the rest of the universe is defined and proclaimed, and whatever strains this relationship has been subjected to in the past year are patched and healed" (Whitthoft 1949:21). Despite its obvious importance to the Iroquois, our knowledge of this rite is less than satisfactory. This is largely due to the fact that while the first part, as still practiced today, does deal with renewal and has a dream-guessing component as older rites, the second part is given over to dances and other rites introduced by Handsome Lake. These may partially be reworked older rites themselves. And some former procedures have lapsed at present. Moreover, probably both it and the Green Corn rite were solstice observances which, over time, then became identified with seasons of agricultural surplus and animal abundance, given as they were at harvest time and after the main hunt of the year. Then, in modern times, these associations were also lost. Strong war associations may also formerly have been a part of it. Therefore, the best we can do is briefly paraphrase a modern account, adding a few reconstructions in the process.

Elizabeth Tooker (1970) has provided data on this rite for the Iroquois in general and we can extract from her accounts of it at various reservations. In the past, either on the first day or prior to it, babies were named if they had been born since the Green Corn festival. Others had been named at that time. Two special leaders dressed in costume went around to the long houses notifying people there that a new year had begun. They also gave instructions for participation at this time and stirred the ashes in the fires. One or more white dogs (unblemished) were strangled to death and hung up on poles. Other functionaries may have stirred the ashes again on this day. The next day was a time for special songs and/or speeches of thanksgiving to all supernatural beings as well as the creator. On this day "Four faithkeepers, a man and a woman from each moiety, next go around to each of the houses and give thanks that they are still alive and to stir the ashes..." (Tooker 1970:53). Other persons may also have done this in the past. Members of the medicine societies might also make a circuit of the houses at this time, blowing ashes on various persons. Dream guessing, previously described, occurred. Today, visiting between houses occurs, as probably in the past, and dances may be carried out.

On the next day the main performances of the curing societies took place; treating those persons whose dreams revealed a need for their membership in such societies as well as those who had become members the previous year. A sacred bowl game was also played and other religious societies staged performances. Dream riddles were recited and bands of young people, impersonating members of a curing society, went about begging or stealing food. This latter activity apparently occurred on a number of days in the past. On the fifth day of the Midwinter festival, the dog or dogs were decorated and then burned as an offering to the creator along with speeches and dances of thanksgiving. Personal chants were also sung. Curing rites continued both in the council house and in the long houses. The next day the bowl game continued and more dances and curing activities occurred. Eventually the game was concluded, final dances were completed, along with speeches, and a food distribution ended the ritual sequence. On most evenings throughout this rite more social dances took place. In general, not only have thanks been expressed to the creator and other supernatural entities in this context but through the dream-guessing and curing procedures the world had been set right once again for the coming year. Specific rites apparently fell on somewhat different days for different Iroquois groups. Before we look at curing aspects in more detail, we can briefly turn to periodic types of festivals among the Huron.

The Huron, like the Iroquois, also had festivals at which feasting was incorporated. Like the New York State groups, different Huron tribes had somewhat different customs in this respect although they appear to have all lacked the cycle of thanksgiving feasts previously described. For them perhaps the most important rite was the Ononharoia. "While this festival appears to have taken place at least once each year in each major village, it does not seem to have been a strictly calendrical observance. The reason given for performing...was either that many of the people in the village were sick or else that some important man or woman was ailing and the ceremony would help to cure them" (Trigger 1969:96-97). It was held sometime in the winter and occurred over a three-day period. People who were sick or disturbed in some fashion went through the village making noise and calling attention to themselves. They returned the next day to announce that they had dreamed of some object and asked for guesses as to the nature of these. Riddles were given, as elsewhere, as hints. Presents were given to such people and eventually the dream object itself came into their possession which was taken "...as a sign that the troubles that were threatening...had been averted" (Trigger 1969:97). Eventually such dreamers went into the forest for a period of time to lose their problem completely and then returned the presents except for the dream object itself. Such acts were like the Midwinter rite without all the other associations and may reflect an ancient core of religious culture in this region. More formal curing rites also took place among the Huron and these will be dealt with presently.

The spirit entities related to in Huron rituals also seem to have been generally comparable to those of other Iroquoian-speaking groups. Supernatural beings of thunder and winds, the sun and moon and the sky were common conceptions. Many of them were believed to be specifically responsible for the growth of corn and other agricultural products, good hunting, and other important activities. Not surprisingly, there was also a war deity. However, all of these seem somewhat less personified than among the New York State groups. Other rites of a general nature also occurred among the Huron. What are called Singing Feasts took place on an annual schedule as part of political confederacy meetings. They were given prior to going to war and at the installation of new chiefs; or even if some individual chief wished to gain in status. They required substantial amounts of food to be collected to feed the many guests who were invited. Singing and dancing occurred, led by chiefs inside a long house structure with only persons specifically invited by formal procedures being permitted inside. The feast itself seems to have been the highlight and accounts suggest that all the food had to be consumed by the participants. A more limited ritual endeavor along these lines was the Thanksgiving Feast given by an individual to celebrate some personal good fortune in hunting or other related activity. Such a person would give a feast for friends and relatives or perhaps even for a whole village. A person who had successfully recovered from illness might also be prompted to this act.

We can now examine a second variety of Iroquoian rituals, those having to deal with fear and loss (as it was put by Wallace). We can begin here with a discussion of shamanistic curing societies. Among the New York State Iroquois much of curing was conducted by members of special medicine societies who would diagnose the cause of an illness and placate the spirit entities involved or do the other therapeutic aspects necessary to restore health. Such endeavors might be done on behalf of individuals at any time, they were incorporated as we have seen into the Midwinter festival, and public exorcisms of disease were also performed in the Spring and Fall. Many such medicine societies existed, each with its own distinctive regalia, songs, ritual maneuvers, associated spirit entities, and myths or legends bearing on its specific origin. Some of these groups were quite ancient, others may have been of seventeenth-century introduction; perhaps from the Huron to the North. Some we know very little about. For example, there was the Little Water society. It cured by using medicines made out of parts of various animals. These were mixed with water and given to their patients. Members also met periodically to renew the powers of such medicines. There also existed a Little People (Dwarf) society which apparently cured with song and dance procedures after dark. A Company of Mystic Animals society gained power from that source, very much as in some other culture areas, and imitated animals in their rituals. Included here were Bear, Eagle, Otter, and Buffalo divisions. The Otter society was composed only of female members. There was also the Chanters For The Dead group, previously mentioned. They also dealt with people troubled by dreams. They sang songs on the evening of the Maple festival and divined which spirits – usually ghosts – might be troubling the dreamer. A feast was then held with food offered at it to that spirit in the effort to relieve such problems.

The most famous Iroquois medicine societies were the masked medicine societies, including the so-called False-faces and Husk-faces. We can discuss these in a little more detail. The False-face society was characterized by the wearing of wooden masks by its members. "They are wooden portraits of several types of mythical beings whom the Iroquois say only a little while ago inhabited the far rocky regions at the rim of the earth or wandered about in the forests" (Fenton 1940:405). They are usually divided into the very powerful leader spirit at the rim and less potent "commoners" who are his followers. These spirits are thought of as deformed and crippled and members of the society who represent them act themselves in such a manner in curing rituals; behaving as though they were the spirits. These entities had the power to control sickness and so were incorporated into rituals to relieve it by the False-face group. The masks worn by members differed in color (black or red) and in the placement and form of features such as mouths and noses. Masks had long (buffalo) hair and were given the names of the spirits they represented. The spirits conferred power upon society members while the masks were being worn. The Husk-faces (Bushy Heads) were another masked medicine society. The masks employed here are made of corn husks braided into the proper form. They too represented supernatural beings. "The Husk faces are a race of agriculturalists. They dwell on the other side of the earth in a ravine where they till their fields amid high stumps...as messengers of the three sisters – corn, beans, and squash – our life supporters, they have great powers of prophecy" (Fenton 1940:416). These spirits were thought to have given humans the knowledge of hunting and agriculture. It should be mentioned that there was also a buckskin-mask type with a long-nose feature which was a clown type used chiefly to frighten children. It was not incorporated into a society.

We can examine the False-face society in somewhat more detail. There may have been two levels of members within it; those who actually did impersonations and those who have been cured by them and who sponsor those rituals. Membership was by dream instructions or by the cure of sickness itself. Illnesses falling to this society often had head and body joint symptoms: swelling, soreness, and the like. A new member either inherited an old mask or had to carve a new one. He would go into the forest, select a suitable tree and pray to it and the False-face spirits. He would then roughly carve the mask on the tree and then remove that block of wood and finish off his work at home. Members also carried wooden staves and turtle-shell rattles as part of their ritual equipment; the noise generated by these was considered as a help in scaring off the spirits that caused illness. Evil influences could also be brushed away with pine boughs. In the Spring and Fall in public rites the society members would put on their masks and, after going through the whole village, they would go to the council house where those who were sick had been assembled. After speeches to the spirits and gifts to the performers, those who wished relief came forward and stood near the fire. "The faces swarmed over them, blowing ashes in their hair, manhandling them....They then danced around the council house to the music of a turtle rattle and a singer" (Wallace 1970:83). The great rim-dweller spirit was then impersonated in a dance by two individuals and then all the people inside the council house danced.

Curing aspects among the Huron were similar in many respects to those of the Iroquoians. Among these people, the unfulfilled desires of the soul could cause illness as could various spirits. Witchcraft too was a greatly feared activity. More natural problems such as wounds received in warfare were treated by herbal medicines, more rationalistically than among Subarctic peoples. Dream difficulties were treated in the winter rite already discussed and witchcraft caused illnesses, caused by spells put on a person by such evil humans, were treated in various ways. Counterspells, for example, were employed to return such a spell to its sender. Efforts were also made to determine the identity of the witch and, if successful, a witch would be asked to remove the spell. If they refused they could be killed with the sanction of the chiefs. The persons responsible for curing activities were shamans of various types. While some functioned only to control weather or predict the future and discover any lost objects, most apparently were connected in one fashion or another with attempts to cure the sick. Some of them were specialists in diagnosis. They possessed helping spirits which could reveal the causes of difficulties to them in dreams. Such shamans could also divine a person's soul desires by gazing into a vessel filled with water and waiting for that desire to manifest itself there; like using a crystal ball. Diagnosticians of these types worked with men who actually employed curing techniques in the event that a person's own actions were not sufficient to rectify the situation. Their powers too were derived from spirit helpers. Power was gained from a dream or vision experience that was ultimately secured by partial fasting in seclusion for about one month.

Many shamans formed themselves into curing societies as in New York State. Each of these groups apparently had a hereditary leader. This man was often a civil chief as well; leading to a reinforcement of both types of power. Each society cured a certain variety of illness or problem through its rituals and members were drawn from the ranks of those who had been cured. Membership might also have been inherited. One of these groups was called the Atirenda. In its major ritual activity members danced about and magically "killed" one another by using charm objects such as bear claws and wolf teeth. "As the members fell under the spell of these charms, blood poured from their mouths and nostrils as they bit themselves or was simulated with red powder" (Trigger 1969:98). They were restored to life as a way of indicating the general powers and abilities of the society. As was so often the case elsewhere, the members of this society were thought capable of causing as well as curing illnesses and so respect mingled with fear in the attitudes people held towards them. Another society was called the Awataerohi. Members of it may have been the shamans most commonly resorted to in cases of supernatural difficulty and illness. Their main technique involved the handling of hot stones and charcoal. In curing they might rub their heated hands over the body of the patient or spit pieces of hot charcoal on him. They also danced holding hot objects in their mouths. They appear to be related to ash-blowing shamans among the Iroquoians. It should also be mentioned that at least one masked type of society existed that imitated deformed spirits while carrying wooden staffs. Certainly a connection existed between them and the false-faces elsewhere. There were also animal societies whose members mimed animals from whom they gained supernatural power. Still other types of societies are mentioned in early missionary period accounts. We can now deal with a second major non-periodic ritual type, that concerning itself with death at the end of the life cycle.

The Iroquois had no real elaboration of childbirth or even puberty rites as such but death occasioned great grief. They feared death and the ghost that might result from it. They were really disconcerted over the death of a league chief (Sachem) and surrounded it with very complex rituals. This was because the death of these leaders also threatened the continuity of their confederacy. A Condolence Council was held as soon as possible after such a death and before any new league business was taken up. This was given by the opposite moiety of league tribes. Representatives of these came to the village of the deceased individual and met the mourning relatives at the boundary between the forest and the village clearing. They then recited the Roll Call of Chiefs, a special eulogy mentioning the names of the league founders and Sachem positions. These were recited in groups of names interspersed with a special sound–"hai hai"–said to represent the noise made by souls of the departed. If this were not done the dead would become unhappy with the living and send them disease or misfortune. A Condoling song, as a farewell to the deceased chief, was also sung. The Three Rare Words of Requickening were then given to the mourners by the condolers. These words were eyes, ears, and throat, and condolers, "...perceiving that the mourners' eyes were blinded with tears, their ears clogged and unable to hear, and their throats choked with sadness so that they could not speak and could breathe only with difficulty, wiped away the tears with the white fawn-skin of pity, cleaned out the ears, and removed the throttling obstructions from the throat" (Wallace 1970:96). They then continued on to the long house of the deceased where a more lengthy Requickening Address was recited as strings of wampum were passed over the fire. This address dealt with twelve separate things and its performance was intended to revive the mourners and lift them out of their grief as well as to remind them of various society obligations.

> With one or two exceptions each word or section of the Requickening Address describes first a particular hurt that has arisen as a result of the grief occasioned by the loss through death. Next mention is made that this hurt is affecting those present, and then that this hurt is now either removed or healed and the person or situation is restored to its former condition....Then, giving a wampum string...to those addressed, the speaker says that the word...is on its way to them (Tooker 1978A:438).

This ended with the identification of the man selected to be the new chief. The mourners then returned the condolences since the condolers themselves were grieving. The new chief was then installed in his position and this was followed by the usual feast activities and social dancing.

Mourning procedures were less elaborate for people who were not chiefs but the ultimate end for all deceased individuals was burial in a grave along with some goods intended for use in the next life. No real consensus existed as to the nature of this continued existence. Funerals were apparently under the charge of women who were conspicuous in their overt expressions of grief; crying, tearing their hair, and often rolling about on the ground. After burial had taken place those close female relatives of the deceased continued weeping activities and other signs of intense mourning for nine more days. The next day a special Ten Days Feast occurred. Survivors and friends feasted, much of the property of the deceased was given away and food was provided to feed the soul of the deceased and send it on its way to the next life. Prior to this it had remained close to the body. Mourners were reminded at this time that they must return to a normal life.

A soul or ghost might still linger about, however, causing dreams, so the Ohgiwe chanters might have to be called in to perform privately as previously described. They performed once or twice a year to deal with this difficulty anyway. A feast was also given one year later on the anniversary of the death.

Huron customs relating to death were much like those of the New York State Iroquoians with significant additions, especially that of the great Feast of the Dead. Upon the death of an individual, persons outside the deceased's group took charge and a wake or Feast of Souls was held for several days. This provided an opportunity for women to weep in a ritualized manner. Others who had previously died might be mentioned at this time. Burial generally took place on the third day. Activities began at dawn to feed both the soul of the departed and the funeral guests and, as usual, all the food was consumed. A procession then went to the burial grounds and the body was most often placed in a bark coffin. This was raised high off the ground on stilts. Property or presents were distributed at this time. For ten days afterwards the surviving spouse had to observe strict behavioral taboos such as laying on a mat with their face against the ground for long periods of time. Such deep mourning then gave way to a year of lesser restrictions and then a return to normal. If a person died a violent death they were buried immediately.

About every ten years, or perhaps each time a village moved its location, the great Feast of the Dead took place. At this time the bodies of those who had been disposed of in the normal manner were recovered from their coffins and reburied together in a large common grave. Each village apparently did this for their own dead independently.

> Only the bodies of those who had died recently were left intact. The rest were stripped of any remaining flesh and skin, which, along with the robes and mats in which they had been buried, were burned. This work was performed by the female relatives of the deceased....After the bones had been cleaned and washed, they were wrapped in fine new beaver skins....Relatives and friends contributed beads and necklaces to the bundle so formed....This bundle was then put into a bag....Then all of the remains of the dead were taken back to the village, where each family had a feast in honor of its own (Trigger 1969:108-09).

Guests from other villages attended these activities and a great deal of feasting and dancing occurred during the time a large pit was being dug. Bundles might also be reopened at this time to permit a last look at the remains and further mourning activities. Poles were also erected on which to hang presents. Ultimately, the pit was lined with beaver skins and the bundles placed within along with some grave goods. It was then filled in with mats, bark and earth. A general feast terminated these procedures. The other tribal groups in the Northeast shared some Iroquoian religious culture traits but also emphasized some beliefs and rituals in a different supernatural direction. We can examine some of these practices to give the flavor of their variety. In the Great Lakes area we can discuss the Algonkian-speaking Menomini and the Siouan Winnebago as more or less typical for that region, and to the south and for coastal Algonkians, the Shawnee and Delaware can be briefly noted.

The quest for a spiritual guardian from which one might receive blessings to give one advantages in life was widespread in the Great Lakes area as elsewhere. For the Menomini it was apparently believed crucial to enhance survival itself Among these people the basis for obtaining it was a Puberty Fast for both boys and girls. In this they received a dream or vision that would give them power and protection. They prepared for the event by undergoing short periods of fasting and practicing austerities and then spent a ten-day period in a small hut to seek the actual vision. Generally an animal appeared and the content of the experience would be interpreted by a shaman later on so that the visionary would know the extent of the powers or abilities he had received, how to deal with them, and the nature of any counter obligations incurred. These latter might include taboos and related negative behaviors. Overall, the dream seems as important here as a basis for action as among Iroquoians.

> It was indicated that children from an early age were encouraged to fast and dream. The special crisis for boys and girls came at puberty in what ethnologists speak of as the dream fast. Each was placed by the parents in a special structure at a secluded spot where...he or she might receive supernatural visions or visitations. By these, or rather by their interpretation, was determined in large the future destiny of the individual in the sight of the powers and of fellow tribesfolk, his or her rights and duties in the religious sphere, fortunes for good or evil and adult status generally (Keesing 1939:46-47).

Winnebago customs were similar. From early on children of both sexes were taught the traditions of their tribe to prepare them for life but it was an absolute necessity that at puberty they would have to go out to some lonely place, fast, and hope to receive a vision. This effort generally began with a short period which, if not successful, was followed by more lengthy endeavors along such lines. Part of the success was believed to be due to the cultivation of the proper religious feeling. As among the Menomini, other people would review a successful experience to determine its true nature and its demand on the youth. Success in life was predicated on such a vision. For example, "No man can hope to go on a warpath and kill an enemy unless he is authorized to do so by a definite blessing received during fasting" (Radin 1923:230).

The types of spirit beings involved in these vision quests and inhabiting the world in general fell into the class of "Manitou" previously discussed for the East Subarctic. In the case of the Winnebago, they were referred to as Wakan, in the same sense as among the peoples of the Plains. Apparently for all groups in this region the world was divided theologically into a number of levels, often both above and below the earth. The spirit entities inhabiting each of these levels sometimes differed in power depending upon their degree of remoteness from humans. For the Menomini, the Sun was very powerful and was perhaps the ultimate creator of all things. In lower levels thunderbirds, war deities, and the Morning Star were to be found. All of these, along with animal spirits and masters of animals, were basically beneficent and most could bestow blessings in visions; the more potent entities giving shamanistic potentials. On the earth itself many more evil spirits, including various cannibalistic types noted elsewhere, occurred. Essentially negative entities were described as being under the earth and included White Bear, Panther, and especially the Horned, Hairy Serpent which inspired great fear and accounted for deaths by drowning and related problems. Winnebago deities were basically similar. Earthmaker (the sun?) had obvious creative powers. Earth and Moon, the Thunderers, and other natural phenomena types were important and evil types including water spirits occurred. An interesting example was Disease Giver, who was more personified, "...his body being divided into two halfs, one half dispensing death and the other life" (Radin 1923:388).

Throughout this area there were various types of shamans and religious groupings. We can briefly examine these for comparative purposes. Some of these were helpful to their tribal groups, others were more dubious. We can use the Menomini as a general example here. A main shamanistic practitioner among these people was the conjurer and he was of the general type we have previously discussed. As elsewhere he consulted with spirits to cure the sick as well as divining the cause itself. This was often attributed to witchcraft as among many peoples in the Northeast. Divination was of the shaking tent variety with wind spirits and the Turtle joining the conjurer inside to reveal the cause of the difficulty. This type of shaman "...would then attempt to coax the soul of the patient to return and enter a small wooden cylinder where it was imprisoned and delivered to its relatives. The cylinder was then attached to the patient's breast for four days, so that the soul could return to his body..." (Spindler 1978:715). Sucking out of disease objects was also common, perhaps by a somewhat different class of shamans. Still another shaman group was the Mide who will be discussed separately. The Wabeno shaman fell into a rather dubious class, one which might help people or could cause evil. They were called "men of the dawn" and apparently received powers from the Morning Star deity. Some accounts suggest they may have received an evil spirit helper as well as a good one from their youthful vision experiences. They seem to have been oriented towards the manipulation of plants and roots and while they could provide herbal remedies and hunting charms for clients they might also give love powders and charms to give people unfair advantages. They might also seek to harm others more directly, often changing their shape into animals to do so. "This belief in the transformation of the Wabeno into some inanimate form, under which disguise he may inflict injury on his victim and immediately thereafter resume his natural form, is still very prevalent..." (Hoffman 1893:152). This was apparently accomplished by putting on the skin of the animal and then imitating its actions. Whether these people were called witches or a separate group of these evil humans existed is not clear.

Much the same difficulty is found for the Winnebago, where herbalists and more purely supernatural healers existed with both good and bad aspects.

Among both peoples quasi-shamanistic groups occurred, very equivalent to such associations among Plains peoples. Among the Menomini there were cults centering on the Buffalo and on Thunder (and perhaps others) whose members had the same guardian spirits from visions. Among the Winnebago at least four such societies existed, some having subgroups. These included a Bear society, Ghost society, Buffalo groups, and the Night Spirit society; the latter being involved with spirits who caused the darkness of night and who were in control of war powers. Rites performed by such groups emphasized the visionary nature of their attachments. The Bear society, for example, periodically put on a bear dance. Depending upon the desires of some sponsoring member they constructed a special lodge structure and placed a mound of earth inside representing a bear's cave. Tobacco and feather offerings were placed upon it and those who had bear power sang and danced both inside and outside of the structure. They imitated bear actions and those who had received slightly different abilities from this spirit incorporated a display of these into their activities. Some competitive aspects may have been involved. "The purpose of the dance was to thank the Grizzly bears for the blessings they had bestowed upon the people" (Radin 1923:300). It is possible that some curing benefits could be gained by ill peoples at these times.

Throughout this region sacred bundle rites were also important. These might be performed by members of kinship groups such as clans for the benefit of their own membership. Among the Winnebago a clan feast was given once a year or more often in the event that a number of clan people were ill or if some other misfortune had befallen them. In the annual case the rite was ostensibly in honor of the clan leader and included exhortations that he successfully carry out his duties of leadership. In more specific cases the intention was to stop the spread of the problem experienced by the group. In all cases tobacco offerings as well as various foods were given to Earthmaker and various other spirits. "These are to be offered to the spirits, and by means of these offerings they expect that their life will be filled with all that is good. It is to obtain these blessings that the feast is given" (Radin 1923:271). It is not clear to what extent members of other clans in the village or their representatives were involved in such rites. Among these people, who seem to have been rather more war-like than others in the area, there were also clan war-bundle feasts (Wagigo). While the clan seems to have been the organizational focus for these they were of wider benefit. Probably such war-power bundles were originally possessed by individuals who lent their potential for enhancing success in battle to others (along Plains lines). As the bundles were generally passed down along family or kinship lines they ultimately came under clan possession as their number decreased in historic times. At any rate, the bundles represented a complex of blessings received from various beings – thunderbirds, Night Spirits and the like – that had control over this activity. The rites associated were very complicated and included a series of speeches followed by song sets and ritual offerings that included deer skins to each set of supernaturals. Smoking of tobacco by participants and feasting on deer meat occurred along with a special dog sacrifice to the deity, Disease Giver. Manipulations of the war bundle were also a focus of ritual activity. It should be mentioned in this connection that war rites both before and after actual expeditions for this purpose were common throughout the area.

Among the Winnebago, a victory dance after war was very important and in fact a kind of ad hoc, temporary society existed to expedite its performance in the Hokixepe dance. It was organized by four men who had counted coup on the last warpath and its overall purpose was to transfer such valor and prowess to someone else in the village. When a man returned from a battle with a scalp he would leave it outside the village. The warriors would bring it in to be given to the selected person who then functioned as a host in the victory dance. War-bundle songs were also sung on this occasion and the scalp was dealt with to make the soul within it less powerful. "Then the dancers and the feasters, indeed all who had counted coup, tried to obtain some of the dead enemies' residuary life. All tried to add some new life to their own" (Radin 1923:333). Prayers to the spirits then requested success and protection in warfare and persons danced with the scalp. This was followed by a special feast. Among many groups a special dance also preceded war activities. In it spirits were invoked and successful warriors attempted to get their own guardian spirits to protect the entire party as they recited their own exploits.

One major religious activity and organization widespread throughout the Great Lakes area was the so-called Medicine Dance or Midewiwin. It occurred among both the Menomini and the Winnebago and was perhaps ultimately derived from Ojibwa groups. It was probably of very early post-contact origin. It was a complicated and tribally variable rite and so only a very brief indication of its structure can be given here. This rite

> ...was the primary ceremony of the Medicine Lodge Society, to which membership was obtained by preliminary instruction and formal initiation. This was done at one of the semi-annual meetings held in late spring and early fall. The instructions and ceremony were under the leadership of a number of recognized priests who were often shamans....It was held in a long, semi-cylindrical lodge that had been constructed for the purpose....It consisted of a pole framework that was left open, except for cedar boughs placed along the sides and up to a height of two or three feet. In former times, some tribes completely covered the Medicine Lodge (Ritzenthaler and Ritzenthaler 1970:88).

The society and its ritual seems to have represented a very collective approach to the supernatural. They attempted not only a cure-all to misfortunes in general and desired to prolong life and insure good health in members but also sought to bestow powers on those people who were initiated into it. Various motives were involved for would-be members. One might choose to enter because of dream advice to do so, as part of being cured of illness, being adopted to fill the vacancy caused by a members death, and other reasons. One had to pay a fee for membership and apparently a number of levels or grades of membership occurred. These were divided among some groups into earth and sky levels with power and fees increasing proportionately.

In the rite a number of days of private instruction occurred in which leaders recited myths connected with the origins of the society. Candidates had the secrets of their grade revealed to them, purifications occurred, and curing knowledge (and perhaps sorcery power at the highest levels) were mastered. Generally, some day or days of more public events took place at which powers of members could be exhibited. Members had or were given a special sea shell of supernatural power and an animal skin medicine bag in which to keep or control it. New candidates were shot by these shells, fell unconscious, and then had them extracted and were returned to life. Among some groups, power, of which the shell was the tangible symbol, may have been left in their bodies. Later on new members could also shoot shells to demonstrate their newly acquired abilities and other shamanistic tricks were performed to impress onlookers. While this rite and organization may have been of more recent introduction to help against the historic misfortunes besetting these peoples, the constituent elements were basically aboriginal. Since life-cycle rites do not depart significantly from Iroquoian practices, we can turn now to Algonkian peoples to the south and east, Shawnee and Delaware, to conclude the present chapter.

Algonkian religious patterns among these peoples are not well known. This is due to the early dislocations and extermination of many tribal units. We are also plagued with poor observations in historic times. Speaking of the Delaware (Lenape) specifically, "religion in the earliest period is poorly known because the Europeans who described it knew little of the system of beliefs as a whole and often misunderstood the significance of the rituals they witnessed" (Goddard 1978:219-20). It is clear, and predictable, that there was a great belief in guardian types of spirits and many prayers and offerings were made to them. The securing of such blessings was a prerequisite for success in all endeavors with perhaps the ultimate favors granted enabling a person to practice shamanism. In this latter case usually more high-powered deities appeared. Procedures followed in these quests approximated those described for other groups.

> Parents were especially anxious, of course, that their sons should have supernatural aid, hence, when a boy reached the age of about twelve years, they would...drive him, fasting, out into the forest to shift as best he might, in the hope that some manito would take pity on the suffering child and grant him some power or blessing that would be his dependence through life. (They were) able to fast...for twelve days, at the end of which time...some had received such power that they were able to...prophesy events a year or two ahead, with the magic aid of the supernatural being that had taken pity upon them (Harrington 1921:63-64).

Some visions apparently occurred in the context of natural sleep and were secured without fasting or might arrive suddenly in the midst of some personal difficulty. In all cases the spirit would first appear in human form, give directions, apply taboos, perhaps suggest some object to be worn as a charm, and would then depart revealing its true shape. Successful visionaries generally also composed special chants that referred to the attributes of their spirit helper or described their visions and these were recited at an annual ceremony.

The types of supernatural entities related to among the Delaware were very comparable to those of other Algonkians. All of nature was under the control of such Manitou. A chief spirit, possibly associated with the sun, was considered as an ultimate creator, doing so directly or through the agency of other spirits. He did receive some prayers although most worship was reserved for less remote beings. Wind spirits representing the four directions were referred to as Grandfathers, the Sun and the Moon as Elder Brothers, and the Earth as Our Mother. Thunderbirds not only brought rain to nourish the earth and fields but were also considered as chief protectors of the Delawares against various evil spirits and monsters. A corn goddess ruled over all vegetation and a chief master of animals (especially deer) occurred. He was called Living Solid Face and was represented by a carved mask and was impersonated in rites. Archaeological evidence suggests a long history for this conception. Evil spirits included the ubiquitous horned water serpent. Most of these beings were arranged in a layered universe consisting of twelve heavens and prayers could pass through these until they reached the creator at the top.

The Shawnee data also reveal a vision quest occurring in the past, often being undertaken shortly before the age of puberty. Spirits appeared in animal form after a period of fasting and praying on the part of supplicants. Instructions were given relative to some area of life in which the visionary would now be particularly adept if proper relations were maintained to the world of the supernatural. As elsewhere, not all seekers were successful. The natures of supernatural beings were very close to those described for the Delaware although some significant exceptions did occur. While there is some indication of a shadowy and remote male creator, in historic times such emphasis shifted to a female deity.

> The Shawnee recognized a large number of deities. Most of these were in some sense controlled, or at least influenced, by the supreme being, a woman usually called Our Grandmother, or the Creator....Closely associated with her were her grandson called Rounded Side...and a small dog. She was also associated with a variety of 'witnesses' she had created as intermediaries between herself and the Shawnee. The most important of these were tobacco, fire, water, and eagles (Callender 1978:628).

As suggested above, this deity was most involved in aiding the Shawnee, especially so in all rites of a communal orientation. Some myths relative to her suggest strong Iroquoian influence. Wind spirits, thunderbirds, Earth, and other supernatural entities also occurred and tobacco offerings, as elsewhere, were common. Mention is also made of a sacred fire that was constantly kept burning in their honor.

Ritual activities varied among these peoples. Perhaps the major Delaware rite was the so-called Big House ceremony. The overall intention of this rite seems to have been to renew the world and please the various classes of spirits within it. It is somewhat reminiscent of the Iroquois New Year festival. "The Big House represented the universe; its floor, the earth; its four walls, the four quarters; its vault, the sky dome where the Creator resided....The centerpost was a staff linking the right hand of the Creator with...(the)...people. At the close of the twelfth night, after the ceremony ended, the Delawares believed they had worshiped everything on earth and that, by pleasing the Creator and the Spirit Forces, their prayers would help all of humanity" (Weslager 1972:71).

The rite was initiated by a special leader; attendants and singers were chosen, special fires lighted, and many prayers offered to the Creator through his intermediaries in the various heavens. Special activities included dancing, feasting on corn mush and deer meat, and the chanting of the personal vision experiences previously mentioned. On the ninth night a special new fire was kindled and the ashes of the old one were carried out of the structure through a special door used only for that purpose. "The new fire seems to symbolize a fresh start in all the affairs of life" (Harrington 1921:101). Myths relative to creation were apparently also recited and on the last night women might also relate visions of their own. Final dances and prayers terminated this ritual and afterwards a sweat bath might be taken for purification. In the spring a specific rite and feast was held among some Delaware groups for the masked being who was the master of animals. Dances in his honor took place and impersonations of him, prayers of thanks for his help, and feasting on corn mush and deer meat were highlights of it. A green corn festival also occurred along with periodic feasts in honor of specific animals such as bears and otters.

The Shawnee also performed an annual cycle of rituals as well as sacred bundle rites similar to those of Great Lakes groups. There were apparently at least five sacred bundles, one for each tribal division. All were believed to have been given by the creator who maintained at least potential control over them; informing humans of desired changes in both contents and in the associated ritual procedures. Each bundle had a special custodian and was kept in his house or in a special structure nearby. Many taboos were associated with them. "The bundles provide the most sacred approach to Our Grandmother as well as the vehicle through which she delivers extremely holy, sometimes esoteric communications to her Shawnee grandchildren....Formerly bundles were opened and their contents manipulated in order to learn the cause of future events" (Howard 1981:214). There were also some private, individually owned bundles used for hunting success and other specific activities. There may also have been a special war bundle employed for group benefit.

Other Shawnee annual ceremonies included a series of dances, the most important of which were Bread dances held in the spring and fall. Both gave thanks to the creator and other deities. The one in the spring emphasized agriculture and was thought to be effective in promoting a good harvest; it highlighted the role of women. The fall rite reflected the male role in hunting and requested the abundance of game animals. In both cases prayers were offered to secure good health. Between these two rites which opened and closed the ritual year, other dances and festivals were held, including a green corn rite as elsewhere. Ball games employing deer hair stuffed balls were played between men and women as attempts to bring rain and promote crop fertility. Life-cycle rites were variable in their timing and for both the Shawnee and Delaware were roughly comparable to elsewhere in the Northeast. We can turn now to the consideration of the Southeast part of the Eastern culture area and briefly sample religious beliefs and practices there.

NORTHEAST BIBLIOGRAPHY AND REFERENCES

Barbeau, M.

1914. Supernatural Beings of the Huron and Wyandot. *American Anthropologist* 16:288-313.

Blau, Harold.

1966. Function and False Faces. *Journal of American Folklore* 79:564-80.

Callender, Charles.

1978. Shawnee. In Handbook of North American Indians, *North East*, Bruce G. Trigger (editor), pp. 622-35. Washington: Smithsonian Institution Press.

Fenton, W. N.

1941. Tonawanda Longhouse Ceremonies. *Bureau of American Ethnology Bulletin* 128:14-166.

1940. Masked medicine societies of the Iroquois. *Smithsonian Institution Annual Report*, pp. 397-430.

1937. The Seneca Society of Faces. *Scientific Monthly* 44:215-38.

1936. An Outline of Seneca Ceremonies of Coldspring Longhouse. *Yale University Publications in Anthropology* 9:1-23.

Goddard, Ives.

1978. Delaware. In Handbook of North American Indians, *North East*, Bruce G. Trigger (editor), pp. 213-39. Washington: Smithsonian Institution Press.

Harrington, Mark R.

1921. Religion and Ceremonies of the Lenape. *Indian Notes and Monographs* (Heye Foundation) 19:1-249.

Hoffman, W. J.

1893. The Menomini Indians. *Bureau of American Ethnology Annual Report* 14:11-328.

Howard, James H.

1981. Shawnee: The Ceremonialism of a Native American Tribe and Its Cultural Background. Athens: Ohio University Press.

Jones, W.

1939. Ethnography of the Fox Indians. *Bureau of American Ethnology Bulletin* 125:1-156.

Keesing, Felix M.

1939. The Menomini Indians of Wisconsin. *American Philosophical Society Memoirs* 10:1-261.

Kinietz, W. Vernon.

1965. The Indians of the Western Great Lakes. Ann Arbor: University of Michigan Press.

Lurie, Nancy O.

1978. Winnebago. In Handbook of North American Indians, *North East*, Bruce G. Trigger (editor), pp. 690-707. Washington: Smithsonian Institution Press.

Morgan, Lewis Henry.

1962. League of the Ho-De-No-Sau-Nee or Iroquois. Secaucus: Citadel Press (reprint of 1901 edition).

Parker, Arthur C.

1909. Secret Medicine Societies of the Seneca. *American Anthropologist* 11:161-85.

Radin, Paul.

1923. The Winnebago Tribe. *Bureau of American Ethnology Annual Report* 37:33-550.

Ritzenthaler, Robert E.

1953. The Potawatomi Indians of Wisconsin. *Milwaukee Public Museum Bulletin* 19:99-174.

Ritzenthaler, Robert E. and Patricia.

1970. The Woodland Indians of the Western Great Lakes. Garden City: Natural History Press.

Skinner, A.

1915. Associations and Ceremonies of the Menomini Indians. *American Museum of Natural History Anthropology Papers* 13:167-215.

Speck, Frank G.

1937. Oklahoma Delaware Ceremonies, Dances, and Feasts. *American Philosophical Society Memoirs* 7:1-61.

1931. A Study of the Delaware Big House Ceremony. *Pennsylvania Historical Commission Publications* 2:5-192.

Spindler, Louise S.
1978. Menominee. In Handbook of North American Indians, *North East*, Bruce G. Trigger (editor), pp. 708-24. Washington, Smithsonian Institution Press.

Tooker, Elizabeth.
1978A. The League of the Iroquois: Its History, Politics, and Ritual. In Handbook of North American Indians, *North East*. Bruce G. Trigger (editor), pp. 418-41. Washington: Smithsonian Institution Press.

1978B. Iroquois Since 1820. In Handbook of North American Indians, *North East*, Bruce G. Trigger (editor), pp. 449-65. Washington: Smithsonian Institution Press.

1970. The Iroquois Ceremonial of Midwinter. Syracuse: Syracuse University Press.

Trigger, Bruce G.
1969. The Huron. New York: Holt, Rinehart and Winston.

Voegelin, E. W.
1944. Mortuary Customs of the Shawnee and Other Eastern Tribes. *Indiana Historical Society Prehistory Research Series* 2:227-444.

Wallace, Anthony F. C.
1970. The Death and Rebirth of the Seneca. New York: Alfred C. Knopf.

1958. Dreams and Wishes of the Soul. *American Anthropologist* 60:234-48.

Weslager, C. A.
1972. The Delaware Indians. New Brunswick: Rutgers University Press.

Witthoft, John.
1949. Green Corn Ceremonialism in the Eastern Woodlands. *University of Michigan Museum of Anthropology Occasional Contributions* 13:11-21.

CHAPTER XVII

SOUTHEAST RELIGION

The religion of the Southeastern peoples of the Eastern culture area is perhaps the most incompletely known of all the cultural regions of Native North America. Early European contact bringing war and diseases destroyed many groups and others took on European culture very early. This makes reconstruction of aboriginal patterns very difficult. In this very brief chapter we can merely survey some of the topics we covered for the Northeast: gods, major rites, life-cycle observances, and shamanism and related practices.

Lists of gods and other spirits among Southeast peoples are difficult to acquire and often seemingly reflect Christian influences, although some good versus evil aspects seem to have been very early beliefs. The worship of the sun as a major deity may well go back to Formative-Mississippian times in this region. Sun gods seem well attested to in all groups for which we have data. Among the Creek the "...supreme deity was known as Hisagita-imisi, 'the preserver of breath'...who bore a rather close relation to the sun but was not equivalent to it. His representative on earth was the (sacred) fire, and the fire spirit seems to have been in some measure his messenger" (Swanton 1946:773). This connection between heat of the sun and the fire used in ceremonial activity was widespread throughout the region. Among the Natchez there was also a supreme being who lived in the sky and who was resident in or connected to the sun. He was a deity revered in many rites and had a sacred fire kept continually burning in his honor. The chiefs of the Natchez people observed the sun each day, bowing and calling to it and blowing tobacco smoke in its direction. "The culture hero of this tribe was supposed to have come from the sun and, after organizing the Natchez state to have entered or turned into a stone which was carefully preserved in the temple where a fire was kept burning perpetually" (Swanton 1928:206). The sun caste was believed to be descended from him which gave them their very prominent political and religious position.

Among the Yuchi the sun was also the chief deity and they called themselves the children of the sun, likewise tracing themselves to a culture hero who came from the sky to instruct their ancestors in the proper rites of propitiation. Among the Choctaw the sun deity was considered to have the power of life and death as well as being the source for success in warfare and other activities. A sacred fire was considered a manifestation of the sun, along with the former being a messenger to the sun, informing that deity about human behaviors and needs. Finally, the Catawba, a Siouan-speaking group, also accorded the sun, along with the moon, a high and probably creative cosmological position. "It seems deducible also that solar-lunar beings received some forms of adoration as a source of life whose linked symbol, likewise venerated, was fire – their antithesis being death and ashes" (Speck 1939:38-39).

Many other types of supernatural entities occurred in the Southeast. Among the Creek there were two spirits called Yahola and Hayuya closely related to major annual ceremonies. At least the second deity was identical to the four winds or they came from him. Thunder was also represented in spirit form as so often elsewhere in North America. Plants and animals also had spirits and sometimes controlling deities as well and played a great role in shamanism as we shall see later. Water serpents, usually horned and of evil intent, also occurred among these peoples. Sometimes they were associated with rain and war. Giants and dwarfs as well as the ghosts of deceased individuals might cause problems. Among the Cherokee, besides the Sun and Moon, Thunder, and Corn spirits there also existed a host of lesser types. Some of these, called the Immortals and who lived in houses in the mountains, were well disposed towards humans. They might help lost hunters. Other categories such as the little people were more dubious in this respect.

> Like the Immortals, they were invisible except when they wanted to be seen. They were physically well formed, but like European leprechauns and fairies they were no higher than a man's knee, and their hair grew long, like Trolls, reaching to the ground. They lived...in rock shelters and caves in the mountain side...and out in the open....One had to deal with the Little People with some care. They did not like to be disturbed, and anyone who did so might suffer a psychological or physical illness. The Little People could cause a person to become temporarily bewildered, or even to become insane (Hudson 1976:171).

The Cherokee also believed in monster beings, perhaps the best known being Uktena. This creature had the body of a snake, deer horns on its head, and wings like a bird. Like horned serpents it combined different natural categories and so was frighteningly unnatural. It lived in deep pools of water and waylaid the unwary. Even to smell its breath brought death.

Much as in the Northeast, these various beings were assigned positions in a layered universe. Generally this consisted of an upper world above the sky, a place of order and permanence, balanced by an underworld of disorder and change inhabited by evil beings. The world of humans was thought of as flat and crosscut by the directions into quarters with assigned values and symbolism. Again for the Cherokee, "The east was the direction of the sun, the color red, sacred fire, blood, and life and success; its opposite, the west, was associated with the moon, the souls of the dead, the color black, and death" (Hudson 1976:132). Certainly such symbolic patterning had its origins in earlier MesoAmerican thought. We can turn now to a more ritualistic dimension of Southeastern supernaturalism.

Major rituals, with the exception of an annual Green Corn or Harvest festival are not well known for this eastern region. Certainly, as has been mentioned in an earlier chapter, there were special religious structures around which rites were normally held. The Creek, it will be remembered, had both a council house and a public square. A temple was common among the Natchez and most lower Mississippi cultures. The Natchez temple was often on the west side of the main village square and consisted of a wooden frame building covered with cane mats, was perhaps 40 by 20 feet in size and raised up on an earth mound. Bird images were placed on its roof. Benches lined the inside walls and a partition apparently divided it into two interior parts, the second of which was kept shrouded in darkness. The stone representing the culture hero was kept in this inner chamber. In the forepart there was a low table for food offerings and a series of baskets in which the bones of past leaders were kept. There may also have been baskets containing magic crystals and small images of other deities as well as ornaments worn in rituals. The temple was dedicated to the sun deity and daily worship there was part of the "state cult" of these people. This was a preoccupation that probably suppressed many other ritual endeavors. "In this temple a perpetual fire was maintained and preserved by certain guardians, any remissness on whose part was severely punished" (Swanton 1946:779). Pure wood without bark was burned. How many of these priest-like guardians existed is difficult to ascertain. There may have been four or perhaps a dozen who worked in shifts. Special fires may also have been lighted at the door of the structure at sunrise and sunset. Food offerings were given at each new moon and in the morning and evening the highest ranking leader also entered for worship. Making divinatory pronouncements to the people upon his exit. Common people passing by this structure would utter cries of devotion and extend their arms in the direction of the temple. First fruit offerings were also made there by family heads at the proper seasons and seeds for planting were presented for blessing. If the fire in the temple went out it had to be rekindled from that of another such sacred fire. Apparently only one main temple with a sacred stone existed. Certainly such a complex differed from that of other culture areas we have surveyed.

The Natchez celebrated other periodic rituals besides those specifically connected to the sun temple. Some of these were of a political nature. In one, for example, there was a reenactment of a mythic or historic event in which their high leader was almost captured by the enemy. It was held during a special month each year and may have had renewal aspects. In the partial accounts we have of it a mock battle took place around the person of the leader. Actors representing enemies tried to seize and carry him off and supporters managed to recover and save him. Later on he led a procession towards the temple, stopping to throw earth in the four directions and then remaining still for a long period of time. His place was eventually taken by other functionaries. After returning to his own house this chief then dressed up in a costume symbolic of his office, sat on a special seat, and presided over a feast. Despite a paucity of clear information concerning it, this rite does suggest a reestablishment of political power or its affirmation, as well as, perhaps, suggesting that the welfare of this leader and the world itself were interconnected.

We also have among these people conflicting but abundant evidence of some sort of harvest festival possibly equivalent to the Green Corn rite among other Southeastern tribes. According to one source a special field was planted with corn in a special area not previously cultivated. This was done by members of the warrior class led by the highest war chief. These individuals also constructed a special granary and eventually harvested this crop and placed it in this special structure. After notifying the high leader (great sun) of their completion of this task he then commanded that special houses for the leaders of the tribe be constructed by it and people from all the villages of the tribe assembled. The high leader was then carried in on a litter and arrived amidst great pomp and ceremony. After some circuits of the area he ordered a special sacred fire to be lighted. Prayers were offered in thanksgiving and the grain was ritually distributed and consumed. As gathered from early French accounts:

> During the time of the thanksgiving, the four warriors with their great chief having arrived, each ascends a ladder, they quickly take the covering off the granary,...and give grain to the female Suns and afterwards to all the women who present themselves....They empty it on skins and husk it quickly....The pot is on the fire with boiling water....They throw this meal into it and hasten to cook it. As soon as it is cooked they await the word to eat it, and they never touch any of it before....When they see that all is cooked...they bring it to the great chief in two plates....He rises. They give him one of these dishes. He goes out and presents it to the four quarters of the world, then sends it to the great war chief...and then it is that everyone eats (Swanton 1911:115-16).

Songs followed this feast and a speech by the war chief. Warriors then recited their exploits and struck a war post that had also been constructed in the area. At night many torches were lighted and a dance was performed by men and women in concentric circles around a single drummer. The next day warriors played a ballgame interspersed with war dances. Such activities lasted until all the corn had been consumed. First fruits saved from the previous year were also eaten. People then returned to their respective villages. This rite bears a strong resemblance to activities among the Creek which are somewhat better known by piecing together accounts from different villages and times.

The annual harvest festival of the Creek was called the Busk or Boskita, "Act of Fasting." It was held in July and the general function of the rite was to propitiate all of the gods and to mark the passage of time from one year to the next. "In the ceremonial inauguration of the new Creek year man renews his worn and strained spiritual relationships with his environment" (Whitthoft 1949:69). When the village leader considered the corn ready for harvesting he decided on a day for the rite to begin and the population came and camped about the public square. They put out their own house fires before leaving. Leaders and warriors occupied special positions. Taboos such as one on the use of salt were placed on behavior. The Black Drink – a concoction causing vomiting for purification – was prepared. Most of the initial day was given over to dances and a series of these were held, most of which had their own songs and gestures. These had as their function the expression of gratitude to various spirits both good and evil. They were performed on the square ground and apparently anyone wishing to do so could participate, although some sources suggest that each clan may have had its own performance. Some of these dances were simply for the amusement of spectators, like the Crazy Dance; others, like the Drunken Dance, may have been in honor of deities controlling childbirth and may have involved sexual activities. On the second day the Black Drink was consumed. Leaders first drank and then others in turn. "It is a quick and rapid emetic and drank for that purpose by all the men and nearly all the women wash their children with it" (Swanton 1925:569). Consumption of this liquid was not only for purification and strength but was felt to be pleasing to the corn deity. Other dances occurred at this time including some by women.

After this, first ashes from previous fires in the square were swept up by the town leader who then kindled a new fire which was taken by the women to their own houses. This new fire rite marked the actual bringing in of the new year. "After this all personal differences, previously standing unsettled and liable to provoke disputes, were effaced and everyone began a new season of peace and friendship" (Speck 1907:142). The previously performed dances were repeated and a ballgame was played. There may also have been war dances and recitation of exploits as among the Natchez. It should also be mentioned that from time to time during the course of this ritual young men were given new names; losing their childhood designation and assuming one by which they would be known the rest of their lives. To accomplish this a leader or a warrior would stand and call a name and the young man so designated would go to him and receive a new name along with a symbolic change in costume. This was, in effect, an initiation rite since they could now marry, sit in a man's place in the shelters about the public square and take an active part in civil and military affairs. Eventually a feast of corn and other foods was held, the participants having fasted for the several main days of the Busk rite. They then returned to their homes, but after a few days reconvened in the town square for another Black Drink purification. Most groups in the Southeast had some version of this type of ritual.

Southeastern groups not only had major, periodic festivals but also, as elsewhere, observed many passage rites. These were tinged with special rules and avoidances. These included the usual birth-related magical activities to ensure the success of that endeavor and to promote growth in the newborn as well as observances at girl's puberty when they were subjected to special care and attention. Menstrual taboos and related restrictions also pertained to women later in life. Generally speaking they had to remain in isolation in a hut for several days – as did warriors leaving for a raid or persons about to engage in any special activity. Isolation was also a prerequisite for purification in general as was bathing in water which was believed to add to one's longevity. Naming and boy's initiation have already been mentioned. Of all of life's phases, however, death called forth the greatest ritual efforts and historical Southeastern peoples were in this case no doubt serving as the inheritors of the earlier mound-building preoccupation with it. As one scholar has generally summarized such customs:

> First of all, the Southeastern Indians believed that some part of a person, which we may call his spirit, lived on after death. Second, the living had to show respect to spirits and take their wishes into account. Third, some individuals were accorded far more ceremony at death than others, and in some cases, after their bodies had lain in a grave or on a raised platform for

> some time, their bones removed and placed in a temple or ossuary (Hudson 1976:327).

We can examine a few cases of such beliefs and practices.

Choctaw customs are fairly well known. If a sick person was said to be incapable of recovery he might be killed (as elsewhere in the East) and when a person did die his dwelling and any foodstuffs it contained would be burned or given away. The corpse would then be placed on a scaffold near the house along with certain items of property. The head of the deceased was painted red and the body covered with animal skins. The scaffold might also be specially decorated if the deceased were a high-ranking male. A small fire was kept burning underneath it for four days. A fence or mud wall set the scaffold area off as a special place and benches were placed nearby on which the mourners might rest. These individuals probably cut off most or all of their hair to symbolize their grief. After a period of time for the flesh to decay a special functionary called the Buzzard Man or Bone Picker came and removed the flesh from the bones. He accomplished this task to the accompaniment of songs by the assembled mourners. The bones were then given to the family of the deceased person who put them in a basket which was then placed in a special mortuary structure. If the dead person had been a chief it is possible that the bones were placed in a more special house. The flesh from the bones was burned. These dispositions were then followed by a feast.

When such charnel houses were filled with bone boxes the Buzzard Man of an area carried them to a central location and piled them up and then heaped earth over them to form a large mound. In some cases, perhaps, the charnel house itself might have been covered over when full. In late fall and sometimes also in the spring there was a feast of the dead which provided an opportunity for families to visit the burial mounds and again pay respect to the dead. As among Northeastern Iroquois, opposite moieties mourned each other's dead at these times. As elsewhere, too, death beliefs were predicated on the survival of a soul. "Each Choctaw is believed to have two souls that survive his death. One of these is the Shilombish, an outside shadow which in life always follows him, and after death remains in the vicinity to frighten his survivors by moaning at night....The second soul is the

Shilup, an inside shadow or ghost, which at death goes to the afterworld" (Campbell 1959:149). This afterworld was located on earth but was considered to be a great distance away. Its nature, about to be described, suggests some penetration of Christian belief but, from various sources of evidence, it seems to represent truly aboriginal beliefs.

Soon after death the Shilup soul began its journey, taking a path towards the afterworld. The approach was blocked by a deep chasm with a fast river at its bottom and to arrive there one had to cross over a log bridge. Actually two afterworlds existed (or there were two parts one might enter). The good afterworld was described as a land divided into square plots by a system of streams with a pool of pure water in each. Game was abundant along with wild plants. Continual sunshine, cool breezes, and eternal spring prevailed. People remained forever young. The bad afterworld had thorny brush, eternal gloom and never enough to eat. All those who dwelt there were constantly at war and were, vainly, trying to escape their fate. If one had been good in life, and sources are not clear on what constituted this, one crossed the bridge over the chasm without difficulty; if bad, one fell into the chasm and was swept away into the bad afterworld. Many other southeastern tribes shared this belief in a dual future existence of reward and punishment.

Somewhat comparable customs relating to grief expression and the disposition of the body occurred among most other groups in this region.

> Along the lower Mississippi the symbols of grief were much the same as those exhibited farther east. The hair was singed or cut off, the face was left unpainted, and the mourner stayed away from all dances and assemblies. The corpse was laid out in the best clothing with arms and such other articles as a kettle and provisions by its side. After burial the relatives repaired to the grave morning and evening to bring food and to weep, mentioning as they did so their degree of relationship. The food was placed at the feet of the corpse (Swanton 1946:727-28).

Descriptions of the funeral of Tattooed-serpent, the high war chief of the Natchez, who died in 1725, are frequently cited in this connection since these people were perhaps the last Southeastern people to have the full Mississippian complex. When he died, people in all the villages of the tribe were informed of his death. Relatives cut their hair and his property was destroyed. After laying in state for three days his body was placed on a litter and was carried towards the temple in a spiral fashion to prolong the time of the procession. Along the way there were scaffolds on which were standing a number of persons who would join this leader in death. These included his wives, some of his assistants and others who wished to obtain honor by dying at this time. These people were strangled by means of cords after first being rendered unconscious or stupefied by swallowing balls of tobacco. Their bodies were placed on the scaffold and that of Tattooed-serpent was subsequently removed and placed in a basket in the temple. Mourners cried for four days.

We conclude this very brief chapter with a discussion of shamanism and related activities. The Creek had several different types of supernatural practitioners. "Just as among beings and objects in nature there were certain which possessed or acquired exceptional supernatural powers, so there were certain men who were possessed of such power or were mediums for its expression" (Swanton 1925:614). One class of these people was called Knowers and membership was apparently limited to males. Only a few of these persons existed in any one village or area. While such practitioners might engage in actual healing, their chief function was as diagnosticians; to determine the nature of the illness afflicting a sick person. This was accomplished primarily by examining the clothing and perhaps other possessions of the patient. Such persons were also prophets in the sense that they might also predict the future. They were born with this power.

The curing shamans were called Isti Poskalgi, "fasting men," because they had fasted to receive their powers in visions or before undergoing formal training. In this the novice was required to drink special medicines which would help him to master the words, songs, and other knowledge imparted to him. Such Creek shamans apparently specialized in curing particular diseases. Cures commonly included rubbing medicines on the patient, giving him some medicines to drink, dancing to weaken evil influences, and sucking out disease objects. Among the Creek, "All bodily affliction is believed to come from the presence of some foreign and harmful matter in the system, placed there by either some animal spirit or a conjurer. So long as this substance remains in the body it cannot be cured..." (Speck 1907:121).

As among many Southeastern peoples, animals, based on mythic accounts, were said to cause illness and plants were often the source of the remedies. Different plant medicines countered different animal diseases. There were apparently also special dances caused by the ghosts of people not properly buried. Shamans who dealt with disease also engaged in contests as elsewhere and could also supply charms to common people. These charms were crystals divided by color into male and female and kept in bags. They were used in conjunction with spells to secure supernatural aid. A class of weather shamans may also have existed among the Creek. The Natchez also had rainmakers. When desiring rain these men filled their mouths with water and blew this into the air through a reed with several holes on the end (like a sprinkler). To end rain they stood on the roofs of their houses, danced and sang, and blew tobacco smoke. Many early accounts suggest that they might be killed in the case of failure. In fact, curers themselves might have had vengeance taken against them if they were unsuccessful. Natchez curers (Alexis) also removed disease objects. They sucked blood from the patient through a horn tube or directly with their mouths and used various herbs boiled in water as a liquid medicine. Steam baths were also employed. The patient was placed on a bed of canes and covered with moss, except for his face. A charcoal fire was then built under this and the patient was smoked until heavy sweating occurred. It is not clear as to the degree of specialization of Natchez shamans in these different techniques. Possibly the theocratic aspects of their religion somewhat suppressed shamanism as it did other ritual activities.

Divination procedures of various types were also found throughout this Eastern region. As in the Northeast and elsewhere dreams were thought to reveal much hidden knowledge; especially relative to the future. Water and fire types were common. Among the Catawba, for example, a diviner might place magic herbs in water in a container and then blow his breath into it through a cane tube. He would then observe the bubbles and ripples on its surface to determine the desired information. The Cherokee may have been the most developed in such arts. Among them a diviner would stand in a river and place a special stick in his mouth with its other end in the water. He would then swirl this stick around in a counter-clockwise circle several times while reciting the appropriate spell, eventually bringing the stick to rest in its center. He then studied the water in the area of the circle to see the movement of minnows or crayfish or look to see if birds were flying overhead. Such phenomena reflected predetermined answers. In a similar fashion tobacco could be placed in a fire and the results of its burning, smoke direction and the like were used to provide divinatory meanings. The Cherokee also employed quartz crystals for seeing into the future.

In sum, it can be stated that Southeastern peoples had many of the same concerns as elsewhere in the Eastern culture area. Their gods and spirits rather closely resembled those of the Northeast as did various life-cycle observances and harvest festivals. In the case of the latter we may be observing a ritual complex that dispersed with the notion of corn agriculture itself. Shamanism, likewise, was not particularly different or developed. The emphasis on death and its related customs were perhaps more elaborate as were the uses of temples, purgatives, sacred fires, and supernatural expressions related to social rank. Certainly supernatural beliefs and rituals in this region must have been much more complex than what the available evidence permits for reconstruction. We can turn now to the last culture area for Native North America, that of the Northwest Coast.

SOUTHEAST BIBLIOGRAPHY AND REFERENCES

Campbell, T. N.

1959. The Choctaw Afterworld. *Journal of American Folklore* 72:146-54.

Foreman, George.

1934. The Five Civilized Tribes. Norman: University of Oklahoma Press.

Gilbert, W. H.

1943. The Eastern Cherokees. *Bureau of American Ethnology Bulletin* 133:169-414.

Hudson, Charles.

1976. The Southeastern Indians. Knoxville: University of Tennessee Press.

Mooney, James.

1894. The Siouan Tribes of the East. *Bureau of American Ethnology Bulletin* 22:5-101.

1886. The Sacred Formulas of the Cherokees. *Bureau of American Ethnology Annual Report* 7:301-97.

Speck, Frank.

1939. Catawba Religious Beliefs, Mortuary Customs, and Dances. *Primitive Man* 12:21-57.

1909. Ethnology of the Yuchi Indians. *University of Pennsylvania Museum of Anthropology Publications* 1:1-154.

1907. The Creek Indians of Taskigi Town. *American Anthropological Association Memoirs* 2:99-164.

Swanton, John R.

1946. Indians of the Southeastern United States. *Bureau of American Ethnology Bulletin* 137:1-943.

1931. Source Material for the Social and Ceremonial Life of the Choctaw Indians. *Bureau of American Ethnology Bulletin* 103:1-282.

1928. Sun Worship in the Southeast. *American Anthropologist* 30:206-13.

1927. Social and religious beliefs and usages of the Chickasaw Indians. *Bureau of American Ethnology Annual Report* 44:169-273.

1925A. Religious beliefs and medical practices of the Creek Indians. *Bureau of American Ethnology Annual Report* 42:473-672.

1925B. Social organization and social usages of the Indians of the Creek Confederacy. *Bureau of American Ethnology Annual Report* 42:23-472.

1911. Indian tribes of the lower Mississippi Valley and Adjacent Gulf of Mexico. *Bureau of American Ethnology Bulletin* 43:1-387.

Whitthoft, John.
1949. Green Corn Ceremonialism in the Eastern Woodlands. *University of Michigan Museum of Anthropology Occasional Publications* 13: 11-21.

CHAPTER XVIII

THE NORTHWEST COAST CULTURE AREA AND RELIGION

The Northwest Coast is the final culture area to be surveyed in this book. In geographical terms it runs along the Pacific coast and inland a short way from approximately Yukatat Bay in Southeastern Alaska down towards Northern California. This is a region of heavy forests and an irregular coast-line with offshore islands. Because of a fortuitous concentration of marine resources an extremely complicated level of culture was achieved in this area – a development usually only associated with advanced agriculture and domesticated animals. While some of the more northern tribes were most typical and the originators of many developments, most groups did manifest variations of an overall cultural pattern and specific religious beliefs and practices. Rather considerable linguistic diversity occurred. In the north, Athabascan languages were spoken by groups such as the Tlingit and Haida. In the central region Wakashan languages prevailed. The Kwakiutl and Nootka are famous examples of these peoples. Salishan languages were spoken towards the south, for example among the Tillamook. Penutian languages with ties to California peoples were also mixed in here and there. Such linguistic variety suggestions the attractiveness of the area to many peoples over a considerable period of time.

Fishing was the basis of life in the Northwest Coast. A number of species of salmon migrated up the streams in this region as part of their spawning cycle and schools of halibut, cod, herring, and smelt could be taken along the coast. While some fish resources were seasonal, good preservation techniques permitted their year-round contribution to the diet. Many techniques for exploiting them developed: fish dams, basket traps, dip nets, and harpoons. Rake-like tools were used for literally harvesting herring and drawing them into boats. Along with fish, shellfish varieties such as clams, mussels, and abalone could be collected. Sea mammals such as whales, seals, and sea otters were hunted by some tribes. The use of harpoons cast from canoes was a common technique for obtaining these. In addition to this bounty of sea resources many groups also did hunting on land for bear, deer, elk, and smaller game such as beaver and mink. Bow and arrow hunting and the use of traps was widespread. Various bird species and migratory waterfowl were also taken. Wild plant resources were available but generally were unimportant.

Just as animal skins formed a resource for technological constructions and creativity among Plains peoples the great abundance of wood, especially from cedar trees, in this region provided raw materials for many material items of culture. Dishes, boxes for storage, mats and clothing were all constructed of wood or its derived fibers. Sturdy houses which were large and had gabled roofs were also made as well as large canoes some of which had the capacity to hold a large number of people. Wood carving for decoration and to create masks with religious significance reached the level of a great art tradition. The well-known "totem pole" was a hallmark of this region. Masks were outstanding in the details of their construction and will be dealt with in the context of religious beliefs and behaviors. Material paraphernalia was certainly highly developed in the Northwest Coast.

Social life in this culture area was very diverse probably due to linguistic and historic variations and perhaps also due to the geographic isolation feature of the region itself. Local groups were an important social level, existing above the family but below the tribe. While local groups might combine for religious, military, or specific social functions, feelings of real tribal identification were underdeveloped among most groups. Local groups were based on kinship ties and comprised lineages and larger descent aggregates. In the North, for example, where matrilineal descent prevailed, the residence unit consisted of men and their sister's sons and in-marrying wives. These comprised a whole village or a series of houses built close together. Local groups had chiefs who coordinated technological and social activities of the members and who were custodians of group property such as fishing stations, ocean-going canoes, and the like. Such chiefs had real political power at least with respect to their own groups. A rank system also existed and was defined rather individually in degrees of direct heredity from the founders of descent groups. This system is generally characterized as comprising chiefs, nobles, and commoners with differences in the prestige and associated prerogatives of such positions. Success in warfare or in craft activities might have somewhat altered one's rank in this system as did becoming a shaman of great repute.

High rank was conferred and exhibited at feast activities called potlatches. These were give-away events at which new chiefs were presented to invited groups, rituals occurred along with dispersal of food and property, and, among other functions, the rank of the entire group might be advanced. Slaves also occurred in most groups. They were persons either forced into this condition due to debt or were persons captured in war. They were outside the class system but might be sacrificed to enhance group status. War in this culture area was common although the level and intensity of it was higher in the North than in the South where it was generally limited to feuding situations. Such feuds were motivated by trespass of group territory and were sustained by revenge attacks over long periods of time. Payment of wealth might lead to their resolution. Where war was more complex the motives might, on the surface, be to attack another group when precipitated by grief resulting from the death of an important person but covertly involved driving off or killing off another group to acquire their lands and other wealth as well as for slaves. Victims were often beheaded and some groups also took scalps. We can now examine the religious beliefs and behaviors of this area.

Religion, like the rest of Northwest Coast culture, was very complex. It was also somewhat localized due to the ecological isolation of many of the tribal groups in this area. Nonetheless, one noted scholar has suggested that:

> Native religious beliefs and practices on the Northwest Coast revolved about a series of patterns and concepts shared by all or nearly all of the groups participating in the areal culture. There was, of course, a good deal of variation in the detailed manifestations of these basic tenets, but from the broad point of view these differences are quite superficial. These fundamental principles that combined to give the Northwest Coast religion its distinctive cast were: lack of systematization of beliefs on creation, cosmology, and deities; a rather vague notion of a remote, disinterested Supreme Being or Beings; a set of beliefs revolving about the immortality of certain economically important species of animals, combined with a series of ritual practices to ensure the return of those creatures; and finally, the concept of the possibility of lifelong assistance by a personal guardian spirit (Drucker 1963:151).

We can add to this statement the usual observances of the life cycle of birth and death, puberty rites for girls, a well-developed complex of shamanism and curing, and major rituals that were performed during the winter season. As Drucker noted, the concept of a supreme being so well developed in many Eastern areas was only vague; such beings were remote and only poorly conceptualized. The emphasis, as was so often the case in North America, was on the more immediate types of supernatural entities; those who lived in forests and mountains and in the ocean. As suggested, many of these were potentially of the guardian spirit variety and could be helpers of shamans; others might bring benefit to whole groups of people. An example of the second type were Salmon spirits who became fish at spawning time to migrate up rivers to form an important part of the food supply. Other spirits brought blessings during the winter to those who danced in their honor. Still other supernatural beings were of a more evil variety and often took monstrous shapes as in the neighboring Subarctic area. We can begin with a discussion of shamanism since many beliefs came together in that complex.

Shamans, as in all other culture areas, had as their prime function the curing of sickness. Some also aided in the food quest by luring animals or making hunting charms, influenced weather, divined the future, and assisted against enemies in war. They also engaged in contests among themselves. We can use the Kwakiutl as an in-depth example of such practices. A number of distinct types of shamans occurred among these people. The most potent of these types were those who had not only the power to cure but to also cause disease by "throwing" disease objects into other people. Such were generally also assistants to chiefs and worked harm to enemies on their behalf. Then there were shamans who had similar curing abilities but who were incapable (or unwilling) to cause disease. There were also persons who merely located these problems for others to cure. "A lower class of shamans neither throw or remove disease, but merely discover it, by feeling the patient and locating it. Most of these shamans are women" (Boas 1966:146). To accomplish this one sat near the patient, washed her hands and felt the body. By so doing she could discover where the sickness was located and the type of supernatural power responsible. Such a "feeling" shaman often then suggested that the cure lay in the patient coming to control that supernatural power; perhaps even in becoming a shaman. Other types of supernatural practitioners include the Seer, a person who has the gift for foretelling the future, sorcerers who harmed other people by evil magical techniques (often called witches in the literature), and special people sometimes called dreamers who seem to have been sons or successors of curing shamans. This last type apparently served as scouts, keeping their masters informed on the illness of possible clients.

Among the Kwakiutl a shaman might obtain his position by heredity, a natural enough event given the nature of Northwest Coast society, or he might seek the gift independently or be so chosen by supernaturals. Often in childhood he might have "fainting fits" or act in a wild and uncontrolled manner. Such behavior was interpreted as a sign of shamanistic destiny. Common associated spirits were the wolf, killer whale, and toad and the overall format involved making the person sick with the power and then curing him in a somewhat hyperdeveloped vision quest-like sequence of events. The novice was taken to a lonely place believed inhabited by spirits. There a hut was built for him and he waited in isolation for about four days or until hearing the song of his spirit helper. This spirit then placed a quartz crystal in which shaman power resided into the body of the novice, giving him a special name and other instructions. Older shamans then retrieved the novice and brought him back to his house. They dressed him in hemlock rings having sacred significance for curing. While an audience drummed the novice danced and sang songs given to him by his helping spirit. He might have displayed his power at this time or he went back for another short period of time in isolation to gain further control over it. Eventually the hemlock rings were burned and he did display his power to cure sickness. He did have to observe many taboos for up to four years after this event; not even being able to mourn deceased relatives during this period. He might also not be able to request payment for cures at this time.

Curing activities of shamans among these people were somewhat different than elsewhere. "The most important ceremonial implement of the shaman is the purification ring....The essential feature of the use of the ring is that the patient must be passed through it. The ring is made of hemlock branches...large enough to be passed over the head and down the whole body of the patient" (Boas 1966:136). Crosspieces on it represented arms and legs. Rattles were also used and masks, which will be discussed later on. Cures were public events to which elderly people were invited even if not relatives of the patient. Younger people were generally excluded as their sexual activities or menstrual cycles might adversely affect the success of the proceedings. Drummers formed a line opposite the house fire and the patient was placed between while observers sat at the rear of the dwelling. The shaman often performed in a contorted posture, his body trembling violently in seemingly uncontrolled fashion.

The format of the cure itself reflected the suspected cause of the illness. For the Kwakiutl, and most other groups in this culture area, the two chief causes of illness were the intrusion of disease objects or entities sent by sorcerers, other shamans or supernatural beings, and soul loss. This latter cause often was the result of some sudden fright in the patient. In the case of object intrusion the shaman eventually came to sit near the patient. He felt the body to locate the source of the problem if necessary, then moistened his lips and sucked out the disease – represented by a splinter of bone or other materials. Generally these emerged from the shaman's mouth covered with blood. This was then disposed of, often by the shaman himself swallowing it. Cases of soul loss involved somewhat more complicated manipulations. After singing to call his helping spirit a shaman in these cases sang a second time to call souls and ghosts. He held his hemlock ring as he did this and continued singing until the soul of the patient became attached to it. He sang a third time to encourage the soul to remain on the ring and made a number of circuits around the interior of the house. Eventually he returned to the patient and passed the ring over that person and then rubbed it against the sick person's body. The patient then rose and stepped out of the ring in a prescribed manner. This was repeated four times, the soul becoming smaller each time and eventually reentering the patient. The shaman then divined the success of his cure. Sorcerers might also be discovered and killed in the event they were related to the causes of illness in any way.

We can more briefly examine some other examples of shamanism since it was such a basic feature in this area. Among the Tlingit, shamans (Ichta) had a number of spirit helpers and masks to represent them. They also maintained a wild, dirty appearance. They never cut their hair, letting it fall in long strands or doing it up in a knot at the back of the head. They wore necklaces of bones and did wild, contorted dances like the Kwakiutl. They were especially interested in obtaining split animal tongues to increase their powers. Some spirits were hereditary in families provided the spirits would accept the novice. "Who ever wishes to become a shaman goes alone into the forest or the mountains far from human contacts for a period of one week to several months, during which time he nourishes himself on roots....The shorter or longer period in the wilderness depends on the appearance of the spirit. When he finally meets the spirit he can count himself among the lucky if he gets a land otter in whose tongue is contained the whole secret of shamanism" (Krause 1956:195). Tlingit shamans apparently had relations to three kinds of spirits (Jek). Upper spirits who were the souls of persons who died in war and appeared to shamans as warriors, Land spirits who were the souls of persons who died naturally and appeared as land animals, and Water spirits who were the souls of water animals. A shaman had to maintain proper rapport with these spirits or they might kill him. He could also "throw" them into an enemy or a person expressing disbelief in his activities.

Tlingit shamans were considered especially effective at exposing sorcerers who were men or women who had learned their skill from a mythic being. In harming others they sought to obtain something belonging to their victim and then to place it near a dead body while reciting an evil spell. The shaman would manipulate the body of the patient to determine the identity of the sorcerer and then accuse someone. If such a suspect confessed he had to show the shaman the possessions of the victim he had taken and these were then purified to relieve the distress. If he failed to confess apparently he was starved to death or drowned. Among the Tlingit guardian spirits also occurred, giving other than curing powers and abilities and this distinction seems to have been fairly typical for the whole Northwest Coast area.

Among the Salishan speakers around Puget Sound there were two basic classes of spirits. Sklaetut were guardian spirits thought capable of bringing luck in acquiring wealth and rank or success in war. Xudab spirits were beings who controlled illness and could aid shamans in curing. All such spirits had their own special songs and traveled around the earth, returning to the villages of humans during the winter. People gained spirits for one or another purpose by becoming "sick" and then singing and dancing to please them. The guardian spirits left part of each year but shamanistic types remained with their owners so they might function on a year-round basis.

Salish peoples in this area had two types of shamans "...those who sucked in curing and those who cured without touching the patient. The former could also look for souls....The distinction between the two kinds of shamans depended on the kinds of spirits he had and what they had taught him" (Haeberlin and Gunther 1930:76). The same spirit might not teach different shamans the same things. Generally speaking, a shaman would seek a helping spirit early in life but would not actually practice until about twenty-five; after acquiring six or more spirit entities. As elsewhere these shamans might eventually become wealthy. Their cures involved the return of lost souls and removing disease objects by sucking, pulling out with the hands, bathing the patient with cold water, striking the patient's body, and bleeding. Shamans might also kill other people if offended by them as well as other shamans in contests of their abilities. In the extreme south of the Northwest Coast culture area the complicated aspects of shamanism declined and even guardian spirits may not have been universally shared. Among the Takelma, for example, "The shaman obtained his magical power to cause and cure sickness from one or generally several guardian spirits...as a rule animal spirits or natural objects and forces....It is to be carefully noted that guardian spirits were not possessed by the great run of people..." (Sapir 1907:41-42).

Catching disease objects and removing them was standard procedure among these people and several classes of shamans existed as elsewhere in this area.

Ritual behaviors separate from curing activities also occurred in this area. Two major complexes are generally highlighted in the literature. One of these was the World Renewal type of ritual of the Yurok, Karok and Hupa tribes which we discussed as part of Californian religion. The second complex consisted of a series of performances revolving around supernatural beings and according to one scholar these fell into three types "...which comprise a series in complexity of elaboration of the basic theme" (Drucker 1965:97). The first of these he calls the Spirit Singing complex where individuals demonstrated the result of their guardian spirit quests by exhibiting songs and dances or special powers they had so acquired. Among some groups such as those around Puget Sound, these semi-competitive displays were the highest level found. A more complex type of performance was the Crest Dance. In it the performer exhibited songs and dances or powers which were his heredity right by virtue of having been bestowed upon an ancestor by some spirit entity. The most elaborate performances were the Dancing Society complex in which not only the hereditary gifts given by spirits were displayed but the vision-quest episode itself was acted out with great drama and stagecraft. The basic plot here was "...the protagonist's encounter with a spirit who kidnaps him, bestows supernatural powers upon him, then returns him to his village, repeating the experience of the ancestor from which the performer inherited the right to the performance" (Drucker 1963:164). To accomplish this and to heighten the ritual drama and effects, elaborate costumes were worn, houses had trap doors to aid actors in appearing and disappearing, speaking tubes were used to make voices come from various directions, and masks were employed. These last were so well made that we can briefly discuss them.

The masks were carved out of wood, chiefly red cedar and alder and were constructed after obtaining the wood, estimating shrinkage and then letting the finished product dry out for its final form after which it could be painted. Generally the carvers were high-ranking males belonging to the ritual societies who used the masks or a shaman having spirit power to do so. Actual construction might occur in the house of the person requesting a mask or in the forest and the carvers did this work as a part-time activity. "A man was recognized for his special abilities, but he lived much as others lived, following traditional subsistence activities....But a gifted carver was respected for the power he had acquired, power to see what others could not see, and power to transform what they were unable to transform" (Malin 1978:18). Three basic types of masks existed. A single face mask represented one spirit. Mechanical masks had only one face but had some movable parts to enhance the aspects of the spirit represented. The most spectacular creations were the transformation masks which comprised one or more spirit faces hidden behind an outer design which was hinged to swing open at a critical dramatic moment to reveal what was within. Masks were held on with cords around the wearer's head or in the case of very large types, by a webbing of bent twigs inside. Apart from shamanistic use and a few social/non-ritual types, the use of masks was restricted to the sacred season and the ritual events held at that time.

We can discuss the Kwakiutl as an example of such dramatic performance among Northwest Coast peoples. Among them specifically the rituals and their organization were perhaps the most complex. The time period for their rituals was the Winter sacred season (beginning in November), a time when supernatural beings were near the villages and quarrels and other secular things had to be forgotten. Many different activities occurred along the lines previously mentioned but they were all coordinated together into one overall cycle of dramatic performances. This required a great deal of management and so:

> The whole tribe is divided in two groups: the uninitiated, secular, who do not take any active part in the ceremonial, and the initiates. The latter are subdivided into two groups, which I will designate...the Sparrows...and the Seals. The Sparrows are the managers of the ceremonial. All the officials are Sparrows. The Seals are those who are under the influence of the spirits of the winter ceremonial and act according to the forms characteristic of the spirit under whose influence they stand (Boas 1966:174).

The Sparrows who coordinate the activities gained their position by heredity; a few became officers directly, most by having first been Seals. This gave them shaman-like powers enabling them to serve as spiritual guides and managers. They formed themselves into a number of societies which were age graded like some of those in the Plains area. Some were female but most were male. In addition to other responsibilities they also performed in a comic fashion prior to the start of the formal proceedings and feasted themselves periodically.

The Seals represented the various supernatural beings and involved people belonging to many different descent groups who had generally acquired their position by marriage ties. More than fifty separate spirit entities were impersonated. Further, "All the spirit impersonators fall into two hierarchical divisions. The highest are the Laxsa...and include all dancers who came under the influence of Man Eater at the Mouth of the River....In ritual these dancers actually disappear into the woods and need to be captured. All other dancers are Wixsa...they need not leave the ceremonial house at all" (Goldman 1975:89). Laxsa members performed the major ceremonies and apparently consisted of three separate societies or divisions as impersonation groups. Wixsa also had several divisions, one of which, the Nutlmatl or fool dancers, acted as police in enforcing discipline in the rites and as contraries; again in Plains fashion. Among some Kwakiutl groups these two different sets of impersonators performed at different times.

We cannot in the present work discuss the Winter ritual in descriptive detail. We can give, however, a brief sample of part of it. One of the most important and dramatic performances of the Laxsa division was the Hamatsa or cannibal dance. Persons involved in this rite were possessed by a violent desire to consume human flesh and were taken away by the highest cannibal spirit. Novices involved here had to remain in isolation in the woods during most of the winter period. When one returned, acting out the basic dramatic format, he came to the village crying out the distinctive word Hap–"eating"–a number of times. Assistants to such novices were then supposed to obtain food for them. "Then he returns and attacks every one upon whom he can lay his hands. He bites pieces of flesh out of the arms and chests of the people" (Boas 1895:438). Then special functionaries came to such possessed individuals, shook rattles to pacify them, and formed a protective circle around them to prevent further attacks. Apparently in the more remote past slaves were killed and at least part of their bodies eaten by the Hamatsa. Corpses were also eaten in these performances, pieces of which were cut by the main ritual leader and ingested without chewing.

> After this part of the ceremony is finished...(the assistants)...drag them to the salt water. They go into the water until it reaches up to their waists, and, facing the rising sun, they dip the hamatsa four times under water. Every time he rises again he cries hap. Then they go back to the house. Their excitement has left them. They dance during the following nights. They look downcast and do not utter their peculiar cries....After the close of the ceremonial the hamatsa by the payment of blankets indemnifies those whom he has bitten and the owner of the slaves who he has killed (Boas 1895:442-43).

As in most dances in the winter ritual of the Kwakiutl specific movements and actions reflected mythic attributes or adventures of the impersonated spirits.

Among other groups the number of separate dance societies was compressed. The Nootka, for example, had but a single group, the Wolf Dancers, who reenacted a mythic episode by carrying off novices, generally young children. Persons of high rank could be carried off a number of times to receive additional spiritual benefits. The start of their rite was heralded by the blowing of wooden horns miming the cries of wolves and men wearing wolf disguises then captured a number of young persons, eventually taking them behind a partition in a ritual house. There they were instructed while adults engaged in feasting and social dance activities. Eventually the wolf impersonators appeared with the children and these were then rescued after a mock battle. The novices were then painted and given an ornament symbolic of the powers or privileges the wolf spirits were supposed to have given them. They were then purified to return them to the secular world and they then displayed their supernatural gifts.

Rituals other than those associated with winter drama cycles also occurred among Northwest Coast peoples. Despite the relative ease with which food supplies were obtained rather magical activities were employed to ensure the success of such endeavors. Most of these techniques were the property of chiefs and hereditary in such families. They were used to improve hunting, fishing, and collection activities of their local groups. The most dramatic of these among the Nootka were magic procedures designed to cause dead whales to drift onto beaches owned by local groups. This was done as an alternative to harpooning them from canoes. "The ritual whaling technique revolved about a shrine constructed by the chief and his trusted aides in a secret spot in the woods. Human corpses or mannikins, carved of wood or formed of bundles of brush and surmounted by human skulls, were set up around the image of a whale, often arranged as though dragging the whale with a rope. The corpses and skulls were stolen by the chief and his helpers from burial places" (Drucker 1965:156). The chief, after prior ritual cleansing and purification, then prayed and chanted at this shrine in the belief that the dead had power over whales. As in California, salmon (and often other fish as well) were also ritually treated. They were welcomed when they first appeared, the first ones were ritually caught and their bones were returned to the water amidst great taboo observances. They were thought of as a race of supernatural beings in animal disguises. Comparable, if less developed and more individually employed, rites occurred to secure success in hunting land animals.

Life-cycle observances were another focus of ritual activities. In the Northwest Coast culture area the notion often involved was that the person undergoing such rites of passage was "unclean" in the supernatural sense or was surrounded by special supernatural powers at such times. Birth rites were somewhat more complicated than in many other regions of North America, often actively involving the father as well as the mother and child. Among some Salishan speakers for example, when a "...woman was about to give birth to a child she went out to a little lodge built away from the communal houses....The woman stayed in her lodge twelve days. During this period her husband stayed there with her...he brought her water and tended the fire" (Haeberlin and Gunther 1930:43). Magic medicines were taken to hasten delivery and the mother-to-be sat on mats with covered hot stones to keep her blood thin and prevent any difficulty at the time of birth. After birth, various bathing procedures had to be followed by the mother and child and for some groups the husband also had to observe these. Generally both parents had to observe taboos, especially with references to food, for about a month after the child was born.

Among the Tlingit, a woman was also isolated in a small hut for about ten days. She was attended by a midwife. "As soon as he entered the world a child's navel-string was cut off, placed in a bag made especially for it, dried inside of this, and hung about the child's neck until he was eight days old. In the case of a boy...(it)...was placed under a tree on which was an eagle's nest, so that he might be brave when he grew up" (Swanton 1908:429). A baby was also not allowed to nurse until it was forced to vomit in the belief that this would purge the individual of future illness. The child was given a name soon after birth and then, later, a second name in a feast given to honor dead relatives. A father among the Tsimshian also took an active part in such proceedings, staying outside the house and wearing ragged clothing. He also had rather severe food taboos after birth, having to avoid all fatty foods such as seal and whale.

Among the Kwakiutl when a woman became aware of her pregnancy many special procedures had to be followed. She had to refrain from hard work lest she endanger the life of the child, and, among other things, she had to open the house door first each morning so as to ensure an easy delivery, as well as avoid salmon eggs because they are sticky and would keep the child in her body. The father had to follow many similar behaviors. Medicines were also taken to ensure an easy delivery. Birth took place in isolation, even if this required everyone to leave the house, and while the woman was in labor her husband had many things to do to assist the delivery. One of these involved entering each house in the village and then leaving by the back door to aid in the ease of birth. Many observances took place after the birth of the child, most focusing on the newborn. For example, "Ten moons after birth, a festival is celebrated, at which straps are put around the ankles of the child, under the knees, around the wrists, and above the elbows, at which time his or her face is painted and the hair singed off. The paint and the smell of singed hair is a protection against disease and pains" (Boas 1966:364). Most or all of these rites were essentially private observances with family members, relatives, and perhaps a shaman in attendance.

While puberty rites for girls occurred throughout this culture area, boys' rites as such did not exist except that groups did begin the toughening-up process for later vision quests at this time. Girls' rites were fairly comparable throughout this area and did not substantially differ from those found elsewhere in North America. Among the Tlingit girls were secluded in a little hut made of branches at the time of their first menstrual period. In past times this may have been for up to a whole year. They could leave only at night and their mother brought them food and gave advice and instruction. Many taboos had to be followed such as sipping water through a drinking tube and not looking up at the sky. At the start of their period of seclusion their lower lips were pierced for the later insertion of a plug or labret and there was a feast at the conclusion of the period of confinement.

Among the Kwakiutl the girl at puberty was first restricted to the house for four days after which a lengthy period of purification began. During it she was first ritually bathed by a female relative a number of times over a forty-nine day period. Such activities were done to ensure that she would live to be old, have a good marriage, and otherwise be successful, healthy, and hard-working throughout life. At some point she was also secluded in a small room inside the house and observed various taboos, attended by her mother as elsewhere. Eventually a feast was held and the girl received a special name. Among the Tsimshian:

> Numerous ceremonies must be observed when girls reach maturity. When about thirteen...they begin to practice fasting...as very severe fasting is prescribed at the time when they reach maturity. It is believed that if they have any food in their stomachs at this time, they will have bad luck in all the future....At the end of this fasting they are covered with mats and held over a fire. It is believed by this ceremony her children are made to be healthy....The girl is not allowed to look at fresh salmon...for a whole year, and has to abstain from eating it...and she must not look at men....Her mother's family gave a great feast and...at this feast her ears are perforated, and she is given ear ornaments....When the festival was held, slaves were often given away or killed (Boas 1916:531).

Later on in life notice-taking also occurred at the time of menstruation. Generally a lodge or special room was used to isolate the woman whose condition was inimical to the success of male activities and offensive to animals and spirits. Bathing and various taboos usually accompanied these brief periods of seclusion.

A great number of rituals occurred at the end of the life cycle; at the time of death. Among the Tlingit relatives began to wail as soon as a person died. The body of the deceased person was prepared by female relatives and placed in a sitting position against the back wall of the house. Mourning activities then commenced and lasted for four nights. They consisted of wailing, singing and dancing, and involved considerable feasting (the memorial feast) and the giving of gifts to guests from other tribal divisions. Mourners cut their hair short and painted their faces black. The body was removed through a hole cut in the wall of the house and was taken to a place nearby where it was to be cremated. After speeches extolling the accomplishments of the deceased, especially if he were a chief, the corpse was placed in the center of a criss-cross of logs which were lighted. As the fire consumed the body of the deceased person the mourners and onlookers quietly left the scene. Later on a few bones were removed from the ashes and were wrapped in a skin and placed in a wooden box. This was then placed in a "grave house," a little building often raised up on posts. This was believed to protect the soul from cold. Sometimes the bones were placed in a grave post carved like a totem pole. When chiefs died, sometimes a special separate memorial pole was carved and slaves were sacrificed. Special potlatch feasts would follow. If a shaman died additional customs were also observed. Passersby might leave offerings at the grave houses of these latter individuals. The soul concept of the Tlingit was called the Qatuwu – "what feels," and at least some local groups believed it traveled to an above world.

Among the Puget Sound groups, each person became a ghost at the time of death, ultimately going to an afterlife described as being much like life itself. This place was located in the west and one account suggests that two roads led there; a long road if one had been sick for some time, another short one if death were sudden. Mention is also made of having to cross rivers or other barriers to reach it. These people were less elaborate in their disposition of the corpse, higher ranking group members being wrapped up and placed in canoes which were then placed upon scaffolds. Their bodies might first be kept in the house for a period of mourning with a shaman to watch over them. A commoner or slave usually was simply placed on a platform built in a tree and might be kept outside of the house until the time came for disposal. Some of these people used graves. Sacrifices also accompanied the deaths of important people. If a chief died at least two slaves were killed, wrapped in mats, and placed in the canoe with him. An extensive amount of property was also given away at a memorial feast and relatives had to observe the customary death taboos. Other groups had comparable behaviors. In sum, life-cycle observances, shamanism and curing, and dramatic winter ritual performances formed complexes of Northwest Coast supernatural beliefs and behaviors and with their description we have finished the survey of areas of aboriginal Native American culture. Because new religions have also been exhibited by these people we can conclude this book by presenting a brief description of some of these in a final, concluding chapter.

NORTHWEST COAST BIBLIOGRAPHY AND REFERENCES

Amos, Pamela.

1978. Coast Salish Spirit Dancing: The survival of an ancestral religion. Seattle: University of Washington Press.

Barnett, Homer G.

1955. The Coast of British Columbia. *University of Oregon Monographs* 4.

Boas, Franz.

1966. Kwakiutl Ethnography (edited by Helen Codere). Chicago: University of Chicago Press.

1916. Tsimshian Mythology. *Bureau of American Ethnology Annual Report* 31:29-979.

1895. The social Organization and the Secret Societies of the Kwaliutl Indians. *Reports of the United States National Museum*, pp. 311-738.

Drucker, Philip.

1965. Cultures of the North Pacific Coast. San Francisco: Chandler Publishing Company.

1963. Indians of the Northwest Coast. Garden City: Natural History Press.

1951. The Northern and Central Nootkan Tribes. *Bureau of American Ethnology Bulletin* 144.

Frachtenberg, L. J.

1921. The Ceremonial Societies of the Quileute Indians. *American Anthropologist* 23:320-52.

1920. Eschatology of the Quileute Indians. *American Anthropologist* 22:330-40.

Goldman, Irving.

1975. The Mouth of Heaven: An introduction to Kwakiutl religious thought. New York: John Wiley and Sons.

Gunther, Erna.
1927. Kallam Ethnography. *University of Washington Publications in Anthropology* 1:171-314.

1926. An Analysis of the First Salmon Ceremony. *American Anthropologist* 28:605-17.

Haeberlin, H. K.
1918. A Shamanistic Performance of the Coast Salish. *American Anthropologist* 20:249-57.

Haeberlin, H. K. and Gunther, Erna.
1930. The Indians of Puget Sound. *University of Washington Publications in Anthropology* 4:1-83.

Krause, Ariel.
1956. The Tlingit Indians (translated by Erna Gunther). Seattle: University of Washington Press.

Malin, Edward.
1978. A World of Faces: Masks of the Northwest Coast Indians. Portland: Timber Press.

McIlwraith, T. F.
1948. The Bella Coola Indians (2 Volumes). Toronto: University of Toronto Press.

Olson, R. L.
1936. The Quinault Indians. *University of Washington Publications in Anthropology* 6:1-190.

Sapir, Edward
1913. A Girl's Puberty Ceremony among the Nootka Indians. *Proceedings and Transactions of the Royal Society of Canada* 7:67-80.

1907. Religious Ideas of the Takelma Indians. *Journal of American Folklore* 20:33-49.

Smith, H. I.
1925. Sympathetic Magic and Witchcraft among the Bella Coola. *American Anthropologist* 27:116-21.

Swanton, John R.
1909. Contributions to the Ethnology of the Haida. *American Museum of Natural History Memoirs* 8:1-300.

1908. Social Conditions, Beliefs, and Linguistic Relationship of the Tlingit Indians. *Bureau of American Ethnology Annual Report* 26:391-486.

CHAPTER XIX

RECENT CULTS AND RELIGIOUS MOVEMENTS

We noted in chapter one that Native American peoples developed in the New World through a series of five culture stages. These went from the stage of early hunters to that of the Post-Classic civilizations. With the coming of Europeans to the Americas a last stage in development occurred; one that led ultimately to the disruption, dislocation, and destruction of many Indian groups. When Europeans arrived on these shores they were characterized by three motives, all of which worked against the best interests of the populations they encountered. A lust for wealth, often to finance wars elsewhere, led to the plunder of many groups and their enslavement as workers. War between European powers was also carried to the New World where various Indian groups were recruited as allies or were caught in the middle. And finally, religious zeal in converting the "savage" took away a major prop to cultural integrity; this at a time when many Indians were in disarray. To these motives can be added greed for the land itself which led to the greatest problems of all. Land not occupied by Europeans was considered "unoccupied"! Settlers continually poured onto Indian land displacing its former inhabitants by any means possible; a practice that continues to occur at the present time. All this was compounded by the impact of European diseases which decimated many groups inasmuch as they had little or no natural immunity to them.

In North America (United States) as Europeans moved west tribe after tribe was defeated militarily if not culturally. Survivors under the aegis of the Indian Removal Act of 1830 were pushed farther west, Indian lands in the east being "exchanged" for lands of no use to Whites. "Although removal was theoretically based on the consent of those removed, it is clear that the eastern tribes were coerced. The ideal of 'progress' was invoked to rationalize the forced migrations as inevitable and to obscure the material greed of American expansionism" (Civil Rights Report 1981:19). Those groups escaping removal were expected to assimilate into the mainstream of American life. As Whites moved farther west, defeated groups (after the mid-19th century) were placed on reservations and another "dark chapter" in American history began. Such reservations were virtual prisons and a way to deal with the Indian problem in an "out of sight, out of mind" manner. Perhaps, more overtly, such reserves were designed to break the Indian's will. Certainly such areas were to become "slums in the wilderness." Even reservation lands were appropriated as gold or other valuable resources, or simply the land itself, were found useful for Whites.

Ultimately, under the Dawes General Allotment Act of 1887, a plan developed to have Indian lands surrendered and then be divided up into small plots and returned to tribal members on a more individual basis. With such ownership it was felt Indians could be more actively hastened into assimilation. "Allotment and other assimilationist practices received strong support from 'friends' of the Indians. Many believed that these policies represented the only alternative to Indian extinction (Civil Rights Report 1981:21). Conditions however soon worsened on reservations and, of course, much Indian land passed into White hands. By 1934 allotment policies had been judged as failures and the realization developed that most Indians were not ready for full assimilation. The Indian Reorganization Act of that year attempted among other things to improve health conditions for Indians, improve education, restore freedom of religion, and encourage tribal self-government. All of these laudable moves were done, however, with the notion that assimilation was still inevitable. And what was clearly missing was "...a national policy to promote and support the study and understanding of Indian cultures" (Civil Rights Report 1981:22).

Periodically since this time the excessive cost of supporting the Indians has led to one or another form of Termination policy; removing them from Federal support. Clearly many groups were and are unready for this; lacking both the human and economic resources for self determination. And, it should be added, many groups that do wish assimilation also wish to accomplish this without complete loss of self identity; to keep a foot in each culture so to speak. The history of Indian-White relations in this country (and elsewhere) has thus been one of true tragedy resulting in the extinction of many ways of being human. Enough has been indicated here to give a rough impression of it. Throughout its course many attempts were made by populations of Native Americans to reject or accommodate to the encroaching culture of Europeans. When regular military efforts failed these attempts often took the form of religious movements or cults. Since this is a work on Native American religion it is appropriate to briefly comment on these and describe a few of them in some detail.

Religious movements or cults are difficult to define. They are often called movements because of their group nature and due to the generally new aspects of behavior involved and the resistance they often engender from their own or some other society. Ralph Linton called such movements Nativistic Movements because he saw them arising among primitive peoples in response to threats from more powerful, modern societies. He defined such activities as "Any conscious, organized attempt on the part of a society's members to revive or perpetuate selected aspects of its culture" (Linton 1943:230). Certainly many American Indian movements can be characterized along such lines and while other definitions and names do exist – revitalization, transformation, revivalistic, and the like – this is not the place to deal with such scholarly debates. For a brief discussion of such problems see my general book, *Primitive Religion* (Collins 1978). In probably all cases, no matter what classification term is applied to such movements, they are the religious behaviors of oppressed peoples and, as we have seen, the Native Americans clearly qualify in this sense. Historically speaking, we can discuss examples of two different kinds of nativism in this very brief chapter.

> In general, the...movements of North America reveal two principal trends, which correspond to two different phases of Indian history. In the first phase, which was revolutionary and openly hostile to the whites, the religious trend reflects the yearning of the Indians for the recovery of their own culture which was rapidly declining. Such movements...sought to salvage and renovate a culture already in crisis by rejecting the white man and his civilization. This trend is retrospective: for in these movements it is the past that offers the way to salvation. The second phase, which started when the whites had taken and begun to develop the Indian's land, produced a religious trend that called for adaptation...they focus their prophetic sights on change and progress (Lanternari 1963:114-15).

One of the most dramatic examples of the first type of movement that appeared in North America was the Ghost Dance. Many western peoples were swept up in it. It first appeared among the Paviotsos of Nevada in 1870. There in its first phase it was begun by the prophet Wodziwob. He had received a vision in which he saw a railroad train carrying Indian ancestors. They were returning to life and would announce their arrival with a great explosion. In this vision it was also suggested that the world would witness a great cataclysm and that it would open up to engulf the Whites who would then disappear. Their material wealth, however, would somehow remain for the Indians. Even Indians would die in this upheaval but those who followed the new religion would be reborn shortly afterward and live in the company of the Great Spirit in an eternal existence. The basic ritual consisted of men and women dancing around a pole. The dances performed were mostly traditional types but the songs they sang to accompany them were new, having been taught to the participants by the prophet Wodziwob who had apparently learned them during one of his vision experiences.

The early phase of the Ghost Dance had for the most part only a local significance although it did spread to a few other societies. Perhaps its major impact was to stimulate a number of other such movements most of which also predicted destruction, resurrection, and the removal of Whites and had somewhat new ritual activities designed to hasten the appearance of such events. Around 1890, a new and more potent phase of the Ghost Dance arose under a new prophet, Wovoka (John Wilson). This caused a very widespread expansion of this cult. Wovoka was a Paiute and he had been some sort of supernatural leader among these people. His own vision was gained during a period of sickness–which is very common among such people everywhere. This phase of the cult was a little less hostile to Whites although their ultimate removal was greatly desired. James Mooney gives us the best account of this phase and we can quote him on its doctrines.

> The great underlying principle of the Ghost Dance doctrine is that the time will come when the whole Indian race, living and dead, will be reunited upon a regenerated earth, to live a life of aboriginal happiness, forever free from death, disease, and misery....The White race...has no part in this scheme...and will be left behind....All this is to be brought about by an overruling spiritual power that needs no assistance from human creatures....On the contrary, all believers were exhorted to make themselves worthy of the predicted happiness by discarding all things warlike and practicing honesty, peace and good will, not only among themselves, but also towards the Whites, so long as they were together (Mooney 1965:19).

The suggestion here was that the dead were shortly to return and that this would be announced by cataclysms, and that immortality would be the reward of the faithful.

Part of Wovoka's doctrine consisted of a code of ethics. Injunctions were placed upon harming others and on lying and stealing. Followers of the cult were told to love one another, to work hard, and to give up some of the more destructive ritual aspects of their old religion, for example destroying property as a sign of mourning in death rites. He also preached that Indians ought to be peaceful towards the Whites until they would magically disappear on the day of deliverance. It should be mentioned in this connection that this phase of the cult spread rapidly among Plains peoples and that this emphasis clearly went against their focus on militarism. Many of these groups did not accept this part of the doctrine and in fact developed the notion that the special shirt worn in the cult, the Ghost Shirt, had supernatural properties that could protect the wearer against the weapons of White soldiers. Such ideas did stimulate active resistance!

As in the earlier phase the major ritual endeavor in 1890 was a special dance which occurred over a four- or five-day period. Men and women danced in concentric circles. Leaders invoked the ancestors in an opening song and were then joined by other participants who often numbered in the hundreds. Other songs were sung as the dancers circled around the pole. During rest periods between song and dance performances leaders would relate their own trance experiences and engage in sermonizing activity relative to the ethical aspects of the cult. This was a departure from past custom as was the non-use of any musical instruments. As the dancers continued their movements the level of excitement slowly built up until some participants were swept away by the emotional aspects of the endeavor. Such excitement was enhanced by the leaders who attempted to stimulate and "psyche up" such people even further. "For a while the woman continues to move around with the circle of dancers, singing the song with the others, but usually before the circuit is completed she loses control of herself entirely, and, breaking away from the partners who have hold of her hands on either side, she staggers into the ring, while the circle at once closes up again behind her" (Mooney 1965:198). The leaders then further aided such persons until they passed into a trance-like state. In it they too might have the opportunity for communicating with the supernatural world. Ultimately, of course, such magical supernatural efforts were doomed to failure. They did have, however, some positive effects for some groups and we will presently return to this point.

Another example of a cult along the lines of the Ghost Dance was that called the Cult of Dreamers, founded by the prophet Smohalla – "preacher." This movement came into existence among groups living along the Columbia River in Washington and Oregon around 1860. Groups in this region were refusing to move onto reservations provided for them since they feared that to do so would confine them for further assimilation. At this time many local cults were developing (like the Prophet Dance) and these, along with that of Smohalla were attempts to provide hope in the face of increasing White pressures. As in the case of Wovoka, this prophet also claimed to have had special visions. He had been a shaman among his people, the Wanapum. In such a capacity he had engaged in a fight with a rival who had defeated him and left him for dead on a stream bank. Rising waters carried him downstream where he was rescued by a White farmer. After a lengthy period he recovered and then traveled widely throughout California and the Southwest before returning home. When he did arrive there he proclaimed to everyone that he had died and that he had met the Great Spirit/supreme being. This god was unhappy that Indians had taken over White culture and had allowed their own traditions to lapse. If some of the old ways were returned to, then God would remove Whites, return the lost lands of the Indian, and resurrect the dead.

Smohalla's faith was called Washani – "worship" – but became referred to as the Dream Cult after his own designation as the Dreamer. This was due to his frequent trances in which God revealed certain knowledge to him. This information was then passed on to his followers. His theology included the notion that the Creator had made the Indian first, after which came other peoples – French, priests, English, and so on – all in turn from each other. As Indians were first in creation, the only God-created beings, therefore the earth belonged to them. Furthermore the earth itself was a goddess who should not have her breast plowed; farming (and other white customs) becoming a sacrilege. This was also a wrong behavior since it was from the soil that the dead would rise again once they were reanimated by their souls at the time of a cataclysm.

Clearly in this cult wisdom come in dreams but there were also regular ritual activities. These began with a procession of the faithful from a cult house with the leaders carrying a banner with decorations on it symbolic of the earth and sky and the cult house itself. Smohalla also wore a special shirt of symbolic importance. After the procession worshippers returned to their cult house, went inside, and arranged themselves along the walls with the prophet in the center. There was a verbal recitation of dogma, and singing and dancing accompanied by drum music. These latter activities, as in the Ghost Dance, eventually led to trance-like behavior in many participants culminating in dreams which could then be told to fellow worshippers. Special rites might also occur, the most common being a Salmon Dance and a Berry Dance to mark the start of these wild resource seasons. For a while Smohalla gained many converts. In 1877 the Nez Perce tribe was stimulated into military activity but eventually this cult waned. Smohalla died in 1895, was succeeded by his son Yoyoumi and then by a nephew, Puck Hyat Toot whose death led to the final end of a severely declined faith.

In this same general area another cult developed between 1870-1880 among groups such as the Sanpoil and the Spokane. Its prophet and leader was Kolaskin and the cult is named after him. At the age of twenty he became ill and this resulted in a paralysis that lasted for two years. Traditional shamans proved incapable of helping him and one day he lost consciousness. Preparations were made for his funeral but suddenly he regained consciousness and those present believed him returned from the dead. He began to sing a strange new song. This, he revealed, had its origin from the Creator, whom he had met while dead, and he claimed to have revelation from that being which he then imparted. Its general tenor was that Indians "...must change their ways; they must no longer drink, steal, or commit adultery. But it was most important that they pray to their new god" (Ray 1936:68). This god would deliver them from their problems and should be prayed to a number of times daily as well as having every seventh day devoted to him exclusively.

Kolaskin's message fell on sympathetic ears and he was hailed as a prophet; first among his own kin and then, increasingly, beyond them. He also gradually recovered from his affliction. Meetings drew large audiences and were held once or twice each Sunday. When cult members entered the meeting place they all kneeled. One began to pray and the others joined in. Songs were also sung but dances were apparently absent, unlike the other cults that we have examined. The prophet also spoke at each meeting and repeated his own story, suggesting to converts that his recovery from paralysis had been instantaneous. Clearly stimulated by Christian doctrine, Kolaskin had a second revelation. He

> ...announced to his people that at the end of ten years' time the world would be enveloped in a great flood. To avoid destruction, he continued, they were to build a sawmill near the church and saw the lumber for a great boat. Before the end of ten years the boat would be completed and all followers would gather inside at the appointed time. Also, a male and female of every animal and bird would be included. Then the

> rain would come and flood the earth but all those in the boat would be saved (Ray 1936:71).

Shortly after this message, White authorities stepped in to curtail his activities and the boat was never constructed. Later on the prophet was put in jail, returning three years later to claim that his teachings had been untrue. He attempted to disband the cult and he himself became a shaman of some note. Even so, a few followers continued the cult until about 1930. We see in this cult a movement somewhat more accommodating to Whites and we can now examine two last examples which move decidedly in this direction. One of these also demonstrates how the focus of such expressions may change over time when confronted with outside realities.

A religious movement still found among modern Iroquois is the Handsome Lake Religion. Named after its Seneca prophet it is also referred to as the New Religion and as the Gai-wiio or "good message." This movement began among one band of Indians along the Allegheny River in western New York State in 1799. These people, along with other Iroquois, had been severely impaired by effects of European contact. Prior to the end of the French and Indian War (1763) they had maintained their power, lands, and much of their self-esteem. With the British victory they could no longer play off the two sides against each other and in the Revolutionary War most of them backed the British and, as a result, their heartland was devastated and their population greatly reduced in numbers. Now they were confined to reservations with those attendant consequences.

For the Seneca, specifically, most of their land had been alienated by 1797 and they were greatly impoverished. In June of 1799 Handsome Lake, the brother of a local leader, received a vision. Like other prophets he was sick and near death at the time. Recovering, he reported that he had been visited by three angels who told him they had been sent by the Creator to show him how to get well and to tell his people about a message. He was to say that the Creator was angry about evil practices that were going on. These included the use of alcohol, witchcraft, love magic, and sterility magic and "People who are guilty of doing these things must admit their wrongdoing, repent, and never sin again..." (Wallace 1970:241). Confessions of such sins could be made to Handsome Lake himself or, if truly bad, to the Creator.

The Prophet reported this during a ritual, the Berry Festival, which the message also said should continue to be held. The message was also discussed in a council.

Several weeks later a fourth angel appeared to Handsome Lake and he thus had a second vision. In it the prophet was taken on a spiritual journey through heaven and hell and he was given a moral code at this time. This was accomplished through a number of scenarios in which he saw various types of evil persons and the punishments they had received. He even met a disillusioned Jesus; Quaker influence was heavy in this area of New York State. Clearly witchcraft, promiscuity, wife beating, gambling, and the like were behaviors that were causing trouble for the Indians and the angel told Handsome Lake that they had to cease. The Seneca prophet again recounted his vision in a council. In the following year yet a third vision occurred. The three original angels appeared and urged him to carry on his role as one who should spread the good message. Handsome Lake's health continued to improve and he received further revelations, gaining many adherents. He died in 1815.

Anthony Wallace sees two major "gospels" involved in this cult. The first of these was complete at the end of the third main vision. "This first gospel was apocalyptic and contained three major, interrelated themes: the imminence of world destruction, the definition of sin, and the prescription for salvation" (Wallace 1970:249). If Indians did not cease their bad practices and return to traditional religion the prophet himself would die and the earth would be destroyed. The specific sins had been catalogued in the visions and to these were added the failure to believe in the Gai-wiio. Release from sin, salvation, was accomplished by following the path laid down by Handsome Lake. Confession of sins, as previously mentioned, was the crucial element here. The second gospel, a social gospel, followed these teachings. Along with an emphasis upon moral conduct these teachings, again influenced by Quakers in the area, suggested economic and technological efforts such as learning how to farm in a White manner. Ultimately this gospel had more to do with revitalizing the Seneca and providing them with social stability. After his death he was succeeded by his nephew and then other leaders and his message is preached and recited at the Mid-Winter Festival on various

Iroquois Reservations in New York and Canada at the present time. A written code was determined and composed early in the present century.

We can present a final example of a Native American religious movement, again one that continues to the present time and which is the most widespread of such nativistic endeavors. This is the Peyote Cult or Native American Church. This movement basically seeks adjustment to Whites rather than struggle against them and a return to the past. In this sense it is a more rational supernatural effort. Its focal point is the use of peyote in a ritual context.

> Peyote...is a small, spineless, carrot-shaped cactus growing in the Rio Grande Valley and southward. It contains nine narcotic alkaloids...some of them strychnine-like in physiological action, the rest morphine-like. In pre-Columbian times the Aztec, Huichol, and other Mexican Indians ate the plant ceremonially either in the dried or green state. This produces profound sensory and psychic derangements lasting twenty-four hours, a property which led the natives to value and use it religiously (LaBarre 1938:7).

Its early use was as a therapeutic and hallucinatory device: for curing the sick and offering protection as well as alleviating fatigue and as a bridge for contacting the supernatural world. As its use spread into North America it was incorporated as part of a religious movement in response to White domination, becoming popular about the time that the influence of the Ghost Dance was waning. In fact, its first prophet, John Wilson (not the man previously mentioned) was introduced to peyote at a ghost dance and had a vision in which he went to heaven, meeting various supernaturals. He ultimately was informed that God had put part of the Holy Spirit into peyote for use by the Indians. He was also taught songs and other ritual aspects. Wilson then started the cult adapting a strict ethical code to go along with it. As the cult spread many offshoots and other prophets developed; many with a heavy Christian theme, some more aboriginal in nature. Eventually many were merged together (1918) as the Native American Church. Since cult practices do differ somewhat from one group to another we can focus on one example, the Taos Pueblo Indians of New Mexico.

At Taos Pueblo, unless sickness or some emergency is the cause, the rite is performed in response to a vow and will be held on a Saturday night.

It is held in response to the vow of an individual and such vows are made for three main reasons: to gain a supernatural solution to some problem, to show appreciation after its solution, or to gain general blessings and good luck. The person making the vow becomes its sponsor and must provide food, invite participants and select a leader. A tipi as a ritual structure must also be erected and other material paraphernalia obtained and readied. Other leaders are also selected: a fireman who tends a ritual fire, a man who places cedar incense upon it, a special drummer, and a woman who is in charge of water and who will bring in a ritual breakfast at the appropriate time. She is usually the wife of the sponsor. Preparation by other participants who are all male and who number perhaps fifteen individuals is variable but there is a general feeling that behavior should be circumspect on the day of the ritual. Certainly alcohol must not be used.

Ritual procedures run as follows. The participants gather in the early evening and the fireman goes into the tipi and lights the fire which is itself part of an altar complex. Others line up in a special order with the male leaders first. A prayer is offered by the main leader and they all enter the structure. The cedarman places incense in the fire for purification and the peyote is warmed by it. Tobacco is passed, which is made into cigarettes whose smoke can be "prayed through." At this time a formal prayer is offered in which the purpose of the rite is stated. Portions of peyote are then distributed to all the participants and ingested by them, ultimately to produce visions. The leader sings a special "starting song" accompanied by the drummer. Singing and drumming are then also done by the other leaders and by those participants who wish to do so. Prayers are also said privately during these activities. At midnight the leader again sings a special song and water is brought in and passed around. The leader goes outside and prays and upon his return the singing, drumming, and individual praying continue until near dawn. When it is almost sunrise the leader again calls for water and sings a third special song. The water woman enters with the water and after some ritual activity she prays – also relative to the specific purpose of the rite. The leader also offers a formal prayer at this point and the female leader leaves and returns with a special "breakfast" which, like the water, is symbolic of the necessities of life. Food and water are passed out to participants and, after consumption, the leader sings a special "quitting song" and they leave the tipi. Most participants remain in the area until noon when a special meal is served to finally terminate the ritual activities. For more information on ritual details and the intricate symbolism of this cult see Collins (1967,1968).

The Peyote Cult is, as one can guess from this very brief description, an extremely personal kind of experience. One derives from it pretty much what one wishes. As many participants have stated, it is a kind of road that one can follow. In the words of Weston LaBarre:

> Peyotism functions in many other ways as a living religion. Throughout life, peyote offers consolation for troubles, chastens for bad deeds or thoughts, advises and directs behavior through the drug-induced vision, and serves as the focus nowdays for both tribal and intertribal life, thus preserving and reinforcing many of the old cultural and religious values....Thus peyote makes a major contribution toward the preservation of morale of the present day generation, torn as it is between loyalty to two cultures, the native and the white (LaBarre 1947:300-01).

At Taos Pueblo specifically this cult provides a kind of middle ground for religious experience between the older faith, now rapidly declining, and Christianity, which some pueblo members do not respond to as positively as others. In the Peyote Cult both the old and new are integrated together into a ritual endeavor that all can gain benefit from. It does help to reinforce their collective sense of social and cultural identity. As such, it has a positive, beneficial function in their lives.

Movements such as Peyotism, the Handsome Lake Cult, and other rational supernatural approaches do offer hope to the oppressed in a way that the more magical cults such as the Ghost Dance with their elaborate claims failed to do. Ancestors do not return to life; the millenium so devoutly wished for fails to materialize. Yet even in these "far-out" situations some revitalization, some positive effects may be discerned. Among the Pawnee of the Plains, for example, the vision provided by the Ghost Dance failed but, in the process, Pawnee participants in their trances saw the ancestors practicing the older way of life – a way of life largely forgotten or lost by that point in time. Such visions did lead to a resurrection of some of these older elements of culture.

> This effect occurred in the following way: In a vision the subject would see some old way of life which had come to be disregarded. He would remember it. His vision then became a command upon those alive who knew how it must be carried out to do so. Sometimes there were men alive who knew the thing thoroughly and were persuaded by the demand of a supernatural message to begin it again. But often a ritual or dance was only partially remembered. Then many men would get together and pool their memories to revive the affair (Lesser 1933:112).

So the final result was to give the Pawnee a new sense of integrity and solidarity, to revive some of their past even though this was not accomplished in the manner promised by the cult itself. Some positive aspects were obtained. As the pressures on many Native Americans continue to exist one might well expect further religious movements to occur among them, not necessarily only those of a more rational, accommodating type.

RECENT CULTS AND RELIGIOUS MOVEMENTS
BIBLIOGRAPHY AND REFERENCES

Civil Rights Commission Report.
1981. Indian Tribes: A continuing quest for survival. Washington: U.S. Government Printing Office.

Collins, John J.
1978. Primitive Religion. Totowa: Littlefield, Adams and Co.

1968. A Descriptive Introduction to the Taos Peyote Ceremony. *Ethnology* 7:427-49.

1967. Peyotism and Religious Membership at Taos Pueblo, New Mexico. *Southwestern Social Science Quarterly* 48:183-91.

Deardorff, Merle H.
1951. The Religion of Handsome Lake. In W. N. Fenton (editor), Symposium on Local Diversity in Iroquoian Culture. *Bureau of American Ethnology Bulletin* 149:77-107.

Hertzberg, Hazel W.
1971. The Search for an American Indian Identity. Syracuse: Syracuse University Press.

LaBarre, Weston.
1947. Primitive Psychotherapy in Native American Cultures: Peyotism and Confession. *Journal of Abnormal and Social Psychology* 42:294-309.

1938. The Peyote Cult. New Haven: Yale University Press.

Lanternari, Vittorio.
1963. The Religions of the Oppressed. New York: Alfred Knopf.

Lesser, Alexander.
1933. Cultural Significance of the Ghost Dance. *American Anthropologist* 35:108-15.

Linton, Ralph.
1943. Nativistic Movements. *American Anthropologist* 45:230-40.

McNickle, D'arcy.
1973. Native American Tribalism. New York: Oxford University Press.

Mooney, James.
1965. The Ghost Dance and the Sioux Outbreak of 1890. Chicago: University of Chicago Press.

Parker, Arthur C.
1968. The Code of Handsome Lake, The Seneca Prophet. In W. N. Fenton (editor), Parker on the Iroquois (Book 2). Syracuse: Syracuse University Press.

Ray, Verne F.
1936. The Kolaskin Cult. *American Anthropologist* 38:67-75.

Wallace, Anthony F. C.
1970. The Death and Rebirth of the Seneca. New York: Alfred Knopf.

SELECTED BIBLIOGRAPHY

Included below are works that treat the fictive American Indian at least tangentially or have important implications for its literary history: the bibliography in Paula Gunn Allen's *Studies in American Indian Literature* (New York, 1983), pp. 320-61; Jeannette Henry, and others' *Index to Literature on the American Indian,* 4 vols. (San Francisco, 1971-1975); and Arlene Hirschfelder's *American Indian and Eskimo Authors: A Comprehensive Bibliography* (New York, 1973).

Axtell, James. *The Europeans and the Indians: Essays in the Ethnohistory of Colonial North America.* New York, 1981.

Barnett, Louise K. *The Ignoble Savage: American Literary Racism, 1790-1890.* Westport, Conn., 1975.

Berkhofer, Robert F., Jr. *The White Man's Indian: Images of the American Indian from Columbus to the Present.* New York, 1978.

Bierhorst, John, Ed. *Four Masterworks of American Indian Literature.* New York, 1974.

Chapman, Abraham, Ed. *Literature of the American Indian: Views and Interpretations.* New York, 1975.

Dabney, Lewis. *The Indians of Yoknapatawpha.* Baton Rouge, La., 1974.

Driver, Harold E. *Indians of North America.* 2nd. ed. Chicago, 1969.

Dudley, Edward and Maximillian Novak, eds. *The Wild Man Within.* Pittsburgh, 1972.

Elliot, J. H. *The Old World and the New, 1492-1650.* Cambridge, Eng., 1970.

Fairchild, Hoxie. *The Noble Savage.* New York, 1961.

Farb, Peter. *Man's Rise to Civilization.* New York, 1968.

Fiedler, Leslie. *The Return of the Vanishing American.* New York, 1968.

Fisher, Dexter. *The Third Woman: Minority Woman Writers of the United States.* New York, 1980.

Foss, Michael. *Undreamed Shores.* London, 1974.

Fussell, Edwin. *Frontier: American Literature and the American West.* Princeton, N. J., 1965.

Hallowell, A. Irving. "American Indians, White and Black: The Phenomenon of Transculturalization." *Current Anthropology*, 4 (1963): 519-31.

"The Backwash of the Frontier: The Impact of the Indian on American Culture." In Walker D. Wyman and Clifton B. Kroeber, eds. *The Frontier in Perspective*. Madison, Wisc., 1957.

Hanke, Lewis. *Aristotle and the American Indian*. Bloomington, Ind., 1959.

Harris, Helen. "Mark Twain's Response to the Native American." *American Literature*, XLVI (January, 1975): 495-505.

Heard, J. Norman. *White into Red: A Study of the Assimilation of White Persons Captured by Indians*. Metuchen, N.J., 1973.

Hoover, Dwight. *The Red and the Black*. Chicago, 1976.

Huymes, Dell. *"In Vain I Tried to Tell You": Essays in Native American Ethnopoetics*. Philadelphia, 1981.

Jacobs, Wilbur R. *Dispossessing the American Indian: Indians and Whites on the Colonial Frontier*. New York, 1972.

Jennings, Francis. *The Invasion of America: Indians, Colonialism, and the Cant of Conquest*. Chapel Hill, N.C., 1975. Part I & II.

Jordan, Winthrop. *White Over Black*. Chapel Hill, N.C., 1968.

Josephy, Alvin. M. *The Indian Heritage of America*. New York, 1968.

Keiser, Albert. *The Indian in American Literature*. New York, 1933.

"Thoreau's Manuscripts on the Indian." *Journal of English and Germanic Philology* XXVIII (April, 1928): 183-199.

Larson, Charles. *American Indian Fiction*. Albuquerque, 1978.

Levernier, James A., and Hennig Cohen, eds. *The Indians and Their Captives*. Westport, Conn., 1977.

Lincoln, Kenneth. *Native American Renaissance*. Berkeley, 1983.

Nash, Gary. *Red, White, and Black: The Peoples of Early America*. Englewood Cliffs, N.J., 1974.

Pearce, Roy Harvey. *The Savages of America: A Study of the Indian and the Idea of Civilization*. Baltimore, 1953. Rev. ed. titled *Savagism and Civilization: A Study of the Indian and the American Mind*. Baltimore, 1965.

"The Significances of the Captivity Narrative." *American Literature*, 19 (1947): 1-20.

Philbrick, Francis. *The Rise of the West, 1754-1830*. New York, 1965.

Porter, H. C. *The Inconsistent Savage: England and the North American Indian, 1500-1660*. London, 1979.

Rogin, Michael. *Fathers and Children*. New York, 1975.

Rosowski, Susan, and Helen Stauffer, eds. *Women in Western American Literature*. Troy. N.Y., 1982.

Rotherberg, Jerome, ed. *Shaking and the Pumpkin: Traditional Poetry of the Indian North Americas*. Garden City, N.J., 1972.

Sayre, Robert F. *Thoreau and the American Indians*. Princeton, 1977.

"A Bibliography and an Anthology of American Indian Literature." *College English*, 35 (1974): 704-06.

Sheehan, Bernard W. *Savagism and Civility: Indians and Englishmen in Colonial Virginia*. Cambridge, Eng., 1980.

"Indian-White Relations in Early America: A Review Essay." *William and Mary Quarterly*, 26 (1969): 267-86.

Slotkin, Richard. *Regeneration through Violence: The Mythology of the American Frontier, 1600-1860*. Middletown, Conn., 1973.

Slotkin, Richard, and James K. Folsom, eds. *So Dreadful A Judgment: Puritan Responses to King Philip's War, 1676-1677*. Middletown, Conn., 1979.

Stinebeck, David C., and Charles M. Segal. *Puritans, Indians, and Manifest Destiny*. New York, 1977.

Swann, Brian, ed. *Smoothing the Ground: Essays on Native American Oral Literature*. Los Angeles, 1982.

Taylor, Golden, ed. *The Literary History of the American West*. Fort Worth, Texas, 1987.

Trimble, Martha Scott. *N. Scott Momaday*. Western Writers. Boise, Id., 1973.

Turner, Frederick. *The Frontier in American History*. New York, 1920.

Turner, Victor. *The Forest of Symbols*. Ithaca, N.Y., 1967.

Underhill, Ruth M. *Red Man's America: A History of Indians in the United States*. Rev. ed. Chicago, 1971.

VanDerBeets, Richard. *The Indian Captivity Narrative: An American Genre*. Lanham, Md., 1984.

Held Captive by Indians: Selected Narratives, 1642-1836. Knoxville, Tenn., 1973.

"'*A Thirst for Empire*': The Indian Captivity Narrative as Propaganda." *Research Studies*, 40 (1972): 207-15.

"The Indian Captivity Narrative as Ritual." *American Literature*, 43 (1972): 548-62.

"A Surfeit of Style: The Indian Captivity Narrative as Penny Dreadful." *Research Studies*, 39 (1971): 297-306.

Vaughan, Alden T. *New England Frontier: Puritans and Indians, 1620-1675*. Boston, 1965; rev. ed. New York, 1979.

"Pequots and Puritans: the Causes of the War of 1637." *William and Mary Quarterly*, 21 (1964): 256-69.

Vaughan, Alden T. and Francis J. Bremer, eds. *Puritan New England: Essays on Religion Society and Culture*. New York, 1977.

Vaughan, Alden T. and Edward C. Clark, eds. *Puritans Among the Indians: Accounts of Captivity Redemption*. Cambridge, Mass., 1981.

Vaughan, Alden T. and Daniel K. Richter. "Crossing the Cultural Divide: Indians and New Englanders, 1605-1763. *American Antiquarian Society Proceedings*, 90 (1980): 23-90.

Velie, Alan R. *Four American Indian Literary Masters*. Norman, Okla., 1982.

ed. *American Indian Literature*: *An Anthology*. Norman, Okla., 1979.

"James Welch's Poetry." *American Indian Culture and Research Journal* 3, No. 1 (1979): 19-38.

Wallace, Anthony F. C. *The Death and Rebirth of the Seneca*. New York, 1969.

"Political Organization and Land Tenure Among the Northeastern Indians, 1600-1830." *Southwestern Journal of Anthropology* 13 (1957): 301-21.

Washburn, Wilcomb E. *The Indian in America*. New York, 1975.

Red Man's Land – White Man's Law: A Study of the Past and Present Status of the American Indian. New York, 1971.

"The Moral and Legal Justification for Dispossessing the Indians." In James Morton Smith ed., *Seventeenth-Century America: Essays in Colonial History.* Chapel Hill, N.C., 1959.

Wilner, Eleanor. *Gathering the Winds: Visionary Imagination and Radical Transformation of Self and Society.* Baltimore, Md., 1975.

Ziff, Larzer. *Literary Democracy: The Declaration of Cultural Independence in America.* New York, 1981.

Puritanism in America: New Culture in a New World. New York, 1973.

Zolla, Elemire. *The Writer and the Shaman.* Trans. Raymond Rosenthal. New York, 1973.

POSTSCRIPT

This volume represents a very brief attempt to generally characterize the past religions of the Native American peoples north of Mexico. It has indicated both the typical patterns of particular culture areas and some of their variations, a task easier to accomplish for some areas than others. To recapitulate briefly, for the great Southwest culture area we noted a number of different styles of supernaturalism. We saw among Puebloan peoples major ceremonies designed to control the world relative to seasons, crops, and life in general. Varieties of cult organizations occurred including those dedicated to shamanistic pursuits. Almost all such endeavors had collectivistic emphases following the group orientation of the rest of Pueblo culture. Other varieties in that area–Apache and Navaho, Pimans and Yumans also emphasized individualistic attempts at gaining and using power. In Western North America more variety developed with rites in California being most developed and those in the Great Basin and Plateau being heavily individualistic and meager in comparison to elsewhere. Such was the content of part one.

In part two we dealt with the hunting concerns of the Arctic cultures and with the very self-contained, supernatural behaviors of Subarctic peoples. The Plains area was emphasized due to the contrast of activities there, ranging from vision quests, through various associations, to collective-group benefit annual rites. The East was divided into essentially three patterns; in some ways comparable. The Iroquoians emphasized rites of thanksgiving and religious societies for curing, the Algonkians were less developed here and, in the Southeast, sun worship and major rites focused on collective well-being. Finally, the Northwest coast with its emphasis on winter drama cycles completed our picture. For all areas life-cycle observances, shamanism and curing, and the search for guardian spirits or supernatural power were discussed and unique beliefs and practices were highlighted. The careful reader should have become aware of the many dimensions of Native American religiosity. Useful but not complete bibliographies were also provided.

This volume is not suggested as a definitive summation of this topic. To do this adequately, if such an attempt could succeed, archaeological and linguistic evidence would have to be integrated with a much more detailed presentation of these culture areas. A more analytical approach than has been taken here would also be required, one that would take into account the often thorny issues of historical development and influences. Such is far beyond the scope of the present work and the abilities of any single writer. As stated in the introduction the purpose of this volume is merely to provide an introduction to Native American religion for the general reader and beginning student and, perhaps, to stimulate further interest along such lines. One should also be reminded of the irreparable loss of most of these religious expressions and of their place in the history of religion.

Index

Tribes and Language Groupings for whom specific materials are presented

J

K

L

M

N

O

P

R

S

T

Index

Selected Rites and other religious expressions

P

R

S

T

V

W

NATIVE AMERICAN STUDIES

1. John James Collins, **Native American Religions: A Geographical Survey**
2. Maureen Korp, **The Sacred Geography of the American Mound Builders**